MODERN AMERICAN CULTURE:
An Introduction

MODERN AMERICAN CULTURE:
An Introduction

Edited by Mick Gidley

Longman
London and New York

Longman Group UK Limited,
Longman House, Burnt Mill,
Harlow, Essex CM20 2JE, England
and Associated Companies throughout the world.

Published in the United States of America
by Longman Publishing, New York

First published 1993

ISBN 0 582 05111 8 CSD
ISBN 0 582 05110 X PPR

British Library Cataloguing-in-Publication Data

A catalogue record for this book is available from the British Library

Library of Congress Cataloging-in-Publication Data

Modern American culture : an introduction / edited by Mick Gidley.
        p.   cm.
    Includes bibliographical references and index.
    ISBN 0–582–05111–8. – ISBN 0–582–05110–X (pbk.)
    1. United States – Civilization – 20th century. 2. United States –
Civilization.
E169.1.M7145   1993
973.9–dc20   92–28394
                                                                            CIP

set in 10/12 pt Bembo Roman by 8 in B.

Produced by Longman Singapore Publishers (Pte) Ltd.
Printed in Singapore

Contents

Preface

Modern American Culture offers an introduction to the richness and diversity of American culture, especially but not exclusively during the twentieth century. 'Culture' here is conceived in broad terms, to include ideas, social institutions, environmental features, behavioural patterns, and forms of expression. The initial chapters for the most part present historical, economic, political and geographical aspects of culture, while those in the second half treat expressive, often artistic, elements. But these are obviously not hard-and-fast divisions: many 'art' works are referred to in the early chapters, and authors of later chapters have kept in mind issues raised in the opening ones. Since culture is so broadly conceived here – and in general has long been viewed as a notoriously multifarious and complex concept – we thought it worthwhile for each chapter at least to introduce appropriate cultural critics, thus leading towards the fuller-scale treatment of American cultural criticism itself which concludes the book. Throughout there is an emphasis on relationships between ideological assumptions in the culture and their representation in manifold ways.

In sum, the book is interdisciplinary. At the same time, authors of individual chapters, while working to an agreed broad outline, were free to decide what was truly important in each topic and – since different aspects of culture demand their own particular approaches, at least to a certain degree – to use appropriate methods; some chapters, therefore, work through explication of texts, others offer much data in the manner of social science disciplines, while still others are more descriptive or analyse ideas. An introduction cannot aspire to comprehensiveness and one deliberate omission here is a chapter on American fiction; many American novels and stories are featured, of course, but we did not consider it sensible to duplicate in excessively short compass adequate existing introductory texts. In a book of this scope there may be other omissions that readers feel should be made good, so, in the event of future editions, I would be glad to hear of them.

Since the book is organized thematically, it complements the chronological arrangement, and does not duplicate, the contents of *Introduction to American Studies* (edited by Malcolm Bradbury and Howard Temperley, also published by Longman). It is hoped that, like that earlier book, *Modern American Culture* will prove useful both to general readers and to students taking American Studies degrees or courses in institutions of higher education, as well as to those seeking greater contextualization for reading or courses in American history, literature, geography, film, etc., or in such related areas as cultural and media studies.

I have been fortunate in my international team of contributors. While I have been an active editor, pointing up and creating links between chapters, checking references, pursuing leads, suggesting or making changes and the like, the book has also been a genuine cooperative venture in that the contributors, drawing upon their teaching experience in Britain, the United States, continental Europe and beyond, each read and commented upon drafts of one or more chapters by others. I am most grateful to the contributors for the much greater stock of knowledge and insight that this procedure put at my disposal and, in a sometimes rather isolated profession, for the sense of camaraderie that it often produced. I would also like to thank my colleagues at the University of Exeter, especially Richard Bradbury and Richard Maltby, for information and advice. I know that the contributors each appreciated their own 'reader's' comments and, had there been space, some would like to have acknowledged also the help or stimulation of other colleagues; similarly, several of us would have liked to include more personal acknowledgements. The individuals warranting such acknowledgement doubtless know who they are; we hope that this general statement of good intentions will serve as a substitute. Thanks are due to Joe Britton for compiling the index. Finally, I would like to say that I am very grateful to have been able to complete the editing of the book while enjoying a Fellowship granted to me by The Netherlands Institute for Advanced Study, during research leave given by the University of Exeter.

Many of the contributors are directly indebted to the late Marcus Cunliffe for scholarly help or professional advice, and most of us were beneficiaries of his writings on aspects of American culture; it seemed fitting, therefore, for us to dedicate this book to his memory.

Mick Gidley
Wassenaar, November 1991

Acknowledgements

We are grateful to the following for permission to reproduce copyright material:

Campbell Connelly and Co Ltd for an extract from the lyrics of the song 'Jet Song' by Leonard Bernstein and Stephen Sondheim, copyright © 1957 (renewed) Leonard Bernstein, Stephen Sondheim (Jalni Publications Inc, USA and Canadian publisher/G Schirmer Inc, worldwide print rights and publisher rest of the world) Campbell Connelly and Co Ltd. International Copyright Secured. All Rights Reserved; Carcanet Press Ltd and New Directions Publishing Corporation for the poem 'On the Road to the Contagious Hospital' by William Carlos Williams from *Collected Poems*, US title *Imaginations*, copyright © 1970 by Florence H Williams; Faber and Faber Ltd and New Directions Publishing Corporation for the poem 'In A Station of the Metro' by Ezra Pound and an extract from the poem 'A Pact' by Ezra Pound from *Collected Shorter Poems*, US title *Personae*, copyright 1926 by Ezra Pound; International Music Publications for an extract from the lyrics of the song 'Summertime' words by Dubose Heyward, music by George Gershwin, © 1935 Gershwin Publishing Corporation, USA/Chappell Music Ltd, London/International Music Publications; the author's agent and New Directions Publishing Corporation for the poem 'Advent 1966' by Denise Levertov from *Selected Poems* (Bloodaxe Books Ltd), US title *Poems 1968–1972* copyright © 1967 by Denise Levertov Goodman; New Directions Publishing Corporation for the poem 'A Language of New York' by George Open from *The Collected Poems of George Oppen*, copyright © 1974 by George Oppen and extracts from the poem 'Paterson' from *Paterson* by William Carlos Williams, copyright © 1944, 1962 by William Carlos Williams; Polygram Island Publishing for an extract from the lyrics of the song 'Ol' Man River' by Oscar Hammerstein and Edna Ferber.

In Memory of Marcus Cunliffe
American Studies Scholar 1922–90

CHAPTER ONE
The American Difference

Stephen Fender

Almost as soon as it was discovered, the New World began to arouse the intense interest of European travellers, historians, philosophers, statesmen, speculators and visionaries of various kinds. Along with the Marquis de Barbé-Marbois, whose 'queries' about America prompted Thomas Jefferson's *Notes on the State of Virginia* (1785), all Europe wanted to know. The United States had opened for business as a sovereign state in 1776, not just as another country, but, to borrow the title of Seymour Martin Lipset's seminal book on the subject, as *The First New Nation* (1963): a political, social (and hence cultural) dispensation qualitatively different from anything that had preceded it in history.

The Europeans' idea of what made America different depended of course on their own interests, and was articulated in terms of comparisons with what they knew at home. In *Letters from an American Farmer* (1782), St John de Crèvecoeur noted the emergence of a dominant American middle class of craftsmen, traders and farmers owning and improving their own property: an emerging bourgeoisie rapidly supplanting the European extremes of peasantry and aristocracy. For Alexis de Tocqueville the salient difference was the American cult of individual enterprise, independent of political and social constraints and obligations, combined paradoxically with great conformity of thought and behaviour. 'I know of no country', he wrote in *Democracy in America* (1836), 'in which there is so little independence of mind and real freedom of discussion as in America.'[1]

These are just two early reactions. The assumption of American exceptionalism, and the attempt to define it, has continued to the present day. Among the economic, political and cultural features said to distinguish the United States from less fortunate nations are a relatively open access to land (later, wealth in general), education and the law; a high value placed on individual effort; an egalitarianism in politics and society; a high proportion of elected officers at all levels of government; the faith in future possibilities; a generally unpromising environment for socialism and corporatist structures.

Naturally Americans have collaborated willingly in these attempts to define their unique dispensation. They have stressed the abundant natural materials of the American continent – their compensation for the relative lack of the deeply ingrained cultural institutions of Europe. Early narratives of exploration frequently catalogued the animals, plants, minerals and topographical features which might supply the new settlers and provide their trade. Above all, American models of the distinctive national identity tend to involve the idea of process – of movement and renewal – through a time of trial. To become American is to be initiated into a higher state of existence. (Even the idea of 'becoming' a particular nationality can almost be said to have been an American invention.)

Renewal could take the form of a religious reformation. In 1630 the Puritan settlers of Massachusetts Bay (now Boston and its environs) braved the Atlantic crossing to establish what their governor, John Winthrop, called a 'city on a hill': a reformed community open to the critical gaze of all and a model to the unregenerate world left behind them. Or the reformation could be more secular and individualistic in emphasis. In an enormously influential lecture delivered at the Chicago World Columbian Exposition in 1893, the historian Frederick Jackson Turner argued that the American identity had been formed by countless individual confrontations with the frontier, where the settler underwent an initiation forcing him or her to 'strip . . . off the garments of civilization' and 'put on the hunting shirt and moccasin'. As they transformed themselves, 'so little by little [they] transform[ed] the wilderness'. The result was 'not the old Europe . . . [but] a new product that is American'.[2]

AMERICA AS A STATE OF MIND

But are Americans 'really' different? The question is meaningless, since the wish to become American and the sense of being so, is such a large part of the fact. 'America – love it or leave it', the conservative car bumper stickers used to say during the domestic protest over the Vietnam War. It is hard to imagine that slogan adapted to British politics, any more than (for all its inequities) the British political establishment could have thrown up a parliamentary select committee on un-British activities. A British subject is British by virtue of being born in England, Wales, Scotland or Northern

Ireland. By contrast, America was and is a state of mind; you could stop being American by dissenting from that consensus. The question 'Are Americans different?' is unanswerable because so many of the possible answers are implicated in an American drive to assert a distinctive, collective identity under the rubric 'American'. The United States, the first new country in modern history, had to constitute itself by separation from a parent culture, which spoke and presumed to set the standards of the same language. 'America' and the Americans were different by definition.

Of course, there is an objective, legal distinction between the United States and Great Britain. In the present-day world, though, this difference tends to make Great Britain, rather than the United States, look unusual. America has a written constitution; Britain doesn't. This is not just a nominal difference, and it is by no means remote from day-to-day experience. It is often argued that the very invisibility of the British 'constitution' is its biggest advantage, providing great flexibility of interpretation and sensitivity to individual nuance. Advantage to whom, though? Not, assuredly, to the man or woman lacking the means to pursue a case through the courts. 'Can then Mr Burke produce the English Constitution?' asked Tom Paine in the first chapter of *The Rights of Man* (1791–92). 'If he cannot, we may fairly conclude, that though it has been so much talked about, no such thing as a constitution exists, or ever did exist.'

THE COLLECTIVE SINGULAR

But even this apparently objective difference rests on the foundations of an American metaphor – and therefore on a figurative construction produced by one of the two parties to the debate. The British are subjects of the queen; they are governed by the sovereign in parliament. This sovereign is a real person to be located in time and space, and she can be seen in her proper governing function every time she opens parliament surrounded by the descending ranks of Lords and Commons. Even when she is absent – that is, when the real work is done – she is present by metonymic extension, in the form of the throne on which she sits at the State Opening, and to which all Peers bow when entering or leaving the chamber of the Upper House.

The Americans, on the other hand, are governed by the sovereignty of the people. This formulation is more abstract than the British model of government, because through the agency of a figure of speech which we

3

might call the 'collective singular', it suggests a whole population somehow sitting on an imaginary throne. The idea is also paradoxical, establishing the governed as also the governor. All the people stand in for one 'sovereign'; in respect of their governing function, all the people *act* as one. A good many of the books about America start from this premise of the collective singular. Consider just the titles of some of the better known: *The Lonely Crowd: A Study of the Changing American Character*; *American Humor: A Study of the National Character*; *And Keep Your Powder Dry: An Anthropologist Looks at the American Character*; *American Tough: The Tough-Guy Tradition and American Character*. It is as though it were possible to talk of the whole diversity of American society as one human personality. 'You might think that with such a varied nation there couldn't be one . . . character' President Reagan remarked to an audience in Shanghai, China, in 1984, 'but in many ways there is . . . . We're idealists . . . . We're a compassionate people . . . . We're an optimistic people . . . . Like you, we inherited a land of endless skies, tall mountains, rich fields, and open prairies. It made us see the possibilities of everything.'

In the American Constitution itself the sovereignty of the people is established and maintained through the voice of the collective singular: 'We the People . . . do ordain and establish this CONSTITUTION for the United States of America.' In another such preamble, to an equally inclusive and innovative discourse of and by America, Walt Whitman begins *Leaves of Grass* (1855) with an apparent impossibility in English usage: 'One's-Self I Sing, a simple separate person,/Yet utter the word Democratic, the word En-Masse'. It makes sense only if 'one's self' understands how deeply the collective singular is grooved in the American consciousness. Americans have always had great faith – many British would say a touching and even peculiar faith – in constitutions. Constitutions were what Americans did before they encountered the unknown. The Mayflower compact was drawn up on board the ship of that name before the first settlers set foot in Massachusetts in 1620. More than 200 years later, Forty-niners about to set off across the country to look for gold in California formed themselves into companies with printed constitutions containing clauses like: '*Resolved* that the Christian Sabbath shall be observed, except where absolutely necessary to travel. *Resolved* that each and every member shall pay strict and proper respect to the feelings of each and all the Company.'

Clearly, not all of these regulations were equally practicable and enforceable. What they had in common, though, was a set of *a priori* formulations posed as a verbal stockade against the unknown. Though drawing on precedent and past experience, constitutions are also a programme for the future. So the Constitution of the United States drew specifically on the English Bill of Rights of 1689 and, more generally, on what American colonists took their rights to be as British subjects before (as they saw it) parliament began to strip those rights away, but it also addressed the future of a newly independent republic anxious to define itself as legally and politically distinct within the linguistic and cultural field controlled by the old metropolis.

FOUNDATION AS FRAGMENTATION

So the Americans constituted themselves as a single character – and one cut off from the continuum of British history – and even American books about the American founding premise have been premissed in turn upon the founding premise itself. Consider two contrasting theories about how America came to be – one American and one not. *The Machiavellian Moment* (1975) by J.G.A. Pocock, a Londoner educated in New Zealand and at Cambridge, traces the idea of the American republic through James Harrington's *The Commonwealth of Oceana* (1656) back to the sixteenth-century theorists of the Italian city state, Machiavelli and Leonardo Bruni. In *The Liberal Tradition in America* (1955), and later in a collection of essays of which his was the salient one, *The Founding of New Societies* (1964), Louis Hartz imagined America as a branch off the European tree; or, more radical still, a *fragment* (his word) which, when it 'leaves Europe . . . cuts short the process of European *contagion* at the point of leaving. When it leaves its first antagonist, it leaves all of the future antagonists that the first inspires.'[3] On the basis of this image of catastrophic separation Hartz erects his well known theory of America as a fly fixed in the amber of Lockean free-enterprise, property-valuing liberalism. The country turned out like that because it broke off from Great Britain when those values were in their ascendancy. In so severing itself, the United States ceased to function in the dialectic of history. Time, in a sense, stopped for it. After that it was no longer a part of the continuum assumed by Pocock.

The relative virtues of these hypotheses, or even their full exposition, are beside the point here. What matters is that the non-American theorist of American foundation could easily conceive of the country in history, as it were: as one more term in a sequence of political and intellectual events in time, while the American found it more difficult to imagine the foundation process as other than qualitatively different from everything that went before it. Not that Americans themselves are incapable of imagining themselves into both sides of the debate over whether the thinking behind the Constitution owed more to republican (public) or Liberal–Lockeian (private) values. Contemporary historians have lined up behind Pocock and Hartz, with (roughly speaking) Bernard Bailyn, Gordon Wood and Garry Wills following the line of the republican synthesis, and Carl Becker, John P. Diggins and Isaak Kramnick taking the neo-liberal case. But this dispute is one over content rather than process. What most of them share – and what makes their debate so urgent – is the assumption that America jumped off predominantly from one tradition (whichever it be), which worked unchanged thereafter so as to determine its political character. Their argument is partly over issues begging the question of American exceptionalism in the first place: What is the true nature of America? What sort of country ought it to be? What makes it distinct? Astonishingly (given the enormous success of the American political dispensation), American historians sometimes seem still to be searching for a usable tradition of political philosophy.

As with the foundation theories of the American republic, so also the hypotheses defining and explaining the unique trajectory of American literary history. Leslie Fiedler, Richard Chase, R.W.B. Lewis and others wrote the influential books on the distinctiveness of American literature, especially that kind of American literature selected by (among others) Leslie Fiedler, Richard Chase and R.W.B. Lewis to be taught in the universities as distinctively American. Writers such as these – among the most imaginative and learned of their generation in the universities – set out to ask, not if American literature was different, but why. Fiedler started his now legendary *Love and Death in the American Novel* (1960) by admitting the bias in his sample. He wanted, as he says in his preface, 'to define what is peculiarly American in our books'. What he found is that American literature is characteristic in being unable to portray a satisfactory heterosexual relationship between partners of the same race and class. In *The American Novel and its Tradition* (1957) Chase says that American fiction dramatises radical forms of alienation, contradiction and disorder and, unlike English fiction, refuses to resolve these tensions, characteristically leaving its protagonists to light out for the Territory, like Mark Twain's Huckleberry Finn, at the end of the story.

Again, the exceptionalist premise is built into the question. Suppose there is nothing 'characteristic' about American novels? Is there anything characteristically English in Dickens, Evelyn Waugh, Graham Greene, Anthony Burgess and Margaret Drabble? If so, could any book about this characteristic be a worthwhile project? What looks like a description of American literature turns out to be its prescription, its constitution, as it were. It is not necessarily American literature, but its meta-literature that is characteristic. Yet that too must be accounted for. In fact, the first of these exceptionalist hypotheses – that American literature would be different in that it would imagine characters who made themselves different – was constructed (again) by de Tocqueville: 'Man himself, taken aloof from his age and country, and standing in the presence of nature and of God, with his passions, his doubts, his rare prosperities, and inconceivable wretchedness – will become the chief, if not the sole theme of poetry among these nations.'[4] By 'poetry' he means imaginative literature, and 'these nations' are democracies. But de Tocqueville was constituting, not describing. He wrote and published this before he had seen anything he recognized as 'poetry' in America.

A DISCOURSE OF DIFFERENCE

If we are going to describe the American difference, then, we must begin by recognizing that what we are discussing is not an actual difference but the idea of one. Americans are different because they think they are – have constituted themselves as distinct not only in the Constitution (itself a set of ideas, of course), but also in the idea that constitutions matter. This is not an insignificant fact in itself, but it calls for another kind of history to supplement that grounded, for example, on the material facts of topography. What idea, or complex of ideas, constitutes the dominant thesis of the American ideology of identity? Perhaps the sense of being American has been most closely associated with the shared (or inherited) experience of emigration. This is not to say that the one caused or conditioned the other, but that emigration and American-ness were both constituted by the same discourse, which itself has a history. The narrative by which the country has come to define itself – even the assumption of American exceptionalism and the recurrent image of American 'character' – is part of that which moved people to go there in the first place.

In tracing that history the first thing to establish is that the idea of the American difference began as a European construct, not an American one. Long before the continents of North and South America began to be settled, European explorers tried to explain what made the New World so unusual. In a letter of 1502 Amerigo Vespucci wrote of the Amerindians, 'We did not learn that they had any law . . . [or] offered any sacrifice: nor even had a house of prayer . . . they use no trade, they neither buy nor sell.'[5] This was not a 'discovery', nor even a new idea. Classical authors had used the same beneficent negatives to describe life in the Golden Age, when men lived happily without laws, borders, trade, warfare or the need to travel, and when nature gave forth her bounty of nuts and berries without the need for laborious cultivation. So 'America' was first imagined as different because it had somehow escaped the Fall. The idea took hold, even (perhaps especially) among those who had never gone there. Montaigne's essay 'On Cannibals' (1580) expanded Vespucci's paradisal negatives about the Indians, adding detail from Ovid; Thomas More used the same trope for the inhabitants of his *Utopia* (first published in an English translation in 1551), and Shakespeare, cribbing from Florio's English translation of Montaigne, used it for Gonzalo's ideal commonwealth in *The Tempest* (1611).

When the Europeans began to think seriously of settling and colonizing America, their reports became more materialistic and scientific – more 'realistic' in one common use of the word. Now interest in the Indians faded, and people began to ask questions about American nature in its non-human aspect: What can we know about it? How do we know we know it? (and above all) How can we use it? Now the descriptions of the New World became a list of positives. *A Brief and True Report of the New-Found Land of Virginia* (1588), by the scientist John Hariot, and Captain John Smith's *A Description of New England* (1616) were only two of the many accounts that catalogued the exploitable raw materials of profuse American nature: its timber, minerals, animal life, climate. Though still conditioned by classical and medieval formulas for describing the realm of the goddess Nature, the positive catalogues now adjusted themselves to what was actually there on American soil.

The New World became, indeed, the focus of the British ideology of empire. Treatises by Richard Hakluyt (*Discourse on Western Planting*, 1584), Henry Robinson (*England's Safety in Trade's Increase*, 1641) and others argued for American colonization in order to extend the reformed religion as a counterbalance to Spain's intention to convert the South American Indians to Catholicism; to replace other British trade routes made 'beggarly or dangerous' by Spanish explorations; to employ 'numbers of idle men' made homeless by the enclosures of the late sixteenth century; to discover a north-west passage to the Orient; and above all, to supply the British demand for raw materials from her own dominions while establishing, in turn, captive markets for the British manufactured goods that would result.

THE EUROPEAN USE OF THE AMERICAN 'OTHER'

So the idea of the New World began as an idea of its difference. That idea was European at first, but it soon became American as well. Early

Massachusetts was settled by English Puritans who had come to feel increasingly alienated within the Anglican establishment at home. In 1620 a band of separatists who had already fled to Holland landed on Cape Cod and later settled on the mainland at Plymouth. Ten years later the much larger and better financed Massachusetts Bay Company established itself in what is now Boston and its surrounding communities. Strictly defined, these were sects, and sects define themselves by difference. Even the Boston settlers, though theoretically still communicating with the Church of England and therefore not separatists, were a beleaguered group of Puritans who had been made very unwelcome by Bishop Laud of London and his pursuivants, who interrupted their services and prohibited them the use of Anglican churches.

If the Puritans thought of themselves as different in their religious practice, the British authorities certainly thought them different in their politics – and dangerously so. In 1665 a delegation of Royal Commissioners visited New England to hear various grievances and settle territorial disputes between the colonies. Most of the settlements protested their loyalty to the king – indeed all, with one notorious exception:

> They of this colony [Massachusetts Bay] say that King Charles the First gave them power to make laws and to execute them, and granted them a charter as a warrant against himself, and his successors, and so long as they pay the fifth part of all gold and silver ore which they shall get, they are free to use their privileges granted them, and that they are not obliged to the King, but by civility . . . .[6]

'A charter as a warrant against' the King's personal fiat – authority grounded in the law rather than in the individual: this was and remains the core principle of constitutional government. The Commissioners knew that Massachusetts Bay was heading for rebellion when it began to call itself (as the State of Massachusetts does to this day) a 'Commonwealth'.

When in 1776 the other American colonies joined Massachusetts in declaring their independence from Great Britain, they not only cut themselves off from the rest of the British Empire, including British North America, but also struck out in a new constitutional direction (see Chapter 3). A democratic republic, in which sovereignty was vested in the people, now confronted an oligarchic monarchy taking its authority from the sovereignty of the king in parliament. The War of 1812 served to reinforce the hostilities between Britain and the United States begun with the American Revolution.

And so began the third stage in the European construction of the American difference. Here the facts of history – at least as suggested by the statistics of emigration – and the dominant discourse of the American difference are sharply divergent. By the end of the first quarter of the nineteenth century a substantial minority of British subjects (not citizens – that was another difference) had grown disaffected and alienated: unenfranchised British labourers, tenant farmers, artisans and merchants, peasants who had been displaced by a renewed cycle of enclosures in the eighteenth century and handloom workers beginning to be thrown out of work by the factory system. Many of them did emigrate. But where? To America, the country offering the vote to the common man and cheap land to those who would work it? Only up to a point. In the seventeen years of British domestic unrest between the end of the Napoleonic Wars and the passing of the first Reform Bill of 1832 well over half a million people emigrated from United Kingdom ports to the United States, Canada and (from 1821) New Zealand and Australia. But while around 206.5 thousand went to the United States, over 334 thousand emigrated to Canada, and another 14.2 thousand to Australia and New Zealand. In other words, total emigrations to the United States were little more than half of those to Canada alone.

Yet in the same period the contemporary books and pamphlets rushed onto the market to argue the case for or against emigration concentrated almost exclusively on emigration to the United States. That, and not the question of removing to the Colonies, was the dominant issue in the discourse. Why? Because by now the whole issue of emigration had became part of the debate for and against the extension of the franchise and reform of the tax system. Loathe it or love it, the United States was now the 'other' – the alternative, radical dispensation. Hardly one of the many British books of travels in America published in the first half of the nineteenth century failed to include the question of emigration among its observations on the new country, and scarcely a tract promoting American emigration, or a guidebook showing how to go about it, omitted its critique of the depressed condition of the voteless British poor paying their tithes and taxes to a hard-hearted parish, a distant Church authority and an unrepresentative government. If the disadvantaged could not vote in a ballot, they could at least vote with their feet.

But there would be little point in going through all the trauma of emigration only to wind up in an equally reactionary British dependency overseas. Hence the salience of the United States in the British political debate. William Cobbett, the radical agitator for reform, had been sceptical at first of what he called the 'transalleganian romance' of English schemes to settle emigrants in Illinois Territory, but by 1829 he felt pressed to issue his own guide to emigration, illustrated by letters from happy settlers in the States. His strongest advice concerned the 'worthlessness' of the 'English colonies', and the need for the emigrant to go to the United States if at all possible.

THE RHETORIC OF EMIGRATION

This is how British emigration to the United States and the idea of the American difference became inextricably tangled up with one another. It would be impossible to say which came first, which 'caused' the other. The idea conditioned the psychology of emigration to America; emigration and its psychology helped to form the idea. In other words, it would be far too simple to assert that emigration to the United States *converted* British peasants into American farmers, craftsmen, managers of small business, and other sorts of entrepreneur. The enclosures of common lands at the end of the sixteenth and eighteenth centuries, the Highland clearances, the growth of the factory system – all had contributed to the uprooting of a traditionary British peasant class, turning them into vagrants and labourers, forced to move where the food and work was to be had. Even before the industrial revolution Great Britain had a high rate of internal migration compared to the rest of Europe.

In other words, when one talks of the 'psychology' of emigration, one is discussing how the idea was advertised in prospect and described in retrospect: not what 'really' went on in the minds of the emigrants – for who can know? – but what the propagandists said in its favour and the participants wrote home of the experience. How then might that psychology be described? Its first ingredient is the sense, whether justified or illusory, of choice. The emigrants might have been rich or poor, adventurers of greater or lesser means, or indentured servants, or whole communities pushed out of their homes by political, social, financial or even military persecution. In any case, they had to be convinced that they were making the decision to emigrate for themselves. African slaves and English criminals sentenced to penal servitude were therefore not emigrants in the sense that produced and participated in the dominant founding discourse, but Russian Jews escaping the pogroms of the late nineteenth century were, because though constrained and even terrorized by their native environment, they still had the choice of whether to go or not. Narratives of Jewish emigration to the United States, like Mary Antin's *The Promised Land* (1912) and Anzia Yezierska's *Bread Givers* (1925), all speak of advance planning, of money set aside, of families and even communities clubbing together to send one or a few representative members over.

What attracted them? The appeal was (it is a cliché of the dominant discourse) the 'American Dream'. The American Dream, first articulated by Englishmen trying to get other Englishmen to go to America, then sharpened by the British political debate over reform, was the opportunity for the poor to employ the one resource they had in good supply – their labour – and through it to escape from their feudal dependency, taking

11

their part, finally, as full citizens in the polity of their adopted country. And the 'dream' is essentially bourgeois (which is to say that in the seventeenth, eighteenth and early nineteenth centuries, it was radical). American society is often said to be one large middle class. If this generalization serves, it does so not only because America split off from Europe at the moment when Europe itself was going through a phase when the dominant values were bourgeois, or because the timing of the American Revolution happened to coincide with the emergence of European capitalism, but also because the very thought of becoming American promoted and reinforced those qualities which we call bourgeois: enterprise, the accumulation and investment of capital, the taking of risk, the deferring of gratification, the faith in future possibilities.

So much for the dream. What did the emigrant imagine he or she would have to give up for it? The protection and physical convenience of city walls, solid houses, public meeting places; the parish church, with its social networks and spiritual comfort; friends, gossips, the emotional, moral and material support of the extended family (for typically it was the individual or nuclear family only that made the trip, perhaps financed by the larger kinship group); the transmission of a whole culture of cooking and household management, childbirth and child-rearing (most of which lore is handed down in extended-family societies from generation to generation by example and word of mouth). Emigration threatened to put all these comforts, and more, at risk. Not that the threat wasn't posed almost to the same extent by the prospect of moving from the country to a city or a mill town, but that the prospect of emigration to the United States was more daunting than that of moving to, say, London, or Northern Ireland, or even to Canada and New Zealand. To become an American was not just to distance the metropolitan centre where standards of language, custom, faith and fashion were set; it was to cut oneself off altogether from the imperial network, to repudiate the very hereditary hierarchy by which that empire was authorized.

A PORTABLE FAITH/FAITH IN THE PORTABLE

To bolster his or her confidence the emigrant needed an ideology of the portable, arguing the possibility – perhaps even the desirability – of leaving all these things behind. The ideology required a belief that challenged the importance of accumulated traditions – institutional and architectural.

Historians sometimes complain at the extent to which the New England Puritans have hogged the attentions of America's mythographers. And after all, why should the Puritans have assumed such importance out of all proportion to their numbers, wealth and power? The country was settled by people of so many faiths: by Anglicans in Virginia, Catholics in Maryland, Quakers and German enthusiastics in Pennsylvania – and by others of no particular religion at all. But Puritanism so exactly fits America's idea of itself because it was the most articulate expression (just as its followers were the most deliberate and self-conscious exponents) of the essential ideology of emigration, the thesis of portability:

> But now we are all in all places strangers and pilgrims, travellers and sojourners, most properly, having no dwelling but in this earthen tabernacle; our dwelling is but a wandering, and our abiding but as a fleeting, and in a word our home is nowhere, but in the heavens, in that house not made with hands, whose maker and builder is God, and to which all ascend, that love the coming of our Lord Jesus.

Thus Robert Cushman's sermon trying to persuade the English Puritans of the 'Lawfulness of Removing . . . into the Parts of America' (1622).[7] America, in other words, was for the Puritan nothing more or less than the world properly understood: with its 'worldly' trappings stripped away; fallen from that primacy of place and status to which God had assigned Eden before the Original Sin, and to which idolatrous men still exalt the vain metropolises of king and Pope; yet redeemable under republican principles – and above all, as Milton says after the Fall in *Paradise Lost*, lying 'all before them, where to choose, and Providence their guide'.

And the transatlantic voyage, charged with the significance of the biblical type of the Israelites crossing the Red Sea, became a one-way pendulum in the narrative of the New England providence. The Journal of John Winthrop, the Governor of Massachusetts Bay, makes a note of every ship that arrives in the Bay Colony bearing supplies and – most importantly – new settlers from England. Typically these vessels are said to have come 'through many great tempests; yet through the Lord's great providence, her passengers all safe'. But with equal regularity these same ships get dismasted, or founder with the loss of all hands, on their return voyages. Winthrop catalogues their loss as lovingly as he does their bountiful arrival.

William Hubbard's *General History of New England* tells of a ship returning to England that was wrecked on the notorious lee shore of the Bay of Biscay:

> Amongst them that were lost, was one Pratt and his wife, that had lived divers years in New England in much discontent and now went to provide better for himself in his old age, fearing he might come to want afterward; but now he wanted nothing but a grave being buried in the rude waters.[8]

To the topic of the return to the Old World it is God's Old Testament justice that applies, not the mercy of his New Covenant. The transgressor gets just what he deserves (and no more). The savagery of remarks like these suggests that Winthrop, Hubbard and other New England settlers just could not countenance the retrograde motion of the transatlantic return. This was not only because they were desperately defensive about their precarious enterprise, or even just because they were Puritans steeped in the justice of God's providence, but because at that time the journey backwards was literally unimaginable within the plot they were living. And that plot was not only a providential reformation of the spirit but also, more generally, a rite of passage to a new stage of life. And rites of passage, since they celebrate irreversible processes like birth, adolescence and death, point forward only.

REFORMATIONS AND TRANSFORMATIONS

What about the waves of nineteenth-century emigrants to America? Did they see the enterprise as just the chance to improve their material prosperity? There is evidence that even among emigrants not obviously 'religious' in outlook or reference, the journey was considered an irreversible passage to a higher state of awareness, a greater maturity. Letters to the extended family back home speak frequently of improved health and an altered state of mind. 'I myself am very well in body, mind, spirit quite stout. I weigh 182 lbs so you may think how I am, a man of my size. Am very corpulent', wrote a man in 1826, when 'corpulence' was a badge of well-being.[9] 'Tell aunt she need not be in any trouble about her sons', wrote a woman in the same year, 'for they are doing very well. Tell her she would not know John if she was to see him; for he is altered both in speech, looks and dress: *he is very polite.*' And another woman wrote, in 1829, 'I could never go to England to live now after being here in Kansas. The air is so light here. I suppose you will be planting potatoes by this time. We shall plant this week.' The letter is not without nostalgia, but remains buttressed by the conviction of change for the better – not a spiritual 'better' exactly, but certainly not just material.

A common feature in emigrants' letters home to England is an unwarranted concern for the future of the country they had left behind them. Repeated pessimism was expressed as to whether the Reform Bill would be passed. One correspondent in 1837 doubted whether 'a girl of eighteen' would be able 'to rule the destinies of a hundred and fifty millions of free men'. The reason is obvious enough. The pattern required that the old life had to be outmoded, stuck in the past. How unbearable, after all the trauma of separation and resettlement, if the Old Country should turn out to have a future after all: if the bill to widen the franchise should become law and Queen Victoria grow up to reign over the most powerful empire in the world's history.

Another feature common to these letters, and growing out of the strenuous conviction to which they needed to hold – that they had made the right move – was a general contempt for those who had tried the experiment, and failed. As one man wrote to his brother in 1850:

> if your prospects are so gloomy as you forebode, it is about time you tried another country where you can get your children educated for nothing, and so enable them to work their way in the world; but . . . you must make up your mind . . . if you wish to succeed you must learn to conform to the people in the host country as soon as possible. I really have no patience with such chicken-hearted people. Henry Clarke is one of that kind. He came here bragging about what he would do. He knew every thing about the country, and nobody could tell him any thing . . . got scared and went home without trying any thing . . . .

Another, writing in 1831, told of two men who landed in Philadelphia, stayed 'about two weeks and got drunk almost every day and then began to curse the country and all that was in it. They went back . . . So I leave you to guess what tales they would tell when they got home.' Within the rhetorical complex of the rite-of-passage narrative, people don't return because of illness, bad luck or bad management. They return because they fail. And they fail because they are too 'chicken-hearted' to cope with the adventure in political and economic enterprise, or too lazy. They can't leave the nest, can't embrace the unpredictable challenge of fresh experience – in short, they have never grown up.

In fact – as nearly as one can tell from the statistics – return migration has always been much more common than allowed by the foundation discourse. Around a quarter of the sixteen million European immigrants to the United States in the first three decades of the twentieth century returned home in the same period. A recent history of migration to New England in the seventeenth century estimates that around 7,000 out of 21,000 (one in three) returned home from Massachusetts Bay in the first decade of the colony's settlement. But in the rhetoric of American foundation, the back migrants do not find a voice. There seems no very substantial body of data comprising first-hand accounts of their experience. Perhaps their families thought their letters shameful and discarded them, so

15

they didn't get passed on in turn to the local record office, university library or genealogical society.

Most probably, the 'failed' emigrant didn't write home in the first place. How do we know? There is the positive evidence of those who did succeed – that they often didn't write until they had good news to report: often years went by before what proclaimed itself to be the emigrant's first letter home. A woman in 1881 was quite explicit about this: 'Dear Brother . . . We have had two very bad years out here; but we have pulled through them and this year is better so far. We are very busy harvesting wheat.' And so was another in 1823: 'I would have wrote before this, but could not write pleasant news; as Stephen has been so unhappy in a strange country, but is now contented and doing well.' The act of writing home, therefore, was a trophy of the emigrants' success in their own terms. The text itself was the badge of the initiate.

Initiation, transformation, perhaps even reformation: these seem the appropriate words to describe the psychology of emigration to America. It is worth pausing a moment at the word 'reformation', because it helps to explain the Americans' fondness for the figure of the collective singular: the 'American character' and the sovereign people. If 'reform' usually applies to a public, even political act (the reform of the franchise, of the civil service, or whatever), 'reformation' is both personal and communal, private and public. Of course, it had to be promulgated by one or more originators: Luther, Calvin, the many British and American evangelists from the eighteenth century to the present day. But to succeed it had to be taken up by millions of individuals. The Reformation as proper noun was actually the sum of countless personal reformations in the common sense. How could it be otherwise, given the Protestant theology of man's direct access to God, without the mediation of Church structures, the parish priest, liturgy, the mechanism of salvation?

The experience of emigration, as considered and remembered, was like this too: a mass movement at times – sometimes, as in certain utopian ventures, undertaken communally – but one motivated by a multitude of *individual* decisions, acts of forward planning, achievements and setbacks, endurance and imagination. You had to do it for yourself. Every emigration, however commonplace when considered statistically, was charged with immense drama. And even today every American life seems to replicate the founding process. The American emigrant makes his country by going there. His or her rite of passage is also that of his or her country. The founding of a new life is also the founding of a new country. And this drama of the individual transformation is, in turn, reinforced by the sense that the enterprise of the individual and the country are somehow coterminous.

THE INDIVIDUAL ON THE FRONTIER OF EXPERIENCE

If people tell stories to make sense of their lives, then these narratives, properly examined, will reveal something about the people who tell and hear them. But to examine the imaginative literature of a whole country in close detail, it is first necessary to select and highlight, to canonize a representative sample of texts. The fiction of alienation, the novel that refuses to close with an accommodation to contemporary society, the 'poetry' of 'man himself, taken aloof from his age and country, and standing in the presence of nature and of God', may indeed represent the characteristic literary production of the United States. Or it may represent what Americans (and others) have 'constituted' that literature to be. All we can suggest with any conviction is that such writing is part of a dominant discourse of American identity which has been conditioned by the communal experience of uprooting, of moving on when life (including contemporary social relations) becomes constraining – in short, that American literature, as described or prescribed, is connected with the psychology of emigration.

But suppose we sidestep 'American literature' for a moment – that canon embracing Benjamin Franklin's *Autobiography*, *The Scarlet Letter*, *Moby Dick*, *The Portrait of a Lady* and *The Sun Also Rises* selected as somehow characteristically American – and look briefly at another sample approved more objectively (or at least more communally) by the sovereignty of the people: American bestsellers. Perennially the most popular American stories dramatize the experience of (male, usually) initiation, the irreversible rite of passage into a higher state of consciousness. They do so even in places where the story would seem to suggest other themes. Some of the most popular American fiction conforms to one of two plot paradigms: Turner's paradigm of the individual initiated through exposure to danger on the frontier, and the story of the good bad boy. In the first category comes the western, starting as early as Captain John Smith's *The General History of Virginia* (1624), in which the protagonist ventures out from the English camp, is captured by the Indians, 'married' to the American wilderness through the love of the Chief's daughter, Pocahontas, then released from his ordeal to resolve the divisions between factions of those settlers left behind. From Smith the theme of the isolated frontiersman's initiation can be traced through John Filson's biography of Daniel Boone in his *Discovery, Settlement and Present State of Kentucke* (1784), James Fenimore Cooper's Leatherstocking tales (1823–41), and on to the popular almanacks and dime novels, down to western movies of the 1940s and 1950s. The good bad boy is an innocent rebel at odds with grown-up society. Twain's *Huckleberry Finn* (1884), J.D.

Salinger's *The Catcher in the Rye* (1951) and Philip Roth's *Portnoy's Complaint* (1969), are all dramatizations of adolescence necessitating the act of lighting out from constraints of family life and often, in Freudian ritual displacement, killing their fathers in the process.

STORIES OF CAPTIVITY

Common to many popular American narratives is the theme of captivity. The captors may be Indians, as in *The General History* and Cooper's *The Last of the Mohicans* (1826), or the South Sea Islanders of Herman Melville's *Typee* (1846), or the white planters in Harriet Beecher Stowe's *Uncle Tom's Cabin* (1852), or even the ancient Romans of General Lew Wallace's *Ben-Hur* (1880). Properly understood, even the bestsellers set in or around the Second World War come into this category, for in Thomas Heggen's *Mister Roberts* (1946), Norman Mailer's *The Naked and the Dead* (1948), James Jones's *From Here to Eternity* (1951), Herman Wouk's *The Caine Mutiny* (1951) and even Joseph Heller's *Catch-22* (1961) the protagonists are imprisoned, in one way or another, by officers and men of their own military forces.

Of course, to an extent these stories simply reflect the objective challenges faced by Americans at various points in their history: settlement, conflict between whites and Indians, slavery and emancipation, international warfare. But consider how the narratives warp their settings. Fictional cowboys, for instance, are rather like lone detectives, putting right the world's wrongs, often in face of the defiance, or at least the indifference, of the majority of solid citizens and salaried law-enforcement officers who might be expected to keep the peace – then riding off into the sunset. But real cowboys worked and lived in communities; they cooperated as part of a tightly-knit, well-organized group. (To get the idea, try rounding up two thousand or so head of cattle on your own, then driving them from Texas to Abeline, Kansas.) Again, the historical captors change, but the theme of captivity always bends history to its dominant discourse. In the popular war fiction the imagined enemy is always on one's own side. The historical conflict with the Japanese and Germans is moved to the margins of the story, displaced by a crisis of separation: the irreversible development of an individual's adolescence, or some other experience that transforms the personality utterly. As with the canonical texts, these more popular American fictions can be explained in the context of the psychology of emigration. Dramas of adolescent rebellion, contemporary public events displaced and reinscribed in private reformations of the individual consciousness – both motifs may be seen as oblique expressions of the American collective singular: a nation pulled out of history to reform itself through individual endeavour.

Why should Americans have been so perennially fascinated by narratives of captivity? One possibility is that in the Land of the Free, confinement is almost the worst nightmare. The stories, in other words, pleased their readers by 'telling it scary'. Another is that settlement in the New World, especially on the frontier or in small towns far from older and more built-up communities, is liberating in prospect but confining in actual experience. Traditional communities in Europe or on the American East Coast may have been sufficiently claustrophobic to prompt the emigrant to light out for the frontier, but the uncleared forest could induce another sort of confinement, at least as strong. Even cleared and cultivated, the distant settlement, given the primitive state of travel and communications, allowed the settler little variety. However far he or she could travel in any direction, the sights, sounds and company would remain much the same.

Significantly, emigrants to Canada could admit to this feeling. In her *Life in the Clearings versus the Bush* (1853) Susanna Moodie could write about having suffered 'the green prison of the woods' of the Canadian wilderness, after her petition to the Lieutenant Governor of Upper Canada had secured her husband the position of Sheriff in a 'more settled part of the country'. But for the majority of Americans such feelings ran too strongly counter to the ideology of their migration. Unlike Moodie, they had burned their boats: not only left their neighbours and extended families but also cut the ties of imperial hierarchy and government preferment. There was no governor for them to appeal to. They had undergone a reformation of behaviour, belief and expectation. How unbearable, then, if the new lives for which they had risked everything should turn out to be as restricted (though in a different way) as the old. So the dominant discourse had to displace that disappointment into stories of confinement, in which the villainous captors were agents of the 'other': Indians, French Jesuits, or other Americans acting in an un-American way, like aristocratic slave-holders or officers in a rigid military hierarchy.

On reflection, then, perhaps it is a bit hard to blame the theorists of the American difference for describing what they have already prescribed. Even the more objective sample of the people's choice seems to confirm the exceptionalist rule that American literature, like the culture of which it is a part, is a theatre of exceptions: the drama of the imperative to separate from a society imagined as retrograde and confining; of the individual crisis appropriating the more public historical setting. American culture has defined itself through the act of separation, of difference in action. The curiously reflexive ideology of the American difference is both expressed and reflected not only in its history and literature, but in the history of its literature and the history of its history. The analysis of the condition is itself part of that condition. Americans are different because they think they are, or wish to be, and the wish has always been father and mother to the fact.

NOTES

1. Alexis de Tocqueville, *Democracy in America*, trans. Henry Reeve, ed. Phillips Bradley (New York, 1945), vol. I, p. 263.

2. Frederick Jackson Turner, 'The Significance of the Frontier in American History', in George Roberts Taylor (ed.), *The Turner Thesis* (Boston, 1956), p. 2.

3. Louis Hartz, et al., *The Founding of New Societies: Studies in the History of the United States, Latin America, South Africa, Canada and Australia* (New York, 1964), p. 7; my emphasis.

4. Alexis de Tocqueville, *Democracy in America*, vol. II, p. 81.

5. 'Amerigo Vespucci's Account of his First Voyage', in Charles W. Eliot (ed.), *American Historical Documents* (New York, 1910), pp. 35–6.

6. 'Report of the Royal Commissioners in 1665 . . .', British Library, Egerton MAA 2395, fos. 434–4b.

7. Robert Cushman, 'Reasons & Considerations touching the Lawfulness of Removing out of England into the Parts of America', in Dwight Heath (ed.), *A Relation . . . of the Beginnings and Proceedings of the English Plantation Settled at Plymouth in New England* (New York, 1963), pp. 89–90.

8. William Hubbard, *General History of New England*, Collections of the Massachusetts Historical Society, 2nd series, VI (1815), p. 525.

9. This and other extracts from immigrants' letters quoted here are taken from Charlotte Erickson (ed.), *Invisible Immigrants: The Adaption of English and Scottish Immigrants to Nineteenth-Century America* (London, 1972; reprinted Ithaca, NY, 1991).

SUGGESTIONS FOR FURTHER READING

The history of ideas about American exceptionalism, and the present-day debate on the issue, are surveyed in Daniel Bell, Andrew Greeley, Seymour Martin Lipset, et al., *Is America Different?*, ed. Byron E. Shafer (Oxford, 1991). Theories of American foundation can be sampled in Seymour Martin Lipset, *The First New Nation: The United States in Historical and*

Comparative Prospective (New York, 1963); Louis Hartz, et al., *The Founding of New Societies: Studies in the History of the United States, Latin America, South America, Canada and Australia* (New York, 1964); Michael Kammen, *People of Paradox: An Inquiry Concerning the Origins of American Civilization* (New York, 1972); J.G.A. Pocock, *The Machiavellian Moment: Florentine Political Thought and the Atlantic Republican Tradition* (Princeton, NJ, 1975); Benedict Anderson, *Imagined Communities: Reflections on the Origin and Spread of Nationalism* (London, 1983); and John Harmon McElroy, *Finding Freedom: America's Distinctive Cultural Foundation* (Carbondale, IL, 1988). The issue of the 'American character' is surveyed in Rupert Wilkinson, *The Pursuit of American Character* (New York, 1988).

The debate between American historians over whether the American polity owes more to Lockeian or republican ideas is set out in (for the republicans): Bernard Bailyn, *The Ideological Origins of the American Revolution, 1776–1789* (Cambridge, MA, 1967); Gordon Wood, *The Creation of the American Republic* (1969; 2nd edn, New York, 1972); and Garry Wills, *Inventing America: Jefferson's Declaration of Independence* (New York, 1978); (for the Lockeians): Carl Becker, *The Declaration of Independence: A Study in the History of Political Ideas* (New York, 1922); John P. Diggins, *The Lost Soul of American Politics: Virtue, Self-Interest and the Foundations of Liberalism* (New York, 1984); and Isaak Kramnick, *Republicanism and Bourgeois Radicalism: Political Ideology in Late Eighteenth-Century England and America* (Ithaca, NY, 1990).

An indispensable survey of British theories of colonialism is Klaus Knorr, *British Colonial Theories, 1570–1850* (London, 1983). Facts and figures on British emigration to America and the colonies can be found in Wilbur Shepperson, *British Emigration to North America* (Oxford, 1957) for the nineteenth century; Bernard Bailyn, *Voyagers to the West: Emigration from Britain to America on the Eve of the Revolution* (New York, 1987) for the eighteenth century; and David Cressey, *Coming Over: Migration and Communication between England and New England in the Seventeenth Century* (Cambridge, 1987) for the Massachusetts Puritans.

This essay concentrates on the discourse of emigration – its psychology and the rhetoric in which it was promoted and described by native English speakers. Most historians have tended to analyse the phenomenon from the point of view of its material causes. Their argument has focused on whether emigrants were 'pushed' or 'pulled': that is, whether they were victims of religious persecution and poor peasants forced out by economic necessity; or relatively mobile workers, craftsmen, small farmers and traders able to dispose of their labour where they wished, and thus responding of free choice to the relative economic, social and political attractions of the New World. Advocates of the 'push' thesis include William Forbes Adams,

Ireland and the Irish Emigration to the New World from 1815 to the Famine (New Haven: Yale Historical Publications, Miscellany 23, 1932); and Oscar Handlin, *The Uprooted* (2nd edn, Boston, MA, 1973); the 'pull' argument is best put by John Bodnar, *The Transplanted: A History of Immigrants in Urban America* (Bloomington, IN, 1985). But see also the full discussion and suggestions for further reading in Chapter 7 here. A full and well-annotated sampling of British emigrants' letters home from the United States in the nineteenth century can be found in Charlotte Erickson (ed.), *Invisible Immigrants: The Adaptation of English and Scottish Immigrants to 19th Century America* (1972; reprinted Ithaca, NY, 1991).

Classic definitions of 'American literature' can be found in Richard Chase, *The American Novel and its Tradition* (New York, 1957); R.W.B. Lewis, *The American Adam* (Chicago, 1955); and Leslie Fiedler, *Love and Death in the American Novel* (New York, 1960). The theme of captivity in American fiction has been carefully examined and subtly contextualized in Richard Slotkin, *Regeneration Through Violence: The Myth of the American Frontier* (Middletown, CT, 1973).

CHAPTER TWO
Religious America

Ferenc M. Szasz

FIRST CONTACT

Present-day visitors to the United States are often astonished by the public display of religion. Lapel badges, licence plates, billboards, and car bumper stickers proclaim that 'God Is Number One' or 'Jesus Is My Best Friend'. Radio and television evangelists command an extraordinary amount of air time, not just on Sunday mornings but every day of the week. On a typical Sunday, about 40 per cent of the nation participates in some form of formal worship. (In England, the figure is less than 10 per cent.) Pollsters have discovered that 98 per cent of Americans believe in God; about one-third confess to some type of mystical experience; and 60 per cent state that they would never vote for an atheist. Why is the United States one of the most religious countries of the industrialized world? Why the ever ongoing ferment in American religious life? The answer lies in the complex course of American religious history.

Only twenty-five years after Columbus set foot in the New World, Martin Luther set forth his famous ninety-five theses. Within a generation, the Catholic Reformation also began in earnest. Thus, when the Europeans brought their animals, plants, insects, technologies and viruses to the New World, they also brought their theologies and church organizations as well. From first contact until the late eighteenth century, American religious history largely revolved around the planting of mature European faiths in a new environment, and the reaction of the Native Americans to these imported ideas.

It is virtually impossible to separate politics from religion for the sixteenth, seventeenth and most of the eighteenth centuries. The Spanish Conquistadors and Franciscan friars of the American Southwest were opposite sides of the same coin. For the Puritans of Massachusetts Bay,

Calvinism served as the core of their social identity. The Puritans, as Chapter 1 reminds us, journeyed to America to establish 'a city upon a hill', by which the rest of the world might judge itself. These early missionaries came not simply to minister to their own peoples. Columbus's discovery of the numerous nations of Native Americans proved almost as astonishing as the discovery of the New World itself. For centuries, the Europeans viewed the American Indians as 'pagans' and actively sought to 'Christianize and civilize' them. Not until late in the nineteenth century and early in the twentieth century would anthropologists and historians realize fully that these native groups possessed religions of their own, which involved both complex patterns of ritual observance and sophisticated cosmologies and systems of belief. Thus, the first 'cultural clashes' came when Catholic and Protestant missionaries confronted Native American shamans on the theological battleground.

The Indian faiths varied considerably from one region to another, depending on geography, economy and social structure. But, at the risk of oversimplification, generalizations are still possible. For the Native Americans, 'religion' meant less a church or a theology than an entire view of the cosmos. The Europeans restricted their 'sacred space' largely to specific locations: an altar, church building, or a cemetery; but the Indians' sacred space coincided not only with such sites as burial grounds but also encompassed the land itself. For the Europeans, humankind had been created to rule over the animals and the land; for the Indians, people were but one part of a continuum that included both living and non-living things. The Native Americans' goal of life was to place themselves in harmony with the forces of nature, and this could be done only by proper ritual enactment of traditional ceremonies.

Although the written sources regarding this encounter are entirely European (the Indians had no written language), they nevertheless often reveal a vigorous theological interchange. Both the Jesuits in New France and the Puritans in New England engaged indigenous religious leaders in extensive dialogue about matters of faith. Each side viewed the other with considerable suspicion. From the Indian point of view, the results of this encounter might be best summarized in one word: synchronization. Everywhere the faiths overlapped and merged with each other. Nowhere is this mixture of native faiths and Christianity more evident than among the Indian groups of the American South-west. In 1680 the Pueblo Indians of the Rio Grande Valley drove the Spanish conquerors back to El Paso and held them there for a decade. When the Spanish returned in the 1690s, they also silently acknowledged the religious accommodation that one finds yet today. For the Pueblo Indians, traditional faiths and Roman Catholicism intermingle at every juncture. Today the ancient Native planting, harvest, and other festivals bear Catholic saints' names, but the dances to celebrate them date back to pre-contact times. The cross, the church, corn pollen and eagle feathers are all present in the ceremonies. Respect for both the 'Corn Mother' and 'Padre Jesus' have existed side by side in this region for almost four hundred years.

All the major versions of English Christianity were also transplanted to the New World. The Church of England formed the established Church (the church supported by taxation) for the Southern colonies. Most of the colonial gentry were at least nominal members. The only region where the Church of England failed to exert much influence was New England, where in 1620 the Puritans established a way of life that endured for almost 200 years. Lord Baltimore began the Colony of Maryland (probably named for the Virgin Mary) as a haven for persecuted Roman Catholics. English and Scottish Presbyterians found homes in New York, New Jersey and Pennsylvania. From the outset, New York City boasted a bewildering array of faiths: Dutch Reformed, Swedish Lutherans, Huguenots, Sephardic Jews, Presbyterians, Catholics, Puritans, etc. The English colonial world contained a vast spectrum of contemporary religious life, far greater than the Catholic Spanish or French colonies.

The colony of Pennsylvania best illustrates this diversity of faiths. From its origins in the 1680s, Pennsylvania bore the mark of its two Quaker founders, George Fox and William Penn. Fox rejected both the elaborate formalism of the Church of England and what he saw as the dry scholasticism of the Puritan reformers. Instead, Fox founded his faith on human experience. He argued that every man and woman had within themselves an 'Inward Light' – a reflection of the central light of the universe – to which each person could look for guidance on all moral and ethical questions. The radically democratic implications of this position, plus the Quakers' pacifism, made them *personae non gratae* for most of the seventeenth century. King Charles II (who owed William Penn's father a great debt for helping him secure the throne) was delighted to be rid of them by giving Penn land in the New World. Since the Quakers were too few in numbers to populate the colony, Penn began to advertise the virtues of Pennsylvania among like-minded pietists on the Continent. His offers of cheap land, promises of religious freedom, the lack of an established Church, and an enlightened legal code found a ready response among the Mennonites, Amish and other German peasants of the Rhine Valley. These migrants, who proved to be excellent farmers, came to be known over time as 'The Pennsylvania Dutch' (a corruption of Deutsch). Their folklore, idioms, hex signs and 'archaic' horse-drawn carriages and clothing still give a highly distinctive touch to the visual landscape of eastern Pennsylvania today. For the eighteenth century, moreover, the colony of

Pennsylvania served a very important role. Pennsylvania became living proof that society did not *need* a state-supported Church to guarantee either moral or economic stability. It also probably provided the 1787 Constitutional Convention with its model for the new, federal church–state relationship.

THE GREAT AWAKENING

Perhaps the most significant pre-Revolutionary colonial religious experience came with the religious revival that began in 1734 with the fierce sermons of Jonathan Edwards, including 'Sinners in the Hands of an Angry God' (1741), and swept the colonies in the mid-1740s. Historians have labelled this 'The Great Awakening', and it led to a comprehensive realignment of the Colonial social order. The 1739 arrival of English Methodist evangelist George Whitefield transformed a series of local revivals into a colony-wide movement. Preaching in churches, chapels, and often in open fields, the charismatic Whitefield criss-crossed the land with his simple message: all people were sinners but God's grace was available to whoever would have it. Thousands came to hear him, many of them drawn from the lower social classes: slaves, indentured servants, and miscellaneous dissenters. Although the colonial clergy initially welcomed Whitefield, they soon turned against the excesses, as they saw it, that his revival spawned. But the clerical denunciations of the revival had little effect. The Awakening had assumed a life of its own. In New England and the Middle Colonies, numerous congregations split over whether they should be 'Old Light' or 'New Light'. The fledgling (and lower class) Baptists and Methodists grew rapidly from this movement, as 'come-outers' steadily swelled their ranks.

Historians Rhys Isaac and Patricia Bonomi have shown that the rise of religious dissent spawned by the Great Awakening severely disrupted the established social order, especially in the leading southern colony, Virginia. There the Baptists' insistence on God's free grace, their refusal to acknowledge the legitimacy of the established Church of England (which resulted in subsequent persecution), their suspicion of 'learned clergy', plus their vigorous attacks on gambling, horse-racing, and fancy-dress balls all represented, in Bonomi's words, 'a standing rebuke to the social style of the Virginia Tidewater'.[1] The movement also left a political legacy. The Great Awakening introduced mass meetings, public controversy, dynamic speakers, pamphleteering, and vigorous name calling into American life. While these reflected religious themes in the 1740s, the subsequent generation would turn them to political purposes.

THE REVOLUTIONARY ERA

In addition to the revivalism that in America found expression in the Great Awakening, the late eighteenth century produced a quite different mode of social/religious thought that historians have termed the 'Enlightenment'. American Enlightenment thinkers such as Thomas Jefferson and Benjamin Franklin argued that human beings had been gifted with reason and natural rights, and that the sole purpose of government lay in the protection of those rights. They agreed that no religious question could be settled entirely by an appeal to reason. To some extent, the rise of Unitarianism at that time, with its denial of the traditional Christian belief in the mystery of the Trinity of God the Father, Son and Holy Spirit, and a parallel stress on the power of individual reason, may be seen as an appropriate religious response to the thrust of the Enlightenment (see also Chapter 4 for another view). In general Enlightenment thinkers allowed that churches taught a common morality that the state might find useful, but they stopped there. They expressed little concern over such traditional Christian religious concepts as sin, grace or redemption.

Enlightenment thought formed the basis for the American Revolution of 1776, but the churches soon threw their support behind the movement. New England Congregational ministers backed the revolutionaries from the onset, and they emerged from the war with renewed strength. Catholics, Presbyterians and Jews also supported the rebels. The Quakers found themselves caught on the dilemma of freedom versus pacifism, but their problems were minuscule compared with those of the Church of England. Because of its obvious ties with the Crown, the Anglican Church found itself on the defensive from the beginning. From 1776 onward, popular pressure began to force Anglican church closures all over the colonies. Tory Rector Samuel Seabury once preached with two loaded pistols by his side. At the time of the Peace Treaty of 1783 the Church of England lay in ruins; its privileged position had been destroyed. Consequently, when the Virginia House of Burgesses began to discuss probable future church–state relationships, few urged a direct re-establishment of the Anglican Church. But what other options were there? Some urged the creation of a 'comprehensive establishment', where every denomination would receive a share of state taxes. Thomas Jefferson and James Madison, however, fought vigorously against this. Finally, after over a decade of debate, they pushed through an alternative: the 1786 Virginia Statute of Religious Freedom stated that there should be freedom of worship, with no state support for *any* denomination.

The following year, the delegates to the Constitutional Convention in Philadelphia wrestled with a similar problem, but this time for the entire nation. What should the church–state relationship be for the proposed American federal republic? Clearly the English model of an established Church with tolerated dissenters would not suffice. The Congregational establishment seemed secure in New England, but it had no following elsewhere. So, the delegates looked to the recently enacted Virginia statute and to the example of Pennsylvania for their models. Their 1789 Constitution stated: 'No religious test shall ever be required as a qualification to any office or public trust under the United States.' Then, in 1791, the first Amendment of the Bill of Rights added: 'Congress shall make no law respecting an establishment of religion or prohibiting the free exercise thereof.' With great skill, the creators of the federal Constitution had sidestepped the most volatile of social issues, those dealing with religion. Individual states might, if they chose, keep a religious establishment (Massachusetts did so until 1820). But the *nation* would have no established Church. On the national level, all faiths would be created equal. One should not suggest that the American founding fathers 'invented' the concept of religious freedom. Rather, they 'discovered' it, in Pennsylvania, New York City, Rhode Island, Virginia and elsewhere. This 'discovery' they then applied to the new American republic.

But how could a new nation hold together without a shared religious faith? Virtually no Enlightenment figure wanted to create a completely secular society. Rather, they tended to agree that a highminded morality among citizens was essential to the health of a democratic republic. If the churches were no longer to play this role, who would teach the symbols, myths, icons, meanings to holidays, moral fables, preferred codes of morality and public behaviour that such thinkers generally agreed that a nation – in order to be a nation – must share? Within a generation, the answer had emerged: the American public school system. By the 1830s, the emerging public schools had taken over much of the role of the earlier 'established Church'. It was through the schools that the children learned the panoply of communally understood signs and beliefs that bind a nation together. And it was through the schools that they learned the common faith: the religion of democracy.

Historian Sidney Mead has argued that the decade of the 1780s formed the crucial era of American religious history. Prior to this, the churches could often rely on the arm of the state to achieve their goals. Afterwards, they were on their own. Henceforth, all religious bodies had to rely solely on their ability to *persuade* others – 'voluntarism' – that their cause was just and right. Since the art of 'persuasion' had become crucial to church expansion, the churches began to experiment with various modes of it. In the pre-Civil War world, the most effective means of persuasion lay with the institutions of the revival and the camp meeting.

THE RISE OF EVANGELICAL AMERICA

After the Revolution, thousands of settlers poured west across the Appalachian Mountains to the new lands of Kentucky, the deep South, and the Ohio River Valley. But neither of the old, established churches (the Congregationalists and the Anglicans, now reconstituted as the Protestant Episcopal Church) could keep up with this migration. Aided by revivals and camp meetings, other denominations, such as the Baptists, Methodists, Presbyterians and Disciples of Christ gathered thousands of converts to their ranks. These early evangelical churches – with their suspicion of a 'learned clergy', their emphasis on the literal word of the King James Version of Scripture, and their simple message of sin, grace and redemption – especially moulded the culture of the South and became one of its primary aspects.

As this Southern evangelical culture evolved, however, it revealed, as later chapters of this book will also underline, two distinct components, one black and one white. While the eighteenth-century world of the Enlightenment left little room for black participation, the later evangelicalism of the antebellum era did provide cultural space for the slaves. Although stripped of much of their African religious heritage, the slaves mingled retentions of their original beliefs and practices with evangelical Christianity to produce an 'Afro-Baptist' faith that is still very much alive today. From the 1780s onward, the church played a crucial role in the African–American experience. The African emphasis on oral culture had given a special role to the person who had 'the gift of words', the 'singer of tales', the *griot* celebrated by such present-day black American writers as Toni Morrison. Traditional songs, dances and festivals also merged easily into the evangelical framework. The 'call and response' form of worship (an old African custom) remains central to many black services today. Perhaps it is no accident that two of the most significant and famous black political leaders of the late twentieth century, Martin Luther King, Jr and Jesse Jackson, both came from ministerial backgrounds.

North of the Ohio River, the religious enthusiasm of the antebellum era took on even more varied forms. The frontier of western New York soon became known as 'the burned over district' because of the large number of revival fires that swept through the region. From the enthusiasm of 'Freedom's Ferment' came numerous religious alternatives to the Protestant mainstream: the Millerites, or Adventists, followers of Baptist preacher William Miller who predicted that Jesus would return in 1844/45 to end time; the Oneida Community, founded by John Humphrey Noyes, where every member was 'married' to all others of the opposite sex and children raised communally; the Shakers, founded by British immigrant Ann Lee, who practised absolute celibacy, equal rights for women and pacifism, and whose community created simple but elegant crafts and furniture; the Seventh Day Adventists, led by Ellen White; the Spiritualists, a popular mid-century crusade that promised communication with the dead, initiated by Kate Fox in upstate New York; and a host of other, lesser known movements.

Antebellum women were excluded from the realm of politics, but, as the above mention of certain prominent figures indicates, they frequently played major roles in the parallel world of religious life. From Colonial times onward, women formed a majority of the nation's churchgoers. Many served as teachers on the Home Mission frontier, as well as overseas. Former Unitarian minister Ralph Waldo Emerson tried out many of his ideas, in the form of public lectures, on largely female audiences. In time, as Chapter 4 elaborates in some detail, these concepts would form the heart of the movement known as Transcendentalism, and one of its innovative thinkers was Margaret Fuller. Later, in 1879 – though its lineaments were sketched earlier in her life – the Church of Christ, Scientist was founded in Boston by Mary Baker Eddy.

None of the antebellum religious movements has been as enduring or as successful as the Latter-day Saints, or Mormons. Historian Gordon Wood has tried to place the emergence of Mormonism within the social boundaries of antebellum frontier life. The raw democracy of the era, Wood maintained, combined with popular evangelicalism to mount an attack on all previous forms of authority and hierarchy, whether secular or religious. Within a generation after the Revolution, many of the institutional supports that had linked people together for centuries had burst asunder. To whom should one go for answers to life's fundamental metaphysical questions? The bewildering cacophony of voices offered little assurance to the earnest seeker. The prophet, Joseph Smith, Jr, who grew to maturity in this milieu, in a family where spiritual healing through the laying on of hands and anointing with oil was practised, forged his own answer. Confused as to which church to join, Smith said that he received a visit from an angel, who eventually led him to Hill Cumorah, outside of present-day Rochester, New York, where he dug up a set of golden plates, eight inches square and six inches thick. Seated behind a curtain, Smith 'translated' these plates into a 568-page *Book of Mormon*, which was published in 1830. This was the new nation's first indigenous Bible.

The *Book of Mormon*, by the power of revelation, served for many as a set of answers to the religious questions of the day: God had again spoken to His people through his latest prophet, Joseph Smith, Jr. With Smith's message, the true Church, the Church of Jesus Christ of Latter-day Saints, had been restored to earth. The Mormons began proselytizing immediately and many missionaries found a ready response to their message in the British Isles. From Liverpool, Wales, the Midlands and elsewhere, thousands accepted the new prophet and journeyed to, first, Nauvoo, Illinois, and, later, after Smith's assassination in 1844, to the Valley of the Great Salt Lake in Utah. Once the Saints had arrived there, under the able leadership of Smith's successor, Brigham Young, they officially confirmed what had earlier been only a widespread rumour: based on an early Smith revelation, polygamy had become an official tenet of the new Mormon faith. As we have seen, other communitarian ventures of the period also initiated what were regarded as unconventional sexual relationships, partly out of idealism, partly to increase numbers of adherents quickly, but none became as well-known as the Mormons; within a decade, the practice of polygamy brought the Latter-day Saints to the attention of the world. More important, the Utah Mormons forged a unique identification with the ancient Hebrews. Salt Lake City became their Zion, and they were the Latter-day Saints; the rest of the world became 'Gentiles'. From the 1850s onward, the Mormon Church emerged as the single most important force in the settlement of the Intermountain West. Even today, it is the most powerful institution in the region.

The antebellum era also witnessed a steady immigration of German Jews and German and Irish Catholics to the New World (for more detailed data see Chapter 7). The Jews, who at this time entered the United States in comparatively small numbers, merged relatively easily into American life, but the rapid growth of the Catholic Church, with its predominantly immigrant hierarchy and burgeoning congregations, occasioned periodic bursts of anti-Catholicism, including a few riots and a short-lived political party, the 'Know Nothings'. Yet Protestant–Catholic tensions formed but one aspect of the antebellum 'wars of religion'. During that era, Calvinist disputed with Arminian, Shaker debated Disciple, and Freethinker took on Christian in a wide range of popular, public confrontations. Indeed, these popular religious debates formed a lively part of life, especially on the frontier. The reason was obvious. Everything had become 'democratized'. No traditional hierarchy was viable, even in the realm of faith. Let the two sides present their cases; 'the people' would decide the issue for themselves.

By the 1850s, these public disputations over religious truth began to give way to discussions over slavery. Clerical voices proved vital here, too. Northern evangelists began to crusade vigorously against slavery, while their southern counterparts wrote at least half of the pamphlets that defended the South's 'peculiar institution'. Clearly, the words of the Constitution, like those of Scripture, could be read in several different ways. In the antebellum world, the two major institutions that bound the North and South together were the two political parties (Whigs and

Democrats) and the evangelical churches. The latter proved more sensitive as barometers of public opinion, for the churches split over a decade before the upheavals of the 1850s divided the political parties. The Methodists split in 1844; the Baptists in 1845; the Presbyterians in 1837, and, after a reconciliation, again in 1861. Each division in one way or another involved the issue of slavery. Historian C.C. Goen has argued that these denominational divisions – accompanied by heated words and bitter accusations – paved the way for the Civil War. They did so, largely, by setting the wrong example. The bloodless division of the three evangelical churches led the southern leaders to assume that they could similarly secede in the political realm. In this, of course, they were sadly mistaken.

THE GILDED AGE, 1865–95

The Civil War, which cost more American lives than all the nation's other wars combined, cast a severe cloud over the nation's much vaunted role as a 'City upon a Hill'. Although touring revivalists continued to reap conversions among the Confederate soldiers, the Northern troops seemed less susceptible to their appeals. For both sides, the chaos of the battle of the Wilderness, Antietam and other clashes cast doubt about the workings of Divine Providence. As one Confederate soldier put it, 'ware is very unsertin'.[2] The foremost rabbi of the time, Isaac M. Wise, however, was unwilling to dismiss the city on the hill concept entirely. The Civil War, Wise observed, had become a tragic necessity. The war had to be fought so that slavery could be destroyed. Afterwards, America would assume a new role. She would become an 'immigrant-receiving country' for the rest of the world. Rabbi Wise's prediction came strangely true, for the story of immigration and the problems of ethnic assimilation formed a central theme for the entire last half of the century.

In the crowded cities of the east coast, the immigrants tried to recreate as many Old World institutions as they could. Soon local neighborhoods abounded with ethnic bakeries and restaurants, foreign language news-papers, fraternal organizations, and ethnic churches or synagogues. In the more isolated sections of the Great Plains, however, the most portable (and often the sole) immigrant institution became the church. Thus, in the West, the ethnic church took on a multitude of functions: it preserved the language of the group, taught the youth, comforted the elderly, and generally served as social cement to reinforce the concept of ethnic communal identity. The self identity of (say) a Norwegian Lutheran, Danish Lutheran, Swedish Lutheran, Bavarian Catholic, Czech Catholic, or

Hungarian Reformed community on the upper Great Plains revolved primarily around the Church and its activities. In those regions, the churches and ethnicity kept each other alive.

The most dramatic overlap of faith and ethnicity may be seen in the saga of the Mennonites and Hutterites. Descendants from the radical Anabaptists of Reformation times, these Germanic, communal peoples had been universally despised by all the rulers of Europe, both Protestant and Catholic. Finally, in the 1760s, Catherine the Great invited them to settle the southern steppes of Russia. Catherine promised them that they could create German-speaking, communal enclaves within the Russian state. She guaranteed them freedom of worship and amnesty from military service. In return, they were to share their agricultural skills with the Russian peasantry. For over a century, this system worked rather well. In the 1870s, however, Tsar Alexander II decided to 'Russify' these groups and gave them ten years to conform to national norms or depart. Dismayed by the new decrees, Mennonite and Hutterite scouts came to America, where they met an especially vigorous entrepreneur, Carl Schmidt, who, as it was commonly said, 'sold Kansas to the Russian Germans and the Russian Germans to Kansas'. The combination proved especially fruitful, as the agricultural skills of these immigrants meshed well with the harsh demands of the Northern Plains; in time they helped turn that region into America's 'bread basket'. Descendants of these Russian Germans, both those practising a powerfully communal life style (Hutterites) and those established more as individual farmers (most Mennonites) are much in evidence on the Great Plains today.

The Russian Tsars inaugurated yet another religious exodus to the United States by their policy toward the Jews. From 1881 onward, increased anti-Semitism sent perhaps two million Jews from Russia/Poland to the shores of the New World. In *World of Our Fathers* (1976), literary critic Irving Howe has chronicled the lives of these immigrants. Originally rural, poor, and often very religious, they settled in tightly knit ethnic enclaves up and down the East Coast. For those who rejected religious orthodoxy, socialism or political radicalism often became what might be called a 'substitute faith'. The first-generation immigrant Jews viewed themselves as 'strangers in a strange land'. The more acculturated German Jewish community was not pleased by this rapid influx of their coreligionists. Fearing the rise of anti-Semitism (which did occur), they began a series of programmes to move the Russian Jews out of the urban slums and settle them in various agricultural communities (none of which succeeded). Interestingly, the tension between the two Jewish communities was often as much religious as ethnic. By the 1880s Reform Judaism, headquartered in the Hebrew Union College in Cincinnati (founded in

1865) had virtually become *American* Judaism. Many of the newcomers, however, denounced Reform Judaism's accommodation to Christian Sunday worship, rejection of the old dietary laws, suspicion of Zionism, and liberal theology. In turn, they founded their own institutions. Thus, conservative Jews created the Jewish Theological Seminary in New York City in 1886, and ten years later, Orthodox Jews began Yeshiva. Thus, by the turn of the century, the three major branches of American Judaism – Reform, Conservative, and Orthodox – had all put down firm institutional roots in the New World.

The vast majority of immigrants, however, came from Roman Catholic countries. From the 1870s until the 1930s, the American Roman Catholic hierarchy wrestled with a number of complex issues – establishing a parochial school system, creating a Catholic University in the nation's capital and coping with divisive theological quarrels. But no issue proved more baffling than that of Catholic ethnicity. By about 1890, the American Church hierarchy was largely Irish and German. Yet the waves of Polish, Italian, Sicilian, Hungarian, Spanish, Mexican, Romanian, and French Catholic migrants all wanted priests from their own group. A French parish in Denver, for example, once threatened to 'secede' unless the German bishop gave way to their demands. Although the official Church position held to the universality of the Catholic faith, the wiser bishops of urban dioceses usually bent with the prevailing ethnic winds. Thus, in the larger urban areas, distinct ethnic parishes emerged, many of them virtually independent enclaves within the dioceses. These enclaves boasted their own schools, orphanages and cemeteries. One Polish parish in Chicago, for example, sponsored seventy-four different clubs or organizations. This pragmatic compromise allowed the Church to remain intact, for no defection of any size ever occurred. But, as sociologist Andrew Greeley has noted, American Catholicism remained a church in the grip of the immigrant experience until after the Second World War.

Since the mainline urban Protestant churches had become largely middle-class institutions by the 1880s, they had difficulty in responding to the needs of the urban slums. The depression of the 1890s catapulted them into action, however, and from about 1895 to 1920, they instituted a vigorous programme of social involvement that is usually termed the Social Gospel. Baptist scholar Walter Rauschenbusch served as the major theologian of the Social Gospel movement. In several works, especially *Christianity and the Social Crisis* (1907) and *A Theology for the Social Gospel* (1917), Rauschenbusch criticized traditional Protestantism for concentrating too exclusively on individual salvation. God had sent Jesus to earth, Rauschenbusch argued, to save both the individual and the social order. Any society that harboured great social wrongs within it was violating the

laws of God. As the mainline protestant denominations – Con-
gregationalist, Methodist, Episcopalian, Baptist and Presbyterian – entered
into an urban ministry, they developed a new agency: the Institutional
Church. Really a settlement house with a denominational affiliation, this
church remained open seven days a week. It also boasted a variety of new
social services: gymnasiums, swimming pools, nurseries, lecture halls, public
health officials, and, sometimes, an employment agency. The ministers
who led these down-town churches worked closely with Salvation Army
officers (who had arrived from Britain in 1880) and related organizations,
such as the Volunteers of America or the Goodwill Society. Thanks in part
to their increased social concern, the American clergy received a great deal
of favourable publicity during the *fin-de-siècle* years. By about 1910, they
found themselves at what would prove to be the apex of their influence
during the twentieth century. Rabbi, priest, liberal Protestant, conservative
evangelist – all were engaged in a common effort: helping to bring in the
Kingdom of God.

The early years of the century, while a period of profound investigation
of religion for some, as in *The Varieties of Religious Experience* (1902) by the
Pragmatist philosopher William James, also saw this broadly 'evangelical'
rhetoric spill over into politics. When Theodore Roosevelt, after defecting
from the Republican Party, forged a splinter Progressive Party in 1912, he
gave his followers a 'Confession of Faith'. The campaign song for this new
'Bull Moose' Party was 'Onward Christian Soldiers'. Democrat Woodrow
Wilson defeated Roosevelt in that election, but his speeches reflected the
same moralising, evangelical rhetoric. The culmination of this crusading
temperament, ironically, led directly into America's entry into the First
World War. As Wilson reminded his listeners, America entered the war for
no selfish purposes. Instead, she hoped to make the world 'safe for
democracy'.

RELIGION AFTER THE FIRST WORLD WAR

The cynicism of the period after the First World War not only destroyed
the Kingdom of God ideal, it also played havoc with the world of
American religion. A wave of nativism, centred in the Ku Klux Klan, arose
to attack Catholics and Jews as 'unAmerican'. Many of the mainline
Protestant denominations broke into warring factions over the issues of
higher criticism of scripture, evolution and the Social Gospel. As
Fundamentalists and Modernists denounced each other on the front pages
of the nation's dailies, a Catholic priest observed in a common expression

of the time that this marked 'the death knell of Protestantism'. While that may have been an exaggeration, the Fundamentalist–Modernist controversy of the 1920s did signify the demise of Protestant hegemony in America. After this, the mainline Protestant churches had a very difficult time maintaining that they were the chief bearers of the American cultural tradition.

Religious concerns often appeared in the media during the 1920s, but – from the religious point of view – for all the wrong reasons: bitter quarrels over theology; controversies over which group would 'control' a denomination; a variety of church scandals; and, finally, in July 1925, the famous 'Scopes Monkey Trial' in Dayton, Tennessee, over whether the doctrine of evolution should be taught in the public schools. A wave of 'naturalism' or 'indifferentism' swept across the nation's college campuses, as a generation of young people rejected institutional church or YMCA work for more earthly pursuits, and Sinclair Lewis's popular novel *Elmer Gantry* (1927) presented a fictional charismatic preacher as even more prone than other mortals to succumb to the temptations of the flesh. Historian Robert Handy has argued that, to match the economic Depression, there was an 'American Religious Depression' that began in about 1925 and extended well into the ensuing decade. One might see signs of this 'depression' in the vacuity of the religious writings of the 1920s. The best example is Bruce Barton's classic bestseller, *The Man Nobody Knows* (1924), which portrayed Jesus as a business executive who understood the virtues of efficient organization and sound management.

The 1920s also saw the unprecedented growth of advertising, and, in many cases, religion became simply another 'product' to sell to reluctant consumers. Churches experimented with movable signboards, catchy sermon titles, neon crosses, and painted messages on barn doors. Conservative evangelical ministers realized the power of radio, and quickly utilized the medium to spread their message. Unlike the mid-eighteenth century, the antebellum years, or the Progressive era, the churches of the 1920s no longer moulded the social order (some rural areas excepted). The dominant shapers of culture – film, radio, the newspapers and magazines – were all predominantly secular. Consequently, the churches began to take their cues from the culture, rather than vice versa, or to use their influence more indirectly, as when, for instance, they urged censorship of the film industry (see Chapter 10). The silence of the theologians, literary critic H.L. Mencken observed, was an ominous sign of the times.

Contrary to the prediction of the pundits, however, post-First World War religion showed no signs of actually 'disappearing'. Instead, it assumed a variety of innovative forms. An example may be seen in the first colourful (and controversial) 'superstar' of American religious life, Aimee Semple

McPherson. A young widow with two small children, Sister Aimee arrived in Los Angeles in 1918 to establish her own Pentecostal denomination, the Four Square Gospel, which, she said, had been revealed to her in a vision. With dramatic sermons, often in costume, plus a simple message of hope and redemption, McPherson drew a steady round of followers. Visitors to Los Angeles would no more have missed attending one of her services than they would have passed up a walk down Hollywood Boulevard. One historian has estimated that from 1926 to 1937, Sister Aimee appeared on the front pages of the Los Angeles *Times* on the average of three times a week. Even her dramatic 'kidnapping' (when she disappeared for a tryst with her married radio operator), failed to dampen her followers' enthusiasm. McPherson received a less publicized (although perhaps more substantial) following during the Great Depression of the 1930s, when she gave away tons of free food and ministered especially to the Hispanic *barrios*. With all her contradictions, Aimee Semple McPherson represented a new type of figure on the American religious scene.

Perhaps surprisingly, the economic depression of the 1930s brought forth no national religious revival. Instead, middle-class readers found solace by reading best-selling religious novels, such as Lloyd C. Douglas's *Magnificent Obsession* (1938) or Sholem Asch's *The Nazarene* (1939), the first of volume of a trilogy by the Yiddish writer which attempted to portray early Christianity from an ecumenical viewpoint. On another social level, Pentecostal and Holiness groups forged distinct religious subcultures in the rural areas of Washington, Oklahoma, California, and Missouri. In the predominantly black inner cities, clergymen such as Father Divine, Sweet Daddy Grace and Adam Clayton Powell, Sr merged individual salvation, dreams of prosperity, and free food and shelter to create strong local followings. Catholic convert Dorothy Day helped forge both Catholic pacifism and Catholic radicalism, although the full impact of her ideas would not be felt for a generation. While the religious world of the depression seemed calm on the surface, underneath it was churning rapidly.

In the academic sphere, several theologians began reaching out to the depression generation in a movement that has sometimes been labelled 'neo-orthodoxy'. The most influential spokesman was Reinhold Niebuhr, the American-born son of a German Reformed pastor. A prolific writer, Niebuhr attacked both Christian Liberals and Fundamentalists for failing to understand the human condition. Arguing for a return to biblical revelation, Niebuhr denied the prevailing optimism about human nature, the belief that humanity had become master of its own fate. He argued for the reality of sin, and pointed to the rise of Nazism in Germany as an example of the intrusion of the demonic into the flow of history. He insisted that God's grace was still needed, on both an individual and social level. Widely acknowledged as the most significant American religious thinker of his day, Niebuhr influenced a generation of writers, intellectuals and political statesmen. As one rabbi quipped, 'Thou shalt love thy Niebuhr as thyself.'

RELIGION AFTER THE SECOND WORLD WAR

The onset of the Second World War continued the reorientation of American religious life. The use of the atomic bomb, the disclosure of the Holocaust, the collapse of Western Europe, the dismantling of the British Empire and the sudden rise of the United States to superpower status presented a variety of unanswerable questions, all of which had religious components. Although the complexity of these issues was bewildering, the dominant thrust of American religious life from 1945 to the mid-1960s proved just the opposite. To many historians of religion these were the years of 'the cult of reassurance'. Virtually all religious groups in the late 1940s and 1950s drank deeply from this spring. The 'reassurance' took on several forms: mustard seed jewellery, 'prayer cards' on restaurant tables with 'suggested' Protestant, Catholic and Jewish graces; popular music that crooned about 'The Man Upstairs'. The culmination came in 1954 when Congress officially added 'under God' to the Pledge of Allegiance. Evangelist William (Billy) Franklin Graham formed a central part of this post-war movement, with his simple, yet sincere, call for individual and national repentance.

In 1955, Sociologist Will Herberg published his influential *Protestant–Catholic–Jew*. In this study, Herberg accurately summarized several of the main religious themes of his day. The chief question of existence for post-Second World War Americans, he argued, was that of 'identity'. Since the legendary 'melting pot' of immigration had never insisted that a person give up his or her personal faith, religion had emerged as the chief focal point of identity. Through the Church or synagogue, children learned who they were as individuals. The three great historic faiths of his title had become three equally valid ways by which one could become 'American'. Herberg's observations were borne out by later developments. By the late 1950s, American Protestantism had been forced to share its cultural hegemony with its Catholic and Jewish counterparts. The common enemy, of course, was 'Godless Russia'. By the 1950s, also, the 'immigrant ghetto world view' that had so moulded both American Catholicism and Judaism had begun to collapse. It faded with the slowing of immigration and the rise of a college-trained generation of young people. A 1974 Carnegie

Institution report confirmed that American Catholics had become as middle-class as any other religious/ethnic group. In fact, the survey revealed that Catholic youth were actually attending university at a higher rate than their Protestant counterparts. The Catholic monk and poet Thomas Merton was extremely influential among educated people of all persuasions. In his advocacy of the need for meditation in such books as *Seeds of Contemplation* (1948) and in his recognition of the efficacy of oriental spiritual practices he struck chords that continued to resonate, especially in the counterculture of the 1960s. The 1960 election of John F. Kennedy proved that the Catholic faith was no longer a barrier to the highest office of the land. The end of the Second Vatican Council in 1965 introduced cooperation with Protestants and Jews that would have been unheard of only a decade before. By the 1950s the Catholics had been 'mainstreamed'.

The same mainstreaming affected America's Jews. By 1945, Jewish intellectuals had become major forces in journalism, the arts, and cultural criticism. Like the Catholics, their sons and daughters escaped the conflicts of their parents' generation through university education. The creation of the state of Israel in 1948 also helped blur the ethnic/theological divisions within the Jewish community. Since Israel looked first to the United States to guarantee its territorial integrity and to support it with arms and financial aid, it also forever entwined American political fortunes with the increasingly volatile Near East. By the 1960s, colleges had lifted their restrictive 'Jewish quotas' and surveys showed that Jews rivalled Asians for the highest percentage of youth seeking advanced schooling. The Jews, too, had become part of the American mainstream.

Two decades later, however, after all the turmoil caused by America's pursuit of the Vietnam War – as fierce within organized religion as beyond it – all three branches of the religious mainstream found themselves in serious difficulty. With anti-Semitism a negligible force, Jewish periodicals worried aloud about an intermarriage rate that approached 38 per cent. While Vatican II reforms allowed Catholics to interact with American society on numerous levels, they also destroyed the Church's traditional unity of purpose. Prominent laymen and clerics publicly disagreed with the official Church position on a variety of issues: divorce, birth control, celibacy for priests, the sanctuary movement for Latin American refugees, ordination of women, the charismatic movement within Catholicism and abortion. For the first time in modern history, American Catholics could no longer agree on the answer to the question: What does it mean to be Catholic? Mainline Protestants fared no better. According to a 1990 G.I. Lilly report, all the major Protestant denominations had lost vast numbers during the previous two decades. In one year, for example, 174,000 left the

Methodists, 104,000 the Presbyterians, and 70,000 the three leading Lutheran bodies. The aging liberal Protestant denominations found it difficult to establish a meaningful theological framework and keep the loyalty of their youth. By 1985, one out of every three people had left the denomination into which they had been born.

The groups that gained from this realignment were usually conservative ones. Within Judaism, this meant either the Orthodox or Conservative branches; within Catholicism, it meant a growth of the Traditionalists, who resisted the Vatican II reforms. In terms of pure numbers, however, the groups that benefited most from the troubles of the mainstream were the conservative evangelical Protestant groups. In the 1970s, for example, the Evangelical Free Church, the Church of the Nazarene, the Latter-day Saints, the Pentecostals, and the Southern Baptists all experienced rapid growth in membership. Some of these denominations boasted 'mega-churches' with over 2,000 members each. A 'third force' of Christendom had entered on the scene. Although conservative in theology, these evangelicals were quick to utilize the electronic media of the day. Soon they commanded the lion's share of religious broadcasting, with surveys showing that one-third of the nation watched them 'occasionally'. The scandals involving sexual and financial improprieties on the part of TV evangelists during the 1980s have dampened, but not halted, this movement. It is the upsurge of these conservative evangelical groups that largely accounts for the current popular display of religious messages. The billboard and the bumper sticker have become the modern version of the revival and camp meeting.

Sociologist Dean Kelley has tried to explain this shift in America's religious outlook. He has argued that the conservative evangelical message of biblical literalism, repentance, God's free grace, and individual salvation was not just a 'reaction' to the political traumas of defeat in the Vietnam War and the supposed ascendancy of 'liberal' views, but essentially provided a network of *meaning* for people caught in modern anomie. As Emerson said of the Calvinism of his generation, the evangelical message pinned each member to the 'canvas of the universe'. In a world seemingly out of control, the conservative evangelical interpretation of Scripture offered contemporary citizens a similar 'anchor'.

During the 1960s and early 1970s, non-traditional groups such as the Unification Church (the 'Moonies'), the Hare Krishnas, Scientology, the Native American Church (with its ritual use of peyote) and a wide range of utopian communes received a vast amount of publicity. The holy books of religions formerly alien to the mainstream tradition, such as *The I-Ching*, or celebrated Native American-originated texts like John Neihardt's *Black Elk Speaks* (originally published in 1938) and Frank Waters' *Book of the Hopi*

(1963) were widely disseminated. All fed into a predominantly youth-orientated quest for 'expanded consciousness' which, in the media, was frequently associated with 'hippies' and other exponents of the counterculture, which in turn was partly propelled by opposition to America's prosecution of the Vietnam War. The African–American Nation of Islam, led by Elijah Muhammed, but whose foremost religious/political spokesperson until he left the movement was Malcolm X, demanded upright behaviour from adherents, a land base in America on which to found a new, separate nation and, in general, a rejection of the white 'devils' and their Christianity. The publicity, as well as the membership of these groups had fallen off sharply by the late 1980s. Although the movements show no signs of disappearing, they have experienced little growth of late. Interest in communal living has also fallen off. The young people of the 1980s and 1990s, according to many observers, seem to be searching in more material directions.

The rise of the New Age movement has had considerable appeal for this group. 'New Age' is an umbrella term that draws from a wide variety of belief systems, including eastern mysticism, Theosophy and Native American faiths. New Age shows a concern with environmentalism but also celebrates the private individual, often providing the opportunity for each person to create his or her own 'reality'. What impact it will have in the long run is not yet clear. Two other rapidly growing groups of the 1990s should be mentioned. First are the 'nothingarians', or the secular constituency. It is virtually impossible to count this segment, as it avoids any formal church organization, but sociologists agree that many people who leave the mainline groups will probably never return to any organized church. Second are those individuals who acknowledge themselves as having a strong personal 'faith', but not one that aligns itself easily with any organized group. Sociologist Thomas Luckmann has termed this America's 'invisible religion'. And Robert Bellah, in a variety of sociological studies, has argued that such private, diverse beliefs have come close to being the norm of today's religious world (see also Chapter 16).

America in the 1990s, therefore, presents a vast smorgasbord of religious positions. They range along a social and theological spectrum from extreme 'Left' to extreme 'Right', with most groups clustering in the middle. At last count there were over 1,700 American religious organizations. No one objects to these groups organizing, worshipping, and trying to persuade others to adopt their position. That's how the religious game has been played for over 200 years. The main problem lies in another area. Since all religious groups are equal in the eyes of the state, crucial questions of public policy have usually been constructed so that they did not offend anyone. The end result of this, however, has been to create 'a naked public square' – that is, public issues with minimal moral/religious content.

But separation of church and state has never meant separation of religion from the social order. Much of the current religious controversy comes from various churches' attempts to fill the 'public square' with their own specific positions. Sociologist Robert Wuthnow has argued that as the mainline groups (Protestants, Catholics, Jews) have drawn closer to one another, there has been a drastic 'restructuring' of American religion along a Conservative/Liberal axis, usually involving 'single issue' causes. Issues such as abortion, birth control, human sexuality, the position of women in society, the policies of the state of Israel, euthanasia, AIDS, nuclear armaments, and toxic waste disposal all contain legitimate 'religious' dimensions. But which point of view will dominate in the future? The jury is still out on these issues. Judging from the past, all one can say is that the future of American religious history is bound to be both provocative and interesting.

NOTES

1. Patricia U. Bonomi, *Under the Cope of Heaven: Religion, Society, and Politics in Colonial America* (New York, 1986), p. 184.

2. Cited in Lewis O. Saum, *The Popular Mood of America, 1860–1890* (Lincoln, NE, 1990), p. 24.

SUGGESTIONS FOR FURTHER READING

The most comprehensive overview, almost an encyclopedia of the subject, is Sydney E. Ahlstrom, *A Religious History of the American People* (New Haven, 1972). An equally valuable account is: Edwin S. Gaustad, *Historical Atlas of Religion in America* (New York, 1976). For connections between American political and Christian religious ideas, see Sidney E. Mead, *The Old Religion and the Brave New World: Reflections on the Relation Between Christendom and the Republic* (Berkeley, 1977). For surveys of the three major faiths, try: Martin E. Marty, *Righteous Empire: The Protestant Experience in America* (New York, 1970); Jay P. Dolan, *The American Catholic Experience: A History from Colonial Times to the Present* (Garden City, NY, 1987); and Nathan Glazer, *American Judaism* (Chicago, 1957). The foremost historians of the field today are Martin E. Marty, Sidney E. Mead, and Edwin S. Gaustad. All of their works are worth reading.

Colonial America mixed religion and politics in roughly equal proportions. A fine introduction to the religious life of the South-west is John L. Kessell, *Kiva, Cross and Crown: The Pecos Indians and New Mexico, 1540–1840* (Albuquerque, NM, 1980). For the East, see Patricia U. Bonomi, *Under the Cope of Heaven: Religion, Society and Politics in Colonial America* (New York, 1986) and Rhys Isaac, *The Transformation of Virginia, 1740–1790* (Chapel Hill, NC, 1982). An overview of Indian religions is provided by Ake Hultkrantz, *Belief and Worship in Native North America* (Syracuse, NY, 1981) and for Indian–white interaction, see Henry Warner Bowden, *American Indians and Christian Missions* (Chicago, 1981) and Robert F. Berkhofer, Jr, *Salvation and the Savage* (New York, 1972). Raymond J. DeMallie and Douglas R. Parks (eds), provide a case study in *Sioux Indian Religion* (Norman, OK, 1984). A dramatic statement from the Indian point of view is Vine Deloria, Jr, *God Is Red* (New York, 1973).

The religious excitement of the trans-Appalachian era may be sampled in: John B. Boles, *The Great Revival, 1787–1805: The Origins of the Southern Evangelical Mind* (Lexington, KY, 1972); Whitney R. Cross, *The Burned Over District* (New York, 1965); Mick Gidley with Kate Bowles (ed.), *Locating the Shakers: Cultural Origins and Legacies of an American Religious Movement* (Exeter, 1990); Gordon S. Wood, 'Evangelical America and Early Mormonism', *New York History* **61** (October, 1980), 359–86; Donald G. Matthews, *Religion in the Old South* (Chicago, 1970); Albert J. Raboteau, *Slave Religion: The 'Invisible Institution' in the Antebellum South* (New York, 1978); and C.C. Goen, *Broken Churches, Broken Nation: Denominational Schisms and the Coming of the American Civil War* (Macon, GA, 1985).

The post-Civil War religious world may be explored in: Ferenc Morton Szasz, *The Protestant Clergy in the Great Plains and Mountain West, 1865–1915* (Albuquerque, NM, 1988); Charles H. Hopkins, *The Rise of the Social Gospel in American Protestantism, 1865–1915* (New Haven, 1940); Robert T. Handy, 'The American Religious Depression, 1925–1935', *Church History*, XXIX (1960), 3–16; and Irving Howe, *World of Our Fathers* (New York, 1976). Will Herberg's *Protestant–Catholic–Jew: An Essay in American Religious Sociology* (Garden City, NY, 1955) is discussed in the text. Martin E. Marty has begun a projected four-volume history of Religion in the Twentieth Century with *Modern American Religion: The Irony of it All* (Chicago, 1986). The writings of America's most significant modern theologian have been collected in Robert McAfee Brown (ed.), *The Essential Reinhold Niebuhr: Selected Essays and Addresses* (New Haven, 1986).

For insights into the more recent era, one turns chiefly to sociologists. The best are Peter L. Berger, *The Noise of Solemn Assemblies* (Garden City, NY, 1961); Clifford Geertz, 'Religion as a Cultural System', in *Anthropological Approaches to the Study of Religion* (London, 1966); Patrick H. McNamara (ed.), *Religion American Style* (New York, 1974); Andrew Greeley, *The American Catholic: A Social Portrait* (New York, 1977); Thomas Luckmann, *The Invisible Religion: The Problem of Religion in Modern Society* (New York, 1967); Dean M. Kelley, *Why Conservative Churches are Growing* (New York, 1972); and, Robert Wuthnow, *The Restructuring of American Religion* (Princeton, NJ, 1988). One should especially highlight Robert N. Bellah. All of Bellah's work bristles with insights, most noticeably Robert N. Bellah, et al., *Habits of the Heart: Individualism and Commitment in American Life* (New York, 1985).

CHAPTER THREE

The American Democratic Tradition

Martin Crawford

THE TRADITION

The democratic tradition in the United States has derived both its strength
and its frailty from the relentless dynamism of American development.
From its beginnings in the early seventeenth century American society
exhibited rapid geographic, demographic, and material growth; after 1783
this process accelerated with unparalleled vigour, fuelled by a high birth
rate, large-scale European immigration and seemingly boundless land
resources. As Carl Degler has observed, within the lifetime of a middle-
aged individual, the United States after 1800 expanded in size by
approximately 300 per cent. As it expanded, the new nation also became
more culturally diverse and more economically differentiated, a process
which the North's unifying victory in the Civil War by no means reversed.
After 1880 the waves of non-Anglo-Saxon, non-Protestant immigration
into the United States provoked new concerns, especially among more
established groups, for the long-term stability of American society and for
the values it was intended to embody.

During the formative Colonial and Revolutionary eras, democratic
values struggled to compete against the countervailing forces of social
hierarchy and prescriptive rule, but by the 1830s, the Jacksonian era, the
belief in the people's innate right and ability to govern themselves had
triumphed, reshaping local and national political institutions and extending
into every area of American life. Indeed, the onset of political reform in the
United States was inconceivable without a concomitant movement for
greater social, economic, religious and cultural democracy. In all of these
areas ideas of democracy fused with – and in certain crucial respects,
countermanded – the other cherished values of the post-Revolutionary
experience: liberty and equality. At the same time this was not primarily an

intellectual movement. Although American intellectuals played a key role in shaping a new national culture after 1789, it was their more vulgar compatriots in the newspaper offices, the counting houses and on the political hustings who were ultimately responsible for the promulgation of democratic values in the United States.

In reality, democracy proved far easier to articulate than to establish. Already by the 1830s, contradictions in the emergent democratic polity were to pose serious challenges to the long-term survival of the American republic; throughout the rest of the nineteenth century, as American society continued to transform itself, the optimistic faith in the perfectibility of popular government in the United States gradually receded. Westward expansion, mass immigration, racial and ethnic antagonisms and the transformation of the economic order all conspired to frustrate the simple application of democratic ideas, while in the winter of 1860–61 the secession of the Southern states revealed fundamental ambiguities in the American system which were only resolved, if at all, after colossal expenditure of human and material resources. As the twentieth century dawned, democracy itself looked an increasingly casual garment, to be donned or discarded at will, whenever the temperature required it.

REVOLUTIONARY ORIGINS

While every aspect of American society had come under democratic scrutiny by the second quarter of the nineteenth century, the assumptions underlying the new creed would be most severely tested in the political arena. Following independence from Great Britain in 1776, Americans set about constructing new political institutions in accordance with the principles enunciated by the Revolutionary leadership and vigorously defended by patriot soldiers from New England to Georgia. It was these 'republican' principles that were to provide the foundation for the emergence of a democratic political culture in the United States, although at the onset of the Revolutionary war such an outcome was by no means assured. Late eighteenth-century republicanism defined itself through the protection of liberty and public virtue and not through the promotion of individual or group interests. As Michael Heale has observed, few Americans in 1776, least of all those in authority, were prepared to equate republicanism with democracy.

The long-term impact of republicanism upon the evolution of

American democracy, however, should not be underestimated. Henceforth, government in America – national, state and local – would be based upon the consent of the governed, expressed through free elections and representative institutions. Without that consent, government ceased to have legitimacy and could be replaced, either through the orderly transference of power or, as in the case of British rule, by the use of force. The basic function of republican government was to protect the liberty of the people, whose virtuous character would in any case provide the most effective guarantee against renewed tyranny. In repudiating British rule, Revolutionary Americans were not repudiating authority itself, merely the principle upon which it rested and the source and direction from which it flowed.

After 1776 Americans worked feverishly to give practical shape to republican ideals. Firstly, new state constitutions were drafted. In two cases, Connecticut and Rhode Island, where governors and other officials were already elected by the end of the colonial period, minor amendments to existing charters proved sufficient; but in the majority of states the Revolutionary transition necessitated entirely new constitutions in which the powers of government and the rights of individual citizens were carefully delineated. The overriding concern throughout the complex deliberations of state-constitution-making was abundantly clear: how best to protect the people against the abuse of power. To this end, government would be divided into its separate powers – executive, legislative and judicial – thus ensuring that none would achieve undue dominance over the others. Not unexpectedly, it was the fear of executive encroachment that most exercised the Revolutionary generation, and consequently they sought to expand legislative authority while simultaneously limiting the power of state governors. Two state constitutions, North Carolina and New Jersey, denied their governors any control over appointments, while a third, Pennsylvania, remarkably eliminated the executive office altogether. As a final guarantee, most of the new constitutions also included a Bill of Rights designed to protect individual freedoms from both executive and legislative violation.

Concurrent with the creation of state constitutions was the need to provide a new framework of national authority. The preceding chapter contains a discussion of the religious aspects of these processes. More generally, in the Articles of Confederation, originally drafted in 1776 but not ratified until 1781, the powers already assumed by the Continental Congress in coordinating colonial actions against the British were given revised and more permanent status. Unmistakably the creation of the individual states, the new government attempted to reconcile republican principles to the practical demands of wartime administration. The lack of coercive authority, particularly in fiscal matters, proved a serious impediment, however, and in May 1787 fifty-five delegates from the various states met in Philadelphia 'for the sole and express purpose' of revising the Articles of Confederation. Instead, an entirely new structure of national government was created. The Federal Constitution of 1787 embraced the fundamental principle of the separation of powers, but it did so under the aegis of a supreme national authority instead of a voluntary association of independent states. Some advocates of the new constitution were even to argue that the government was more republican than its predecessor precisely because it restored that essential principle, since under the Articles, executive, legislative and judicial authority had all been exercised by a single body, the Confederation Congress.

However plausible, these and other arguments could not disguise the fundamental shift that had occurred in the nature of political organization in the United States. Prior to 1787, the principle motive for the establishment of new governments, whether state or national, was to protect the rights of individual citizens from internal and external subversion. The Federal Constitution, however, while not abandoning that belief, was built to a more ambitious design, as contemporary opponents such as Patrick Henry were quick to point out. Addressing the Virginia Ratifying Convention in June 1788, Henry argued forcefully that the new 'consolidated' government created at Philadelphia represented a profound break with the past, 'a revolution as radical as that which separated us from Great Britain'. Like other so-called 'Anti-Federalists', Henry was alarmed that the function of government itself had been altered and he charged his fellow-countrymen not to be seduced by arguments for enhanced prosperity and national prestige. Moreover, convinced that state legislatures were the true embodiment of the representative principle, Anti-Federalists looked with alarm at a constitution which sought to bypass state authority and to act directly upon 'the people' of the nation at large. 'Who authorized them to speak the language of *We, the people*, instead of *We, the States*', Henry demanded angrily. 'States are the characteristics and the soul of a confederation. If the States be not the agents of this compact, it must be one great consolidated National Government, of the people of all the States.' Certainly, he concluded, it 'is not a democracy, wherein the people retain all their rights securely.'[1]

For Patrick Henry and other leading Anti-Federalists, the struggle against the 1787 Constitution involved more than the theoretical defence of abstract rights: at stake was the future of popular government itself, or 'democracy', as Henry termed it. Yet the word democracy cannot be understood independently of the social assumptions that governed political behaviour in late eighteenth-century America. Despite the absence of a hereditary aristocracy, few Americans prior to 1776 seriously doubted that political leadership was best left to those traditionally most accustomed to exercising it. Throughout the American colonies, therefore, political authority resided in the hands of the social and economic élites. This 'gentry' class, superior in wealth, education and family background, was bound to its neighbours by complex ties of deference and reciprocal obligation, thus protecting and advancing both its interests and those of the community at large. The precise character of élite authority varied from colony to colony and from region to region. In South Carolina and the Chesapeake Bay colonies, planter domination was sustained by the twin pillars of inequitable landholding and slave labour, but even in New England, a small number of families effectively controlled the management of political affairs.

Colonial America's deferential political culture, with its implied interdependence of social interests, was formally acknowledged in the theory of mixed or balanced government. This classical prescription, most clearly identified in the English constitution, divided government into three ideal forms: monarchy, aristocracy and democracy. Each form possessed its own discrete qualities, all of which were required for stable government. As Gordon Wood has shown, the theory's attraction was largely due to its social embodiment, to the reassurance it provided that all interests within the state would be adequately represented. During the nineteenth century, as American society broke loose from its colonial confines, this identification of government and society would diminish, but to most eighteenth-century Anglo-Americans at least, it remained the vital touchstone of their political culture.

The coming of Revolution after 1763, however, provoked a fundamental challenge both to the supremacy of American élites and to the theory of mixed government. Historians now perceive more sharply the democratic pressures that shaped the Revolutionary struggle. Well before the final conflict with Great Britain, lower class deference to established authority had already begun to erode. Immigration, westward expansion, and the spiritual upheavals of the Great Awakening all encouraged this development, the wider implications of which would not become apparent until the Stamp Act crisis of the mid-1760s, when popular radicalism transformed colonial opposition to British policy. After 1765 thousands of ordinary Americans took direct action to protest against imperial restraints upon their liberty and, in the process, helped to further undermine the values and institutions of the deferential society. The social challenges of the pre-Revolutionary decades, moreover, were but a prelude to the fundamental repudiation of established authority that occurred after 1775. For by challenging British rule, colonial Americans were also challenging the hierarchical assumptions that sustained it and to which they themselves had invariably subscribed. At every level, the traditional ties that bound the gentry class to its social inferiors were becoming unravelled. For some members of the colonial governing class, the change proved unacceptable: during the Revolutionary War an estimated 100,000 Loyalists left America, unwilling to adapt to the new egalitarian ethos which the conflict had fomented.

The political institutions that were created after 1776 reflected both the new republican ideology and the social transformation of the Revolutionary era. Without the latter, in fact, implementation of the former would hardly have been necessary. While the distribution of wealth in America had not substantially changed as a result of the revolution, a profound alteration had taken place in the relationships between the various classes. No longer would ordinary people – farmers, artisans and clerks – automatically defer to or be governed by their social superiors. Instead of the prescriptive rule of monarchs and aristocrats, government henceforth would be based solely upon popular consent. As the Declaration of Independence insisted in July 1776, the people themselves were now the only legitimate source of political authority.

These radical assumptions were clearly in evidence during the writing of the new state constitutions. As we have seen, these documents were designed above all to protect the liberty of the citizen from the arbitrary abuse of power, but they also reflected the growing determination of the common people to participate in the political process. While most states sought to apply the lessons of mixed or balanced government, efforts to reproduce the traditional model of monarchy, aristocracy and democracy conspicuously failed. New limitations on executive power have already been noted; equally significant was the failure to create a separate aristocratic estate in the upper houses of the legislature. Three states – Georgia, Pennsylvania and Vermont – declined to establish upper houses at all. Simultaneously, lower-house authority was strengthened through the elimination of many of the constitutional restraints of the pre-Revolutionary era. As a result, elected representatives were now more responsive to public opinion and, equally important in the emergence of a democratic political culture, also possessed the power to implement it through legislation. As Jackson Turner Main concludes, before the Revolution 'a great many measures desired by the majority of voters could never have become law; after it they seldom failed.'[2]

Even before the break with Britain, the American electorate was considerably broader than that of any comparable society, indicative of the wide degree of property holding in the colonies. After 1776 suffrage requirements were further liberalized, although the actual increase in voting as a result of the new state constitutions was probably small. Property holding continued to dictate the ability to vote and to hold office, but in a number of states, North Carolina and Pennsylvania, for example, it was granted to all taxpayers, an important step on the road to a democratic suffrage.

Of potentially greater significance than the suffrage were changes in the bases of political representation. As the central bone of contention in the dispute with England, representation was the focal point for much democratic energy both before and after 1776. The root cause of the issue was the demand of more recently settled communities in the interior for equal representation in the state legislatures. In reality, they were demanding a greater share of power, which the established seaboard interests had traditionally denied them through inequitable apportionment. As the American population expanded westward, the call for equal or 'actual' representation was bound to intensify and, as with the suffrage, the response of individual states varied considerably. In all states, however, western representation increased under the new constitutions, resulting in a sizeable growth in the number of representatives and a recognizable change in their social composition.

Political change in the new republic was neither uniform in its application nor uninterrupted in its progress. Democratic initiatives varied from state to state and, as in the case of Pennsylvania, whose radical constitution was replaced in 1790, were always likely to be overturned by conservative counter-reaction. Nor did the republican Revolution completely extinguish the deferential political culture of the colonial era. Wealthy merchants and landowners continued to hold office in disproportionate numbers, even though they were now forced to compete in the electoral arena with men of lesser social standing. Moreover, large segments of American society – women, blacks and Native Americans – remained barred from political participation. In the Southern states, thousands of black slaves were refused any civic rights at all, while for free blacks the post-revolutionary era proved a stumbling block to their democratic aspirations. Although most new state constitutions did not exclude free blacks from voting, legislative action in the early nineteenth century quickly reversed the situation. Native Americans had even fewer opportunities for democratic progress: denied citizenship, the continent's original inhabitants were usually unable to resist the erosion of their land resources, their distinctive cultures and the tribal identities that sustained them. Native American powerlessness would be dramatically confirmed in the 1830s, when thousands of members of eastern tribal nations were forcibly 'removed' to 'Indian Territory' (now Oklahoma) in the trans-Mississippi west.

Clearly, democracy had not yet triumphed in the new republic. In fact, for the majority of revolutionary leaders, such a condition was profoundly to be avoided. Fears of unfettered popular or 'mob' rule were rampant after 1776 and played a key role in constitutional deliberations, where the Republican vision of a disinterested citizenry, free from selfish pursuits, was challenged by the growing democratic insistence on equal representation, with its barely disguised defence of local interests. The more American society expanded and the more competitive it became, the more it appeared to deviate from the classical republican model, in which the interests of all people were presumed to coincide. Of course, such an idealist vision was easier to defend from the vantage point of economic privilege, as much of the criticism of state legislative excesses in the 1780s revealed. Anti-democratic concerns were by no means confined to a reactionary economic élite, however, but embraced a wide spectrum of political opinion that would ultimately find expression in support for the new Federal Constitution in 1787.

POST-REVOLUTIONARY ARGUMENTS

The conflict that developed over the Federal Constitution was of profound consequence to the history of American democracy. The Philadelphia document was designed both to remedy the defects of the existing Articles of Confederation and to create a new national authority under whose aegis the excesses of democratic politics could be curbed. The 'Federalist' advocates of the new constitution were particularly alarmed by what they considered the irresponsible behaviour of the new state governments, where the creation of paper money and the passage of debtor relief laws evidenced a selfish disregard for the economic interests of the society as a whole. As such, the movement aroused wide support from wealthy commercial and other creditor interests, as well as from those broader sections of American society anxious to provide for more assertive national government. Although the Revolutionary principles of popular sovereignty were not abandoned under the new constitution, its architects did intend to provide protection against the self-interested demands of democratic society.

Both Federalists and Anti-Federalists derived their legitimacy from a common republican tradition: where they diverged was in their attitude towards democratic politics. For the majority of Federalists, popular involvement was to be carefully mediated through continuing deference to élite authority, which would best be maintained by strengthening the national at the expense of state government. Without that constraint, they argued, American republicanism would soon be transformed into a corrupt squabble for self-advantage. Anti-Federalists, on the other hand, saw their republican inheritance in a very different light. In their view, liberty was best protected and the interests of ordinary Americans advanced through state and local government, where more democratic representation would inevitably prevail.

The battle lines of 1787–88 would remain virtually intact for several generations after the ratification of the Federal Constitution. In fact, the ideological cleavage between the conservative nationalists and their democratic, locally orientated rivals would become more sharply defined under the administration of the first president, George Washington, who assumed office in 1789. The immediate catalyst was Alexander Hamilton, Washington's first Secretary of the Treasury. Hamilton's neo-mercantilist programme for economic development, which included a protective tariff, the establishment of a new national bank and the assumption of state Revolutionary debts, provoked fierce opposition from former Anti-Federalists and significantly also angered many, like James Madison, who had helped to engineer the passage of the Philadelphia document.

Hamilton's ambitious design to link the economic and political fortunes of the new republic to those of its wealthy commercial élites was likely to offend large sections of the population, whose democratic energies were now being stimulated by the rapid expansion of American society. By 1796 the original thirteen states of the Union had increased to sixteen with the admission of Vermont, Kentucky and Tennessee; a quarter of a century later the number had mushroomed to twenty-four. As American society grew and became more diversified, it generated new sources of economic and cultural competitiveness. A rapidly multiplying number of social groups now vied for political attention, thereby placing unprecedented demands upon the existing representative structures. The result was a resurgence in democratic politics and the creation of a new institution, the political party, through which popular interests could be channelled.

Political parties did not emerge overnight in response to Hamilton's economic programme. Conflict over the issue initially developed within Congress, but then gradually dispersed into the states as legislative leaders sought wider endorsement for their respective positions. Soon, rival factions within the governing elite became consolidated into larger organizations, designed to mobilize electoral support throughout the expanding nation. Those in favour of Hamilton's programme, including the majority of those who had earlier endorsed the Philadelphia constitution, adopted the familiar sobriquet of 'Federalist'; their opponents, led by Thomas Jefferson and Madison, began to call themselves 'Democratic-Republican' or simply 'Republican'. Federalist support was concentrated within the more established, commercially orientated populations, notably in New England, whereas Republicans appealed more to the plantation and farm districts of the slave South and on the newly settled western frontier.

It was not Hamilton's economic programme, however, but the outbreak of the Franco-British war in 1793 which proved the major catalyst to party development. As Paul Goodman and others have shown, the ideological and diplomatic crisis generated by the war helped arouse a largely indifferent electorate by simplifying and dramatizing the issues which had polarized Congressional leaders as a result of Hamilton's initiatives. The more Federalist leaders demonstrated their sympathy for Great Britain, the more Republicans became convinced that Hamilton and his friends were bent on returning the United States to monarchical, anti-republican rule. Equally, Republican support for revolutionary France was viewed with alarm by Federalist leaders, who saw in it confirmation that the struggle for liberty, if not properly supervised, would quickly degenerate into anarchy and terror. The conflict came to a head in 1795 in the fight over John Jay's Treaty with Britain, which its Federalist architects regarded as a diplomatic necessity to guarantee continued American trade with Britain through the difficult period of Britain's war with France (in which it had interfered with American shipping), despite the fact that the treaty resolved only a proportion of America's grievances. The treaty's opponents could see it only as capitulation to the pro-British monarchical interest. Three years later, the Federalist passage of the defiantly partisan Alien and Sedition Acts confirmed the bitter divide that now existed between the governing 'party' and its Republican opposition.

The bitter partisan battles of the 1790s were in many respects as crucial to the history of American democracy as the Revolutionary movement that preceded them. In their opposition to Federalist rule, a growing majority of Americans sought to extend the democratic commitments of the Revolutionary era, which they saw threatened by the actions of self-perpetuating élites. While Federalists may have conceded that ultimate authority resided with the people, too often their actions during the decade, including the suppression of the so-called Whiskey Rebellion of western Pennsylvania farmers in 1794, suggested that the 'people' themselves were not yet ready to exercise it. Popular fears were particularly aroused by the Federalists' determination to strengthen central government at the expense of the states, which were regarded as the essential protectors of democratic liberties. This concern was especially strong in the South, where the fight for local autonomy would soon be linked to the defence of black slavery. In 1798 Jefferson and Madison drafted their powerful Kentucky and Virginia Resolutions, which outlined a 'States' rights' or 'strict construction' interpretation of the Federal Constitution as the best defence against anti-republican consolidation.

In their attacks upon the 'aristocratic' interest, the Republicans continued to profit from the social changes that were transforming American society. The more Americans distanced themselves from the population centres of the north-east and middle states, the more impatient they became with Federalist governance and the paternalistic assumptions sustaining it. As the United States expanded, new élites emerged to challenge for political supremacy, more popular in their orientation and more diverse in their backgrounds and ambitions than those they sought to replace.

In fact, westward expansion was only the most dramatic aspect of the social transformation of the early nineteenth century. By 1820 extraordinary changes had occurred in the cultural and economic fabric of American life, all of which contributed decisively to the decline in traditional politics. Expansion west and the increasing demands of eastern and European consumers helped fuel a dynamic market economy, which in turn promoted the development of urban society. In the north-eastern states, the growth of household manufacturing signalled the emergence of mature capitalist relations, while to the south 'King Cotton' and a reinvigorated slave system were beginning their inexorable march westwards, eating up new lands and ruthlessly displacing their Native American occupants in the process. The loosening of traditional bonds was further aggravated by new waves of religious revivalism that swept many areas after 1800. The seeds of the 'Great Revival' were first sown in the West, but its impact soon spread throughout the nation, as established religious authority succumbed to popular demands for greater spiritual self-determination.

Although the full force of these and other changes would not be felt for several generations or more, the election of Jefferson to the presidency in 1800 was early testimony of their impact upon American politics. While not the 'revolution' that some historians have claimed it to be, Jefferson's victory nonetheless denoted the clear repudiation of Federalist policies and attitudes by an increasingly self-confident electorate. Over the next two decades Federalist political fortunes went into terminal decline, and by 1824 the party was effectively dead, although some of the values it embodied still remained to be buried.

The Republican triumphs of the early 1800s should not be regarded as signifying the full emergence of democratic politics in the United States; rather, they were vital steps in an evolutionary process that was to reach its climax during the 1830s and 1840s. For one thing, attitudes to political parties, even among Republicans, remained wedded to eighteenth-century beliefs, which equated them with corrupt factionalism, and were therefore inappropriate in a society dedicated to harmony and virtue. Political leadership at both the state and national level, moreover, continued to reside in the hands of the gentry élite. Despite their ideological differences, Federalist and Republican leaders shared certain hierarchical assumptions that, as Robert H. Wiebe has described, set them apart from the mass of their countrymen. Jefferson was, after all, a wealthy Virginia planter and slaveholder who defended the mixed constitution and remained lukewarm to the introduction of universal manhood suffrage. For all his democratic instincts, Jefferson continued to believe that only those blessed with breeding, education and property should qualify as political leaders. It was hardly a prescription for plebeian rule.

The democratization of American politics, therefore, was not achieved overnight. Traditional beliefs continued to influence political activity for several decades after Jefferson's election and, in at least one region of the United States, the slave South, a conservative reaction would threaten to destroy all that the founding fathers had achieved. But the democratization of American political culture was not to be reversed, despite the uneven progress of the late eighteenth and early nineteenth centuries. By the late 1820s, democratic values were in the ascendant in the United States, refashioning and ultimately transforming the political institutions that had been created during the Revolutionary era.

DEMOCRATIC VICTORIES

The key ingredient in the emergence of unfettered democracy was a new emphasis on equality. Forged in the heat of revolution, egalitarian doctrines had largely been displaced during the formative years of political and constitutional development. But with the freedom generated by rapid social change, the belief in equality soon established itself as a vital force in American popular thought. In great measure, the new egalitarianism reflected the liberalization in political practice that had occurred since the 1780s. Widening of the suffrage through the abandonment of property and taxpaying qualifications was a crucial element in this process: by 1824 only a handful of states still imposed serious restrictions on the voting rights of their white adult male citizens. Other democratic innovations of this era included the popular election of judges, the creation of single-member congressional districts, and the transferring of the election of presidential electors from the state legislatures to the people at large.

The more ordinary Americans were encouraged to participate in the political process, the more they came to believe in their inalienable right, as equals, so to do. And as equals they soon began to insist that the only legitimate way to determine political choice was by following the will of the majority, where the principle of 'the greatest good of the greatest number' would apply. In this sense, the fight for majoritarian rule was a logical extension of the republican crusade against prescriptive authority that had begun before the Revolution. What had changed was the strident egalitarianism in which the calls for greater democracy were now phrased. As Harry L. Watson has observed, the new reform impulse did not supplant Republicanism in American political thinking, but 'significantly shifted its emphasis towards majoritarian democracy'.[3]

Changes in political practice did not create an egalitarian society in the United States; but they did greatly stimulate the belief in the equality of all white Americans, which in turn generated new demands for political reform. By the 1820s the American people were growing impatient with the residual power of the gentry élite. In 1819 a severe economic depression induced widespread misery throughout the nation, further undermining popular confidence in gentry authority in general and in the complacent leadership of the Republican Party in particular. The culmination of these developments was the election of General Andrew Jackson to the White House in 1828 and the creation of a new political organization, the Democratic Party, dedicated to the proposition of 'equal rights for all, special privileges for none'.

Jackson's election followed a decade or more of political transition in the United States. After Jefferson's victory in 1800, the Republican Party gradually dissolved into a *mélange* of competing interests, its loss of unity in part deriving from its acceptance of several key Hamiltonian policies, including the national bank and the protective tariff, the need for which had been keenly felt during the second war with Britain between 1812 and 1815. Out of this confusion emerged a new generation of political activists, determined to revive political conflict along the ideological lines of the 1790s. Pre-eminent among them was Martin Van Buren of New York, the son of a tavern-keeper. Van Buren rejected Republican administration efforts to create a governing consensus after 1815 by arguing that political distinctions must always exist between those who trusted the people's capacity for self-government, the 'democrats', and those who did not, the 'aristocrats'. Van Buren's organizational efforts were particularly geared towards creating a new political alliance between Northern and Southern interests. This would prevent, he hoped, the revival of sectional tensions as had arisen during the Missouri Crisis of 1819–21 over the legal extension of slavery into new states, when the stability of the Union itself was threatened.

Apart from social origin, the most significant difference between this new breed of professional politicians and their gentry predecessors occurred in their attitude to parties. Far from regarding parties as corrupt institutions, Van Buren and his followers now saw them as legitimate, indeed vital, instruments of democratic representation in a free society. Identification with a political party was now to be celebrated not condemned, as it would provide the common people with a means to counter the wealth and privilege of the aristocratic interest and would also help maintain the ideological battle-lines between the people and their would-be masters.

After 1827 Van Buren threw his considerable organizational genius and following behind Jackson, the hero of the Battle of New Orleans. Jackson had already demonstrated his electoral potentiality in 1824 when, after receiving the highest popular vote, he was deprived of the presidency in the House of Representatives by what he and his supporters claimed was a 'corrupt bargain' between his two principal opponents, John Quincy Adams of Massachusetts and Henry Clay of Kentucky. In 1828, however, republican virtue triumphed, with the new Jacksonian organization sweeping to victory against the incumbent Adams, the son of the former Federalist president. The 1828 election dramatically contrasted Adams's well-educated, patrician background with that of his lowly born opponent, setting a pattern for future presidential contests in which the man of action would triumph over the intellectual and the scholar. Four years later Jackson was easily re-elected after waging a popular campaign against the Second Bank of the United States. The era of Jacksonian Democracy had arrived.

Jacksonian Democracy was never as democratic or egalitarian as its most fervent admirers have claimed; but neither was it the unadulterated bourgeois movement invented by the so-called 'consensus' historians. As John Ashworth has described, there was a strong streak of anti-commercialism in the Democratic make-up, indicative of the party's Anti-Federalist and Jeffersonian origins. This hostility achieved its most potent expression in the attack upon the Second Bank, when the full force of Jacksonian fury was roused to defend republican virtue against aristocratic corruption. Less ambiguously, Jackson's victory in 1828 inaugurated a new era of democratic politics, in which the remaining strands of hierarchical authority were largely abandoned.

'Publick opinion is the lever by which all things are moved, in a democracy', wrote the novelist James Fenimore Cooper in 1838.[4] Jacksonian Democracy married the republican concern for the preservation of liberty and virtue to the new, egalitarian demands of a rapidly developing society. The result was an aggressively popular politics, which sought at all times to celebrate the 'common man's' capacity for self-government. Jacksonian Democracy profited by and further encouraged the changes in political practice that had occurred since the Revolution. By the 1830s full white adult male suffrage was well on the road to universal acceptance, although in a number of states tax-paying qualifications remained for local elections. In 1831–32 a significant change took place in the method of candidate selection, with the replacement of the traditional 'caucus' system by new nominating conventions. These were designed to make the process of selection more democratic: in practice they also consolidated control of local and state politics in the hands of professional party managers.

The democratic advances of the Jacksonian era can be gauged by the significant increase in popular involvement in political activity, notably at the ballot box. During the years of Republican one-party dominance after 1815, voter participation in national elections was conspicuously low. Only 27 per cent of eligible electors bothered to vote in the presidential contest of 1824. Public interest soon revived following the resumption of political competition, however, and in 1828 over 57 per cent of the electorate went to the polls. After the creation of a new anti-Jacksonian opposition party, the Whigs, in 1834, interest in national politics was further stimulated, culminating in the colourful election of 1840, when 80 per cent of the white adult male electorate voted. As Michael McGerr has commented, by the 1840s Americans had come to accept 'that white men of all classes should participate in politics by voting'.[5] Over the next five decades voter turnout would remain at a high level, before declining during the early years of the twentieth century.

As a postscript to the democratic era, it is worth reminding ourselves how inextricably linked the Jacksonians were to their republican past. At every stage Jacksonian Democrats continued to insist on the Jeffersonian maxim that the best government is that which governs least. 'All communities are apt to look to government for too much', argued Jackson's successor, Van Buren, in rejecting pleas for intervention following the financial panic of 1837.[6] In the presidential election of 1840, Van Buren was defeated by a rejuvenated Whig Party, who achieved power by aping, often grotesquely, the common-man rituals of their Democratic opponents. Ironically, it was the conservative Whigs who appeared more likely to free themselves from their Revolutionary inheritance by advocating a stronger role for government in the promotion of American economic and social development. Unfortunately, Whig attitudes were often informed by a distrust of popular democracy, which

59

they regarded as incompatible with their vision of a harmonious, organic society. In this regard, Whigs too were captives of their republican inheritance, albeit one of a rather different complexion to that of their Democratic rivals.

By 1840, therefore, political parties had emerged as the prime vehicles of democratic representation in American society. Yet for some Americans the 'second party system', as historians now describe it, proved far from adequate. One intellectual, Henry David Thoreau, author of *Walden* (1854) – which was at once both the record of a period of self-sufficient life close to nature at Walden Pond near Concord, Massachusetts, and a highly self-referential meditation upon a spiritual quest – actually went so far as to write, in the first lines of 'Civil Disobedience' (1849), 'that government is best which governs not at all'. In a text which has proved highly influential in protest movements all over the world, Thoreau argued that in situations where a person believed that the state was itself acting immorally, as in the perpetuation of slavery and the prosecution of imperialistic wars, civil disobedience was more than justified; to him the individual conscience was sovereign. Such ideas could be seen, at one and the same time, both as an extension of the democratic tradition, nurtured by the aggressive championing of the rights of ordinary folk during the Jacksonian era, and in its (potential or actual) defiance of the majority, as a negation of it.

As American society grew and became more differentiated, groups emerged whose demands could not easily be accommodated within the existing majoritarian coalitions. One such group were the urban artisans, whose livelihoods were threatened by changing social relations of production and by the vagaries of the economic cycle. In response, artisans in many north-eastern cities after 1828 formed their own 'working-men's' parties, with policies ranging from bread-and-butter demands for shorter hours and improved working conditions to a more ideological insistence on changes in the economic order. These working-men's parties were closely allied to the nascent trade union organizations, which would re-emerge in the second half of the nineteenth century as vital institutions of working-class representation in industrial America.

In the main, the Democratic and Whig coalitions proved highly adept at absorbing the new economic and cultural demands generated by the transformation of antebellum society. One of the most conspicuous exceptions was the Women's Rights movement which, although it led Elizabeth Cady Stanton to produce the 1848 Seneca Falls 'Declaration of Sentiments', with its opening words a deliberate upstaging of an earlier democratic text ('We hold these truths to be self-evident: that all men and women are created equal'), was not allowed to make a substantial contemporary impact and did not achieve the goal of national women's

suffrage until the Nineteenth Amendment in 1920. Even more conspicuous was the movement to abolish black slavery, which gained new
momentum after 1831. The problem with abolitionism was that it
massively assaulted the economic interests and racial prescriptions of
Southerners, as well as offending large numbers of Non-southerners by its
radical challenge to accepted values and procedures. Initially, abolitionism
eschewed political action in favour of a campaign of moral conversion.
However, the movement's progressive institutionalization soon led anti-
slavery reformers into the political mainstream and by 1840 anti-slavery
parties were contesting for power in national elections.

Abolitionism revealed the strengths and weaknesses of the American
democratic impulse. As moral crusaders, radical reformers such as William
Lloyd Garrison successfully galvanized thousands of Americans into
challenging the political and racial consensus that had nurtured slavery's
growth since the Revolution. Yet in order to achieve its ends, abolitionism
was soon forced to compete in the political arena where moral issues were
invariably susceptible to dilution and compromise. The result was that by
the 1850s the movement to abolish slavery was indissolubly intertwined
with the broader concerns of American development, including westward
expansion and the changing economic character of Northern society.
Increasingly subordinated in this process were the rights of the black slaves
themselves, whose pleas for equality most white Americans would continue
to resist long after emancipation had been accomplished. Moreover, while
the abolitionist movement finally succeeded in its purpose, it did so only
after the collapse of the much-vaunted democratic system and the terrible
confrontation of civil war.

COUNTER-REACTION

America's optimistic faith in its democratic political culture was rudely
shattered during the bitter struggle for sectional supremacy. Over 600,000
men lost their lives during the Civil War, which occurred after the
Southern states refused to accept the verdict of the 1860 presidential
election. Majoritarian democracy, which had finally been achieved after
decades of political evolution, had failed at a critical juncture to satisfy the
interests of a determined minority, anxious to conserve its unique society
against the nationalizing forces that conspired to change it. American
political leaders had long been aware of the inherent problem of minority
regional rights, but it was only after the expansion of American society that
the issue came to a head, notably in the nullification dispute of 1828–33,

when President Jackson threatened drastic measures against South Carolina's opposition to the Federal tariff. Thirty years later, South Carolina led the secession movement which took the Southern states out of the Union.

What then happened to the American democratic tradition after 1865? From one perspective, it had already achieved its aims. Even before the Civil War the United States possessed a more liberal suffrage and more representative institutions than any comparable society, provoking the admiration of European reformers. Other essential democratic attributes such as freedom of the press, of speech, and of religious worship were also guaranteed under the first ten amendments to the Constitution, the Bill of Rights. Moreover, as a result of the North's victory, the issue of majoritarian democracy appeared to have been settled, albeit through the arbitrament of military force. Slavery, the great stain on American society, had been abolished by 1865, and millions of former bondsmen and women granted civil and political rights through the Fourteenth and Fifteenth Amendments. For a time these efforts to extend democratic rights to the freed blacks proved remarkably successful; in the late 1860s and 1870s thousands of black citizens exercised their democratic option for the first time by voting in local, state and national elections. A considerable number of freedmen were also elected to office, although, contrary to white Southern legend, blacks never had political control of any Southern state.

Unfortunately, the democratic progress of the mid-nineteenth century was not sustained. In fact, the post-Civil War period saw a revival of anti-democratic sentiment as American society embarked upon a new phase of economic and social transformation. The growth of anti-democratic sentiment was underwritten by an intellectual counterattack upon American Revolutionary values. Confronted by renewed assertions of popular democracy during the Reconstruction era, conservative lawyers, clergymen and academics sought, in Daniel T. Rodgers words, 'to wrest the language of political legitimacy away from the people'.[7] In place of the familiar lexicon of 'natural rights', 'popular sovereignty', and the 'social compact', a new set of 'obligations' was proposed, designed to limit the people's authority. Foremost among the casualties was the inalienable right to vote, which was now to be regarded as a privilege and hence subject to restriction or withdrawal. By the end of the century, the language of Revolutionary rights had all but disappeared, to be replaced by enthusiastic talk of the 'state' and of the 'interests' comprising it.

The most blatant victims of the anti-democratic movement after 1865 were the newly enfranchised freedmen. After the defeat of Radical Reconstruction and the redemption of the ex-Confederate states for white Democratic rule, black political participation was inevitably vulnerable, notwithstanding the legal guarantees of the Fourteenth and Fifteenth Amendments. During the 1890s, however, black disfranchisement became a key strategy of Democratic party governance in the South, as white supremacists sought to regain their former racial dominance. The southern disfranchisement impulse was greatly stimulated by the continuing electoral influence of black voters, and by the threat posed, in the Populist revolt, by the possibility of a biracial challenge to white upper-class rule. By the beginning of the twentieth century, black democracy in the South was in full retreat, not to be reversed until the Civil Rights era of the 1950s and 1960s.

In an obvious sense, black disfranchisement showed American democracy merely reverting to type, since even at its zenith in the Jacksonian era, the movement for greater political participation was overwhelmingly based on racial exclusivity. It would be a mistake to assume, however, that the anti-democratic impulse was solely directed against America's non-white population: the other major unenfranchised group in the nineteenth century, women, also failed to make any significant democratic progress in the aftermath of the Civil War. As Eric Foner has written, the failure to include a guarantee of women's suffrage in the Fourteenth Amendment left feminist leaders such as Susan B. Anthony 'with a deep sense of betrayal'.[8] Women, as we have seen, continued to be regarded as inappropriate subjects for democratic inclusion, only achieving suffrage in August 1920.

More surprising was the fact that many white males were also regarded in the same light. Not unexpectedly, prime movers in the anti-democratic crusade were the Southern 'bourbon' élites who sought to eliminate 'irresponsible' yeoman and poor white, as well as black, voters from their electoral calculations. But élite suspicion of popular democracy also revived in the rapidly industrializing North, ostensibly provoked by the emergence of labour unions, class violence, and by the arrival of millions of 'new' immigrants from southern and central Europe, whose religion, language and political values, it was argued, did not equip them for full democratic rights (see Chapter 7). During the 1870s patrician reformers such as Charles Francis Adams Jr, great-grandson of the Federalist president, proposed abandoning the principle of universal suffrage through the imposition of educational and other voting qualifications. Only then, they suggested, would municipal government be purified and the deleterious effects of equality checked.

Unlike Southern disfranchisement, the movement to restrict urban voting came to nothing; by the 1890s middle- and upper-class Americans were turning their attention to other areas of reform, including immigration restriction and educational politics. However, the net effect of their activities and of the massive socio-economic transformations of the late nineteenth and early twentieth centuries, several of which are described in Chapter 8, was a decline in mass political activity and the abandonment of the flamboyant popular partisanship of nineteenth-century democracy. It is an ironic fact that during the Progressive era, when efforts were made to restrain the new concentrations of power in American society, and when such democratic innovations as the referendum were instituted, voting in national elections decreased, as political parties appeared to lose their grip upon the American imagination.

However, for those groups who were denied access to the political system, and who also suffered wider discrimination in American society, the right to vote remained a crucial democratic ambition. Following the disappointment of the Fourteenth Amendment, the women's movement had fragmented into competing reform factions and not until 1890 and the founding of the National American Woman Suffrage Association was a unified campaign re-established. Although piecemeal victories were achieved in many western states before 1900 – notably in Colorado, which in 1893 became the first state in which male electors actually voted for women's suffrage – it would be another generation before ratification of the amendment guaranteeing that the 'right of citizens of the United States to vote shall not be denied . . . on account of sex'. Southern blacks, on the other hand, as we have seen, were fighting to regain political rights expropriated during the era of counter-reaction, as well as seeking to end the system of racial segregation imposed at the same time. Like the advocates of women's suffrage before them, black Civil Rights leaders after the Second World War saw voting as a vital weapon in the fight for justice and equality. In August 1965 the campaign achieved a landmark victory with the passage of the Civil Rights Voting Act, which opened the door for the gradual reassertion of black democratic rights.

MODERN DEMOCRACY

Possession of the vote does not guarantee equality or material progress, however, as both women and black Americans have found to their cost. In fact, democracy's limitations were tragically highlighted a few days after the passage of the Voting Rights Act, when rioting broke out in the largely black Watts district of Los Angeles, resulting in thirty-four deaths and millions of dollars of property damage.

How then does democracy fare in modern America? Despite the expansion of the suffrage through the enfranchisement of women,

Southern blacks and, following the ratification of the Twenty-sixth Amendment in 1971, eighteen-year-olds, popular interest in democratic politics shows little sign of revival. Although partisan identification and voter turnout partially revived during the 1930s and 1960s, the long-term trend was unmistakable. In five presidential contests since 1972, average voter turnout has been less than 54 per cent, a far cry from the enthusiastic participation of the middle and late nineteenth century. The rise in public apathy has coincided both with a decline in the influence of political parties and an increase in the power of the state and Federal governments in American life. Election campaigns, so pivotal to the democratic political culture of the nineteenth century, are now regarded as little more than exercises in television manipulation. The recent report of the Markle Commission, set up in the wake of the 1988 election, finds a dispiriting level of public indifference towards the political process. In 1988 37 per cent of the eligible electorate failed to register to vote, the highest percentage of any industrialized nation.

Moreover, it is among the poor and disadvantaged, particularly in the black and Hispanic communities, that public apathy is most prevalent. Two-thirds of unregistered electors in 1988 were below the median income line. As the economy falters relative to its competitors in Europe and the Far East, the gap between rich and poor is likely to widen. In this regard, America's republican inheritance may prove a burden. For a majority of Americans, democracy remains an essentially defensive ideal, a useful weapon in the fight against freedom's enemies, real or imagined. And apparently, among those Americans whose economic and social needs are greatest, it fails to accomplish even that modest aim.

Undoubtedly, democracy as practised in its nineteenth century heyday no longer exists; but neither does the largely undifferentiated society from which it evolved. In late twentieth-century America, with its overarching state and complex economic and cultural fabric, democracy has had to be reconstituted. Simple concepts of majoritarian rule have been replaced by a pluralist vision of competing minority interests. As was pointed out in Chapter 2, fundamental questions – often seen as 'single issues' unrelated to any accompanying political programme, party-inspired or not – continue to be hotly debated, campaigned over, and sometimes resolved, at least temporarily, with proponents and antagonists using the full panoply of democratic means available. Even as they decline to participate in many of its familiar party political rituals, Americans remain firmly committed to their democratic beliefs, and at the state and local level in particular, continue to seek new means of sovereign expression, including most recently, the revival of the popular referendum. Today, self-doubts about the democratic process go hand in hand with what one writer has called a 'compulsive attachment' to it.[9] How and when this paradox will be resolved remains to be seen; in the meantime, the democratic tradition survives in the United States, although in a form that its Jacksonian practitioners would have increasing difficulty in recognizing.

NOTES

1. Samuel Eliot Morison (ed.), *Sources and Documents Illustrating the American Revolution, 1764–1788* (New York, 1965), pp. 309, 321.

2. Jackson Turner Main, *The Sovereign States, 1775–1783* (New York, 1973), p. 206.

3. Harry Watson, *Liberty and Power: The Politics of Jacksonian America* (New York, 1990), p. 51.

4. James Fenimore Cooper, *The American Democrat* (1838; Harmondsworth, 1969), p. 205.

5. Michael C. McGerr, *The Decline of Popular Politics: The American North, 1865–1928* (New York, 1986), p. 5.

6. Quoted in Watson, *Liberty and Power*, p. 207.

7. Daniel T. Rodgers, *Contested Truths: Keywords in American Politics since Independence* (New York, 1987), p. 145.

8. Eric Foner, *Reconstruction: America's Unfinished Revolution* (New York, 1987), p. 255.

9. Michael Foley, *American Political Ideas: Traditions and Usages* (Manchester, 1991), p. 79.

SUGGESTIONS FOR FURTHER READING

An outstanding modern synthesis of early American society and government is James A. Henretta and Gregory H. Nobles, *Evolution and Revolution: American Society, 1600–1820* (Lexington, MA, 1987), while Carl Degler, *Out of Our Past: Forces That Shaped Modern America* (New York, 3rd ed., 1984) is an admirable interpretive survey. The emergence of a democratic political culture is skilfully described in Michael Heale, *The Making of American Politics, 1750–1850* (London, 1976), while Chilton Williamson, *American Suffrage from Property to Democracy* (Princeton, NJ, 1960) provides a readable overview of that broad and important subject.

For a provocative interpretation of the transition from a hierarchical to a democratic society, see Robert H. Wiebe, *The Opening of American Society: From the Adoption of the Constitution to the Eve of Disunion* (New York, 1984).

Standing head and shoulders above all other studies of revolutionary era political thought is Gordon S. Wood, *The Creation of the American Republic, 1776–1787* (Chapel Hill, NC, 1969). It can be usefully supplemented by Jackson Turner Main, *The Sovereign States, 1775–1783* (New York, 1973), which provides a well-rounded summary of local conditions. The revolution and constitution debates can be observed at first hand in Samuel Eliot Morison (ed.), *Sources and Documents illustrating the American Revolution, 1764–1788* (New York, 1965). Colin Bonwick, *The American Revolution* (London, 1991) is an excellent new interpretive text.

An exemplary analysis of the emergence of American parties during the 1790s can be found in Paul Goodman, 'The First American Party System', in Walter Nisbet Chambers and Walter Dean Burnham (eds), *The American Party Systems: States of Political Development* (New York, 1967), which also contains other pertinent essays. Particularly valuable on early attitudes to political parties is Richard Hofstadter, *The Idea of a Party System: The Rise of Legitimate Opposition in the United States, 1780–1840* (Berkeley and Los Angeles, 1969). Harry L. Watson, *Liberty and Power: The Politics of Jacksonian America* (New York, 1990) provides a first-rate new synthesis of democratic politics during the 1830s, while John Ashworth's *'Agrarians and Aristocrats': Party Political Ideology in the United States, 1837–1846* (1983; Cambridge, 1987), is a valuable revisionist essay.

The democratic victories and betrayals of the post-Civil War period are brilliantly examined in Eric Foner, *Reconstruction: America's Unfinished Revolution* (New York, 1987). Anti-democracy in the South is further investigated in J. Morgan Kousser, *The Shaping of Southern Politics: Suffrage Restriction and the Establishment of the One-Party South, 1880–1910* (New Haven, 1974). Kousser's book should be read in conjunction with Michael E. McGerr, *The Decline of Popular Politics: The American North, 1865–1928* (New York, 1986). On women's suffrage, see Eleanor Flexner, *Century of Struggle: The Women's Rights Movement in the United States* (Cambridge, MA, 1959).

Daniel T. Rodgers, *Contested Truths: Keywords in American Politics since Independence* (New York, 1987), offers an outstanding overview of rhetorical transformation. For valuable introductions to the central themes of American political thought, see Michael Foley, *American Political Ideas: Traditions and Usages* (Manchester, 1991). Finally, two classic nineteenth-century works which provide a wealth of contemporary insight into early American democratic values: James Fenimore Cooper, *The American Democrat* (1838, Harmondsworth, 1969); and especially Alexis de Tocqueville, *Democracy in America* (1835, 1840; 2 vols, New York, 1945).

CHAPTER FOUR

Transcendentalism and Pragmatism

Douglas Tallack

INTRODUCTION

There are no rivals to transcendentalism and pragmatism as the most famous philosophical movements in the United States between the 1830s and the 1930s. Any checklist of leading American thinkers would almost certainly be headed by Ralph Waldo Emerson, William James and John Dewey, and strong support could be mustered for Charles Sanders Peirce and possibly Henry David Thoreau. However, over the past forty years, the Emerson, James and Dewey line of thinking has been eclipsed by the astounding professional success of Anglo-American analytical philosophy. This has meant more than a simple change of philosophical personnel; rather, the effect has been to downgrade transcendentalism and pragmatism *as philosophy*. By 1981, Stanley Cavell could observe of the transcendentalists Emerson and Thoreau that 'it is hard to imagine any writers more foreign to our currently established philosophical sensibility'.[1] The neglect of James and Dewey is, if anything, more startling, given that at their deaths (in 1910 and 1952, respectively) they stood for so much of what American philosophy was supposed to be.

If the transcendentalism–pragmatism line had completely come to an end, this essay would be solely a chapter in the history of American philosophy. But during the 1980s – and in some ways related to the larger cultural and political debate over postmodernism – new interest has been shown in the 'classic' thinkers. The revival sometimes goes under the heading of neo-pragmatism, though Emerson has also been excitingly reread in an effort to raise – yet again – definitional questions about philosophy, but from a distinctively American point of view. The revival has been led by a few well-known, if somewhat unorthodox, neo-pragmatist American philosophers. In 1981 Cavell expanded *The Senses of*

Walden (a 1972 book on Thoreau) with two essays on Emerson, and has maintained his interest in *Conditions Handsome and Unhandsome: The Constitution of Emersonian Perfectionism* (1991). In *Consequences of Pragmatism* (1982) Richard Rorty rehabilitated Dewey and James at the expense of 'professionalized Philosophy'. In *Philosophical Profiles: Essays in a Pragmatic Mode* (1986) – written from a political position more to the left of Rorty's liberalism – Richard Bernstein has reconsidered Dewey and Peirce (and engaged with Rorty) in the context of modern and contemporary European thought. And in *The American Evasion of Philosophy* (1989), Cornel West has retraced the 'genealogy of pragmatism' from Emerson through Peirce, James and Dewey to Rorty and (more surprisingly) to West's own philosophical project as a black, neo-Marxist liberationist theologian.

By picking up cues in the current re-evaluation of transcendentalism and pragmatism, the present essay goes against the grain of existing studies – and does so in two main ways. First, it has to be accepted that little justice will be done to the rather precious New England atmosphere and localized contexts of transcendentalism and early pragmatism. For the record, these contexts are – in the case of transcendentalism – the debate within the Unitarian churches of Boston between the 1820s and 1840s and the important institutional structures of transcendentalism: *The Dial* magazine (1840–44); the Transcendentalist Club (founded 1838); and Brook Farm utopian community (1841–47). For pragmatism, the local context is the division within the profession of philosophy, and, indeed, within the Harvard Philosophy department. Hopefully, the bibliographical essay will help readers to situate my own, more argumentative, approach.

Second, those recent critics and philosophers who have taken another look at transcendentalism and pragmatism have found similarities rather than differences between the two movements. Here, they have respected James and Dewey, who certainly thought they were in Emerson's tradition. Nevertheless, a postmodern reading of Emerson, which doubts whether there was such a break between the soaring idealism of antebellum transcendentalism and the more empirical, low-key writings of pragmatism, is bound to seem provocative. Emerson is, after all, almost the type of a foundational thinker, that is, one who believes there is, in God, the self or nature, a final truth. Yet it is precisely in reading Emerson against the grain that we can appreciate the claims now being made that transcendentalism and pragmatism amount to a very significant American critique of philosophy; almost an anti-philosophy, according to some commentators.

As the accompanying suggestions for further reading confirm, the topic of transcendentalism and pragmatism has a well-trodden feel to it. Some retreading will still be necessary, for the sake of clear exposition and also because we need to know what the traditional wisdom is if we are going to argue that there is an anti-tradition (or anti-philosophy) at the heart of American philosophy. Moreover, the move from philosophy to the broader cultural concerns of Rorty, West, Cavell and Bernstein has (ironically) to be argued through with some traditional rigour. The need to do justice to ideas, even as context becomes more important than text, also justifies a concentrated focus upon the three representative figures: Emerson, James and Dewey.

EMERSON AND TRANSCENDENTALISM: 1830s–40s

Transcendentalism began when Emerson resigned as a Unitarian minister in 1832. Unitarianism was a stage on the way to transcendentalism, especially in the thought of William Ellery Channing, in that the exercise of human reason increased as the total power of the Calvinists' God grew less. But Emerson, in his 'Divinity School Address' (1838), and Theodore Parker, in his sermon, 'The Transient and Permanent in Christianity' (1841), objected that Unitarians had rendered the link between the human and the divine a matter of education and not revelation or intuition, so that, paradoxically, only literal miracles could bridge the gap, rather than the miracles of 'the blowing clover and the falling rain'.[2] Emerson described the rational, liberal theology of orthodox Unitarianism as 'corpse cold', while Parker found no inspiration in 'the dry leaves' of theology.

Unitarianism was the late eighteenth- and early nineteenth-century successor to the rationalistic, legalistic wing of seventeenth-century Puritanism. Right from the beginning that rational tradition of thinking stood out against the kind of self-empowerment which surfaced briefly during the Antinomian Controversy of 1634–38. At her trial in 1637, Anne Hutchinson horrified the Puritan establishment in Boston by claiming 'an immediate revelation' from God which bypassed all of the rational structures of belief embodied in seventeenth-century congregationalism. She resisted a strong interpretive impulse which entered Puritan theology in piecemeal fashion as many early New England ministers sought to transform the theological doctrine of Calvinism into a moral blueprint for social life in New England townships. Literally, 'antinomian' means to oppose the moral law of society with a higher or transcendent truth. In modified form, the Antinomian or intensely spiritual wing of Puritanism runs through the many separatist challenges to Puritanism and the arguments for the spirit made so powerfully by

Jonathan Edwards during the Great Awakening of the early 1740s. In the most widely accepted tellings of Colonial intellectual history Edwards is juxtaposed with Benjamin Franklin, with Franklin's journey from Boston to Philadelphia, as recounted in his *Autobiography* (1791), signalling his move to the eighteenth-century Enlightenment and to secular, practical achievements. The Antinomian strain bypassed Franklin to re-emerge in the 1830s and 1840s in the central transcendentalist claim for the self's knowledge of its own thoughts: that is, self-consciousness.

Transcendentalism becomes part of the broader context of modern American culture, as well as joining with the international movement of romanticism, in *Nature* (1836), when Emerson fastens on to the central philosophical relationship of mind to itself and its world, the 'NOT-ME', in Emerson's expression. This was also the common ground between Emerson, Parker, Orestes Brownson, George Ripley, and other Unitarian ministers, and free-floating intellectuals like Bronson Alcott, Margaret Fuller, Elizabeth Peabody and Thoreau. However, if we closely follow Emerson as he argues out the case for the common ground of a transcendent truth, we can also identify certain problems with his foundational metaphysics and it is these which will help us to trace the route towards pragmatism.

Emerson begins *Nature* with the proposition that the past, and specifically the past inscribed in texts ('biographies, histories, and criticism'), be replaced by 'an original relation to the universe'. The model for this unmediated relationship is nature, which 'is already, in its forms and tendencies, describing its own design'. A person's 'nature' is similarly directly accessible, providing we eschew interpretive detours to knowledge: 'Every man's condition is a solution in hieroglyphic to those inquiries he would put. He acts it as life, before he apprehends it as truth' (*SE*, pp. 35, 36).

In *Nature* the drive for cultural independence from Europe (announced the following year in 'The American Scholar') is quickly subsumed within Emerson's pursuit of a transcendent truth which will resolve the division between mind and matter so famously identified by Descartes, and then confirmed, but reorientated, by John Locke. Locke's influence in America had led many thinkers, including Channing, to believe that knowledge could be derived from the sensations which the mind, as a *tabula rasa*, registered in its contact with the external world. Emerson addresses both the Cartesian and Lockean versions of the great divide by promoting intuition as *the* way of knowing, including the knowing of oneself. He adds that we know ourselves most fully when we are alone and surrounded by nature: 'I am not solitary whilst I read and write, though nobody is with me. But if a man would be alone, let him look at the stars' (*SE*, p. 37).

Emerson expands upon this theme in a passage which culminates in his most memorable transcendental image:

> Crossing a bare common, in snow puddles, at twilight, under a clouded sky, without having in my thoughts any occurrence of special good fortune, I have enjoyed a perfect exhilaration. I am glad to the brink of fear. In the woods, too, a man casts off his years, as the snake his slough, and at what period soever of life is always a child .... . Standing on the bare ground – my head bathed by the blithe air and uplifted into infinite space – all mean egotism vanishes. I become a transparent eyeball; I am nothing; I see all; the currents of the Universal Being circulate through me; I am part or parcel of God.
>
> (*SE*, pp. 38, 39)

In 'The Over-Soul' (1841) Emerson explains that 'we distinguish the announcements of the soul, its manifestations of its own nature, by the term *Revelation*. These are always attended by the emotion of the sublime' (*SE*, p. 214). Nature is revealed as the idea of God. It is no surprise, then, to find Emerson, in 1842, defining 'what is popularly called Transcendentalism among us [as] Idealism' (*SE*, p. 239) having, in *Nature*, defined idealism as follows:

> Idealism sees the world in God. It beholds the whole circle of persons and things, of actions and events, of country and religion, not as painfully accumulated, atom after atom, act after act, in an aged creeping Past, but as one vast picture which God paints on the instant eternity for the contemplation of the soul.
>
> (*SE*, p. 70)

There is an unimpeded movement back and forward between God, matter, ideas and the soul. In describing the self as a soul, Emerson, in common with all of the transcendentalists, is saying that subjectivity and objectivity can be united by tapping the divine spirit in every person. In case there is any confusion of terminology, it is worth explaining that Emerson uses the word 'reason' where other romantics would use 'imagination' to describe the faculty through which transcendental union is to be achieved.

If we now bring back our starting hypothesis about American philosophy as anti-traditional, it would seem that Emerson does not fit. It is difficult to think of a body of writing which is more traditionally metaphysical than Emerson's, and appending the adjective 'American' to his work only underlines this ideal quality: 'The foundations of man are not in matter but in spirit' (that which is meta-physical), and 'the thought is always prior to the fact; all the facts of history preexist in the mind as laws' (*SE*, p. 149). This could almost be a philosophical gloss on the views of American literature's great idealist, Scott Fitzgerald's character Jay Gatsby, who, it will be remembered, 'sprang from his Platonic conception of himself'.[3] Moreover, while Emerson set himself against European traditions he also readily acknowledged his affiliations with Platonic thought and, nearer to hand, with German idealism – notably Kantian philosophy – and the romantic poetics of Coleridge and Wordsworth.

In the 'transparent eyeball' passage, the eye which sees innocently can transcend mundane circumstances as well as the fragmenting of nature under the rule of property. Emerson thinks of a nearby landscape, divided into farms, but his vision does not correspond either to what is palpably there or to the historical process which produced these property divisions, but goes beyond and through it to create an instant picture. By rapidly shifting the point of view from the foreground to the horizon, the fences, hedges and, indeed, the concept of property are blurred, thereby recreating the whole, original landscape. Another Fitzgerald character from *The Great Gatsby* (1925) – Nick Carraway – performs the same feat when he makes the past replace the propertied present by imagining the 'fresh green breast of the New World' that the first Dutch settlers saw (p. 187).

To see in this way requires an exercise of self-reformation, a process that Emerson describes in great detail in 'Self-Reliance' (1841), a compendium of his most ringing pronouncements:

> Nothing is at last sacred but the integrity of your own mind.
>
> No law can be sacred to me but that of my nature.
>
> What is the aboriginal Self, on which a universal reliance may be grounded?
>
> To believe your own thought, to believe that what is true for you in your private heart is true for all men – that is genius.
>
> Speak your latent conviction, and it shall be the universal sense; for the inmost in due time becomes the outmost, and our first thought is rendered back to us by the trumpets of the Last Judgement.
>
> (*SE*, pp. 178, 179, 187, 175)

Emerson is a very inclusive writer, and we can see why he inspired Walt Whitman, the most all-embrasive of poets (see Chapter 15). Still, there are more hesitancies in Emerson than in Whitman. Discriminations have to be made in Emerson's work, and not only those between his work up to, and then after, the mid-1840s. For example, in the above statements collected from 'Self-Reliance', we ought to distinguish between Emerson relying on the self (as in the first two statements) and Emerson seeking to ground self-reliance upon some more aboriginal essence: '*self*-reliance as opposed to God-reliance, though Emerson thought the two were the same', to borrow a pithy formulation from the critic Harold Bloom.[4] Emerson seeks to reconcile the celebrations of self-reliance with the vision of nature as the unified thought of God. In 'History' (1841), he envisages the individual mind as a medium for a pre-existing unity, with other minds: 'What Plato has thought, we may think'; and with God: 'this universal mind' (*SE*, p. 149).

My prejudice against this most metaphysical, most foundational, Emerson, who is supremely confident in 'the final cause of the world', is not just a late twentieth-century, or even a pragmatist one. Nathaniel Hawthorne, a contemporary of Emerson, parodied the transcendentalist faith in a principle of unity flowing through every phenomenon: in 'The Celestial Railroad' (1843) we meet 'Giant Transcendentalist', whose 'form', 'features', 'substance', and 'nature' no one can describe. 'He shouted after us, but in so strange a phraseology that we knew not what he meant.'[5] There is a more telling critique of transcendental coherence in *The Scarlet Letter* (1850), because the letter 'A' remains so ambiguous, and in Herman Melville's *Moby Dick* (1851), when no one can agree on the meaning of the hieroglyphic markings on the doubloon nailed to the mast of the Pequod. A generation on, Emerson's foundationalism was also criticized, but more constructively, by the philosopher George Santayana. In 'The Genteel Tradition in American Philosophy' (1911), Santayana regrets a degeneration into what he calls 'the transcendental myth', and blames the influence of the German Romantics, who 'wished to make not only their own knowledge but the whole universe centre about themselves . . . . It occurred to them and to some transcendentalists to imagine that all reality might be a transcendental self.'[6]

Emerson's metaphysics of the self are so affirmative that the relationship between self and other is barely recognized as a problem. Difficulties in explaining how the self has knowledge of what is outside it are resolved by embracing the opposing terms within a larger principle of unity, which Emerson often calls 'the Over-Soul'. 'Nature', Emerson states, 'always wears the colors of the spirit' and, more ambitiously still: 'Thus inevitably does the universe wear our color.' The circle of self and other is then closed with evidence of beneficent design: 'Nature never wears a mean appearance' (*SE*, pp. 39, 307, 37). In 'Experience' (1844) Emerson touches on the danger of solipsism, the thought that he might be trapped in his own world, a 'prison of glass which we cannot see' (*SE*, p. 290). His self-confidence carries him past this momentary doubt, but, interestingly, the more he relies upon the self, the more we must wonder about the order of priority in his thinking: is the universe (and nature) a construction of the self whom Emerson, more than any other American thinker, empowers? Or does the universe pre-exist the individual mind?

After all this, it is somewhat surprising that Santayana has any sympathy for transcendentalism. Yet in what he calls 'the transcendental method' he finds an important check upon the kind of all-embracing mythic thinking which ignores the problem of priority outlined in the above questions: 'Transcendentalism is systematic subjectivism. It studies the perspectives of knowledge as they radiate from the self; it is a plan of those avenues of inference by which our ideas of things must be reached, if they are to afford any systematic or distant vistas' (Santayana, p. 41). As we shall see, it is William James who employs *method* most systematically to dismantle the traditional opposition between subjectivity and objectivity. In Emerson's own time it was Thoreau, rather than Emerson, who most determinedly tested out knowledge against the self's experiences: when he went to Walden Pond in 1845, but equally when he left two years later, to try out some new way of life. Nevertheless, in Emerson, too, there is a questioning of transcendental myth-making, as we can appreciate if we look, once more, at the opening of *Nature*.

Even in Emerson's most affirmative text there is a tension between the philosophical foundationalism which we have clearly identified and the text as a *performance*; between a form which is already there (the book of God) and a form (Emerson's essay) which has to make its own beginning. The injunction to forget the past and look to nature, followed by the account of crossing Boston Common, only to be whirled up in 'the currents of the Universal Being', precipitate testing questions about the relationship between self and other. Both experiences – dispatching the past and communing with the Universal Being – effectively deposit the knowing self into a lonely situation where no coordinates for knowledge exist: 'The name of the nearest friend sounds then foreign and accidental: to be brothers, to be acquaintances, master or servant, is then a trifle and a disturbance' (*SE*, p. 39). Similarly, in 'Circles' (1841), Emerson pictures himself as 'an endless seeker with no Past at my back', though in the previous clause – 'I simply experiment' – he seems to suggest that the performance continues beyond the cosmic union which is the ostensible climax of the Boston Common experience (*SE*, p. 236). Significantly, it is Rorty who recommends turning our attention from the moments of communion and nationalistic freedom, to the finite moment of aloneness, 'the sense that there is nothing deep down inside us except what we have put there ourselves, no criterion that we have not created in the course of creating such a practice'.[7]

Cornel West opens up the context for the transcendentalist *constitution* of the self when he remarks that

> market forces [such as were newly operative in the 1820s and 1830s] tend to undermine authority, thwart tradition, and throw the burdens once borne by these onto the individual. Once freed from such superegos, the self can be seen to be a rather contingent, arbitrary, and instrumental affair, a mobile, performative, and protean entity, perennially in process.[8]

Intervening to negate the past, as Emerson in effect does when he represents all history as the individual's, is at least as much an act of willing the self into intentional action as it is an encouragement to enter a state of receptivity: 'Let us demand . . . . Let us interrogate . . . . Let us inquire' rather than 'We must trust the perfection of the creation' (*SE*, pp. 35, 36). Will creates the conditions for experimentally *constructing* truth, rather than finding it where – beneath the gathered weight of the past – it had lain since an original moment; that was the moment when – to invoke a founding transcendental myth – God gave the truth to Adam.

As an indication that there are further differences in the transcendental moment of the American Adam, we can turn briefly to the self-engendering process in Margaret Fuller's *Woman in the Nineteenth Century* (1845). Lacking the confident authority of Emerson, and more aware of the constraints upon women, Fuller's discussion of the theme of self-reliance takes longer to get going, requiring a preface, a persona, and the calling up of historical and literary precedents. So male-defined is self-reliance, and so under-written by economic considerations, that Fuller has to contemplate celibacy: 'Union is only possible to those who are units.' Much of the book remains under the influence of Emerson, but in contending with male definitions of women, she enters a question mark against Emerson's essentialist thinking:

> But it is no more the order of nature that it should be incarnated pure in any form, than that the masculine energy should exist unmingled with it in any form.
> Male and female represent the two sides of the great radical dualism. But in fact they are perpetually passing into one another. Fluid hardens to solid, solid rushes to fluid. There is no wholly masculine man, no purely feminine woman.
> History jeers at the attempts of physiologists to bind great original laws by the forms which flow from them.[9]

Stephen Whicher's canonical reading of *Nature* is that Emerson's 'revolt had been designed to cut the traces that bound him to history and bring him to live, not in the kingdom of time, but in direct contact with the divine life beyond and above time'.[10] An antithetical interpretation – which can be supplemented by a reading of Fuller's *Woman in the Nineteenth Century* – suggests that *Nature* is a first step towards recognizing the self's position in history, with a consequent need to 'build therefore your own world' and 'read history actively and not passively' (*SE*, pp. 81, 152). This human, historically located Emerson interested Dewey more than the metaphysical transcendentalist soaring above or immanent in every particle of the universe:

The Platonist teaches the immanence of absolute ideas in the World and in

Man, that every thing and every man participates in an absolute Meaning, individualized in him and through which one has community with others . . . . But to Emerson all 'truth lies on the highway' . . . . The Idea is no longer either an academic toy nor even a gleam of poetry, but a literal report of the experience of the hour as that is enriched and reinforced for the individual through the tale of history, the appliance of science, the gossip of conversation and the exchange of commerce.[11]

Dewey makes Emerson into a virtual pragmatist and goes on to distinguish him from the 'remotenesses' of the transcendentalists. We must be careful, though, not to modernize Emerson too hurriedly, even as we argue that he anticipates a particularly modern 'evasion' of philosophy now associated with American pragmatism. As we shall see when we look at Emerson's later work, he became more aware of constraints upon the self which further removed him from transcendental vagaries. But, writing in the heady, optimistic atmosphere of the 1830s and early 1840s, Emerson's insights into a possible lack of ultimate unity and the consequent need to construct the ground under one's own feet were hardly likely to coalesce in open disagreements with the very idealist tradition of thinking going back to Plato which had (*pace* Dewey) so encouraged him in breaking with Unitarianism. Instead, differences between Emerson and a foundational philosophy often appear in the way he and Thoreau write and structure their texts. Cavell comments on their 'interest in the fact that what they are building is writing, that their writing is, as it realizes itself daily under their hands, sentence by . . . sentence, the accomplishment of inhabitation, the making of it happen, the poetry of it' (Cavell, p. 134).

With Emerson, more than with any of the many other stylistically extravagant American writers, we can explore the relation between 'literary' concerns and philosophy, or at least a way of doing philosophy. Against the standard romantic view of an Emerson text as organic ('Nature is already, in its forms and tendencies, describing its own design'), there are the discontinuities, even in Emerson's own analogy for organic form: 'Who looks upon a river in a meditative hour and is not reminded of the flux of all things? Throw a stone into the stream, and the circles that propagate themselves are the beautiful type of all influence' (*SE*, p. 49). Emerson's question is far from rhetorical. It announces an interpretative gap during which we might wonder how a stone can have anything to do with propagation. Emerson picks up his image of concentric circles in 'Circles': 'The eye is the first circle; the horizon which it forms is the second; and throughout nature this primary figure is repeated without end' (*SE*, p. 225). But Emerson's own style is discontinuous in the extreme: sentences are often discrete and do not, as has frequently been remarked, form themselves into paragraphs, let alone into an organic structure. When Emerson writes, in 'Circles', that 'every action admits of being outdone'

(*SE*, p. 225), the principle of out-doing (sentence to sentence, circle to circle in the stream) is closer to the arbitrariness of interpretation in time than to the spatial ideal of all-at-onceness.

Cavell draws an important cultural conclusion from Emerson's phrase, 'onward thinking': 'it is our [Americans'] poverty not to be final but always to be leaving (abandoning whatever we have and have known): to be initial, medial, American' (Cavell, p. 137). Medial is to be in the midst of 'Life', defined by Emerson as 'a train of moods like a string of beads, and as we pass through them they prove to be many-colored lenses which paint the world their own hue, and each shows only what lies in its focus' (*SE*, pp. 288–9). For all the transcendentalists' flights into a new realm, the experience of reading Emerson, sentence after sentence, essay after essay, is not of blinding epistemological insight, as on Boston Common, but of 'moods' (Cavell) or 'figures of will, and not figures of knowledge' (Bloom, p. 170).

To talk about an evasion of philosophy through style, form and mood does Emerson an injustice if it implies escapism. A more appropriate explanation is that Emerson's stylistic revisions keep his thought on the move and guard against the purity of metaphysical argument. Far from being escapist, Emerson's medial outlook can attend to 'the task of onwardness'. It is future-orientated – to be verified, if at all, only by the future, and can therefore be energizing, propelling the transcendentalist into critical engagement with the events of the time: 'The self-reliant man would utter opinions on all passing affairs, which being seen to be not private but necessary, would sink like darts into the ear of men, and put them in fear' (*SE*, p. 178). Rorty calls this transcendental *culture* (rather than philosophy), adding that 'the kind of name-dropping, rapid shifting of context, and unwillingness to stay for an answer which this culture encourages runs counter to everything that a professionalized academic discipline stands for' (Rorty, p. 65). We meet this quality again in James and Dewey, but before doing so, it is important to try and understand how far Emerson moved towards a reorientation of transcendental idealism, but also why he stopped short of the more significant break-out from metaphysics achieved by the pragmatists. The text which no reader of Emerson can avoid is 'Fate'.

TRANSCENDENTALISM/DARWINISM/PRAGMATISM

During the 1830s and early 1840s Emerson's confidence in an ultimate unity was not some variety of boosterism, in league with a business and expansionist ethic on the rise during Jacksonian America. Nevertheless, his confidence was – reasonably enough – in tune with a vision of American material abundance which could absorb property divisions and create space enough for the individual to recover from personal disasters. Between 1843 and 1847, however, his journal entries indicate that the formulation 'Transcendentalism as Idealism' was being challenged by external events, among them, the Abolitionist crusade against slavery, the expansionism of the US government, and the growth of industry and, with it, the concentration of supposedly free individuals within a factory system. By 1860 and 'Fate', Emerson can openly ask whether transcendentalism is an adequate response to a world which seemed to be in the grip of great forces and new intellectual explanations.

The challenge of Darwinism to Emerson's earlier celebration of nature informs virtually every image:

> The way of Providence is a little rude. The habit of snake and spider, the snap of the tiger and other leapers and bloody jumpers, the crackle of the bones of his prey in the coil of the anaconda, – these are in the system, and our habits are like theirs . . . race living at the expense of race.
>
> (*SE*, p. 364)

Apart from the frightening vision of a dangerous and impersonal world, with its 'shocks and ruins', 'the system' is the very antithesis of a divinely-planned, organic unity. Where Emerson had once dismissed works of natural history as 'dry catalogues of facts' (needing the infusion of spirit to become meaningful), now the interconnections explained by Darwin determine humans as well: 'At the corner of the street you read the possibility of each passenger in the facial angle, in the complexion, in the depth of his eye. His parentage determines it' (*SE*, p. 366). In 'Fate', nature is not present to the individual all at once but is strung out on a relentless narrative line whose mechanism is survival of the fittest: 'The book of Nature is the book of Fate. She turns the gigantic pages, – leaf after leaf, – never re-turning one' (*SE*, p. 369).

Confronted by necessity and limitations, how can Emerson move forward, how can he loosen the opposition between freedom and fate? At its greatest moments, 'Fate' demonstrates an exercise of sheer will, of going on, together with a stern relativism, that can be barely glimpsed in Emerson's earlier works: 'If we must accept Fate, we are not less compelled to affirm liberty' (*SE*, p. 362). At its worst, though, 'Fate' falls back on a slack optimism: 'The adaptation is not capricious. The ulterior aim, the purpose beyond itself . . . will not stop but will work into finer particulars and from finer to finest' (*SE*, p. 384). There is much more potential for 'onward thinking' in a question which Emerson asks and answers in 'Experience': 'Where do we find ourselves? In a series of which we do not know the extremes, and believe that it has none' (*SE*, p. 285). From such a medial location, origins are more like arbitrary beginnings than part of a grand design: 'Did our birth fall in some fit of indigence and frugality in nature . . . that we lack the affirmative principle?' (*SE*, p. 286).

To understand where an 'affirmative principle' might be found, we can call again on Santayana's 'The Genteel Tradition in American Philosophy'. This tribute to William James, who had died the year before, is still the most perceptive explanation of the changes in American thought between the seventeenth century and the end of the nineteenth. We can also formally introduce Dewey through his 1909 essay, 'The Influence of Darwin on Philosophy'.

Santayana applies to the sphere of all of post-Civil War American culture the idea of a 'dual world' which we have noticed in Emerson's 'Fate':

> The truth is that one half of the American mind, that not occupied intensely in practical affairs, has remained, I will not say high-and-dry, but slightly becalmed; it has floated gently in the backwater, while, alongside, in invention and industry and social organization, the other half of the mind was leaping down a sort of Niagara Rapids . . . . The one is all aggressive enterprise; the other is all genteel tradition.
>
> (Santayana, p. 37)

A once-powerful idealism had become a mere academic exercise, a genteel 'backwater' in which nothing significantly critical was being said to, or about, the unthinking commercialism of the Gilded Age: roughly the period from the 1870s to the early 1890s, when, as two later chapters of this book demonstrate, the United States urbanized and industrialized at a phenomenal rate.

Santayana delivered the lecture on the West Coast, and, in these concluding observations, recalls the Emerson who goes out into nature on Boston Common:

> When you transform nature to your uses, when you experiment with her forces, and reduce them to industrial agents, you cannot feel that nature was made by you or for you, for then these adjustments would have been pre-established. Much less can you feel it when she destroys your labour of years in a momentary spasm . . . . It is no transcendental logic that [forests and sierras] teach; and they give no sign of any deliberate morality seated in the world.
>
> (Santayana, pp. 54–5)

Santayana's philosophical naturalism is the counterpart to the literary naturalism of Theodore Dreiser, Frank Norris, Stephen Crane and Jack London. Dreiser's novels, such as *Sister Carrie* (1900) and *An American Tragedy* (1925), tend to have urban settings but present us with a similar impersonal universe which his characters must negotiate. Certainly, the naturalism of Santayana and these American novelists is quite different from a transcendentalist philosophy of nature. To adopt Santayana's terminology, we view nature anthropomorphically and not anthropocentrically; that is to say, humans are in nature but not at its centre. The self makes progress, Santayana argues, by adopting the 'transcendental method' of testing itself against the environment, but with an understanding that the self does not follow a 'transcendental logic' separate from the environment.

In Dewey's 'The Influence of Darwin on Philosophy' (an essay written on the fiftieth anniversary of *The Origin of Species*, and in Dewey's fiftieth year), Darwin is credited with inaugurating 'a new intellectual temper' and a new phase in the methodology of the social as well as the natural sciences. Darwinism challenges a philosophical search for 'the fixed and the final' which looked to nature for a foundation.[12] Prior to evolutionary thinking human beings were treated as unchanging essences. Once Darwin had even partially traced our lineage through the geological record, humans became *forms* undergoing change. Of course, Darwinism could – and did – lead to a deterministic outlook which encouraged both excessive pessimism at humans' lack of power and excessive optimism at their survival. In contrast, Dewey gained from Darwinism a theory of mind arising out of, and not pre-existing, the evolutionary process. Knowledge (including knowledge of ourselves) derives from a continuing and active interaction between an organism and the environment. In consequence, Dewey felt able to talk of freedom, freedom to make ourselves as we make our environment. To this extent, he articulates a 'pragmatic' outlook that had motivated generations of settlers and which found voice in Franklin's *Autobiography*, with its plastic concept of the self and society. In other words, genuine open-ended change – this being the real significance of Darwin's work – has epistemological possibilities undreamt of by an idealist philosophy with its 'logic of the changeless, the final, and the transcendent' (Dewey, p. 16).

WILLIAM JAMES AND PRAGMATISM

The Penguin edition of Emerson's *Selected Essays*, edited by Larzer Ziff, has on its cover a detail from William James Stillman's painting, 'The Philosopher's Camp in the Adirondacks' (c. 1857–58). The second chapter of James's *Pragmatism* (1907), entitled, 'What Pragmatism Means', begins with James telling of a camping trip in the mountains which was punctuated by 'a ferocious metaphysical dispute' about a squirrel clinging to a tree. (Stillman's complete painting depicts a group of men gazing at the trunk of a tree.) If a man walks round the tree but the squirrel 'always keeps the tree between himself and the man, so that never a glimpse of him is caught ... *does the man go round the squirrel or not?* He goes round the tree, sure enough, and the squirrel is on the tree; but does he go round the squirrel?'[13]

In this instance, nature ('the unlimited leisure of the wilderness') does not provide answers in the manner that Emerson had hoped, and James is obliged to introduce a degree of relativism: ' "Which party is right", I said, "depends on what you *practically mean* by 'going round' the squirrel" ' (James, p. 42). In successfully evading the issue of truth, he assists this group of philosophers to go home better equipped to deal with a crowded and contentious world, very different from the open world of the transcendentalists. Pragmatism proposes a method for negotiating a world in which people physically and intellectually fought for space. The initial step is illustrated by the example of the squirrel, namely the settling of 'metaphysical disputes that otherwise might be interminable. Is the world one or many? – fated or free? – material or spiritual?' All the time that Truth, with a capital letter, is thought to be the end of philosophical enquiry, then 'disputes over such notions are unending' (James, p. 42).

In the previous chapter of *Pragmatism* James generalizes the problem of the squirrel into 'the present dilemma in philosophy': how to choose between powerful idealist and materialist traditions of thought: the 'tender-minded' and the 'tough-minded' are James's more colloquial terms, while Santayana talks of the 'American intellect' and the 'American will'. Transcendentalism – in most accounts – would be on the tender/intellectual side, so we need to understand how it is that James, who is scathing about idealism's failure to address the realities of contemporary life, seems to be just the right person to deliver the 'Address at the Emerson Centenary in Concord' in 1903. The answer can be baldly stated and then explained. James, like Santayana, admired the open-minded Emerson, the champion of 'experience' and temperament, rather than the philosopher of the 'Over-soul'.

James's own fascination with experience, with in-betweens rather than origins and ends, is very apparent in his *Principles of Psychology* (1890) and *The Will to Believe* (1897). In the latter, James maintains that while idealism (the transcendental ego of Kant or the Absolute of James's own colleague, Josiah Royce) and materialism (best exemplified, for James, by the British social philosopher, Herbert Spencer) seem to be opposing positions, they both posit closed or 'block' universes. Where Emerson, in 'Fate', sought to harmonize these positions, giving each its due, James seeks to dislodge them. He initially achieves some room to manoeuvre by lowering the stakes and preferring the Darwinian notions of 'chance' or 'indeterminism' to the 'eulogistic' word 'freedom'. 'Chance' is not a possibility in a world determined either by the iron laws of evolution or by an all-knowing mind which operates with first and last principles. Chance proves helpful to James, however, because it is 'a purely negative and relative term' and 'not the unconditional property of the whole'. Its character is that it is 'disconnected with something else'.[14] James reveals the existence of chance by asking his audience to imagine the two routes by which he could return home after the lecture. Once chosen, that route, for the idealist or materialist, is the only possible route. Yet there was always the chance that the other could have been taken because both routes are rational choices. James draws a number of lessons from his trivial example and these are intimately bound up with his developing pragmatism.

First, James believes at the very least in a will to believe in free will, as he had when recovering from near-suicidal depression in 1870. We have detected something of this willing oneself into consequential action in Emerson.

Second, James finds in chance a reason for defending 'the ambiguity of future volitions', whereas, for the determinist 'those parts of the universe already laid down absolutely appoint and decree what the other parts shall be'. Chance gives James sight of 'a pluralistic, restless universe, in which no single point of view can ever take in the whole scene; ... to a mind possessed of the love of unity at any cost, it will, no doubt, remain forever inacceptable' (*Will*, pp. 158, 150, 177). It is important to register that James's commitment to a 'multiverse' rather than a 'universe' derives from his (and Dewey's) realization that the chief philosophical significance of Darwin lay in substituting an explanatory mechanism (natural selection) for the big question of where evolution is taking us.

Third, an unfinished world could be a spur to action. Philosophers preoccupied with certainty and essence did not, James asserts, respond well to the need for action. In *Pragmatism* he quotes a long description of the realities of life in Cleveland for the poor, and asks what kind of practical response can we expect from an idealism which remains aloof from the world or which, in the manner of Royce's absolutist philosophy can argue the existence of 'the eternal order' from 'the very presence of ill in the temporal order' (James, p. 32). Before action can take place in the economic and political sphere James and, more explicitly, Dewey insisted on 'first freeing the mind'.

And, finally, James derives from his trivial example the confidence to investigate the fleeting, the insubstantial, the taken-for-granted in experience. In *Principles of Psychology*, a book which directly influenced Dewey's turn to Pragmatism, James provides an analysis of the experience of consciousness which proves to be of particular relevance to his later *Pragmatism*, and to the larger problem of the relation between thought and its object. Here, again, we can see the connection with Emerson in his less blithe moments. In 'The stream of thought' chapter in *Principles*, James observes that 'within each personal consciousness thought is sensibly continuous'. We are reminded of the stream of consciousness fiction of James Joyce, Virginia Woolf and, in America, William Faulkner, especially his novel *The Sound and the Fury* (1929). According to James, time-gaps, such as sleep, or other perhaps violent interruptions of the thought process do not cause a break in the stream: 'the consciousness after the gap feels as if it belonged together with the consciousness before it, as another part of the same self'.[15] To hold such a view requires close attention to the multitude of seemingly unimportant intermediary stages. Our feeling of happiness is also a feeling of the sadness which may have just passed. It is an awareness of the reality of relations or transitions that gives consciousness its aspect of flowing continuity.

In some respects, though, we have come only a little further than Emerson opting for experience when recognizing that we are 'in a series of which we do not know the extremes' ('Experience'). James's version of 'onward thinking' is that 'we live, as it were, upon the front edge of an advancing wave-crest, and our sense of a determinate direction in falling forward is all we cover of the future of our path'. We are, in effect, only virtual knowers, and 'the immensely greater part of all our knowing never gets beyond this virtual stage'.[16] However, in a world of competing ideas and one in which intelligence needed to be applied to pressing social problems the precise mechanism for taking one action rather than another needed stating, and this James does in *Pragmatism*. Pragmatism and the Progressive movement of reform were roughly coterminous, though the connection only became direct in the work of Dewey.

James's example of the squirrel and the tree introduces 'the pragmatic method', which tries 'to interpret each notion [in a philosophical argument] by tracing its respective practical consequences' (James, p. 42). Even Emerson resorted to this mundane solution on occasions: 'Speak rather of that which relies because it works and is.' James goes further: 'The whole function of philosophy ought to be to find out what definite difference it will make to you and me, at definite instants of our life, if this world-formula or that world-formula be the true one' (James, p. 45). When we apply the pragmatic method to the existence of God – Emerson's foundation – we get this advice from James: '*If theological ideas prove to have a value for concrete life, they will be true, for pragmatism, in the sense of being good for so much*' (James, p. 57). The 'good' is of more value than the 'true'.

The pragmatic method is put into action in the company of others, rather than (as in Emerson) in isolation. Truth is the property of a community rather than an individual, though James is less a philosopher of community than his predecessor, Peirce, and successor, Dewey. James's image is of a (potentially solipsistic) individual coming out of a hotel room into a corridor full of other individuals, each with a particular truth and accompanying philosophical baggage. Clearly, running the gauntlet of truths (in the plural) is not an easy philosophical option, but it establishes the necessity for communication.

James's appears a modest enough proposal but it aroused controversy among philosophers because it undermined Truth, with a capital letter, and did so by positioning the self firmly in experience. Pragmatism may be a 'new name for some old ways of thinking', particularly in practical, anti-intellectual America, but it was 'news in heaven' (in James's Emersonian phrase) to the extent that it accepted one of the premises of Darwinism, namely that humans are a part of nature, not *a priori* above it. No truth could be an absolute truth, no theory a comprehensive transcript of reality, because reality is in the making and it is being made partly by acting in it.

DEWEY AND INSTRUMENTALISM

Within our context, the differences between James and Dewey are of degree. However, Dewey's preference for the term instrumentalism rather than pragmatism does point to the expanded role for the philosopher which stems from the long process by which American philosophy came down to earth. Dewey's philosophy is the most explicitly social of all the pragmatists:

> Interest shifts from the wholesale essence back of special changes to the question of how special changes serve and defeat concrete purposes; shifts from an intelligence that shaped things once for all to the particular intelligences which things are even now shaping; shifts from an ultimate goal of good to the direct increments of justice and happiness that intelligent administration of existent conditions may beget . . . .
>
> (Dewey, p. 20)

Dewey even approximates Marx's call to change the world, not to interpret it, when he observes, in his more low-key, reformist manner, that 'to idealize and rationalize the universe at large is after all a confession of inability to master the courses of things that specifically concern us'. According to Dewey, philosophy should 'humble . . . its pretensions to the work of projecting hypotheses for the education and conduct of mind, individual and social'. He adds that 'in having modesty forced upon it, philosophy also acquires responsibility' (Dewey, p. 21).

Dewey took that responsibility very seriously in his work on education, beginning with his direction, in the mid-1890s in Chicago, of the 'Laboratory School'. Both at home and, after the First World War, on extensive tours to China and Japan, Turkey, Mexico and the USSR, Dewey pioneered progressive education. The link with his instrumental philosophy is evident in that he concentrates upon the environment of education, both the school and its community, and, inside school, changes in classroom practice and design, and adaptations of the curriculum to new student-centred needs and social tasks. If education – on an analogy with philosophy – is the process and not the ends, then it is not primarily about the acquisition of knowledge *per se*. Knowledge resides in relations, and so Dewey could be said to be a pioneer of inter-disciplinary study, as well as of learning by doing. Schools would be model places of dialogue in which decisions would be reached by the exercise of intelligence.

The extent of Dewey's work was phenomenal, and did not respect accepted boundaries. He made his presence felt by signing petitions; forming and supporting groups (for example, the American Civil Liberties Union); and joining, and disaffiliating himself from, political parties. Alongside his many books and articles in learned journals, Dewey maintained a career as a free-floating intellectual, known to the public through his journalism in (mainly) the liberal magazine, *The New Republic*, which was founded in 1914. He consistently had things to say on the domestic and international events of his time, in the process learning from experience: in 1917 he supported America's entry into the First World War, but strongly criticized the peace treaty, which was one of the consequences of the decision to go to war. In the 1920s, he led a move for the outlawing of war. In 1937, aged seventy-eight, he again engaged with public life by going to Mexico to chair the Commission of Inquiry into the Charges against Leon Trotsky. Having read Emerson with pragmatism in mind, and explored his impulse towards engagement rather than withdrawal, we could probably imagine Emerson drawn to such a situation. And we know of Thoreau's willingness to speak out in public, not only in the essay on civil disobedience discussed here in Chapter 3, but also, for instance, on behalf of John Brown at the time of his trial and execution for leading the Harpers Ferry raid in 1859. It is a sign of the difference that pragmatism made, however, that we could not imagine transcendentalists *sustaining* Dewey's level of involvement. Even less could we imagine that a philosopher could have had the kind of prolonged influence on public life that Dewey had achieved by the 1930s.

Pragmatism aims to keep possibilities open, including 'the road not taken', as in Robert Frost's 1916 poem of that title. In concluding this mostly sympathetic account of Dewey with a criticism, it is appropriate to consider a road he did not take. In four articles written for *The New Republic* in 1917, Dewey claims (after much agonizing) that American intellectuals could not – if they were pragmatists – stand aside from the First World War but should seek to influence it from within the circles of government. His argument is also one of consequences: the need to make the world safe for democracy, to cite Woodrow Wilson's justification for American involvement. More particularly, Dewey distinguishes between force and violence, the latter being wasteful and unintelligent, the former being so neutral and ever-present, even in conversation, that Dewey can state that 'No ends are accomplished without the use of force.' Emptied of its content, turned into simply a method, force can then be examined scientifically: 'The criterion of value lies in relative efficiency and economy of the expenditure of force as a means to an end. With advance of knowledge, refined, subtle and indirect use of force is always displacing coarse, obvious and direct methods of applying it.'[17]

Dewey's opponent in the debate was Randolph Bourne, a follower of Dewey and an admirer also of James. In his replies, published in *The Seven Arts* during 1917, Bourne fully acknowledges the achievements of pragmatism in progressive education and in freeing the mind from the cant of *laissez-faire* economics, so that reform could be intellectually justified. But war, he argues, was so powerful that acting critically and creatively from within to convert war into a social instrument was impossible. To join with war was tantamount to acquiescing to it. He accuses the so-called 'war liberals' gathered round *The New Republic* of becoming experts, not intellectuals:

> What is significant is that it is the technical side of the war that appeals to them, not the interpretive or political side. The formulation of values and ideals, the production of articulate and suggestive thinking, had not, in their education, kept pace, to any extent whatever, with their technical aptitude.[18]

For Bourne, Dewey's articles signalled the end of the era dominated by pragmatism, and the need for an alternative: 'If your ideal is to be adjustment to your situation, in radiant cooperation with reality, then your success is likely to be just that and no more. You never transcend anything. You grow, but your spirit never jumps out of your skin to go on wild adventures' (Bourne, p. 344).

A similar argument might be mounted against the work-orientated, vocational side of Dewey's philosophy of education. It can be narrowing and directed towards fitting in with a society interested primarily in training rather than education. This would be unfair to Dewey, but it is a possible consequence of his philosophy. So is Bourne calling for idealism, once more? His language must remind us of transcendentalism (especially Thoreau), and elsewhere in his 'war' essays he sets poetic vision against goal-directed pragmatism. However, it can also be argued that Bourne is reminding Dewey of the claims that, whatever else it was doing, pragmatism sought to keep options open. Bourne's apparent about-face and call for 'wild adventures' is a pragmatic assault, a use of transcendentalist rhetoric but in circumstances which gave new meaning to tired poetic phrases. Bourne did not want intellectuals to turn their backs but to be yet more active, looking for new solutions, ways of revealing the mixture of motives in war-aims, even when the build-up to war seemed inexorable.

POST-PHILOSOPHICAL RECONSIDERATIONS

In this postscript, no attempt is made to do justice to contemporary neo-pragmatism. Instead, the aim is simply to suggest why pragmatism and – to a lesser extent – transcendentalism have undergone a revival over the past decade. Very briefly, there have been a set of challenges to the mainstream of philosophical thinking. Among the challenges have been arguments within the philosophy of science which have clustered around, or been stimulated by, Thomas Kuhn's *The Structure of Scientific Revolutions*, published in 1962. Kuhn argues against a progressive view of truth based on the model of science. According to Kuhn, what counts as a true description of the facts in scientific investigation depends upon a set of assumptions, a 'paradigm' of 'normal science'. This paradigm even determines which areas of science are to be investigated.

Outside of the physical sciences the challenges to foundational thinking and to grand narratives of truth and progress have come more easily but have still been controversial. One example would be the mostly French movements of structuralism and post-structuralism, which directed attention away from the origins of actions and beliefs (away from the individual, intending self, for instance) and towards semiotic structures, in which the meaning of any element derives from its relationship to other elements, rather than from any reference to something outside the structure. Kuhn's paradigm functions in broadly the same way and suggests a provisional, experimental approach to knowledge.

Much more impressionistically – but related in some way to these intellectual challenges – the social and political changes which we loosely date from 'the sixties' have been away from established, unitary authorities towards different groups and their cultures. Within the sphere of education, for example, there has been a blurring of disciplinary boundaries as institutions have taken some notice of different kinds of students. The overall effect has been to reinforce a growing awareness of an inescapable relativism in our actions and beliefs. Absolute standards are more difficult to assert and maintain, and in this postmodern crisis of legitimation, as it has come to be called, transcendentalism (as understood in this essay, at least) and pragmatism have something to offer by way of an analysis of experience, process and the communities of discourse within which we make decisions. Lest all of this sound too promising, I should add that those who have argued – in a postmodern vein – for pluralism, localism, more choice and (to maintain a Deweyan interest) educational programmes which are skills-based and relevant, rather than knowledge-based and academic, have frequently found themselves in some unhappy alliances. (For further commentary on such issues, see Chapter 6.)

Although many of these changes have been loosely philosophical, philosophy as a discipline continues to be seen as a bastion of truth in the midst of the cultural diversity (or confusion) of a postmodern era. Of course, contemporary Anglo-American analytical philosophy, which has largely supplanted the pragmatic tradition of James and Dewey, finds the mainstream of philosophy lacking in rigour and in need of technical refurbishment. Nonetheless, there is continuing agreement about what are philosophical problems. Philosophy is still engaged with *epistemological* questions, the aim being to refine a theory of knowledge. Whether philosophy comes from the empirical/positivist side or the idealist side, whether it pursues a correspondence theory of truth or maintains there is more to truth than meets the scientific eye, philosophy is thought to be *foundational*. It has an object of knowledge in here, out there, beyond this, or before that. Notions of universality or necessity (again depending upon whether one takes the idealist or empiricist route) set limits on how far in, out, beyond, or before one must go in search of Truth. Truth, that is, has a nature, an essence, and philosophy's task (unlike, say, literary criticism's) is to formulate better and better arguments for reaching it. This re-establishment of philosophy's Great Tradition has been chiefly at the expense of a different way of thinking about philosophy held by pragmatists, while the transcendentalists have been firmly consigned to literary or American studies.

However, as we noted at the outset, philosophers like Rorty, Cavell, Bernstein and West are now insisting that transcendentalism and pragmatism matter precisely because they challenge, or evade, philosophy and its aims. So much so that Rorty differentiates between 'Philosophy', with a capital letter, and 'philosophy', the latter describing what he and other latter-day pragmatists do. For while James, Dewey and Peirce were professional philosophers (Peirce, in terms of recognition, a singularly unsuccessful one), and the writings of Emerson and his contemporaries are packed with the staples of philosophical discourse, the current hypothesis is that, generically, transcendentalist and pragmatist works are models for what philosophical writing might be when it is not exactly philosophy. Cavell, who seems to have instigated this backhanded revival, tells us that 'study of *Walden* would perhaps not have become such an obsession with me had it not presented itself as a response to questions with which I was already obsessed: Why has America never expressed itself philosophically? Or has it?' (Cavell, pp. 32–3). Dewey himself makes a related point: 'It is said that Emerson is not a philosopher. I find this denegation false or true according as it is said in blame or praise' ('RWE', p. 24).

Transcendentalism and pragmatism are being reread as part of the 'end of philosophy' debate, and connected to an anti-tradition of thinkers which includes Marx, Nietzsche (*the* connection for Emerson and James), Freud, Saussure, Wittgenstein, Heidegger and, most recently, the French post-structuralists, Derrida, Foucault and Lacan. A current area of interest is to detail this connection to see whether there is a definable American contribution, one which might mitigate against the excesses of a wholly relativistic outlook by providing non-absolutist, non-foundational bases for action and decision-making at both personal and policy levels. In some respects, then, the postmodern crisis of legitimation resembles 'the present dilemma in philosophy' to which James and Dewey responded.

Distinctions are also being made within neo-pragmatism, between, for example, the liberalism of Rorty and the neo-Marxism of West. Whether we follow West and call the latest phase of this anti-tradition 'post-analytic philosophy', or prefer Rorty's 'post-philosophical culture', we are dealing with a way of doing philosophy which questions, dismisses, seeks to destroy, or, in its latest version, deconstructs both the truth-claims made by philosophy since Plato, and philosophy's claims to be an autonomous professional discipline, known for its technical skills of argumentation and its alliances with mathematics and the physical sciences. Cavell takes us closer to the specific transcendentalist and pragmatist challenge to philosophy when he notes that 'we are by now too aware of the philosophical *attacks* on system or theory to place the emphasis in defining philosophy on a product of philosophy rather than on the process of philosophizing' (Cavell, p. 129). Or, as Emerson has it, the interest lies in 'man thinking' rather than thought *per se*. Cavell, Rorty, Bernstein and West are among those who have found common cause with Emerson, James and Dewey in urging philosophy to abandon its analytical vacuum and adopt a cultural, inter-disciplinary focus in order to 'make a difference', as West puts it, echoing William James.

NOTES

1. Stanley Cavell, *The Senses of Walden: An Expanded Edition* (San Francisco, 1981), p. 148; subsequent references in the text.

2. Ralph Waldo Emerson, *Selected Essays*, ed. Larzer Ziff (Harmondsworth, 1982), p. 114; subsequent references, to *SE*, in the text.

3. F. Scott Fitzgerald, *The Great Gatsby* (Harmondsworth, 1950), p. 105; subsequent reference in the text.

4. Harold Bloom, *Agon: Towards a Theory of Revisionism* (New York, 1982), p. 145; subsequent reference in the text.

5. Nathaniel Hawthorne, *The Celestial Railroad and Other Stories* (New York, 1963), p. 194.

6. *Santayana on America: Essays, Notes, and Letters on American Life, Literature, and Philosophy*, ed. Richard Colton Lyon (New York, 1968), p. 42; subsequent references, to Santayana, in the text.

7. Richard Rorty, *Consequences of Pragmatism: Essays, 1972–1980* (Minneapolis, 1982), p. xlii; subsequent reference in the text.

8. Cornel West, *The American Evasion of Philosophy: A Genealogy of Pragmatism* (Houndsmills, 1989), p. 26.

9. Margaret Fuller, *American Romantic: A Selection from Her Writings and Correspondence*, ed. Perry Miller (New York, 1963), p. 172.

10. Stephen E. Whicher, *Freedom and Fate: An Inner Life of Ralph Waldo Emerson* (Philadelphia, 1953), p. 98.

11. John Dewey, 'Ralph Waldo Emerson', in *Emerson: A Collection of Critical Essays*, eds Milton R. Konvitz and Stephen E. Whicher (Westport, CT, 1978), p. 28; subsequent reference, to 'RWE', in the text.

12. John Dewey, *The Essential Writings*, ed. David Sidorski (New York, 1977), p. 13; subsequent references, to Dewey, in the text.

13. William James, *Pragmatism and Four Essays on the Meaning of Truth* (New York, 1974), p. 13; subsequent references, to James, in the text.

14. William James, *The Will to Believe and Other Essays in Popular Philosophy* (New York, 1956), pp. 153–4; subsequent references, to *Will*, in the text.

15. William James, *The Principles of Psychology* (2 vols, London, 1901), **1**, pp. 225, 237.

16. William James, *Essays in Radical Empiricism*, ed. Ralph Barton Perry (London, 1912), pp. 69, 68.

17. John Dewey, *Characters and Events*, 2 vols, ed. Joseph Ratner (New York, 1929), p. 787.

18. Randolph Bourne, *The Radical Will: Selected Writings, 1911–1918*, ed. Olaf Hansen (London, 1977), pp. 342–3; subsequent reference in the text.

SUGGESTIONS FOR FURTHER READING

The starting point should be the transcendentalist and pragmatist writings cited in the notes, plus *The Woman and the Myth: Margaret Fuller's Life and Writings*, compiled by Bell Gail Chevigny (Old Westbury, CT, 1976); Henry David Thoreau, *Walden and Civil Disobedience*, ed. Owen Thomas (New York, 1966); *The American Transcendentalists: Their Prose and Poetry*, ed. Perry Miller (New York, 1957), which, in addition to Emerson and Thoreau, includes writings by Alcott, Brownson, Fuller, and Parker; John Dewey, *Reconstruction in Philosophy*; *Pragmatic Philosophy: An Anthology*, ed. Amelia Rorty (New York, 1966), which, along with James and Dewey, covers Peirce (including his 'How to Make Our Ideas Clear' – the official beginning of pragmatism), and some twentieth-century critics and neo-pragmatists; and *Pragmatism and American Culture*, ed. Gail Kennedy (Boston, 1950), a less specialized collection than Rorty's.

My approach through the texts and via a late twentieth-century revival of transcendentalism and pragmatism needs to be balanced by more historical studies. George Hochfield's 'New England Transcendentalism', in *American Literature to 1900*, ed. Marcus Cunliffe (London, 1975) is thoughtful and reliable. Readers interested in comparing transcendentalism as an aesthetic, intellectual and social movement should consult Lawrence Buell, *Literary Transcendentalism* (Ithaca, NY, 1973); Paul F. Boller, Jr, *American Transcendentalism, 1830–1860: An Intellectual Inquiry* (New York, 1974); and Anne C. Rose, *Transcendentalism as a Social Movement, 1830–1850* (New Haven, 1981). A number of different approaches are represented in Brian M. Barbour (ed.), *Transcendentalism: An Anthology of Criticism* (Notre Dame, IN, 1973). My enthusiasm for the transcendentalists is aroused most by the secondary texts cited in the notes, especially the speculative readings by Cavell, and by Bloom's *The Ringers in the Tower: Studies in the Romantic Tradition* (Chicago, 1971). However, this bias ought to be countered by the following excellent studies: Paula Blanchard, *Margaret Fuller: From Transcendentalism to Revolution* (New York, 1978); Irving Howe, *The American Newness: Culture and Politics in the Age of Emerson* (Cambridge, MA, 1986); F.O. Matthiessen, *American Renaissance: Art and Expression in the Age of Emerson and Whitman* (New York, 1941); Michael Meyer, *Several More Lives to Live: Thoreau's Political Reputation in America* (Westport, CT, 1977); Sherman Paul, *Emerson's Angle of Vision* (Cambridge, MA, 1965) and *The Shores of America: Thoreau's Inward Exploration* (New York, 1958); and Joel Porte, *Representative Man: Ralph Waldo Emerson in His Time* (New York, 1979). *Emerson: A Collection of Critical Essays*, cited above, is a wide-ranging collection which reprints early essays by James, Dewey and Santayana.

A good way to move between study of James's texts and secondary works is Ralph Barton Perry's *The Thought and Character of William James* (2 vols, Boston, 1935), which includes many extracts from James's writings, especially his letters. Gerald E. Myers' *William James: His Life and Thought* (New Haven, 1986) is the modern version of Perry's book. See, also, Graham Bird, *William James* (London, 1986), which puts pragmatism at the centre of James's work. Charles Sanders Peirce is too complex a thinker and, in a way, too idiosyncratic to accommodate within the broad focus of the present essay. Good work is being done on Peirce (see Hoopes, below); at the moment, the best introduction is Christopher Hookway, *Peirce* (London, 1985). Dewey is difficult to introduce because of the breadth of his interests. Two collections make some attempt to cover the ground: *John Dewey: Philosopher of Science and Freedom*, ed. Sidney Hook (Westport, CT, 1976) and *New Studies in the Philosophy of John Dewey*, ed. Steven M. Cahn (Hanover, NH, 1981), especially Richard Rorty and Frederick A. Olafson on, respectively, Dewey's metaphysics and philosophy of education. Two recent monographs are: J.E. Tiles, *Dewey* (London, 1988), and R.W. Sleeper, *The Necessity of Pragmatism* (New Haven, 1986). Lively broader introductions other than those discussed in the text are George Novack, *Pragmatism versus Marxism: An Appraisal of John Dewey's Philosophy* (New York, 1975), Morton White, *Social Thought in America* (London, 1949). *Twentieth-Century America* (London, 1991) puts pragmatism into an intellectual and cultural context.

In connecting transcendentalism and pragmatism and re-assessing their legacy, I have been most enlightened by the following: Paul K. Conkin, *Puritans and Pragmatists: Eight Eminent American Thinkers* (Bloomington, 1976); James Hoopes, *Consciousness in New England: From Puritanism and Ideas to Psychoanalysis and Semiotic* (Baltimore, 1989), in which careful analysis of texts helps the reader over some difficult conceptual problems; and R. Jackson Wilson, *In Quest of Community: Social Philosophy in the United States, 1860–1920* (New York, 1968), pp. 1–59. Anyone interested in the current revival of pragmatism should read Bernstein, Rorty and West, and dip into *Post-analytic Philosophy*, ed. John Rajchman and Cornel West (New York, 1985).

CHAPTER FIVE
Regions and Regionalism

Christine Bold

REGIONALISM AS MOVEMENT

'Regionalism is a way of life; it is a self-conscious process', declared the National Resources Committee in 1935, lending official voice to the white-hot political debate of the period. Continuing its definition, the committee judged that regionalism results when there is

> a clustering of environmental, economic, social and governmental factors to such an extent that a distinct consciousness of separate identity within the whole, a need for autonomous planning, a manifestation of cultural peculiarities, and a desire for administrative freedom, are theoretically recognized and actually put into effect.[1]

In other words, regionalism is much more than a vague identification with a certain geographical unit; it is an act of perception or a discursive practice, one way in which humans categorize (and thereby attempt to control) the world around us. As such, 'regionalism' is a historically specific movement (or series of movements) which needs to be distinguished from bare 'region'.

Michael Bradshaw – among others – has shown that regions of land form, climate and cultural practices existed in America from pre-Columbian times, from the point when human beings began to interact with their natural environment. The very varied groups of Native American peoples occupied what anthropologists have called 'culture areas' – such as the Plains, the Eastern Woodlands, and the Plateau – and within these even tribes who spoke languages totally alien one to another exhibited similar patterns of life. In the (predominantly white) 'mainstream' culture of the United States the consciousness and discourse emerging from the interaction between people and particular landscapes developed much later, under the pressure of ideological and cultural anxieties. By sketching the rise of these regionalist agendas, we can appreciate the politics of space in America, the ways in which American place and space came to be converted into political and personal power. That chronological narrative, on regionalism as movement, in turn informs the brief case-studies of specific regions which form the second half of the chapter.

The post-Civil War era

Given that regionalism is a cultural construct, it is inevitable that there are competing versions of its origins. One argument is that a regionalist consciousness first became pronounced in the wake of the Civil War. The terms in which political confrontations of the mid-nineteenth century and then the war itself were articulated heightened public awareness of sectional difference. The opposing demands of South, North and West in terms of enslaved versus waged labour, of agricultural versus industrial expansion emphasized the degree to which parts of the nation differed in values, priorities, social structures. The war's conclusion did not erase those differences – if anything, defeat made Southern practices more entrenched than ever, the metropolitan North's industrial momentum speeded up exponentially, and Western expansion with its attendant cultural vision took off; in the period of Reconstruction, it became clear that somehow the federal system would have to harness differing regional priorities and loyalties. At the same time, in the face of the rapid industrialization and urbanization of the later nineteenth century, various localities – the North especially – felt the onrush of a standardized mass culture which threatened to obliterate the particular characteristics of individual communities.

Explicit and implicit fictions of this era both expressed and countered these apprehensions by making a virtue out of difference. Regionalist writers emphasized the impact of landscape on a district's customs, dialect, costume, kinship and, in turn, the effect of these cultural practices on the natural environment; in other words, they encoded the power of the local. In literature, this vision was most notably affirmed by the 'local colour' writers, as they were called. Working with the short story form particularly, these writers focused on various geographic locales: Bret Harte (whose story 'The Luck of Roaring Camp' (1868) is often considered the first of this genre) composed sentimental tales of life in the Far West; Edward Eggleston and Hamlin Garland documented rural conditions in the Midwest with varying degrees of realism; Mary Wilkins Freeman and Sarah Orne Jewett vivified the tensions of rural New England life; Kate Chopin and George W. Cable explored the social mores of Louisiana; and many critics categorize O. Henry as a local colourist for his detailed representation of white-collar culture in New York City. These authors portrayed the minutiae of landscape (or cityscape) and period, demonstrating the ways in which setting and culture affect each other. For example, Mary E. Wilkins Freeman's story 'The Revolt of "Mother" ' (1891) tells of a confrontation between a New England farmer bent on building a new barn and his wife to whom he had promised a new house for their growing family. The dimensions of the struggle and its outcome are located in and structured by specific farming practices, domestic exigencies and economic pressures in a particular time and place. We can read the story as a demonstration of the impress of landscape on the formation of individual, family and group identities.

Constructing a narrative of a different order, the turn-of-the-century historian Frederick Jackson Turner explained his country's development exclusively in terms of its spawning of sections, first in 'The Significance of the Frontier in American History' (1893), the lecture quoted in Chapter 1, and then, with full-blown attention to region, in *The Significance of Sections in American History* (1932). Essentially, Turner's argument was that America's uniqueness lay in the historical and geographical pattern of its frontier expansion. Section by section, the country forged its identity out of repeated confrontations with the wilderness, with the result that the nation became a patchwork of distinctive regions with different economic and cultural bases.

None of these narratives, whether codified as historical description or presented as overt fiction, was neutral or innocent of ideological impetus. In each case, by emphasizing the importance of regional roots, the writer is arguing a kind of exceptionalism, claiming centrality for her or his area, whether that be rural New England or the American nation. That strategy could be used to legitimize a range of aberrant social and political practices. As Catherine and John Silk have shown, regionalist rhetoric in the postbellum South served as an apologia for racism, sexism, and class-based oppression. Such transgressions against humanity could be normalized as the colourful idiosyncrasies of a charming community, refigured as the life-blood of local difference.

The 1930s

In the 1930s, regionalist discourse became much more overtly political, more scientific in its aspirations, and its most fervent adherents claimed that the regionalist movement proper began only in that decade. Certainly, it was a time of intensive redefinition. The Great Depression burst more than the bubble of economic speculation so rampant in the 1920s: it undermined the whole capitalist ethos on which America had staked its confidence. At the same time, the land itself was ravaged by the Dust Bowl, the erosion of the soil throughout the Plains caused by a combination of drought and overly intensive farming. This conjunction of economic, social and natural disasters focused the attention of politicians, social scientists, unionists and artists on the domestic scene, and a range of recovery projects was developed in response. Such national self-scrutiny brought a heightened awareness of the qualities and significance of individual regions and a reinforcement of the ties among members of communities as they looked to the resuscitation of their own landscape. At both the regional and the national level, what was underway was, in Warren Susman's words, a 'complex effort to seek and to define America as a culture'.[2]

Two distinct schools constructed agendas out of regional cultures in the 1930s. On the one hand were the conservative Agrarians, a group of Southern intellectuals centred on Vanderbilt University in Nashville, Tennessee, who articulated their aesthetic project in their periodical *The Fugitive* (1922–25) and their 1930 symposium *I'll Take My Stand*. Most famous of the group were the writer-critics John Crowe Ransom, Allen Tate, Donald Davidson and Robert Penn Warren. They had in common a yearning for an agrarian, pre-industrialized, antebellum South which they envisaged as an organic, integrated community endowed with stability and a respect for tradition which the modern, disjointed age sorely missed. Out of this idealized vision they forged heroic subject-matter specific to the region's history, and a literary style and critical precepts which privileged traditional forms, lyricism and organic unity. The Agrarian project was essentially nostalgic, developing maxims for moral behaviour and high literature by idealizing the values of a fictionalized, glorified community from the past.

Opposing this version of regionalism was what Michael O'Brien has called 'the liberal sociology of Chapel Hill': a visionary programme led by Howard Odum of the University of North Carolina and articulated most emphatically in his monumental works *Southern Regions of the United States* (1936) and *American Regionalism: A Cultural–Historical Approach to National Integration* (1938, with Harry Estill Moore).[3] Working separately from Odum, in New York City, but thinking along similar lines, was Lewis Mumford: as one of his numerous penetrating works declared, 'The re-animation and re-building of regions, as deliberate works of collective art, is the grand task of politics for the opening generation.'[4] These 'new regionalists', as they styled themselves, were the polar opposite of the 1930s

Agrarians and the nineteenth-century local colourists. Working with a visionary sense of the industrialized future, rather than an attachment to a dying or vanished past, Odum denied even the name of regionalism to these other movements, criticizing them as 'sectionalism' which commemorated the idiosyncrasies of decaying communities and promoted rivalry among the nation's regions. In contradistinction, argued Odum and Mumford, stood regionalism proper, which was dedicated to developing the distinctive strengths of each area in order to forge at the national level an integrated whole which would balance agricultural and industrial, rural and urban cultures.

This programme fed into the policies of Franklin Roosevelt's administration, receiving its most concrete enactment in a range of New Deal region-based projects: rural electrification, farm resettlement, work relief, greenbelt housing and, most famously, the Tennessee Valley Authority, an experiment in cutting across state lines to develop the natural resources of the valley as a unit (the development of the Tennessee River, for example, integrated flood control, navigation and the generation of electrical power). As well as applying regionalist principles in its social engineering, the New Deal also inculcated a localized sensibility in its cultural projects. Rural resettlement, for example, was supported by the famous Farm Security Administration photography project (see Chapter 13). Photographers fanned out across the country to document the plight and recovery of rural families.

The American Guide Series produced by the Federal Writers' Project divided the country into regions, states, counties and individual communities. Each area was assigned a hefty guide which foregrounded the history and folklore, the personalities, the work, and the material culture which together constituted a 'thick description' (in anthropologist Clifford Geertz's phrase) of the locality.[5] As contemporary commentators endlessly pointed out, this series was America's first complete system of guidebooks: they constituted a number of diversified cultural landscapes by endowing places with newly discovered associations and shaping inhabitants' perceptions of their environment. Similarly, the Federal Art Project promoted the visual representation of localized scenes on the walls of public buildings. The tensions generated within communities by these murals underline the point that such artistic works were not simple reflections of existing regional sensibilities; artists and administrators were creating a regionalist perspective, inevitably shaped by their own agendas. In Karal Ann Marling's (somewhat satiric) words, the cultural wing of the federal government was practising 'regionalism by fiat'.[6]

Government-sponsored projects were not, of course, the only cultural activity of the period. One of the most visible manifestations of region-based expression was the visual art movement known as 'Regionalism' or 'American Scene' painting. In many ways the messiah of this movement was Thomas Craven, the art critic who, from the mid-1920s, exhorted American artists to paint America, specifically their local environments. Craven opposed European traditions and the artistic hegemony of New York City. Firmly convinced that powerful art would flow out of all regions, he marshalled Thomas Hart Benton, Grant Wood and Steuart Curry in evidence. This triumvirate of Midwesterners rejected modernist European forms to concentrate on the land and people around them (see Chapter 13). Although there was no one Regionalist style, such works did privilege formal realism, story-telling and murals or large canvases, and they stressed collective experience either by depicting group activities or by intimating the swallowing up of individual figures into the landscape which they worked. (Benton rehearsed the political and aesthetic implications of this approach in his essay, 'American Regionalism: A Personal History of the Movement', 1951.) Although that last emphasis, plus the implicit respect for folk culture, can be a sign of political radicalism, Benton, Wood and Curry came to be accused of conservative – even Fascist – impulses in their fostering of folksy, nostalgic images, and their nationalist isolationism from international currents. The ensuing controversy, in which the Regionalists' role, as Cecile Whiting has shown, has not always been fairly represented, dramatized the deeply ingrained suspicion of regionalism as a justification of the status quo. By the 1940s, American Scene painting had been buried under the burst of creative activity of Abstract Expressionism, the epitome of the unlocated style.

Regionalist American writers of the period, in contrast, inscribed their radical politics openly in their texts. Various authors worked to create new genres, often in collaboration with photographers, in an attempt to embody the felt reality – which amounted to the grinding poverty – of the far-flung America hidden from Madison Avenue and Greenwich Village. Writers travelled the country, sometimes moving from one area to another but more often soaking in the conditions of a specific geographical area. The quintessential act of personal witness was James Agee and Walker Evans's *Let Us Now Praise Famous Men* (1941). With a combination of prose-poetry, photography and documentary, the work explores the lives of three 'poor white' sharecropper families in Alabama. While the result is a searing indictment of government, the book also rises to lyrical intensity, aiming to construct out of the particularities of habitat and culture a meditation on universal questions of human purpose. The Agee–Evans collaboration proves the radical potential of a regionalist perspective, which can move from the observed details of material, historically specific environment to a panoramic reflection on the human condition. *Let Us Now*

Praise Famous Men was only the most powerful of documentary experiments. Also plumbing the depths of regional experience were John Steinbeck, in numerous fictions set in California; Erskine Caldwell, in his own novels of the South and in collaboration with the photographer Margaret Bourke-White; Paul Taylor and Dorothea Lange, in photo-journalism again; and Nathan Asch, James Rorty, John Dos Passos and others who took to the road to discover how the land and its inhabitants were marking each other under pressure and to create new documentary fictions which would inscribe that interplay in arresting prose.

The post-Second World War era

In the post-Second World War age of the 'global village' and the 'megalopolis', many commentators pronounced regionalism dead. The argument was that the standardization of cultural production through the burgeoning of the mass media and the erosion of individual and community powers by the military–industrial complex removed the conditions necessary to local initiatives. Evidence of this diminution comes in the traces of conservative, nostalgic regionalism in certain commercial cinema projects. In 1984, for example, appeared *Country*, *The River* and *Places in the Heart*: films which look back to the 1930s, in spirit or setting, to dramatize the courage of small farmers battling tornadoes, floods and drought. In their idealization of traditional, rural, family values, these films used regionalist associations both to react against the hard economic realities of Reagan's America and to support the dominant rhetoric of that conservative era.

At the same time, however, regionalism has re-emerged in recent years as a powerful tool for the radical interrogation of the status quo. The explanation for this paradox provided by a leading current theorist of regionalism, Raymond Gastil, is that communities respond to the forces of standardization and regimentation in different, environmentally specific ways which serve to perpetuate and emphasize regional difference. In some cases, what was formerly a general respect for folk life and folk culture became refined into a strategy in support of radical programmes.

One obvious example is the use made by the feminist movement of a regionalist ethos. Some feminist thinkers recognized a parallel between regionalism's celebration of localized, quotidian folk activity and their own project to make visible and to valorize the invisible, undervalued domestic activity of the traditional female sphere. In practice, this attention has resulted in new appreciation for the achievements of women who created artistic and material artefacts out of the stuff of their immediate environments – such as embroideries and, especially, quilts – and who never sustained national reputations. There is currently a vogue for the publication of powerful diaries, letters and oral narratives by women, many of whom are being heard for the first time. For example, Nannie T. Alderson and Elinore Pruitt Stewart detail the opportunities and pitfalls of ranching life for women in the first half of the twentieth century, while Amelia Stewart Knight and Catherine Haun dramatize their experiences on the westward trail to Oregon and the California gold fields in the nineteenth century. Collectively, such authors are now celebrated for creating an alternative vision of the West which challenges the hegemonic myth of masculine adventure; they reject the melodramatic frontier of popular culture to illuminate the drama of the lived West. The gain is an *écriture feminine* carved out of, and empowered by, specific cultural and topographical landscapes.

Similar dynamics emerged with the New Pluralism and the New Ethnicity of the 1960s (see Chapter 7). Various cultural groups rejected the social metaphor of the 'melting pot' (the acculturation of all groups into a homogenized America). They found visibility and legitimacy for their particular customs and values by emphasizing their roots in and their continued identification with specific places. In effect, embattled groups were arguing that their social, political and personal histories were shaped by and inscribed on the landscape. One visionary projection is that institutionalizing regional demarcations would result in less divisive perspectives than the demarcations of race, class and gender. Gastil, echoing in the 1970s his forefathers and mothers from the 1930s, argues that regionalism recognizes individual and social particularities while allowing 'a new synthesis'.

In the academy, this regionalist debate has promoted interdisciplinary perspectives while calling into question conventional assumptions about artistic canons: the privileging of certain works as the 'masterpieces' which transcend place and time to achieve a universal authority. For example, the introduction of diaries and letters into the curricula of English Literature departments has challenged traditional distinctions between the literary and the non-literary, between 'good' and 'bad' writing; by foregrounding political issues, life-writing problematizes aesthetic judgements. The upset of the academic hierarchy in turn spins off into the power structures of government, the economy, class relations and other social formations. 'Universalism' is exposed as not only a myth but a strategy for the dispossession of minority groups. Regionalist perspectives, fuelled by an understanding of environmental influences, can recover and centre voices which, traditionally, have been marginalized by the dominant culture.

SUMMARIZING REGIONALISM

This summary, then, proceeds from the understanding that discourse or language is a major force in constituting (as opposed to simply reflecting or describing) our reality, a case propounded vigorously by Hayden White in *Tropics of Discourse* (1978). Moreover, following the arguments of Michel Foucault on social and political power relations, this synopsis also posits that these discursive practices have everything to do with the maintenance (or overthrow) of power formations. I am arguing that regionalism names and thereby constructs an affective relationship between human beings, as individuals and groups, and the landscape which they inhabit. That relationship is neither simple nor limited, involving as it does culture, politics, social organization, the development of natural resources, economics, and the material institutions of class, race and gender. In the United States, this process of naming and counter-naming has been visible since at least the Civil War. Repeatedly, but with increased radicalism over the decades, individuals and groups staked a claim for their locales, insisting that geographical and cultural difference go hand-in-hand and attempting to write (or speak or paint) their environments into a larger picture of national diversity. In undertaking this self-empowerment, regional groups were implicitly challenging the status quo of political, economic, racial and gender hierarchies. Far from being a quaint or backward impulse, regionalism emerges as a tool for radical interrogation, literally rooted in the palpable spaces, places and landscapes of America.

REGIONS OF AMERICA

The point about the determining significance of perception is underlined when we broach specific regions within the United States. There are as many regions as there are ways of defining them. For example, two major regionalist commentators, Odum from the 1930s and Gastil from the 1970s, disagree radically about the number of regions into which the nation can usefully be divided. Odum defines the 'composite major societal regions' as areas which 'approximate the largest degree of homogeneity, measured by the largest number and variety of indices or units of homogeneity for the largest number of purposes' (Odum, p. 435). He decides on six major group-of-states regions: Southeast (Virginia, North Carolina, South Carolina, Georgia, Florida, Alabama, Mississippi, Louisiana, Arkansas, Tennessee, Kentucky); Northeast (Maine, Vermont, New Hampshire, Massachusetts, Rhode Island, Connecticut, New Jersey, New

York, Pennsylvania, Delaware, Maryland, West Virginia, Washington DC); Middle States (Ohio, Indiana, Illinois, Michigan, Wisconsin, Minnesota, Iowa, Missouri); Northwest (North Dakota, South Dakota, Nebraska, Kansas, Montana, Idaho, Wyoming, Colorado, Utah); Southwest (Texas, Oklahoma, New Mexico, Arizona); and Far West (Washington, Oregon, California, Nevada).

Gastil eschews physiographic and economic characteristics in favour of cultural patterns ('the fundamental lesson of history is that different people make different uses of the same environment'), positing thirteen cultural regions which defy easy correlation with state lines: Northeast, New York Metropolitan, Pennsylvanian, South (including Lowland, Upland, Mountain and Western Souths), Upper Midwest, Central Midwest, Rocky Mountain, Mormon, Interior Southwest, Pacific Southwest, Pacific Northwest, Alaskan, and Hawaiian.[7] Another tack, again, is taken by Joel Garreau in his popular journalistic work, *The Nine Nations of North America* (1981). He perceives Americans and Canadians to cluster into New England, the Foundry, Dixie, the Islands, Mexamerica, Ecotopia, the Empty Quarter, the Breadbasket, and Quebec. There are many different purposes in demarcating regions – practical policy-making or administration, physical or economic geography, commerce, historical enquiry, artistic production, education, cultural analysis – and each purpose shapes a different pattern. Moreover, none of these regions is in fact a homogeneous unit, since they all contain internal varieties of landscape, settlement patterns, commercial activity, or cultural production that could constitute subregions. In considering the 'pressing reality', in Odum's phrase (Odum, p. 423), of specific regions, then, we are still working in the realm of nominalism or naming, and narrative – Hayden White's historical tropes. In order to explore the intersection of geography, history, economy and culture central to the naming of regions, I will follow Odum's scheme of six major areas, because some approximation of his divisions seems most firmly lodged in the popular mind.

In terms of the specific cultural expressions emerging from these constructed regions, I have adopted a broad definition. I consider as regional expression any work whose central or peripheral messages are informed by the landscape or cityscape. For example, a John Ford Western seems to me to convey partial messages about the terrain, ethnic mixture and psychological environment of the Southwest, despite its formulaic adventure narrative whose origins owe much more to the conventions of Hollywood than to the specific conditions of desert life. Also crucial is the constitutive force of such stories. That is, the popular perception of Monument Valley or the Southwest region is strongly shaped by films and tales set in that area, hence they become regionalist expression *de facto*.

The Southeast

Of all the American regions, the Southeast, known also as the South or the Old South, has contributed most to the regionalist debate. This area's highly self-conscious sectionalism results both from internal economics and demographics and from the image of it held by other cultures within and beyond the United States. Both of these forces have much to do with the definitive moment of the Civil War, when the Old South formalized its territorial distinctiveness into the politically independent Confederacy.

The South's distinctive traits were laid long before the mid-nineteenth century, however. From the earliest European explorations of the South in the late fifteenth and early sixteenth centuries, the motive was commercial exploitation of the territory's benign landscape: its rich soils, abundant rainfall, long hot summers and mild winters. The plantation system was a business enterprise which used up land and people ruthlessly in the cause of the colonial economy. A labour-intensive undertaking which came to depend on black slaves, it produced a raw material primarily for export to Britain (predominantly cotton, with secondary development of tobacco, rice, sugar cane and hemp). These two characteristics affected the human geography of the South decisively. The large slave presence inhibited the immigration of non-slaves, with the result that the South had a very small proportion of foreign-born inhabitants right up to the Second World War; one consequence was that colour lines between the Scottish and English strains on the one hand and the black slaves on the other were that much more starkly drawn (limited exceptions to that pattern were caused by Creoles in Louisiana and Spanish settlement in Florida). Furthermore, the export-based economy mitigated against the development of internal markets or economic and transportation links, a lack which fostered rural isolation and strong local allegiances.

Fighting the Civil War in defence of its special economic and social arrangements, the Southern bloc discovered that defeat destroyed its agricultural institutions, its industrial base and its social hierarchy. Nevertheless, the dominant white class used its residual powers to reaffirm the separateness of Southern society. By the end of the nineteenth century a series of 'Jim Crow' laws institutionalizing segregation ensured that Southern blacks remained a disadvantaged underclass. What advances there were in manufacturing technology increased opportunites for whites only, with blacks held in thrall to a sharecropping system which effectively enslaved them as much as ever. Poverty was widespread, with one-crop farming exhausting the land, devastation of the cotton crop by the boll weevil in the early twentieth century, and a general reliance on antiquated practices. Only with large-scale federal intervention in the 1930s, then more rapidly since the Second World War, have the South's traditional composition and enduring poverty been shaken decisively. The Supreme Court decision of 1954, in *Brown* vs. *Board of Education of Topeka*, overturned segregation and led to a gradual racial integration, hastened further by the Civil Rights Act of 1964. Developments in manufacturing have shifted the region away from its predominantly agrarian economy to a much more diversified system.

More dramatic than these changes – and suggesting once again the constitutive properties of discourse – is the reorientation of the Old South into a whole new region: the 'Sunbelt', an area named at the end of the 1960s and inclusive of the eleven Southern states plus Oklahoma, Texas, New Mexico, Arizona and southern California. Slicing the pie in this fashion has delivered a reconstituted South, identified by a vibrant economy, an attractive climate, and the influx of diverse populations (including Cuban refugees from Castro's regime, Mexicans and Puerto Ricans, and retirees from the Northern states and Canada). Moreover, the label implies its opposite: the 'Frostbelt' of the older northern manu- facturing belt, an area seen, in contrast, to be slowing down. This naming has nicely reversed the traditional power balance of North and South.

This new – perhaps temporary – reorientation also suggests that the South has lost its strong difference from the rest of the country, and certainly its distinctive population of blacks has spread out across the country at large. In terms of cultural expression, however, the region's distinctiveness is recurrently reaffirmed on many fronts – as, for example, in the ideological programmes sketched earlier in this chapter. In terms of national politics, too, the South has contributed particular, formative voices, from the Founding Fathers Washington, Jefferson and Madison, through the black activists King and Jackson. In terms of religious practice, Protestant evangelism, as we saw in Chapter 2, has developed a recognizably Southern strain both in black Baptist practices and in the white 'tele-evangelism' which has been brought into such disrepute in recent years.

Music, of course, is the great Southern inheritance to American national culture, with the spread of black blues, spirituals and jazz, as well as white- dominated country music, to the urban north (see Chapter 11). Even as they evolve and change, these forms of cultural expression continue to be marked by their regional origins. The term 'New Orleans Jazz', for example, speaks to the particular cosmopolitan milieu which was the crucible for the birth of jazz and its continued sustenance throughout the modern age. In a different tradition, the country music of 'Grand Ole Opry' continues to negotiate the contradictory imperatives of small-town, folkish informality and urban commercialism that were implicit in its origins as a Nashville, Tennessee radio show in the 1920s.

In literature, distinctive subjects and styles have been forged by white authors such as William Faulkner and Flannery O'Connor who grapple with the inbred isolation of Southern society and the symbolic claustrophobia of its fecund landscape; by the popularizer Margaret Mitchell who idealized the antebellum plantation era in *Gone with the Wind* (1936); and by Eudora Welty, whose strong sense of place informs her fiction, her photography and her famous regionalist statement of 1956, 'Place in Fiction'. Articulating a very different Southern influence are black writers such as Zora Neale Hurston, Richard Wright and Alice Walker (all of whom ultimately migrated northwards), who seek to expose and challenge the racism and sexism which ran through this culture down the centuries.

Different as these voices are, the one constant strain is the biracial composition of the region. One of the complexities attendant on the representation of this area is that the same qualities – its agrarianism, its master–slave relationships, its isolationism, its combination of vast natural resources and enormous social problems – are figured as positive or negative, depending on the voice and the occasion. While, until recent years at least, the South has been the most definite of regions, it has also defied unilingual characterization. What it has done without pause is name its difference.

The Northeast

Of all Odum's demarcations, this region at first seems the most forced yoking together of the dissimilar, incorporating as it does rural and urban New England, metropolitan New York City and the nation's capital, Washington DC. Historically, there are undeniably significant differences between the Puritan stock of New England, whose religious exclusivity preserved a dominant Anglo-Saxonism until the Second Immigration of the late nineteenth century; the ethnic diversity of New York City, cosmopolitan from the coexistence of English and Dutch in the seventeenth century; the tolerant openness of Quaker Pennsylvania, refuge for Puritan outcasts as for fleeing slaves; and the numerically dominant black population of Washington DC. Similarly, the landscapes, from the thickly forested stretches and the mountains of northern New England to the low-lying marshes of Washington DC, created very different environments. Since the urbanization and industrialization of the late nineteenth and twentieth centuries, however, and the major shift in demographics, many of these differences have declined. Cultural manifestations of the larger Northeast region too share some significant characteristics.

The most significant binding of disparate landscapes occurred with the growth of the 'megalopolis', so identified by Jean Gottmann in his 1961 book *Megalopolis: The Urbanized Northeastern Seaboard of the United States*. Essentially, the metropolitan centres up and down the East Coast, from Boston to Washington DC, expanded until they converged, creating one vast conurbation. That development has ensured the industrial and financial predominance of the Northeast over the rest of the country. It has also been accompanied by a thorough ethnic mix as internal immigrants from the South, especially, and external immigrants from a vast range of countries have been attracted by the urban opportunities of these cities. The result is that roughly one-fifth of the US population resides in 1.5 per cent of its landmass.

In terms of cultural expression, the impulse to turn landscape into political power was evident from the earliest stages of white settlement in the Northeast. For example, the seventeenth-century Puritans were convinced that their mission was to plant the new Jerusalem in the New World. In undertaking this task, this group followed its imported dogma, imposing on the landscape a physical system of community expansion and a typological system of symbols which had little to do with the actualities of the land itself. With a similar vision of human domination – though in a very different political context – the city of Washington DC was carved out of the swampland around the Potomac and Anacostia rivers in the eighteenth century to suit the political exigencies of the new Republic. Again, the specific style of that settlement was determined not by topography but by the classical, European models which the founding fathers believed would legitimate their political system.

Moreover, that historical mark put on a recalcitrant landscape has been preserved insistently by those most concerned to give cultural expression to these districts. The township system of government established in Puritan New England, for example, remained a mark of distinction in the 1930s. During the production of the American Guide Series, the Massachusetts Writers' Project director threatened to resign if the central, Washington DC office tried to impose any order other than townships on the Massachusetts guidebook. The cultural manifestations of history are everywhere institutionalized in Washington DC, too, with its continued insistence on neo-Classical architecture which never allows residents or visitors to forget the European origins of this most planned of cities; the public buildings express a historical identity which is hardly appropriate to the crime-ridden, racially tense and bureaucratically determined fabric of the contemporary city.

107

One of the peculiarities of the literary, visual and mass-media works from this environment is that they pretend not to be regional, or they are commonly not considered regional products. For example, reviewers, critics and readers tend not to refer to John Updike novels of small-town Pennsylvania or New England or John Dos Passos's vision of New York City as regional, though in fact these works concentrate on the felt landscape, the quotidian culture of a particular place and time. A similar point could be made about what has been called the 'sordid realism' of the film *Taxi Driver* (1976) or the location footage of the 1970s television series *Kojak*, both set in New York City. Perhaps because of its financial and manufacturing clout, the Northeast has been transformed, implicitly, into a global or universal site. The tendency can be traced historically: the 'American Renaissance' and the 'Boston Brahmin' writers of the nineteenth century tend not to be classified as regional, despite their subjects, style and agenda being heavily conditioned by the New England landscape. (Significantly, those writers readily dubbed 'regional' from this area tend to be women or men whose writing was never canonized by the academy.) If we can say that the Southeast repeatedly insists on its difference through its cultural productions, we can posit the opposite case about the Northeast: its cultural productions deny the difference or even the effective presence of other regions, claiming that this one stands for the whole.

The Middle States

This region, more commonly known as the Midwest or Middle West, consists of a rough triangle of land, approximately bounded by the Ohio and Missouri Rivers east and west and by the southern Great Lakes to the north. Physiographically, it seems a blessed area: its gently rolling, intermittently treed landscape ensures rich soil and natural irrigation; its ample rainfall and long growing season create favourable agricultural conditions for crop and livestock farming; and its natural system of waterways, helped here and there by manufactured canals, facilitated both the movement of peoples west and the transportation of resources back east to metropolitan markets before the continental railway was completed. The result is a region which is a composite of agriculture and urbanism, farms having spread all across the area, small towns having grown up to service these farms, and major cities having developed as both markets and ports for the vast agricultural produce, as well as shipping points for metallic mineral ores.

Demographically, the Midwest's character resulted largely from two waves of immigration. The first influx came in the early nineteenth century, after the government opened up the old Northwest Territory and parcelled it into cheap farming plots to entice settlers. The eager response came both from the previously settled areas of the United States and from north-western Europe, as British, German and Scandinavian farmers, especially, believed that the Midwest offered them familiar land for development. The Second Immigration or 'new immigrants' derived largely from southeastern Europe late in the nineteenth century. Although some Poles and Bohemians managed to find land for tilling, by this stage most of the good land was claimed; the majority of new immigrants (Italians, Slavs, Lithuanians, Greeks, Persians, Syrians, among others) crowded into the burgeoning metropolitan centres of Chicago, Cincinnati, Cleveland and Detroit. As a whole, then, the region is as much an ethnic as a physiographic mixture.

Socio-economically, these conditions fostered certain work habits which prevailed up to roughly the Second World War, when technological and crop innovations created new possibilities. The stock agricultural unit was the family farm, a site of intensive labour; nurturing the soil involved a yearly rotation of corn, wheat or oats, and clover or alfalfa, and many farms also raised cattle and hogs. The urban unit of factory or slaughter house was labour intensive in a different way: poor immigrants with little knowledge of America or its language became the pawns of capitalist barons who could force them to work in any conditions with however inadequate remuneration. (An angry exposé of the Chicago stockyards is Upton Sinclair's *The Jungle*, 1906.) The spread of manufacturing and agricultural technology after the Second World War (plus the development of soybean) improved working conditions in the cities and efficiency on farms but also facilitated consolidation of farms, which meant that family ownership became replaced by corporate or absentee ownership.

From a cultural perspective, what is most significant about this region is the way in which it became idealized as the true America, the place where the American Dream was writ into the landscape. Geographical and historical factors shaped settlement patterns, a work ethic, family solidarity and ethnic mixes which were then refigured as metaphors of moral value. Frederick Jackson Turner portrayed the Midwest as displaying the beginnings of true frontier developments, free of the constricting influence of Europe, and as a new frontier the region spoke to the democratic, egalitarian vision of each person gaining her or his own property, the fundamental necessity for 'life, liberty and the pursuit of happiness'. In the case of popular expression, iconic status was imposed most visibly on the middle of middle America: the small, rural town partway between the agricultural settlements and the burgeoning metropolis. In Frank Capra's popular films *Mr Deeds Goes to Town* (1936) and *It's a Wonderful Life* (1946) the Midwestern town epitomizes the values of community feeling, common sense and material comfort; this vision is then updated only in the size of the urban unit in the Mayfield of the television series *Leave it to Beaver* (1957–63) and the Minneapolis of *The Mary Tyler Moore Show* (1970–77). Mass media won the moral high ground by exploiting the very localized affiliations which its technology could be said to be eroding. Working against that celebration of small-town values are commentators as different as Sherwood Anderson and Garrison Keillor. Anderson's stories of *Winesburg, Ohio* (1919) expose the grotesque underside of rural, close-knit community. Since 1974, Garrison Keillor's radio programme *A Prairie Home Companion* has walked a fine line between nostalgia and satire in tapping the homespun values of his fictional midwestern town, Lake Wobegon.

A more complex translation of landscape into cultural form is decipherable in Frank Lloyd Wright's turn-of-the-century series of Prairie Houses, which are discussed more fully in Chapter 9. Understood as Wright's earliest major contribution to modern architecture, these low, unornamented, open houses were his first steps towards 'organic architecture' adapted to specific environments and local materials. A more tentative regional influence has been identified, too, in the Chicago School architects' emphasis on functional design and stylistic simplicity in the creation of the first skyscrapers. This has been claimed as quintessentially American, embodying an indigenous Midwestern plainness in contrast to 'Europeanized' developments occurring elsewhere in the country. Appreciating the iconology of the Midwest in the twentieth century, then, clarifies the furore over the representations of Benton and other Regionalist painters. When these artists produced controversial symbols or what were seen as ugly styles in depicting their region, they not only offended local pride, they were suspected of attacking the most sacred shibboleth of American identity.

The Northwest

Also known as the Plains, the Great Plains, or the Far West, this is a region whose land form and climate tested human ingenuity from the outset. Stretching approximately from the 98th meridian to the Rocky Mountains, the area is primarily flat (or, more accurately, a plain tilting up from east to west), dry and treeless; the thin, sandy soil and the lack of moisture bode ill for agricultural efforts. Major Stephen Long, whose perceptions were shaped by his Eastern origins, judged the area on his 1820 expedition 'almost wholly unfit for cultivation, and of course, uninhabitable for a people depending upon agriculture for their subsistence'.[8] Indeed, in the first half of the nineteenth century, the entire region was shunned by emigrants labouring to reach the Pacific Frontier as 'The Great American Desert'. Only once the preferred areas of Oregon and California seemed to be filling up did the tide of emigration turn back on itself. At roughly the same time, there occurred expansion from the Midwest and up from Texas, as well as the settling of the Salt Lake City area in Utah by the Mormon pioneers. These various groups carried their distinctive occupations with them and so established the three dominant socio-economic activities of the region.

The most momentous discovery, economically and culturally, was that the grass lands of the mountain belt could profitably support open range ranching of longhorn cattle. This ranching economy was the inheritance of Texas in the years after the Civil War. To feed the voracious appetite of the Northeast, huge herds of cattle were driven north to the railheads in Kansas, with many outfits opting to set themselves up permanently in the more northerly, undeveloped plains, from about 1867 to 1885. With streams scarce and far apart, this ranching was inevitably undertaken on a vast scale, with cattle wandering at their will then sorted out for market in periodic roundups. Farmers gradually discovered that with sophisticated irrigation (including windmills) some areas could be cultivated fruitfully with wheat. And the backwash from Oregon and California included miners who learned that the mining of minerals, coal and, later, oil and natural gas could bring considerable wealth. Thus the Northwest saw cultivation undertaken on many fronts simultaneously, in a greatly foreshortened timespan. The precarious balance collapsed equally rapidly, with the death of open range ranching in the late 1880s – the result partly of widespread overgrazing, partly of the devastating winters of those years, and partly of the increased muscle of small homesteaders with the invention of barbed wire to fence in their crop and livestock operations. These three resource-based occupations still dominate the region today, although ranching has adapted to fences, technology and corporate ownership. What towns there are mostly began as transportation centres and are situated along railroad lines.

The translation of this environment into a set of cultural images took several forms. In the last third of the nineteenth century, pioneer photographers such as Timothy O'Sullivan, Carleton Watkins and William Henry Jackson tried to capture the sweep and scale of wilderness and mountain landscapes. Their works were strongly connected to the land not just in their representation of it, but in their use by governmental explorations and surveys, and in their impact on land development.

Jackson's photographs not only supported railroad publicity directed at potential emigrants, but his depictions of the Yellowstone region were partly instrumental in Congress's decision to create Yellowstone National Park in 1872. Women writers – published and unpublished – also undertook to convey the drama of the Far West. Willa Cather's *O Pioneers!* (1913), for example, constitutes an epic of female heroism in its celebration of one woman's determination and triumphs in running a Nebraska farm. Other women's voices – such as Alderson and Stewart, cited earlier – are inscribed in vivid life writings which demonstrate the quotidian drama of work and family on frontier ranch and settlement.

More popular than any of these versions of the Northwest, however, were the verbal and visual fictions which came to be known generically as 'Westerns' (see Chapter 14). Key to their rise was the rapid urbanization, industrialization and influx of immigrants in the late-nineteenth-century East, which caused members of the élite classes to fear that their hegemony and their vision of a youthful America were coming to an end. Looking for an exemplary alternative, they discovered the open, underpopulated, vigorous West, newly accessible to those with money because of the joining of the transcontinental railway and the development of luxurious Pullman cars. This Far West was heroized most famously by Owen Wister (in *The Virginian* of 1902 and other fictions), Frederic Remington (in his canvases and sculptures of cowboys and Native Americans) and Theodore Roosevelt (in his historical writings and his political rhetoric). These fiction-makers fastened on the open range as the site of rugged individualism where nomadic, independent cowboys mastered turbulent Natives, climate and animals, translating the ingenious exploitation of difficult terrain into an unschooled, natural wisdom. Playing out their personal and class fantasies, these genteel Easterners mythicized the era the more urgently because it was clearly vanishing. Not only was ranching being reduced to familiar agricultural patterns, but this was America's last frontier, 'the end', in Turner's formulation, of the nation's encounter with the wilderness. In the works of these myth-makers, as in 'Buffalo Bill' Cody's Wild West show, and later pulp writing, commercial cinema, popular music, political rhetoric and advertising strategies, the untamed West stands for young America. The landscape is conventionally invested with a moral purity and youthful exuberance which legitimize the violence, imperialism, misogyny and racism which inhered not only in the settlement of the Northwest but in aspects of America's national mission at home and overseas. Product of individual initiatives, commercial promotion and collective wish-fulfilment, this 'code of the West' demonstrates the transformation of a region into a highly stylized, self-serving but undeniably powerful narrative.

The Southwest

The Southwest region is marked by extremes of climate, demography and history, all affecting each other to a degree. Topographically, the area changes from mountains to canyons to plains to desert, with much of this terrain subject to an arid climate with high summer temperatures but a mixture of mild and harsh winters depending on the subregion. This was a landscape habitable to the earliest settlers, the Native groups (including Pueblo, Hopi, Navajo and Apache), and to the sixteenth-century influx of Spanish peoples, as well as the recent wave of 'legal' and 'illegal' immigrants from Mexico. But the 'Anglos' (as they are often known in this area) who came in the nineteenth century found the landscape foreign and recalcitrant to their established agricultural methods. They penetrated the region with uncharacteristic slowness and did not dislodge the Native and Hispanic groups with the ferocity of the Eastern seaboard and Western settlers. One result is that the vaunted 'melting pot' hardly operates here at all, and, though the Anglos dominate economically and politically, the three cultures have marked the environment in quite distinctive ways. Another peculiarity is that the Southwest states are both very young – Texas being admitted to the Union in 1852, Oklahoma in 1908, and New Mexico and Arizona in 1912 – and unusually ancient, the physical landscape marked to a high degree with the ruins and traces of ancient cultures.

Modern white cultures mark the landscape, too, though less harmoniously than Native or Mexican. The economic boom attending the discovery of natural gas and oil resources around the Gulf of Mexico issued in the gleaming new cities of Houston and Dallas. The very scale of skyscrapers, automobiles and other signs of conspicuous consumption is an expression of the business culture asserting itself through the natural and manufactured environment. The contemporary wave of retirees and tourists, responding to the healthy climate and recreational opportunities, also frames the natural beauties of this landscape in particular commercial and architectural ways. The Southwestern landscape is commodified in special-focus communities and, more generally, in the paraphernalia and poses of the tourist industry – witness the activity around Arizona's Grand Canyon, as explicated by Daniel Boorstin in *The Image: What Happened to the American Dream* (1961).

In terms of a more conventional definition of cultural expression, there are significant white creations, from the popular cowboy tales of Will James to Georgia O'Keeffe's feminized desert landscapes. The Taos Society of Artists, cofounded in 1912 by Ernest L. Blumenschein and Bert Phillips, was composed of visual artists sympathetic to the Indian cultures of the region. Working in various styles, painters such as Blumenschein, Joseph Henry Sharp and E. Irving Couse took Pueblo peoples and landscapes as their primary subject. At the other end of the cultural spectrum, the desert and its stereotyped 'savages' have been exploited to adventurous effect in innumerable commercial films and television productions.

From the perspective of the present, however, what seem most urgent are the visual creations and the voices of Native artists, who use the cultural landscape with which they are intimate to forge an alternative, often hearteningly positive vision. One of the most powerful and harmonious of the writers is Leslie Marmon Silko, whose heritage is composed of Pueblo, Mexican and white strains. Her novel *Ceremony* (1977) and multi-genre work *Storyteller* (1981) intertwine the expressive forms of these three cultures to create a vision literally rooted in the particularities of the Southwest landscape, which figures as both spiritual presence and physical nurturance. While these works can certainly be classified as part of Native literature and as part of women's writing, they also belong to the regionalist classification in the degree to which they work with the natural and fabricated environment of a very particular place and time. Many of the regions sketched out here are inevitably defined in denial of the aboriginal experience, past and present, because many of these demarcations follow on non-Native industrial and agricultural developments. In the Southwest, however, the claims and creations of Native groups and individuals have remained insistently audible and visible, prime markers of this region's distinctiveness.

The West Coast

This region – labelled the 'Far West' by Odum but now generally known as the West Coast or the Pacific West – exemplifies the power of naming in extreme form. The human imagination fostered an image of the coastal West as cornucopia, especially in the conventional vocabulary of popular literature, film, advertising and political rhetoric. Despite the proven partiality of that image, it has stimulated large-scale immigration in past and recent times. In turn, that population has worked to mould the reality to the fiction.

Certainly, the landscape is richly varied, incorporating sea, forest, snow, desert, mountains and plateaus. One indication of the region's extremes lies in its incorporation of both Mount Whitney and Death Valley, highest and lowest points in the coterminous United States. A mild climate, wetter in the north than in the south, contributes to the favourable conditions and allows an enormous range of agriculture. North and south, there are hugely productive farms of wheat and fruit, the specialities from California often Mediterranean, as well as dairy cattle in Oregon and Washington. In urban terms, there has been explosive growth since the First World War, especially around the San Francisco Bay Area and the Los Angeles Basin (the area from Santa Barbara to San Diego now qualifying as an automobile-bound 'megalopolis'), and an influx of electronics industries and Pacific Rim business and technology angled towards the Far East. Yet this cornucopia is literally undermined by the chronic lack of water in the south, which threatens the sustenance of both farms and cities, while the fault lines of California and the volcanic peaks of the Cascade mountain range threaten some of the most densely populated of the region's sites. Nevertheless, the image of the Far West playground, location of the good life, remains strong; the coastal areas, especially, remain a mecca for Americans and foreigners from East and West.

Essential to this image is the conviction that human beings can shape the landscape to their purposes, despite the evidence of repeated earthquakes, droughts and eruptions. In the history of the West Coast, the equation between land and money has been unusually direct. In the mid-nineteenth century, tales of the paradisal fertility of the Willamette Valley in Oregon and of the fabulously rich gold mines of California caused thousands to make the difficult continental crossing by covered wagons. Even Nevada attracted large numbers of adventurers intent on mineral extraction, or on selling schemes to inexperienced miners. In recent times, this particular desert has bloomed more profitably with the gambling casinos of Reno and Las Vegas, feeding on the same illusion of easy wealth. Whatever the fictitiousness of these images, they were crucial to the carving out of territory. The influx of miners and settlers enabled America to wrest the southern terrain from Spain and the northern territory from Britain.

The localized literature has retraced the pendulum swing of illusion and disillusionment characteristic of the human relationship with this natural environment. Hot on the heels of the 1849 Gold Rush to California came the sensational dime novels propagating the vision of adventure and easy wealth, a vision then debunked by, among others, Mark Twain in his comic *Roughing It* (1873). That trajectory of attraction and disbelief continues in the contemporary era, from the sentimental film of the California gold fields, *Paint Your Wagon* (1969), to the hard-boiled portrait of Los Angeles as a place of intrigue, incest and corruption, all provoked by the desperate fight for water in the parched land, in *Chinatown* (1974). In the years of the Great Depression, Steinbeck's *The Grapes of Wrath* (1939) movingly depicted the illusions of poverty-stricken Okies, that California is a land of milk and honey (in fact, the family is confronted with poverty, violence and political chicanery). The bountiful farm land of the

115

Willamette Valley gave rise to equally romantic, though less frequent, portraits; see, for example, Emerson Hough's *The Covered Wagon* (1920), made into a film of the same title in 1923, and the manly adventure tale of A.B. Guthrie, *The Way West* (1949; also filmed, in 1967).

The corrective to this vision has not been the harsh debunking of the West Coast's conditions but an exploration of the intersection of real working conditions and masculine mythology, as conducted by Ken Kesey in *Sometimes a Great Notion* (1964), his fictionalization of a part of Oregon famous for having one of the highest suicide rates in America. Meanwhile, in the early years of the twentieth century, Mary Austin gently interrogated prevailing stereotypes of the western desert in her short stories which instead centre woman, nature and Native. From this intimate relationship with landscape, Austin also delivered one of the classic regionalist statements in her 1932 essay 'Regionalism in American Fiction'. A similar attentiveness to the region's natural beauties can be traced in the photography of the f.64 Group (see Chapter 13). Influenced as much by Modernist aesthetics as their appreciation of the landscape, they reproduced the sharpest detail and the most nuanced effects of desert and mountains that phototechnology would allow.

The dominant cultural mythology of the West Coast has survived and flourished in all periods, whatever the dangers of landform, climate or political demagoguery and whatever counter-narratives have been offered. It is no accident that this region spawned two powerful examples of the commercial and political discourse which can be wrought out of the perceived landscape. Hollywood, the centre of the culture industry, is appropriately located at the heart of the Los Angeles megalopolis; and Ronald Reagan, the 1980s 'acting President' (in Gore Vidal's witticism), capitalized on his folksy, Western image as governor of California to become hero of right-wing America.

NOTES

1. Quoted in Howard Odum and Harry Estill Moore, *American Regionalism: A Cultural–Historical Approach to National Integration* (New York, 1938), p. 138; subsequent page references in the text.

2. Warren I. Susman, *Culture as History: The Transformation of American Society in the Twentieth Century* (New York, 1985), p. 157.

3. Michael O'Brien, *The Idea of the American South, 1920–1941* (Baltimore, 1979), p. xxiii.

4. Lewis Mumford, *The Culture of Cities* (New York, 1938), p. 348.

5. Clifford Geertz, 'Thick Description: Toward an Interpretive Theory of Culture', in *The Interpretation of Cultures* (New York, 1973), pp. 3–30.

6. Karal Ann Marling, *Wall-to-Wall America: A Cultural History of Post Office Murals in the Great Depression* (Minneapolis, 1982), p. 83.

7. Raymond D. Gastil, *Cultural Regions of the United States* (Seattle, 1975), pp. 25–6.

8. The words are are those of Dr Edwin James, Long's subordinate, in Reuben G. Thwaites (ed.), *James's Account of the S.H. Long Expedition, 1819–1820*, Early Western Travels Series, Vol. XVII (Cleveland, 1904), pp. 147–8.

SUGGESTIONS FOR FURTHER READING

These notes concentrate on selected artistic forms and more recent discussions of regionalism; 'classic statements' from earlier eras – some of which are cited in the text – are referred to in works included below. The full range of disciplines is covered by the standard bibliography on cultural regionalism, *Regions and Regionalism in the United States: A Source Book for the Humanities and Social Sciences*, by Michael Steiner and Clarence Mondale (New York and London, 1988), supplemented by Clarence Mondale, 'Concepts and Trends in Regional Studies', *American Studies International* XXVII, 1 (April 1989), 13–37.

General discussions of American regions and regionalism abound. Some of the most useful introductions are Michael Bradshaw, *Regions and Regionalism in the United States* (Jackson, MS, 1988); Raymond D. Gastil, *Cultural Regions of the United States* (Seattle, 1975); John Brinkerhoff Jackson, *American Space: The Centennial Years, 1865–1876* (New York, 1972), and *Discovering the Vernacular Landscape* (New Haven, 1984); and D.W. Meinig (ed.), *The Interpretation of Ordinary Landscapes: Geographical Essays* (New York, 1979). Journals worth exploring include *Annals of the American Association of Geographers*; *Journal of Cultural Geography*; *Journal of Regional Cultures*; and *Prospects* (especially Volume IX, 1984).

A number of scholars explore 'mental maps' or the perceptual and discursive construction of the environment: for example, Jay Appleton, *The Experience of Landscape* (London, 1975); Peter Gould and Rodney White, *Mental Maps* (Harmondsworth, 1974); and especially Yi-Fu Tuan, in *Topophilia: A Study of Environmental Perception, Attitudes, and Values* (Englewood Cliffs, NJ, 1974), *Space and Place: The Perspective of Experience* (Minneapolis, 1977), and elsewhere. Other scholars focus on the social and intellectual construction of specific regions; recent exciting studies include

Annette Kolodny, *The Land Before Her: Fantasy and Experience of the American Frontier, 1630–1860* (Chapel Hill, NC, 1984); Richard Gray, *Writing the South: Ideas of an American Region* (Cambridge, 1986); Robert Lawson-Peebles, *Landscape and Written Expression in Revolutionary America: The World Turned Upside Down* (Cambridge, 1988); Catherine P. and John A. Silk, 'Racism, Nationalism and the Creation of a Regional Myth: The Southern States after the American Civil War', in *Geography, The Media and Popular Culture*, eds Jacquelin Burgess and John R. Gold (London, 1985), pp. 165–91; and Richard Slotkin, *The Fatal Environment: The Myth of the Frontier in the Age of Industrialization, 1800–1890* (New York, 1985).

The arts are treated from regional and national perspectives in Charles C. Alexander, *Here the Country Lies: Nationalism and the Arts in the Twentieth Century* (Bloomington, IN, 1980) and Jay Appleton, *The Symbolism of Habitat: An Interpretation of Landscape in the Arts* (Seattle, 1991). Regionalist approaches to some of these cultural fields include David DeLong et al. (eds), *American Architecture: Innovation and Tradition* (New York, 1986); Dell Upton (ed.), *America's Architectural Roots: Ethnic Groups that Built America* (Washington DC, 1986); John Szarkowski, *American Landscapes* (New York, 1981), on landscape photography; Weston Naef and James N. Wood, *Era of Exploration: The Rise of Landscape Photography in the American West* (New York, 1975); Mick Gidley and Robert Lawson-Peebles (eds), *Views of American Landscapes* (Cambridge, 1989); Maren Stange, *Symbols of Ideal Life: Social Documentary Photography in America, 1890–1950* (Cambridge, 1989); William Stott, *Documentary Expression and Thirties America*, rev. edn (Chicago, 1986); George O. Carney (ed.), *The Sounds of People and Places: Readings in the Geography of American Folk and Popular Music* (Lanham, MD, 1987); William Gerdts, *Art Across America* (New York, 1990); Mary Scholz Guedon, *Regionalist Art: Thomas Hart Benton, John Steuart Curry, and Grant Wood: A Guide to the Literature* (Metuchen, NJ, 1982); and Cecile Whiting, 'American Heroes and Invading Barbarians: The Regionalist Response to Fascism', *Prospects* XIII (1988): 295–324, an argument further developed in her *Antifascism in American Art* (New Haven, CT, 1989).

Interesting writings referred to briefly in the text – and recovered for literature – include Nannie T. Alderson and Helena Huntington Smith, *A Bride Goes West* (1942; Lincoln, NE, 1969), and Elinore Pruitt Stewart, *Letters of a Woman Homesteader* (1914; Lincoln, NE, 1961); Amelia Stewart Knight and Catherine Haun, the nineteenth-century figures, are published in Lillian Schlissel, *Women's Diaries of the Westward Journey* (New York, 1982). Regionalist expression in literature is surveyed in Leonard Lutwack, *The Role of Place in Literature* (Syracuse, NY, 1984), and William E. Mallory and Paul Simpson-Housley (eds), *Geography and Literature: A Meeting of the Disciplines* (Syracuse, NY, 1987). Feminist considerations of literary regionalism include Josephine Donovan, *New England Local Color Literature: A Women's Tradition* (New York, 1983); Leonore Hoffman and Deborah Rosenfelt (eds), *Teaching Women's Literature from a Regional Perspective* (New York, 1982); and Emily Toth (ed.), *Regionalism and the Female Imagination: A Collection of Essays* (New York, 1985). Specific regional literatures receive attention in Donovan, Gray, Kolodny and Slotkin, above, and in William Everson, *Archetype West: The Pacific Coast as a Literary Region* (Berkeley, 1976).

CHAPTER SIX
Race and Racism

George Lipsitz

RACE AS A CATEGORY OF DIFFERENCE

The image of America as an ideal community, as a 'shining city on a hill', has permeated American politics and culture for almost four hundred years. From John Winthrop in the seventeenth century to Ronald Reagan in the twentieth, leaders of state have grounded the state's identity and their own consequent authority in one central story, a story of colonists emigrating from Europe to the empty North American wilderness where courage and hard work enabled them to establish an egalitarian, prosperous and free republic.

There is a truth to that story, but it is not the whole truth. Not all of the nation's inhabitants or their forebears crossed the Atlantic to come to America. Some crossed the Pacific, some came involuntarily, others – such as Native Americans and the Spanish-speaking peoples of the Southwest – lost their lands to conquest. American Indians, African slaves, Chinese contract labourers and Mexican field-hands did not come to America; America came to them. It did not come lifting its 'lamp beside the golden door', as the poem on the Statue of Liberty proclaims, but rather with the brutality and sadism of genocide, slavery, exploitation and conquest. The 'empty' North American continent perceived by explorers had in fact been occupied by American Indians for some 20,000 years, and initially only their generosity and knowledge – of plants, foods, medicines and the like – allowed European settlers to survive in the unfamiliar terrain. For this kindness the Indians were repaid with relentless attacks that decimated their numbers and forced them to surrender their land. Slaves from Africa did much of the hard work that built up the economic infrastructure of the United States, but the 'free republic' founded on its shores gave legal sanction to slavery while denying elementary human rights to those whose labour literally built the country.

Herman Melville's observation in *Redburn* (1849) that 'you cannot spill a drop of American blood without spilling the blood of the whole world' dramatically underscores both the central triumph and the central tragedy of the American experience.[1] The definitive social, cultural, and political institutions of the United States owe much to the origins of the American people in nations around the globe and to the resources brought to North America by them. Yet ethnic and racial diversity in the United States has also produced a bitter history of oppression and exploitation, of hatred and discrimination, not only among rival groups of immigrants from Europe, but also between those immigrants and the people of colour whose ancestors came to America from Asia, Africa and South America. We might well wonder how and why this happened.

It is now generally understood that 'race' is a concept with absolutely no scientific or anthropological validity, but it is a powerful 'social fact' nonetheless. What are perceived as racial characteristics – and certainly any assumptions of superiority or inferiority supposedly based upon them: the heart of racism – are not natural givens but historically constructed entities which emerged as a result of economic, political and other factors. Racism has not simply come to people at birth, with their skin colour, so to speak, but has been forged – and often refashioned – by varying circumstances. Racism is more than a matter of personal prejudice; it is culturally derived. Perceptions of racial differences, ethnic rivalries and social stratifications based on apparent racial and ethnic differences appear virtually everywhere in the world; in Europe during the twentieth century, to give an obvious example, extreme nationalisms, such as German Nazism, featured elaborate racist doctrines and murderous practices. In North America they have continually taken a particularly vicious form.

These ideologies of white supremacy served to justify and excuse the genocide, conquest and enslavement of people of colour by Euro-Americans in the early years of settlement, and have worked to perpetuate all kinds of discrimination ever since. Racism in America has not been, though, just a retention of the early experiences of settlement (described in more detail below); it has also been a recurrent creation generated anew, especially in moments of crisis, to perpetuate a broad range of privileges and to undermine efforts at egalitarian reform. It has been both an ideology and a system of control affecting the distribution of material resources, political power and basic human rights. It has been used, especially since the rise of 'scientific racism' (see Chapter 7) – which was also used to justify British and other European imperialisms, the taking up of the so-called 'white man's burden' – systematically to channel benefits to 'white'

121

Euro-Americans while relegating people of colour to positions as second-class citizens, super-exploited workers, and symbols of cultural degradation. Some of the changing ideological complexities of this disturbing phenomenon have been explored at greater length than is possible here, in such works as Thomas F. Gossett's *Race: The History of an Idea in America* (1963).

In America race has been a category with legal, economic and social ramifications. Racially based chattel slavery preceded the American republic and remained a part of it until after the conclusion of the Civil War in 1865. A century later, the 1964 Civil Rights Act finally ended legally mandated segregation between whites and blacks in public accommodations and the 1965 Voting Rights Act terminated policies designed to prevent blacks from voting. But at various times in history, state and federal laws have denied citizenship to 'non-whites', have forbidden inter-racial marriages, imposed special conditions on migrants from non-white countries and have issued a variety of other edicts and regulations that have employed race as a means of distinguishing people from each other. American custom and law have generally assumed the existence of only two groups, blacks and whites, even though the existence of Native Americans, Asian-Americans and Mexican-Americans has often complicated that formula with members of all three of these groups being classified as either black or white under different circumstances. In addition, the tradition of 'hypo-descent' has mandated that people with any black blood in their lineage be considered 'black', although it is well known that extensive intermarriage and inter-racial sex have left only an indeterminate number of people with solely 'white' or 'black' ancestry.

The historical experience of racism alone belies the story of the United States as a shining city on a hill. Thomas Jefferson, the man who wrote the egalitarian phrases in the Declaration of Independence, owned slaves, and the political theorists like James Madison and Alexander Hamilton who crafted the Federalist Papers and the Constitution elevated the property rights of slave owners over the human rights of slaves. Even Abraham Lincoln, the martyred president who signed the Emancipation Proclamation, freed the slaves only as a last resort, and then only in those states in rebellion against the federal government. Rutherford B. Hayes won the presidency in 1877 by promising to betray the policies of Reconstruction. Racism has played a crucial role in so many of the essential decisions that have shaped and transformed American politics. As the twentieth-century African–American poet Langston Hughes explained, 'America never has been America to me.'

Yet, paradoxically enough, American culture has come closest to realizing its utopian aspirations when struggling against racism. Four hundred years of genocide, slavery, conquest and discrimination hardly present a noble example for the world, but four hundred years of struggle by oppressed groups provide ample grounds for inspiration and emulation. If the American Dream seems filled with pretence and self-deception at the centre, it nonetheless permeates the culture of opposition fashioned by black, red, yellow, brown and white enemies of racism. The unremitting and determined resistance to oppression by slaves and free blacks over centuries eventually led union army troops during the Civil War to march off to battle singing hymns comparing the radical abolitionist John Brown to Jesus Christ. Diverse currents of resistance to hierarchy and exploitation mobilized twentieth-century Americans to march behind Dr Martin Luther King, Jr in nonviolent confrontations that ended a century of segregation. By studying racism and anti-racism in the United States we encounter the worst and the best in American culture at the same time – the American Dream and the American Nightmare. There might be other aspects of American culture as important as racism, but surely, none is decidedly more important.

THE SUPPRESSION OF INDIANS AND THE INSTITUTION OF SLAVERY

Europeans often described their arrival in North America as a 'discovery', while in reality, of course, the land had been known and inhabited by its indigenous population for thousands of years. It was in fact an invasion and a conquest. The English colonists justified their conquest on grounds of self-defence, divine will and utility. Initially self-defence was hard to prove since it had not been the Indians who travelled thousands of miles to compete for British territory. But aggressive colonial settlement and intervention in Indian disputes soon led to conflicts in which European self-defence was no small consideration. Divine will emerged as an early justification for the British invasion of America because the colonists reasoned that their efforts would bring Christianity to an inferior civilization. Certain American Indian religious and social practices (including communal bathing, pre-marital and extra-marital sexual encounters and homosexuality) reinforced the British sense of moral superiority. But most important to the settlers was the justification provided by standards of utility; they saw Indian agriculture which produced little surplus wealth as 'unproductive', as squandering the resources of God's commonwealth. The British resolved to do better once they had taken control of Indian land, goods and trade routes.

In the first few years after the founding of Jamestown, Virginia in 1607 as the first permanent English settlement in North America, the colonists faced a severe challenge to their beliefs and to their very survival. They had secured a truce with the local Indians, equipped themselves with the latest European technology and firearms, and had access to the abundant game and fish in Virginia's woods and rivers. Yet they faced starvation as a very real possibility. Some resorted to cannibalism, digging up graves and eating the corpses. Others ran away to live with the Indians who provided the colony with its only adequate food supply. Those who settled in Jamestown aspired to wealth and to live like gentlemen, and arduous labour was not part of their plans. The colonists, relying on Indian supplies, even refused to plant their own corn, preferring instead to go bowling on the lawns at midday. In the summer of 1611, colonial officials dispatched an armed force to two Indian settlements to kill the inhabitants and burn their corn in response to the proud and disdainful answers given them by Chief Powhattan when they asked him for the return of runaway colonists who had taken refuge with the Indians. The next year, the colonial Governor meted out punishments to English colonists which ranged from hanging to burning at the stake to being broken upon wheels for the crime of running away to live with the Indians. Such experiences seriously undermined the arguments of self-defence, divine will and utility that legitimated the colonists' enterprise, but, since economic motives were actually uppermost, rather than rethink their assumptions they devised more elaborate schemes for profiting from the land and labour of the Indians.

In an attempt to make the colony productive for its investors colonial administrators encouraged the planting of tobacco. Colonists sought control over ever greater amounts of Indian land, thus touching off hostilities that wiped out one third of the white population but which took an even greater toll on the Indians. Only eleven of twenty-eight tribes present in Virginia in 1607 remained by 1669. Declining numbers of Indians encouraged the colonists to look to the importation of slaves from Africa and the Caribbean on an ever increasing scale as the solution to their labour problems, and growing class tensions among whites made permanent, hereditary, racially exclusive, chattel slavery an attractive system for the colony's élite. It was not until the 1670s that a series of legislative acts attempted to institutionalize racism in Virginia. Laws prevented blacks and Indians from owning 'Christian' servants but allowed 'thirty lashes on the bare back' as punishment 'if any negro or other slave shall presume to lift up his hand in opposition against any Christian'.[2] In 1705 the legislature authorized the dismemberment of unruly slaves and ordered that any property owned by slaves be given to poor whites. In 1691 new laws demanded banishment from the colony for any white man or woman who married a Negro, mulatto or Indian, and they similarly made it illegal for owners to free their own slaves unless they provided transportation for them out of the colony.

Origins are not destiny and American racism was hardly fixed by 1700. But this brief and undoubtedly oversimplified history of genocide and slavery in Virginia does show that the economic goals and social organization of European settlers laid the groundwork for the anti-Indian and anti-black racism that has played such a fundamental role in framing American identity. Appropriation of Indian land and Afro-American labour brought enormous material rewards to the wealthiest whites while reassuring the poorest that there would always be some level to which they could not fall, always someone worse off and less powerful. Malcolm X, the major black nationalist leader of the 1960s, used to tell a kind of parable to explain how a racist identity was constructed. He said that when immigrants arrived from Europe and learned their first word of English, that word was 'nigger', because it represented the first thing they needed to know about America and their place in it. On leaving Europe they may have been Irish or German or Italian, but on arriving in the United States they became something called 'white', which at the very least meant that they were not black, and therefore entitled to some privileges.

Once underway, the processes of genocide and slavery shaped the experiences and attitudes of individuals, grounding racism in micro-social practice as well as macro-social policy. How else can we explain the actions of the devout Christian slave-owners who brutalized slaves who showed any sign of resistance, or the behaviour of US army troops as they destroyed whole villages of Indians that posed no military threat to white soldiers or civilians? The forced removal of the Cherokee Indians in 1838 to lands west of the Mississippi River (in violation of a 1791 treaty) led to the deaths of 4,000 Cherokees and to an arduous forced march over thousands of miles for 8,000 survivors. Later in that century, US Army troops under the command of General O.O. Howard pursued and captured Chief Joseph and a small band of the peace-loving Nez Perce tribe as they tried to flee to Canada to escape yet another assault on their land. And in 1890 the Seventh Cavalry – which in 1876, when commanded by General George Armstrong Custer, had been badly defeated by a well-disciplined force of Sioux and Cheyenne under Crazy Horse and Sitting Bull – lost control and indiscriminately massacred men, women and children in the notorious incident at Wounded Knee, South Dakota.

Yet – thanks partly to heroic and determined resistance by people of colour – white attitudes and behaviour have not been monolithic. American culture contained, as we have seen, contradictory currents. As individuals some whites allied themselves with Indians and African-Americans, even at great personal risk. Not only the famous white abolitionists like Sarah and Angelina Grimké, John Brown, and William Lloyd Garrison, but in a few sporadic yet significant incidents whites joined Indian communities and even assisted in slave uprisings against local élites. In the years immediately after the Civil War during Reconstruction, Radical Republicans used the power of the state to secure the political and economic rights of blacks, initiating a decade of unprecedented inter-racial cooperation in the states of the Old Confederacy. But just as anti-racist resistance could interrupt the trajectory of white supremacy, white racist responses could wipe away the gains made in periods of progress. After the Compromise of 1877 which returned control of political power in the Southern states to the élites that had dominated the Confederacy, legally mandated segregation separated the races anew, launching an era of debt peonage sharecropping and the 'Jim Crow' system of racial segregation that remained in force for almost a century. Racial violence, such as lynchings by the Ku Klux Klan and other vigilante groups, emerged as a frequent instrument of terror against minority communities seeking to advance their interests, while literacy tests, poll taxes and outright intimidation prevented most black citizens from voting. Even within the modernizing industrial economy, black people served as super-exploited workers, receiving lower pay and less job security than other labourers.

THE HERITAGE OF RACISM

This racism was not simply a matter of black and white. White supremacy as a system trained its adherents to hate Mexican-Americans and Asian-Americans as well. At the conclusion of the Mexican War, the Treaty of Guadalupe-Hidalgo (1848) promised equal rights and respect for the Spanish-speaking inhabitants of the conquered territories, but white Americans never honoured that clause of the treaty. Mexican-Americans lost property, power and position as Anglo administrators assumed control over what had previously been Mexican territory, and it has been estimated that the number of Mexican-Americans killed in racially motivated violence in the American Southwest between 1850 and 1930 was even greater than the number of lynchings of black Americans during the same period. Similarly, the completion of the transcontinental railway system encouraged the importation of Chinese and Japanese labourers to California in the nineteenth century, but state and federal laws denied these immigrants citizenship and served to sanction employer exploitation. White vigilante violence provided another means of controlling these Asian-American immigrants, as sporadic armed attacks on Chinese and Japanese neighbourhoods and households went unpunished by the legally constituted authorities.

The multi-racial character of the United States has been marked by both proud accomplishments and disgraceful acts. Through relentless political struggle and a bloody Civil War, as we saw in Chapter 3, Americans eventually abolished slavery and guaranteed all citizens equal protection under the law with the passage of the 13th and 14th amendments to the Constitution in the late 1860s. One hundred years later, a broad-based civil rights movement secured legislation, presidential executive orders, and judicial decisions which ended *de jure* racial segregation of public facilities, which banned legal barriers against voting by people of colour, and which offered limited redress for past discrimination in education, housing and employment. The birthdays of Abraham Lincoln and Martin Luther King, Jr have legal status as national holidays, and the number of black elected officials in the country has gone from less than 500 in 1965 to more than 7,000 in 1990.

Yet for all of this legacy of ferment and change, racism remains a pervasive and poisonous element in the American political and economic systems. After the mass insurgencies of the 1960s, the melioristic gains of the Civil Rights movement immediately produced a 'white backlash' that severely limited effective implementation of abstract rights affirmed in law. School districts resisted desegregation purportedly in the name of defending 'neighbourhood schools' from having to share their facilities with deprived students from other neighbourhoods, while employers used secret and discriminatory hiring procedures to avoid implementing the fair hiring practices mandated by the 1964 Civil Rights Act. These acts of resistance led federal judges to order 'bussing' (sending children from all-black inner-city neighbourhoods to predominantly white schools) for school desegregation and to mandate 'affirmative action' programmes requiring employers to follow policies designed to guarantee fair access to employment for members of groups previously suffering from discrimination. But neo-conservative political mobilizations denounced these policies as 'judicial activism' and 'reverse racism', claiming that the 1964 Civil Rights Act itself made it illegal for government to use race as the basis for policy decisions and that bussing and affirmative action amounted to racism against whites because they gave benefits expressly to blacks and other aggrieved groups (see also Chapter 7). In addition, major changes in federal taxation and spending programmes after 1969 undermined the few programmes that had been successful in securing increased opportunities for people of colour. At the same time, changes in immigration policy after 1965 had the unintended effect of greatly increasing immigration from Asia, Africa and Latin America which added new dimensions to America's racial make-up and led some to predict that 'whites' would be a numerical minority by the mid-twenty-first century.

The restructuring of the American economy in the 1970s and 1980s into a post-industrial service- and research-oriented structure impacted most heavily on racial minorities, and the rise of a concomitant neo-conservative political ideology further limited the role of the state in redressing historic grievances. By the 1980s, the once narrowing gap between black and white income and schooling began to widen again, so much so that scholars have estimated that it could take at least another hundred years before economic equality is achieved. Although blacks held a greater number of elected offices than ever before, vested interests continued to deny them access to power proportionate to their numbers. In seven Southern states, for instance, black people make up more than 25 per cent of the population but hold only 5.6 per cent of elective offices. In addition, the changing role of the state and recurring budget crises caused by tax policies designed to help affluent property-owners have constrained the ability of elected officials to respond to the social and economic problems of their constituents. Racial violence flared anew on city streets and college campuses, and black leaders warned that the nation was on the verge of reversing most of the progress made over the past fifty years.

Anti-racist and feminist critiques of American culture have brought sharp new directions to American Studies in the 1970s and 1980s. They helped show how seemingly commonplace and ordinary cultural practices might encode larger meanings, and they underscored how narrowly scholars of American culture in the past had defined their tasks. In popular literature and in university curricula, a profound re-examination of American culture has underlined the racially and ethnically mixed heritage of American culture and expression. At the same time, an extraordinary political and cultural mobilization by neo-conservatives in government, the media and in business has attempted to reaffirm the importance of a unified and unifying centre for American politics and culture – usually that evoked at the beginning of this chapter. On the terrain of public policy, they argued that government had to be 'colour blind' and therefore cease affirmative action programmes designed to remedy the legacy of historical discrimination against minority groups and women. In educational matters they attacked expanded school curricula that emphasized American racial diversity past and present, and argued instead for a core curriculum made up of the 'best that has been thought and said' in the western tradition. Often deriding women's studies and ethnic studies as 'oppression studies', the neo-conservatives charged that fragmenting the curriculum only encouraged racial and gender divisions, blocking access to the mainstream for the very constituencies that ethnic studies and women's studies purported to represent. In major public controversies over federally funded research and artistic production, in best-selling books by academic authors, and in bitter fights over curriculum on university campuses, the methods and rationales for studying American culture remain hotly contested.

RACIST IDEAS AND THE REPRESENTATION OF MINORITIES AS OTHERS

In Ralph Ellison's great novel *Invisible Man* (1952), the narrator goes to work for a firm that manufactures white paint for flagpoles, the Liberty Paint Company. He learns that in order to make white paint they must insert a drop of black into the solution. The black is never seen, but it plays an essential role in constructing what people see as 'white'. Like many of Ellison's stories, this incident serves to illustrate the erasure of black identity from American culture. Because white racism systematically prevents black people from representing themselves and their own interests, Ellison organized his critique around the theme of black invisibility.

In another sense, however, certain images of blackness have been all too visible within American culture. One might surmise that the logic of white racism would make white people want to avoid or ignore blacks, and certainly centuries of *de facto* and *de jure* segregation demonstrate an antipathy to face-to-face contact. Yet degraded images of blacks have been pervasive in white culture. Depictions and portrayals of black people as primitive, superstitious, childlike, licentious, cowardly and gluttonous have long been staples in American art, music and literature, while marketing personnel and advertisers have repeatedly adorned products with stereotypical images of servile smiling black men, women and children. For a white American society riddled with divisions caused by ethnic, class and regional antagonisms, degraded images of blacks have served a unifying function, smoothing over other differences and uniting a diverse polity around the fiction of whiteness. Just as the Liberty Paint Company needed that drop of black paint to manufacture 'whiteness', America's white supremacists have harped on black identity as a negative example against which white identity might be manufactured.

The American obsession with race has permeated all forms of cultural expression. It has given rise to a powerful symbolic apparatus designed to legitimate racial hierarchies at odds with the egalitarian rhetoric in much of the rest of American life. Very often this symbolic apparatus has sanctioned the projection on to aggrieved populations of the critique that might otherwise be directed at their conquerors. Thus the white Euro-Americans who systematically violated their treaties with Indians in order to take their land developed a stereotype of the Native American as untrustworthy, as an 'Indian giver'. The folklore scholar Americo Paredes has pointed out that white Southerners portrayed black males as sex fiends when in fact it was white male slave-owners who routinely took slave women as concubines. Similarly, the Anglo-Americans who crossed into Texas illegally to steal lands owned by Mexican citizens later justified their actions by deriding Mexican-Americans as horse thieves and as illegal aliens.

Although minstrel shows predated the Civil War, they became the dominant form of popular entertainment during the age of industrialization in the second half of the nineteenth century. They featured large casts of actors, singers, dancers and comedians – generally white men wearing burnt cork so that they would appear black (or as a caricature of blackness). At a time when industrial time-work discipline revolutionized American culture and forced an entire generation of workers to adjust to the demands of discipline, thrift, sobriety and abstinence, the minstrel show presented all that had to be repressed – laziness, desire, gluttony and licentiousness – as the characteristic qualities of blacks. Thus white audiences learned to ridicule in the 'stage Negro' what they feared most in themselves. Anti-capitalist and anti-industrial impulses became taboo through their association with the despised culture of Afro-Americans. Yet as historian Nathan Irvin Huggins has observed, audiences received a vicarious thrill from these representations of rule-breaking; they returned again and again to witness on stage what they denied themselves in life. So effective were these images that it became increasingly dangerous for the African-American to 'step out of character' either on or off stage. The erasure of Afro-American identity was so complete that when the black entertainer Bert Williams began to attract a following among white audiences in the early years of the twentieth century he had to make up his face with burnt cork to simulate the minstrel mask, to become a black man imitating white men who were imitating black men.

In the twentieth century, cinema established itself as a commercial force in the United States with the popularity of D.W. Griffith's cinematically innovative but vicious *The Birth of a Nation* (1915). The first full-length film to reach a large middle-class audience, *The Birth of a Nation* constructed its audience around the unifying force of white racism. It romanticized and praised the Ku Klux Klan and echoed the conventional historical wisdom of its day by idealizing the slave South and ridiculing Reconstruction. Griffith harnessed the persuasive powers of the medium to reinforce fantasies of a white race under attack by ignorant blacks and their corrupt allies. Completely inaccurate in its historical narrative and so filled with racism that it presented white actors covered with black shoe polish in the putatively African-American roles, *The Birth of a Nation* nonetheless garnered enormous political and critical success. It ran as a first-run feature in Atlanta motion picture theatres for almost ten years, and President Woodrow Wilson lauded it as a kind of history written by lightning. Griffith's success with *The Birth of a Nation* helped legitimate the increasingly segregationist practices of the federal government as well as the 1920s revival of the Ku Klux Klan all across the nation. But it also solidified a pattern within American popular culture, inscribing the basic oppositions of the minstrel show into the emerging forms of electronic mass media.

In popular music, despite the key contributions of black creators, it was white artists who received a grossly disproportionate share of the rewards. The sales of records by black female blues singers, including Bessie Smith, proved the very viability of phonograph records as a commercial product, but her income did not reflect the fact. King Oliver and other black musicians in New Orleans, Chicago and New York started the 'jazz age' celebrated in the writings of F. Scott Fitzgerald, but white artists dominated the radio, recording and live performance sectors of the music industry. Black musicians Louis Armstrong and Fletcher Henderson articulated the basic elements of Dixieland Jazz in the 1920s and swing in the 1930s, but to the public it was white band leader Paul Whiteman who became known as the 'King of Jazz' and the white clarinetist and band leader Benny Goodman who became the 'King of Swing'. The Duke Ellington and Count Basie orchestras attracted a huge black and white following through their radio broadcasts in the 1920s and 1930s and Benny Goodman desegregated the big bands in the 1930s when he hired Teddy Wilson and Billie Holiday, but black musicians never received rewards commensurate with their contributions. One motivation for jazz musicians to turn to bop music in the 1940s was to create a music that would not be appropriated by whites in the industry. In the 1950s Chuck Berry and Little Richard pioneered the development of rock'n'roll, but radio censorship and industry marketing decisions made the white Southerner Elvis Presley the artist presented most accessibly to the public as a rock'n'roll singer. Indeed, the association between rock'n'roll and black artists in the minds of moralists, politicians and business executives led to efforts to censor and repress the entire genre.

Just as images of blacks shaped the determinate contours of the minstrel show, the motion picture and recorded popular music in the United States, they influenced the content of commercial radio as well. The first successful American network radio programme, *Amos'n'Andy*, was a show created and performed by white Southerners pretending to be black. They invoked minstrel-show stereotypes, presenting blacks as lazy and licentious, childlike and cowardly. Despite vehement protests by African-American intellectuals and Civil Rights organizations, *Amos'n'Andy* remained the most popular programme on radio for almost thirty years. It later became one of the first shows placed on commercial network television in the 1950s, garnering a huge audience until protests finally succeeded in getting advertisers and networks to remove the show from production in 1954 and from syndication as reruns in 1966.

Within popular culture racist images of blacks have served to define but not exhaust the process of stereotyping. In theatrical melodramas and Hollywood films, in popular music and on radio or television programmes, Americans have been presented with an almost endless inventory of ethnic slurs. Hollywood presented the genocide of aboriginal peoples as a heroic saga, relegating Indians to roles as either bloodthirsty savages or collaborators with the Euro-American conquest. Every generation since the turn of the century has seen its film about the Battle of the Alamo during the war for Texan independence, and while the particular details changed, the villainy of Mexicans and the virtue of Americans remained a constant in these productions. Asian-American men have seen themselves represented on the screen largely as faithful servants or cunning criminals, while Asian-American females have been portrayed incessantly as exotic objects of white male desire.

Perhaps nothing better epitomizes the way in which racial hostilities have become naturalized in America than an anecdote about the childhoods of two professional baseball players, Kirby Higbe and Satchell Paige. Higbe, a hard-throwing National League pitcher in the 1940s, once explained to reporters that he had developed his powerful arm as a child when he joined other white boys throwing rocks at Negroes. Satchell Paige, a great black pitcher of the same era, attributed *his* skill to childhood days throwing rocks at white boys. Race hatred takes many forms, and in the American context a little stone throwing between boys represents one of the milder and more harmless manifestations of it. But there is something about the seemingly organic and unimpassioned nature of these accounts, their matter-of-fact meanness, that speaks volumes about the breadth and depth of American racial antagonisms, about the heritage of racist ideas, and about the representation of racial minorities as 'others'.

BLACK ASSERTIONS OF IDENTITY

In his 1987 book *Going to the Territory*, Ellison observed that it would be impossible to imagine American culture devoid of the elements brought to it by black people, and one could certainly amend his point by adding to it the contributions by American Indians, Mexican-Americans and Asian-Americans. In the economic and political spheres blacks in America have faced the dilemma encapsulated by historian Eugene Genovese in the questions 'How do you integrate into a country that does not want you? How do you separate from a country that finds it too profitable to let you go?'[3] There are of course many and varied answers to those questions, but one is to claim a place as a legitimate part of the country by articulating one's experience through forms of expressive culture. As jazz critic Albert Murray explains with elegant precision

> Identity is best defined in terms of culture, and the culture of the nation over which the white Anglo-Saxon power elite exercises such exclusive political, economic, and social control is not all-white by any measurement ever devised. American culture, even in its most rigidly segregated precincts, is patently and irrevocably composite. It is, regardless of all the hysterical protestations of those who would have it otherwise, incontestably mulatto.[4]

Yet that 'incontestably mulatto' culture could be forged only through struggle, through the dogged determination by people of colour to be seen and heard and read.

The jazz trumpet player Louis Armstrong used to have a stock answer ready whenever people asked him how things were going. 'White folks still ahead', Armstrong would reply, neatly conflating his own feelings with the social totality. His statement implied that as long as white folks remained ahead in his world, all else would remain epiphenomena. Similarly, in a passage in her moving novel *Ceremony* (1977), Native American author Leslie Marmon Silko relates that American Indians wake up every day to view the land that has been stolen from them. Thus for Silko and for other Indians, the Euro-American conquest is not just something that happened centuries ago; in a certain way it takes place over and over again every day, every time they open their eyes. Yet for all of the suffocating power of white racism, people of colour have nonetheless insisted on speaking out, on making their views known. One source of the sense of entitlement behind such articulations has been the legacy of struggle, the situated knowledge that comes from resistance to oppression.

From the moment of arrival on the North American continent, Africans learned that they would be forbidden to speak their native languages or to practise their traditional religions. In the slave South and in many parts of the North, official statutes made it illegal to teach slaves to read or write, and of course the shackles and chains of slavery prevented African-Americans from the freedom to travel or to congregate in groups. Yet all of these limitations only forced African-Americans to develop a culture of resistance in whatever arenas and cultural forms remained open to them. African languages survived within the speech of slaves and their descendants; slaves known to their masters as 'Joe' thought of themselves as 'Cujo', and a century later jazz musicians might describe one another as 'hip cats', a phrase derived from the Wolof word 'hipicat' – meaning one who has his eyes open. Slaves perpetuated African religious practices during secret night meetings on their plantations, and they brought a decidedly African accent to Christian theology after their masters implemented a policy of coerced conversion. More important, slaves translated the language of deliverance in the Bible into metaphors for resistance to slavery. When their prayers and songs mentioned 'crossing the River Jordan' they often meant escaping to freedom, not going to heaven. Slave-owners may have been reassured by the piety of slaves singing the spiritual 'Steal Away to Jesus', but to the slaves this song often signalled an opportunity to run away.

African cultural practices in the American setting served important political functions. Slaves buried their dead facing the east, facing Africa, to remind them of the continent they had left behind. As long as memories of Africa survived, however tenuously, American servitude could be imagined as provisional and contingent rather than eternal. Secret Africanisms in slave speech and music supported a covert communications network to bolster sagging spirits and to pass along messages about resistance, rebellion and flight. When hundreds of years of slave resistance culminated in the crisis of the 1860s and, specifically, the Emancipation Proclamation, these sedimented communications networks proved extremely effective. Scattered in groups of ten or fifteen on thousands of plantations, forbidden by law to read, write, congregate or travel, slaves nonetheless staged a general strike in the fields that seriously undermined the Southern economy and 200,000 of them ran away to the North and joined the Union army. Their mechanisms of resistance remained hidden, but when the opportunity presented itself they proved themselves capable of extraordinary coordination and unified mobilization.

But African-American culture has not only been important to black people. It has also been a great gift to the society that has so often tried to ridicule and reject it. Music, of course, as Chapter 11 underlines, has been the medium in American culture where African sensibilities have been most prominently displayed. The blues, jazz, and rock'n'roll all build their affects around musical figures of distinctly African origin. Nevertheless, mainstream acknowledgement of the African origins of most American popular music has been given only grudgingly. Throughout the nation's history, white musicians have reaped great rewards by presenting music they copied from black artists as their own. Black music's functional integration with dance and its appeal to the emotions has posed problems for the guardians and gatekeepers of American culture, but watered-down renditions of black music have usually been acceptable. From the compositions of Stephen Foster that romanticized the antebellum South, to the minstrel-show 'coon' songs that ridiculed the bodily habits and desires of 'darkies', American popular music has relied on both appropriation and exploitation of African-American culture. Yet this sad history should not obscure the magnificent creativity of black artists in every genre in fashioning musics that could find their way to larger audiences.

Although music is the form where African contributions to American culture reveal themselves most directly, black artists have drawn on collective memory and sedimented traditions in a wide range of endeavours. Even though racism largely excluded blacks from the conservatories and galleries, visual artists Romare Bearden, Lois Mailou Jones and Jacob Lawrence found ways to present their paintings to appreciative audiences (see Chapter 13). Hollywood hired its first black director – the photographer and writer Gordon Parks – only in the late 1960s, but independent black film makers, including Oscar Micheaux, made motion pictures for black audiences as early as the 1920s. Students of American dance know the contributions to that art fashioned by Alvin Ailey, Katharine Dunham and a legion of popular dancers, such as Bill 'Bojangles' Robinson (see Chapter 12).

Blacks have also made notable contributions to American writing. At the transition between the colonial to the early national period in American history, Phillis Wheatley – who was only fourteen years old when she published her first poem – emerged in her *Poems of Various Subjects, Religious and Moral* (1773) as one of the earliest poets of the new Republic. She paid tribute to the emancipatory powers of imagination in her verse, only to confront critics who accused her of plagiarism because they could not imagine an African-American woman capable of mastering such a cerebral activity as poetry. She and other less privileged black artists who had to communicate by more indirect means found that the obstacles in their paths only reinforced the conviction voiced so forcefully by such contemporary black poets as Audre Lord and Maya Angelou that for subjugated peoples 'poetry is not a luxury'.

A particularly rich strain of African-American art in American culture comes from the first-person narrative and autobiography. In the nineteenth century narratives by former slaves made up a significant genre in popular literature and they expressed important themes from within African-American culture. First-person narratives brought the experiences and interpretations of Sojourner Truth and Frederick Douglass into the mainstream of American politics, and they served as effective encapsulations of complex social problems. The narratives of Mary Prince, William Wells Brown, Harriet Jacobs and Solomon Northup, among others, personalized the injustice and inhumanity of the slave system for a broad popular audience, while at the same time evidencing a form of self-presentation that would have enormous influence on the rest of American literature. The autobiographical presentation of self as a strategy for illumining collective social problems permeates twentieth-century African-American writing, most notably that of James Weldon Johnson, Richard Wright, Zora Neale Hurston, Chester Himes, Ralph Ellison, Malcolm X, Maya Angelou and Alice Walker.

Yet to talk about African-American writing separate from other forms of cultural expression misrepresents the guiding aesthetic behind black literature. Popular speech informs the poetry of Paul Laurence Dunbar and Langston Hughes, while blues and jazz influences pervade the writing of Ellison and Ishmael Reed (see Chapter 14). Toni Morrison's magnificent novels carry this inter-textuality and inter-referentiality to extraordinary heights, writing the history of an entire community through its stories and songs, through its rhymes and remedies. Conversely, black artists in other genres like rap music collapse the boundaries separating music from writing or the visual arts as they draw upon influences ranging from political figures like Malcolm X and Angela Davis, writer-musicians like Gil Scott-Heron, and anonymous graffiti writers, break dancers and fashion designers. The divisions made between art and life and between artistic genres themselves in most post-Renaissance European and Euro-American criticism break down when confronted with the powerful collective memory and mutuality of African-American culture. This blending of forms and crossing of genre boundaries has been characteristic of black dance, music, literature and visual art. It has not only added something of great value to the inventory of American expressive culture, it has also served as a model for artists from other groups interested in challenging the limits of the Euro-American cultural tradition.

RELATIONSHIPS TO OTHER CATEGORIES OF DIFFERENCE

In *No-No Boy* (1976), an impassioned novel (originally published in 1957) about a Japanese–American war resister set shortly after the Second World War, author John Okada has his narrator ruminate on race relations in America. Realizing that everyone he knows feels marginalized in some way, he wonders if there is a centre after all, if maybe the marginal experience is not the modal experience and if the outside is not already the inside. By thinking about the 'minority' experience as perhaps representative of some larger truths about the United States, Okada raised a theme that resonated powerfully for some people of colour in the postwar years. Ellison concluded *Invisible Man* by suggesting to readers that the alienation and anxiety of his African-American protagonist might 'speak for you'. Martin Luther King enlisted Americans in the Civil Rights movement not merely to win rights for black people but to redeem the soul of America by demanding that the nation's practices live up to its promises.

The renewed attention to race generated by the Civil Rights movement and by its attendant cultural expressions played a crucial role in promoting more generalized critiques of American culture and society. Certainly the student protests, anti-war demonstrations and the women's liberation movement owed much to the models of criticism and organization provided by civil rights activists. But while part of a more general social critique about hierarchy, stratification and class, the Civil Rights movement also led to an intensification of identification with race in American society. Mobilization for civil rights coupled with white resistance led to an upsurge in black nationalism during the 1960s, and the example of the Civil Rights movement mobilized Asian-Americans, Mexican-Americans and Native Americans to address long-standing grievances of their own. In some ways the protest movements of the 1960s brought about unprecedented alliances and interactions across racial barriers, but the urban riots of the mid-1960s and the ensuing 'white backlash' also led to intensified polarization of the races. In that era, American culture confronted realities that were as old as European settlement on the continent, but that very confrontation also helped to create a fundamentally new situation within American expressive culture.

For most of American history, people of colour have endeavoured to represent themselves through their own words, images and voices while at the same time struggling to displace the representations of themselves fashioned by others. Even sympathetic whites have often thought of minority communities as mere symbols of broader problems rather than as social actors with their own interests and concerns. As a result of the Black Power and Civil Rights movements of the 1960s, some artists struggled to move beyond simple integration and separatism, and instead to explore forms of cultural expression that allowed them to assert their differences from others without surrendering access to full participation in a larger political and cultural life. In recent years new strategies have emerged in response to a gnawing suspicion that the old battles for autonomy and/or inclusion do not go far enough in challenging the core assumptions behind racist thinking: the contradictory mindset that either denies 'difference' and the accumulated legacy of injustice caused by racism, or else resorts to an 'essentialism' that, as was indicated at the outset of this chapter, asserts the inevitability of division because of putative cultural and/or biological differences between the races.

In the past, minority artists have often felt compelled to represent their communities as more unified and monolithic than their experiences warranted, if for no other reason than to mount a common front against outside hostility. In recent years, however, these traditional representations of race and ethnicity have come under attack especially by women of colour who have complained that existing categories of ethnic identity in America do too little to represent their experiences and aspirations. In the 1960s, the important roles played by black women within the Civil Rights movement made them and their white allies more sensitive to the injustices of sexism, and the increase in female-headed households throughout the postwar period has been an important factor in a generalized increase in feminist consciousness. Feminists of colour have attacked expressions of racial pride which elide gender, which present the community as male, and which measure equality only by the relative status of men of colour in regard to white men. They have pointed out the authoritarian and patriarchal assumptions behind many of the stories structured to signify ethnic identity, asserting that these stories expect them to deny their gender interests in the very act of affirming their racial pride.

Starting in the 1970s a series of extraordinary writings by women of colour problematized the relationship between gender and ethnicity in important new ways. Writers including Asian-Americans Maxine Hong Kingston and Amy Tan, Mexican-Americans Sandra Cisneros and Cherrie Moraga, African-Americans Alice Walker, Toni Cade Bambara and Toni Morrison, and Native Americans Leslie Marmon Silko and Louise Erdrich write about ethnic and racial identity as constructed, contested and composite. Writing about women on the margins suffering the double oppressions of ethnicity and gender, they show how race can be everything and nothing at the same time, how ethnic identity can be surprising and confusing to members of minority communities. Most important, they brought a feminist critique to traditional definitions of their communities and used it to explore the constructed nature of social experience, the creative and active work of ethnic memory, and the ultimate constraints of any essentialist definition of ethnicity or gender. While their writings all clearly challenged racism, instead of simply calling for integration of ethnic minorities into the mainstream of American life these writers demanded equal rights while still celebrating diversity and calling attention to the unique insights and cultural creations fashioned by people who might appear to be outsiders. In addition, they asserted that the 'doubled vision' of those who suffered from oppression by race and gender might provide the basis for a thoroughgoing critique of all hierarchy and exploitation.

In Toni Morrison's novel *Beloved* (1987), she recounts the experiences of newly freed slaves in the mid-nineteenth century. Her focus is on one household and the logic that drove a woman to murder her daughter rather than have her returned to life as a slave. In this book, Morrison attempts to represent the unrepresentable, to bring to the surface the suppressed memories of an American holocaust that previous accounts have been unable to articulate. Morrison's sources of inspiration and enlightenment come from deep rivers of African-American counter-memory as well as from the most contemporary cultural experiments with form that so effectively destabilize history and place. Her work is both emphatically specific to the experience and history of black people, and infinitely generalizable to questions about identity and desire that transcend cultural boundaries. The exhilarating emancipatory potential and the paralysing horror of her book both stem from the same contradictory source – the realities of racism and resistance in post-industrial America.

The novelist John Oliver Killens used to tell an anecdote about a discussion between a father and son concerning the bedtime stories about the jungle that they read together every night. The boy asked his father why it was that the lion was supposed to be the king of the jungle but it was the man who always came out on top in the stories. 'Well, it's going to be that way son,' the father replied, 'until the lion learns to write.' In the 1990s, we know that the lion has learned to write. In fact we are discovering that the lion always knew how to write. It is just that too many of us, too much of the time, have not been adept enough at deciphering lion language.

NOTES

1. Herman Melville, *Redburn: His First Voyage* (Boston, 1924), p. 169.

2. Quoted in Edmund S. Morgan, *American Slavery, American Freedom* (New York and London, 1975), p. 331.

3. Eugene Genovese, *In Red and Black: Marxian Explorations in Southern and Afro-American History* (New York, 1968), p. 144.

4.   Albert Murray, *The Omni-Americans* (New York, 1983), p. 22.

SUGGESTIONS FOR FURTHER READING

Scholarship on race and racism in the United States encompasses many different approaches and methods. Important interpretive works that provide an overview of the problem include Alexander Saxton, *The Rise and Fall of the White Republic* (New York and London, 1991), John Hope Franklin, *From Slavery to Freedom* (New York, 1988), Michael Rogin, *Fathers and Children: Andrew Jackson and the Subjugation of the American Indian* (New York, 1975), Rudolfo Acuna, *Occupied America* (New York, 1972), Sucheng Chan, *Asian Americans* (Boston, MA, 1991), Thomas F. Gossett, *Race: The History of an Idea in America* (New York, 1965), Winthrop Jordan, *White over Black* (Harmondsworth, 1969), Gary Nash, *Red, White, and Black* (Englewood Cliffs, NJ, 1974), and the studies by Morgan and Genovese cited in the Notes.

Historians have made particularly important contributions in the study of black–white relations. Written more than fifty years ago, W.E.B. Du Bois, *Black Reconstruction in America* (New York, 1970) remains a magnificent introduction to the interplay of race, class and politics in industrializing America, and Eric Foner's *Reconstruction* (New York, 1988) succeeds in part because it so skilfully picks up on suggestions advanced by Du Bois. Slave life and culture have been illuminated by George Rawick in *From Sundown to Sunup* (Westport, CT, 1972), which examined slave life from the perspective of workers' self-activity, and by Sterling Stuckey who uses a nationalist frame in his excellent *Slave Culture* (New York, 1987). Important studies of specific topics include Genovese, *Roll, Jordan Roll* (New York, 1974), which presents a detailed description and analysis of the role of white paternalism and black covert resistance under slavery, and Joel Williamson, *The Crucible of Race* (New York, 1984), and George Fredrickson, *The Arrogance of Race* (Middletown, CT, 1988), explore race as an intellectual and social category, as does Nathan Irvin Huggins in his very important *Harlem Renaissance* (New York, 1971). Radical politics and cultures of resistance among twentieth-century blacks provide the focus for Robin Kelley, *Hammer and Hoe* (Chapel Hill, NC, 1990), and George Lipsitz, *A Life in the Struggle: Ivory Perry and the Culture of Opposition* (Philadelphia, 1988).

Sociological studies include Stephen Steinberg, *The Ethnic Myth* (Boston, MA, 1981), which stresses the centrality of race in the construction of economic inequality in the United States. Michael Omi

Race and Racism

and Howard Winant emphasize racism as an ever-changing social process guided and shaped by state policy in their *Racial Formation in the United States* (New York and London, 1987). Aldon D. Morris examines the infrastructures undergirding black protest in *The Origins of the Civil Rights Movement* (New York, 1984), while William J. Wilson examines the relationship between de-industrialization and racism in the post-Civil Rights era in *The Truly Disadvantaged* (Chicago, 1987).

Anthropologists have traditionally been reluctant to work in advanced industrialized societies, but in recent years they have produced enormously perceptive and useful books about ethnicity and race in the United States. Especially noteworthy are Renato Rosaldo, *Culture and Truth* (Boston, MA, 1989), George Marcus and James Clifford, *Writing Culture* (Berkeley, 1986), Carol Stack, *All Our Kin* (New York, 1974), and Micaela di Leonardo, *Varieties of Ethnic Experience* (Ithaca, NY, 1984). Significant folklore studies include Americo Paredes, *With His Pistol in His Hand* (Austin, 1958), Lawrence Levine, *Black Culture: Black Consciousness* (New York, 1978), and Zora Neale Hurston, *Mules and Men* (Bloomington, IN, 1978). Works employing music as a central frame for understanding race in the United States include LeRoi Jones (Amiri Baraka), *Blues People* (New York, 1963), Steve Chapple and Reebee Garofalo, *Rock'n'Roll is Here to Pay* (Chicago, 1977), Nelson George, *The Death of Rhythm and Blues* (New York, 1988), and the Albert Murray book cited above.

Much of the most profound and eloquent evidence about racial matters can best be found in literature. Recent critical studies of particular importance in this area include Henry Louis Gates, *Figures in Black* (New York, 1987), Hazel Carby, *Reconstructing Womanhood* (New York, 1987), Houston Baker, *Blues and Afro-American Literature* (Chicago, 1984), Kenneth Lincoln, *Native American Renaissance* (Berkeley, 1983), and Ramon Saldivar, *Chicano Narrative* (Madison, 1990). Some few specific key works of literature other than autobiographies (and not already mentioned in the text) are: Jean Toomer, *Cane* (1923), Langston Hughes, *The Weary Blues* (1926), Zora Neale Hurston, *Their Eyes Were Watching God* (1937), Richard Wright, *Native Son* (1940), James Baldwin, *Go Tell it on the Mountain* (1953), John Oliver Killens, *And Then We Heard the Thunder* (1963), N. Scott Momaday, *House Made of Dawn* (1968), Maxine Hong Kingston, *Woman Warrior* (1976), Toni Morrison, *Song of Solomon* (1977), Sandra Cisneros, *The House on Mango Street* (1983), and Louise Erdrich, *Love Medicine* (1984).

CHAPTER SEVEN

Immigration and Ethnicity

Berndt Ostendorf and *Stephan Palmié*

OLD AND NEW IMMIGRATION

In 1787 John Jay summed up the prospects for an American state in the *Federalist Papers*. The Americans, he argued, were a people 'descended from the same ancestors, speaking the same language, professing the same religion, attached to the same principles of government, very similar in their manners and custom'.[1] Though Jay's description was already a bit of a myth in 1787 – after all there were at least 200,000 Germans, 250,000 Scotch-Irish, some Sephardic Jews, quite a number of Catholics and a sprinkling of Huguenots in the colonies, not to speak of the continent's aboriginal inhabitants and a sizeable number of African slaves and free blacks – it was way off the mark as a prediction of things to come. Between 1815 and 1980 approximately 46 million people from all corners of the world crossed the seas to settle in the United States and to turn it into a multicultural opposite of Jay's dream.

In order to explain this greatest migration in history it is useful to differentiate between push and pull factors. We should ask what drove people from their homes and what attracted them to America. There were economic, religious and political reasons, and each sending country had its own set of different circumstances. In England, as was pointed out in Chapter 1, the consequences of industrialization and the reorganization of agriculture had made the lot of many common labourers there intolerable. Due to a combination of improved hygienic conditions and better diets the populations of Europe doubled between 1750 and 1850, and this led demographers such as Malthus to warn of the limits of growth as early as 1830. Religious intolerance persisted in many parts of Europe, particularly against Jews. Then a combination of bad harvests and agricultural failures such as the potato blight in Ireland caused widespread famine. The threat of war and conscription drove young men away. High tax burdens convinced youthful entrepreneurs to seek their fortunes elsewhere. Last but not least, the promise of a new beginning made America seem so much more attractive to enterprising individuals.

The stories about America which circulated in Europe were indeed tempting. After the Louisiana Purchase (1803) there was a vast mass of land to be settled, and to own property was the dream of many a second-born son. Moreover, in the 1830s America developed an unquenchable thirst for labour which peaked and sloughed thereafter with the boom and bust cycles so typical of the American economy. Whereas the transatlantic passage had been arduous and dangerous during the eighteenth and early nineteenth centuries, the revolution in shipbuilding and in the transatlantic transport system made the journey both less expensive and quicker. Finally, the promise of the first amendment, freedom of speech and the free exercise of religion were strong enticements for those who wanted more than bread and land.

Old Immigration

Between 1820 and 1880 the majority of immigrants came from northern and central Europe, with the Germans and the Irish taking the lead in 1830 and the English and the Scandinavians running a close second after the Civil War. Two periods, both ones of economic prosperity and expanding markets, saw the highest immigration figures; in the years between 1845 and 1854 and between 1865 and 1875 more than 3.5 million people arrived. Though the Irish and the Germans both came from rural backgrounds their settlement in the United States was remarkably different. The Irish had fled from famine and overpopulation. They brought with them few industrial skills and little or no money and, what is probably more important, little faith in a rural livelihood. They therefore stayed close to their churches in the cities, taking the lowest jobs and working under the most gruesome conditions, particularly in building the transport system – canals and railways – which would in turn provide the basis for the American economic take-off. Eventually the now urban Irish would build what became known as political machines, tightly organized networks of urban political power, firmly committed to the Democratic Party. Most of the Germans of this first immigration phase (among them many German Jews) were not quite as badly off; their decision to emigrate was prompted by more calculated economic motives. As a rule they arrived with some money to move on to the Middle West and, somewhat later, to Texas, where they would buy land and homestead. Then, as increasingly

143

prosperous farmers, they would invite their relatives at home to follow them. Some of them were skilled craftsmen who would find work in the industrial take-off, as carpenters, metal workers, machinists, or as foremen in the mines. Once secure in their jobs these craftsmen would also trigger a chain migration of relatives and friends from their hometowns.

As a rule all immigrants could make more money in America than in their home countries; but they had to accept rather extreme working conditions and little or no job security or safety. Moreover, the quick succession of boom and bust cycles led to a sequence of pauperization of the working classes. The ethnic diversity and constant new arrival of eager foreign workers made it easy for native industrialists to prevent the growth of any long-range solidarity among workers. The successive waves of immigrants into an advancing labour market led to a hierarchization of workers on the basis of ethnic origin and the length of the American work experience. This was the beginning of the fusion of ethnicity and class, sometimes called ethclass by sociologists, so typical of the nineteenth- and twentieth-century American labour market. Important was the continued influx of a reserve labour army which could be used to break any strike. The coincidence of industrialization and immigration had further consequences: first, a radical separation of skilled and unskilled workers; second, the erosion of an independent craft culture. Some craftsmen advanced into the entrepreneurial class, but most experienced social decline.

The immigrants arrived via New York or via New Orleans, which due to its location at the mouth of the Mississippi was before the Civil War the second-largest port of entry. The importance of the Mississippi as a conduit of goods and immigrants to the Midwest declined as the railway system grew from local trunklines servicing the hinterland of cities (1850s) to a national transportation system (1869 onwards). After the Civil War, when Swedish agriculture experienced a depression and the first effects of industrialization were felt in Norway, the numbers of Scandinavian immigrants increased. Like the Germans they settled as farmers in the Middle West, primarily in Wisconsin, Michigan and Minnesota. On the West Coast so-called 'coolie labourers' – that is, Chinese men – were instrumental in building the infrastructure of western expansion in the mines, in canal work and in the railway. They arrived alone, leaving their families behind. As an all-male group, they were objects of fear to the dominant population; this led to an outburst of nativism which in turn prompted the Chinese Exclusion Act of 1882.

After 1845 many of the new Midwestern states such as Michigan and Wisconsin maintained agencies in port cities which would recruit new settlers. Often they made concrete and enticing offers. Kansas exempted

Mennonites from military service, others offered particularly cheap land. After the Civil War, thirty-three states maintained such immigration bureaux. The railroads, which were the largest real-estate owners, also took an active part in settling the newly opened areas. Theirs was an economic interest: the number of settlers stood in direct relation to the value of their land; besides, more people meant more business for the railway. With these methods the populations of such states as Iowa and Minnesota doubled between 1880 and 1900. There were, too, any number of immigration aid societies, semi-philanthropic offices which offered help and information.

The steamship companies also took an active interest. As the number of ships increased and the market tightened a bitter fight for a share of the market ensued. In 1882, twenty-five different lines and steamship companies plied the transatlantic route, which drove down the price of a transatlantic passage from England to between $12 and $15 for a midship passage. The Anchor and Hamburg America Lines ran some 6,500 offices all over the United States where immigrants could prepay tickets for their relatives, thus strengthening the chain migration pattern. Depending on the ethnic groups, between 25 and 70 per cent of the immigrants came to America on prepaid tickets. Until about 1850 a midship passage was at best uncomfortable, at worst hell. Steamships brought radical improvements in comfort, but most of all in time. By 1897 the journey from Liverpool to Boston took a mere five-and-a-half days. Immigration routes were often identical with trade routes. The Irish landed in Boston since this was England's most important harbour with service for Canada. The important cotton trade brought immigrants from Hamburg and Bremen to New Orleans. But New York received the bulk of immigration, up to 70 per cent of the total figures.

The years until 1882 may be called the period of unrestricted immigration. The incoming immigrants were merely registered, not selected according to desirability as new citizens. New York passed a few laws forbidding captains to transport paupers or the diseased. Later, a $1 tax per head was levied to finance hospitals. After 1847 there was a state Board of Commissioners for Immigration. In 1855 Castle Gardens, a former variety hall, was chosen for immigration procedures. Later, after the onset of the New Immigration, Ellis Island was designated for that purpose.

The New Immigration

Between 1880 and 1930, twenty-seven million immigrants came to America, most of them from southern and eastern Europe. The shift is clearly indicated in absolute numbers. Whereas in 1882 of the total number

145

of 788,992 immigrants some 250,000 were German, 32,000 Italian and 17,000 Russian, in 1907 of the 1,285,000 immigrants a mere 37,000 came from Germany whereas 285,731 hailed from Italy and 260,000 from Russia. The effects of European industrialization had reached southern and eastern Europe. Labour migration into the richer parts of Europe, which continued on into America, set in from the poor regions of Sicily and from the Pale, a settlement area in what was then Russia and Austria to which Jews were restricted. A combination of factors – poverty and population increases in Sicily, relatively cheap passage and the expansion of agriculture in the United States – brought three million Italians to the United States between 1881 and 1910.

The second-largest group of about two million were the East European Jews. Among immigrants to America they constitute a special group: they arrived with the experience of having been aliens in their land of birth. Besides, Jewish emigration was not job or gender specific but comprised elements of a complete society, including the intellectual classes. The exodus began after the assassination of Tzar Alexander II in 1881, an event which triggered a series of pogroms. American Jewry changed radically in a mere fifty years. Whereas the number of Jews in America was around 250,000 in 1877, most of whom were German, in 1927 there were four million, most of whom were Eastern European. The third group comprised Slavic immigrants, among them Russians, Ukrainians, Slovaks, Slovenes, Poles, Croats, Serbs and Bulgarians. After 1899 Poles were registered separately; they formed the third-largest group after Italians and Jews. The fourth contingent is made up of Hungarians (one million), Greeks (300,000), Portuguese (146,000), Armenians (70,000) and Japanese (90,000). The First World War interrupted this flow. After the war a wave of those waiting for it to end entered the United States before the doors closed as a consequence of the Quota Act of 1924.

The ratio of men and women differed drastically between groups. Whereas the majority of the Irish were women, most of whom went into domestic service and unskilled labour, the majority of Italians (78 per cent) and Greeks (95 per cent) were men. Only the Jews arrived with entire families. A factor which gets short shrift in immigration studies is remigration. Between 1908 and 1914 the immigration authorities registered 6,709,357 arrivals and 2,063,767 departures. Among these were a large group of Italians who were employed as seasonal agricultural and construction workers, but many central European immigrants also returned home. Not being welcome 'back home', the Jews could not and did not return.

The combined impact of immigration, industrialization and urbanization affected the patterns of growth of major cities such as Chicago and New

York. Of the New Immigration, about 80 per cent settled in the Midwest and Northeast. The great majority ended up working in the large industrial cities. Very few went south. In 1910, 75 per cent of the inhabitants of Detroit, New York, Chicago, Cleveland and Boston were immigrants of the first and second generation, and in 1916, 72 per cent of the inhabitants of San Francisco spoke a foreign language. There is a saying that while not all workers were immigrants, all immigrants were workers.

The reaction of the old stock Americans to what were thought of as these 'hordes of alien vermin' led to a rise in nativism. Of the old immigrants the Catholic and dirt-poor Irish had brought forth a strong reaction which peaked in the middle of the century. Racist books such as Madison Grant's *The Passing of the Great Race* (1916) were written in reaction to the new immigrants, especially the Jews and Italians who would congregate in densely populated inner-city ghettos. Of the two groups, the Italians held on to some of their traditions which were in opposition to the American creed: they remained extremely family centred (some commentators even speak of such ties as 'amoral familism') and clustered around old world networks; their anti-intellectualism kept children from schools; their *padrone* system prevented participation in labour politics; and their distrust of political power prevented the rise of inner-city political machines. Quite differently, the Jews showed a broader social commitment right from the start. The earlier German Jews had set up B'nai B'rith, and by 1909 there were some 2,000 welfare and self-help institutions. Though ostensibly organized like the Italians along regional *Landsmanshaften*, there was a strong sense of togetherness that transcended merely regional loyalties; and, last but not least, Jews had a class of intellectuals and were avid users of the American system of education. By 1915 City College of New York had a student population that was 85 per cent Jewish.

The Chinese Exclusion Act of 1882 marked the beginning of a period when pressure groups began to clamour for restriction to immigration. Much of the nativism directed against the Chinese – and later against the Japanese – was based, as we saw in Chapter 6, on pure racism. But the nativism also contained residues of an earlier anti-Catholic feeling among Protestants that Catholicism presented a menace to American values and institutions. The American Protective Association was founded in 1887; at its peak in 1890 it commanded some 2.5 million members. The Association usually favoured the Republican Party, since most ethnic Catholics voted Democrat. The relatively successful German Jews who had come to America before 1880 encountered little anti-Semitism; but the great mass of East European Jews who started coming after 1880 saw a kindling of a movement for immigration restriction. Economic conflict also strengthened the restriction movement. The Knights of Labor called for a ban on contract labour, and the American Federation of Labor in 1897 supported the introduction of a literacy test as a means of controlling the immigration of unskilled labour. Employers, though in need of a reserve army, were fearful of the politics of labour which 'foreign agitators' imported into their factories. The late nineteenth century saw a rise of pseudo-racial theory issuing from the great universities. This renewed racism was directed mostly against southern and eastern Europeans, who were considered unassimilable. There was also inter-ethnic strife: within the Catholic Church the Poles resented the leadership of the Irish; in Chicago Bohemians and Germans fought over local politics.

In 1907 Congress appointed a Senate-House commission to investigate the immigration problem. In 1911 this resulted in a forty-two-volume report named after the commission chairman, Senator William Paul Dillingham. Congress reacted to the report by passing another literacy bill in 1913. The president vetoed it, but the war drove xenophobic feelings to a feverish pitch, directed mostly against Germans. In the postwar years a 'red scare' led to extensive police raids which rounded up foreigners suspected of political sympathies with labour. The 1920s witnessed a high tide of xenophobia, with the rise of a nativist Ku Klux Klan which claimed over four million members, and with the passing of the Volstead Act which, in inaugurating the Prohibition era, pitted old stock Protestant and 'dry' America against new ethnic urban and 'wet' America. In Detroit Henry Ford's *Dearborn Independent* published vitriolic attacks against Jews. In 1921 Congress passed a law for a one-year period which limited the number of immigrants of each nationality to 3 per cent of the foreign born of that group in America (based on the 1910 census). After extending the law twice until 1924, the Johnson-Reed Immigration Act was passed that year. This cut the number of immigrants to 2 per cent of the foreign born of that group (this time based on the 1890 census). The quota system heavily favoured the old stock groups from northern and central Europe, of course, and further reduced the immigration of eastern and southern Europeans.

Mexican-Americans and Chicanos present a special case in immigration history. The first group of Mexican-Americans was created by the American conquest of the Southwest mentioned in the preceding chapter: between 1845 and 1854 the United States acquired the territory which today comprises California, Arizona, Colorado, Nevada, New Mexico, Texas, Utah and Wyoming. Due to a high birthrate the Mexican population in these states grew rapidly, strengthened by immigration which peaked in the 1920s when almost 500,000 Mexicans crossed the 2,000-mile frontier. Most of these so-called Chicanos were employed as agricultural labourers. During the Depression many of them were repatriated to

Mexico. The end of the Depression and the coming of the Second World War reversed the flow again. In 1942 the Bracero Program was initiated by a Mexican–US agreement. Braceros could enter the United States legally as short-term contract workers. By the time the programme ended in 1947 an estimated 200,000 braceros worked in twenty-one states, most of them in California. The programme was resurrected in 1951 and ran until 1964. In certain peak years (1959) up to half a million braceros, who formed 26 per cent of the agricultural work force, entered the United States. After the programme was officially over, Mexicans continued to come as labourers drawn by an insatiable agricultural labour market.

According to the 1970 census one-third of the entire Puerto Rican population resides in the United States. Of these, 54.8 per cent live in New York City, which has the largest Puerto Rican population of any city in the world. Puerto Ricans have been US citizens since 1917 and can move freely between the Caribbean island of Puerto Rico and the mainland. While in 1930 there were but 50,000 Puerto Ricans in the United States, their number swelled from 300,000 in 1950 to their present 1,391,460. The Puerto Ricans are the reserve army of the working class, most of them employed in menial, unskilled jobs. The islanders came from a culture where colour played an insignificant role; in the United States they were faced by a racial dichotomy which led to an enforced association with blacks.

The new policy of immigration restriction after the First World War combined with the Depression effectively ended immigration to America from all countries but Mexico and Puerto Rico. In 1933 there was a trickle of a mere 23,000. During the Depression more people left than arrived. However, the triumph of fascism in Europe, particularly Hitler's accession to power, brought a highly selective group of European intellectuals to America, a group that would greatly enhance academic and cultural life in the United States. University professors, doctors, lawyers, church leaders, architects, artists and scientists, many of them German Jews, fled to America. Yet, despite the plight of Jews in Europe, the strict immigration quotas remained intact. Nativism was particularly rampant in the case of the Japanese. The attack on Pearl Harbor led President Roosevelt to issue the infamous Executive Order 9066 by which some 110,000 West Coast Japanese, most of them native-born Americans, were rounded up in camps. After the war xenophobic sentiment declined, perhaps due to the postwar prosperity which levelled differences of income and to the massive expansion of the educational sector which made educational advancement possible. The plight of displaced persons due to the war was recognized in the Displaced Persons Act of 1948, which permitted 410,000 people to enter the United States. After its expiration the Refugee Relief Act of 1953 added another 189,000. In 1963 President Kennedy urged Congress to review the national origins system. After Kennedy's assassination President Johnson called upon Congress to enact the Kennedy proposal, and in 1965 it was passed with an overwhelming majority as a new immigration bill.

A NEW 'NEW IMMIGRATION'?

The past twenty-five years have marked yet another turning point in American immigration history. Nowadays, scholars and politicians again find themselves discussing a 'new immigration', while America faces an influx of foreign nationals equalled only by the migration waves prior to the immigration restriction acts of the 1920s. The 'new' immigration differs qualitatively from all preceding waves. Today, the main sources of US-bound migration no longer lie in Europe but in the Pacific region, the Caribbean and Latin America; and the destination of the new migratory flow is no longer the industrial Northeast but urban California, the Sunbelt region, and several largely de-industrialized conurbations like New York, Miami, Washington DC and Chicago.

Students of American immigration largely agree that major, but not exclusive, importance for ushering in the recent immigration waves must be attributed to the 1965 legislation. By the end of the 1950s many organizations were calling for immigration reform, often on the basis that the national quota system not only conflicted with the role of postwar America as a haven for anti-Communist refugees, but also exposed the United States to charges of racist exclusionism. The onset of the Civil Rights movement clearly added another stimulus, but, perhaps most importantly, not only America but most of western Europe was in the midst of postwar prosperity – a fact that made a relaxation of immigration laws appear less of a threat than a benefit to the economy, and reduced the likelihood of such reforms triggering a massive reaction in those (European) countries which, in the past, had served as the main senders.

Thus when in 1965 the national quota regulations were finally replaced by immigration laws rejecting the principle of racial selection in favour of a policy geared towards family unification, the new immigration bill hardly seemed revolutionary to any but the staunchest conservatives. US immigration policy was now to be guided by a preference system allocating 80 per cent of immigrant visas on the basis of kin relations between US citizens or residents and foreign nationals, while merely establishing a 170,000 immigrant limit for the whole eastern hemisphere combined with a non-discriminatory per country ceiling of 20,000. (In 1976 a 120,000 limit for immigration from the western hemisphere was added, and in 1977 a preference system similar to the one applying to the eastern hemisphere was created.)

At the end of the decade, however, it was clear that by their very nature, as well as by their timing, the 1965 immigration reforms had engendered unforeseen results. Twenty-five years of hindsight leave little doubt that the 'New Immigration' was not brought about solely by legislative fiat. Perhaps inadvertently, the 1965 legislators' decisions helped to solidify a new structure of global labour–capital relations – one in which the flow of investment towards peripheral areas of the global economy was paralleled by a flow of labour towards the core. While highly capitalized industrial production tended to move out of the United States and into Third World regions in order to have access to cheap sources of labour, the attendant economic dislocations in those regions drove an increasingly impoverished surplus labour force towards sectors of the US economy characterized by high demand in manpower, undesirable working conditions, and unstable profit rates.

The new 'New Immigrants' arrive

One of the most immediately obvious consequences of the 1965 reforms was a rapid increase in Asian immigration. This was due partly to the lifting of the infamous 'Asian Barred Zone', and partly to the family preference system's potential for stimulating chain migration. Because America's resident Asians had amounted to less than 1 per cent of the national population in 1960, no one had anticipated that Asian immigration would snowball along the lines of extended family networks. Yet this was exactly what happened once a significant number of Asian newcomers gained resident alien status or citizenship, and were thus able to act as sponsors under the preference system.

Perhaps not surprisingly, this pattern assumed its most pronounced form among immigrants stemming from the middle class of Southeast Asian countries like Korea or the Philippines which – in contrast to Japan whose immigration remained virtually at the 1965 level – were experiencing economic slumps at the same time that corporate international investment began to reduce chances for local entrepreneurship, western mass communication rapidly saturated their cultures with images of American consumerism, and cheap airfares became available. By 1970 the number of Filipinos legally admitted to the United States had increased tenfold over the 1965 numbers, while Korean immigration reached a comparable level of increase in 1975, rendering them the second and third most important sending countries after Mexico. In 1980 the Korean-born population in the United States was estimated at almost 355,000, while the nearly 775,000 Filipinos had surpassed the Japanese and now represented America's second-largest Asian minority group after the Chinese, who had also experienced a modest increase. As immigrant groups, both the Filipinos and the Koreans have consistently included a large number of professionals and other qualified personnel and, in general, have evidenced significantly higher than average educational levels. The same appears to hold true for the less significant number of recent Indian and Malaysian immigrants.

Another region to show an immediate reaction to the new legislation was the English-speaking Caribbean. Many of these former British colonies had recently become independent and were, therefore, no longer restricted to the small quota allowances for European dependencies. Instead, they now gained access to equal shares of immigrant visas under the 20,000 per country limit for the western hemisphere. At the same time, Great Britain, which during the 1950s had absorbed large numbers of West Indian migrants, began in 1962 to curtail immigration from the Commonwealth Caribbean drastically. Although aggregate figures are hard to obtain, legal Jamaican immigration into the United States more than tripled during the single year 1966–7, and by 1972 it was estimated that about 315,000 (legal as well as illegal) Jamaican immigrants resided there, most of them concentrated in the New York metropolitan area. Similar trends have been reported for immigration from Barbados and Trinidad/Tobago. The 1980 census counted the foreign-born population from these three islands currently residing in the United States at almost 200,000, while the total number of migrants from the English-speaking Caribbean who came to the United States since 1970 may be as high as 340,000. These numbers are perhaps less significant when judged against total US population figures than when held against the comparatively minuscule populations of these islands.

Less directly affected by the 1965 immigration reforms than by political push factors and, perhaps just as importantly, by global economic trends was the increase in immigration from the Hispanic Caribbean and Latin America. Although traditionally favoured by America's 'Good Neighborhood' policy, and already figuring prominently among the pre-1965 Hispanic immigrant population of other-than-Mexican origin, both Dominican and Colombian entry numbers doubled between 1967 and 1976. The notoriously undercounted figures of the 1980 census indicated a presence of more than 170,000 Dominicans and about 156,000 Colombians. In both cases, however, the increase in numbers was less pronounced than the change in the social composition of immigrants arriving after

1965. While the assassination of the Dominican dictator Trujillo and the aftermath of the 'Violencia' period in Colombia had triggered waves of US-bound élite and middle-class emigration from both countries in the early 1960s, by the end of the decade a steady lowering of educational levels and occupational skills among the incoming population from these regions was stabilizing into a long-term trend. These later-stage immigrants represent but the tip of an iceberg of huge population movements underway in the whole of the Caribbean Basin.

Characteristically, those who turned to the United States for economic and political safety were largely absorbed into low-wage, labour-intensive manufacturing operations or the low-skill service sector, where in the course of the 1970s and 1980s they increasingly replaced better organized and less compliant native workers. Dominicans now dominate New York's formerly floundering garment industry. Large numbers of both Dominican and Colombian women have taken up domestic employment. Similarly, the more recent waves of immigrants from Central American states like El Salvador, Guatemala, Nicaragua and Honduras that were plunged into political and economic crises during the late 1970s and early 1980s appear to have followed the pattern of early élite migration followed by what essentially represents a surplus labour force – created by burgeoning population growth and economic dislocations – driven towards the United States by political violence, severe underemployment and the vague hope of a better life up north.

THE CASE OF MEXICO

Many of the reasons already mentioned help to explain the single most dramatic US-bound migratory outflow from any country to occur in the past twenty-five years: the Mexican exodus. Although the 1965 reforms did not particularly favour Mexico, their coincidence with the end of the Bracero programme had an ominous portent. By the time the programme ended, the inhabitants of literally thousands of villages in the central Mexican highlands had become economically dependent on seasonal labour migration to the United States. In addition, the intrusion of US-based food-processing corporations into Mexico increasingly led to the displacement of small landholdings by large-scale operations, thus turning former producers into wage labourers and potential migrants. Mexico's enormous population growth, the disastrous decline of its national economy (halted only briefly by a short-lived oil boom between 1978 and 1981) and a

153

vertiginous inflation rate have combined to create a situation where –
given the proximity of an almost insatiable market for cheap, legally
unprotected labour beyond an ill-protected border – massive illegal
immigration simply had to occur. While apprehensions of illegal entrants
amounted to a mere 110,000 in 1965, the year the Bracero programme
officially ended, by 1970 that figure had already tripled, and by 1986 it
reached a record high of 1,670,000 apprehensions. In the 1980 census
officials found that more than 50 per cent (that is, approximately 2.2 to 2.8
million) of the total illegal immigrant population counted had crossed the
border from Mexico, while the 1983 Current Population Survey indicated
a clear upward trend in the proportion of illegal to legal Mexican
immigration.

Mexico also represents the most important sending country for *legal*
immigrants. Since 1970 Mexicans have numbered 15 per cent of all legal
US immigrants and more than 700,000 Mexicans have legally acquired
resident status. Few Mexican migrants came entirely unbidden, or entered
the United States in the manner of the proverbial 'mojado' or 'wetback',
and, most important of all, there is no evidence that they are damaging the
economy of their host country. In fact, it is obvious that large parts of the
Sunbelt region and the Mexican border zone now form what has been
called an integrated labour market or even a transnational economic system
based on structured inequality. The so-called 'Texas proviso' taken over
into the 1965 bill ensured that agricultural interests were met by outlawing
undocumented immigration while legalizing employment of illegal
entrants. It thus virtually created an underclass of farm and sweatshop
workers on which Southwestern agrobusiness and manufacture not only
preyed but upon which it became increasingly dependent. This tendency
seems to have intensified: recent studies indicate that most large
Southwestern fruit and vegetable producers and even the Northern
California poultry industry are more dependent than ever on illegal labour
sources. By the end of the 1970s, moreover, large sectors of the small-scale
manufacturing, service and subcontract construction business in the greater
Los Angeles–Long Beach area (where, in 1980, at least 32 per cent of *all*
illegal immigrants were estimated to reside) were vitally linked to ethnic
recruitment networks tapping labour sources below the border. Most
surprisingly perhaps, by the mid-1980s, an estimated 10 to 20 per cent of
illegal Mexican immigrants have found more or less steady employment in
Silicon Valley's high-tech industry. At the same time, many American
firms engage in the so-called 'maquiladora' system, setting up assembly
plants in the northern Mexican border zone. In 1985 such plants were
estimated to employ about 300,000 labourers at a fraction of American
minimum wages. Chances are good that this tendency to enmesh the US

and Mexican economies will continue and, unless Mexico can miraculously rid itself of its dependence on North American capital and create sufficient employment for its exploding population, the US–Mexican border will increasingly become an economic thoroughfare.

THE 'SILENT INVASION' AND THE SIMPSON–RODINO REFORMS

By the early 1980s several factors had combined to create what Wisconsin's Republican senator Alan Rodino referred to as a case of 'compassion fatigue'. Apprehensions of illegal immigrants were running at all-time-high levels. In 1983 Mexico's economy collapsed under international debt, thus arousing fears that the US border would once more serve as a safety valve. The United States themselves were in the midst of a critical recession, with unemployment reaching 10 per cent. In response to affirmative action, some 'white ethnics' were clamouring for 'their share' of recognition and funds. Public outrage erupted over Supreme Court decisions such as *Doe* vs *Plyer*, which granted free public education to children of illegal immigrants (and therefore contradicted the popular impression that illegals caused no public expenditure). Rising crime rates and especially the Latin-American narcotics trade were widely blamed on the new immigration. And increasingly heated debates flared up over the issue of bilingual education for children whose mother tongue was Spanish, and over bilingualism in general. In 1983 a poll on immigration indicated that even blacks and Hispanics solidly favoured both sanctions against employers hiring illegal aliens and more rigorous efforts at controlling the border.

In 1977 President Carter introduced a reform package featuring employer sanctions and limited amnesty for illegal aliens, and in 1981 the Reagan Administration endorsed the recommendations regarding enforcement presented by a House Select Commission. In 1982 Senator Simpson and Democratic representative Romano Mazzoli first introduced a bill specifying such reforms, but it was not until the very end of the 1986 Congress period that immigration reforms (this time co-sponsored by House Judiciary Committee chairman Peter Rodino) came to pass. They featured employer sanctions and amnesty for all illegals residing in the United States since 1982, a 50 per cent increase in funds for immigration enforcement, stronger efforts at registration through Social Security and, in compromise with agricultural interests, an agricultural labour programme reminiscent of European guest-worker schemes. While these measures seem to have taken the edge off some of the worst abuse of illegal labour and slightly reduced the illegal immigrant flow, it is too early to tell whether they have achieved their grand objective.

As from 1 October 1991 a new act of Congress is ushering in changes: raising the quota of highly qualified and skilled workers from 500,000 to 700,000 per annum (the quota for unskilled is unchanged); family reunion is made easier; restrictions on AIDS carriers, homosexuals and politically undesirables are being modified. The act was designed to attract highly qualified scientists and to make the import of investors easier. It should also facilitate the expulsion of alien drug criminals, of which 60,000 are currently in American prisons.

REFUGEES: GENUINE AND SPURIOUS?

The issue other than illegal immigration which probably occasioned the most heated debates about US immigration policy throughout the 1970s and 1980s was that of refugees. And it is here that the inseparability of US immigration from its international context emerged most visibly, and, in many ways, most painfully. Retrospectively, it is clear that some of the major inconsistencies of US refugee policy up to (and even beyond) the 1980 Refugee Act stem from the failure to adjust legal procedures and political guidelines developed during the Cold War era to the pressures and demands of a rapidly changing global scene. As will be clear from what follows, from the onset of Cuban emigration in 1959 through the Indochinese refugee crisis and the Haitian boatlift of the late 1970s, to the Mariel exodus and the ongoing flight from El Salvador, the United States pursued an erratic course, vacillating between wholesale admission of emigrés from Communist countries or collapsing US-supported regimes and denying asylum to refugees fleeing the terror of 'friendly' right-wing dictatorships. In recent years an unfortunate and, in many ways, anachronistic distinction between economic 'migrants' and political 'refugees' has emerged: a distinction between those who seek opportunity and those who seek safety; between those who do not want to leave the United States, and those who do not dare to. Reasonable as these distinctions may seem at first glance, their application has nevertheless given rise to crass injustice and human dramas of massive proportions.

In the early 1960s, US refugee policy still largely centred on the presidential parole power written into law in the 1952 Immigration Act, which was invoked several times in order to admit extra-quota numbers of displaced persons and east European refugees. The Cuban revolution seemed at first to unleash a rather similar influx of 'freedom fighters', such as the landed or professional élite and former adherents of Batista's regime. The abrupt halt to which this early migration came with the Missile Crisis of 1962 appeared to conform to this pattern, so that no special refugee regulations were incorporated into the 1965 immigration bill. However, when regular flights between Havana and Miami resumed in 1966, it was only a matter of time before it became clear that the so-called 'Freedom Flights' (which lasted until 1973) were increasingly bringing in a different set of people. As studies of Cuban immigration show, the phase of the 'golden exile', during which the Cuban exodus was hailed as the largest brain drain in history, ended long before the airlift was finally discontinued. Occupational standards and educational levels steadily declined among the incoming Cubans, while the political aspect of their decision to go into exile became increasingly subject to doubt. It is obvious today that the second major wave of Cuban immigration was largely economically motivated.

Meanwhile, just as the Cubans already in the United States were busily acquiring a reputation as a 'model minority', a wholly different sort of refugee problem rapidly diverted attention from the question of whether Cubans should be granted asylum solely on account of their hailing from a Communist country: at the end of 1975 Saigon fell, and just before the American-supported regime collapsed, the United States agreed to stage a desperate last-minute rescue of those Vietnamese who had worked for the United States. President Ford announced that he would use parole power to admit 130,000 refugees, and before Congress had even decided upon the allocation of funds, even more than this number had already arrived. And this was only the beginning of what turned into an Indochinese refugee crisis. As the United States haggled over parole procedures, in 1978 unprecedented violence erupted in Cambodia and Laos and war broke out between Vietnam and China. By the spring of 1979 the number of refugees pouring out of Vietnam alone had reached a monthly average of 65,000. Neighbouring Asian countries increasingly closed their harbours to these boat people, sometimes – as in the case of Malaysia and Thailand – turning back refugees at rifle point, while the United States gingerly raised its admission rates.

Arriving as they did, in the midst of an economic recession, the Indochinese seem to have been the first group of refugees from Communist countries to experience a cool reception by the US public. The fact that this migrant flow represented a costly legacy of the Vietnam war appears to have rendered the relocation of these 'parolees' difficult, and the difficulty was exacerbated by the enormous cultural distance between some of these migrants and their host society. The large settlements of ethnic groups from the Cambodian and Laotian uplands who fled Pol Pot's reign of terror and of Vietnamese fisherfolk who settled in California and on the coast of the Gulf of Mexico were subjected to intense and sometimes violent reactions. It became clear that the United States was legally as well as socially ill equipped to cope with the sudden massive influx of such newcomer populations without serious policy reforms. By 1980 such reforms had, in fact, been written into law. But only a few months after the Refugee Act of 1980 was passed, a new and truly unprecedented refugee crisis erupted, and the administration failed to enact the new laws.

Essentially, the 1980 Refugee Act brought US law into line with the 1951 United Nations definition of refugee status. A refugee was defined as 'a person who is outside his country of nationality and who is unable or unwilling to return to that country because of persecution or well-founded fear of persecution on account of race, religion, nationality, membership in a particular social group or political opinion'. In addition, federally funded resettlement programmes were instituted and the president's parole power was curtailed in favour of a more active role for Congress in controlling refugee admission. Only a short time after the Act went into effect, however, it was virtually ignored by the Carter administration in the course of the so-called Mariel exodus.

Mariel started out as a modest boatlift of several thousand Cubans who had barricaded themselves into Havana's Peruvian embassy in early April of 1980. Initially the Carter administration declared that the United States would welcome the refugees with 'an open heart and open arms'. However, by summer it was clear that the United States had lost control over the 'freedom flotilla' of small crafts shuttling back and forth between Miami and the harbour of Mariel which Castro had opened for emigrants. In direct contrast to the usual initial welcome given to yet another wave of anti-Communists who had decided to vote with their feet, this time the coastguard was ordered to interdict boats unloading Cubans along the shores of the Florida Keys. Nevertheless, by the time the tide was finally stemmed in September, more than 125,000 had arrived.

But it wasn't only the embarrassing inconsistencies in federal policy that rendered Mariel a political and social debacle; in a clever political move, Castro declared that he intended to use the mass exodus to rid Cuba of undesirable elements. Both the Cuban and the US press reported that he had opened the island's jails and mental asylums and burdened the boats of Miami-Cubans eager to rescue family members with criminals, drug-addicts and psychopaths. As thorough studies of the composition of the 1980 Cubans show, these allegations were far from the truth. While in fact some 2,600 convicted felons were among the incoming population, the vast majority of those who had prison records (16 per cent) had been jailed for political reasons. Similar controversial treatment to that meted out to the Marielitos by both the administration and the American public, only worse, was experienced by Haitian boat-people who arrived at about the same time.

The tragedy of the flight of perhaps as many as 40,000 Haitians from a country which the cleptocratic terror regime of the Duvaliers had reduced to the poorest nation in all of the western hemisphere was driven home to the American public in the late 1970s and early 1980s when small, overloaded and ill-equipped boats trying to cross the 700 miles to Florida were shipwrecked, washing ashore scores of emaciated black bodies. Even those Haitians who survived the perilous voyage faced an uneasy fortune. Since the United States had declared Haitians not eligible for wholesale asylum as a group, every apprehended Haitian had to prove that a 'well-founded fear' of political persecution had driven him or her to seek asylum in the United States. If they were lucky enough not to be caught by the coastguard and forced to return while still at sea, they were detained in overcrowded camps or even jails, awaiting individual hearings for sometimes more than a year. As early as 1976 a House Committee charged that hearings were conducted irregularly and that most of these illiterate peasants, who spoke only Kreyol, the Haitian creole language, were hardly in a position to present their cases. At the same time, vast numbers of Cubans and Indochinese found asylum in the United States without any sort of case-by-case screening. In 1979 a State Department commission reiterated the opinion that Haitians, as a group, did not face persecution upon deportation, and therefore were not eligible for refugee status. But opposition was mounting. In July 1980 a class action suit filed against the US Immigration and Naturalization Service on behalf of the Haitians finally established that INS had pursued a highly discriminatory policy and was guilty of 'wholesale violation of due process'. This case may have been influential in shaping the Carter administration's decision to circumvent the 1980 Refugee Act by creating an artificial 'Cuban–Haitian entrant' status for both the Marielitos and some 30,000 Haitian immigrants who had arrived since about 1978. This move, however, was an attempt on the part of the federal government to buy time and save money, for under this regulation neither group was eligible to full asylum or resident alien benefits. While little is known about the fate of the Haitian group, it is clear that the Mariel entrants, on the whole, fared rather badly.

Available data indicate that regardless of the 1980 reforms, the United States continues to pursue a selective, politicized and morally problematic refugee policy. While the INS approved 60 per cent of Iranian, 51 per cent of Romanian and 45 per cent of Czechoslovakian applications for asylum filed between 1983 and 1986, only 2.6 per cent of Salvadorean, 2.5 per cent of Honduran, 1.8 per cent of Haitian and 0.9 per cent of all Guatemalan applicants were granted asylum. In 1986 the rate of approvals for Nicaraguan applicants was hiked up to 60 per cent, giving clear proof that unsettled conditions (which plagued the whole region and were probably worst in El Salvador, where death squads ravaged the countryside) counted as acceptable grounds for 'well-founded fears' only if these conditions existed in a Communist state. In response to this policy, since 1981 the Sanctuary Movement – a heterogeneous coalition of human-itarian organizations, churches, synagogues and even single city and state governments – has been charging the United States with the violation of human rights. Sanctuary proponents argue that the United States bears responsibility for much of the unrest, injustice, poverty and violence in Central America and that refusing asylum to refugees from that area equals illegal deportation under the Refugee Act. That reforms will emerge from the current debate seems unlikely at the present time.

America is probably facing a long-term trend which can be neither explained nor averted by focusing on national policy alone. For as the increasing globalization of labour–capital relations fostered world-wide migration flows, so have these migratory streams brought forth new patterns of identity transcending single cultures, ethnicities and nationalities. Instead of immigrants more than willing to Americanize if given a chance, America now faces migrants who – sometimes self-consciously, sometimes by force of circumstance – continue to straddle different cultural worlds.

THE RISE OF ETHNICITY AND ETHNIC CULTURE

Richard Polenberg, in *One Nation Divisible* (1980), points to a paradox. In the 1930s America was characterized by sharp regional contrasts in language, cuisine and lifestyles, yet its population stood unified behind the universalism of the American creed. By the 1990s American everyday culture, with its landscape of TV-networked motels and identical suburban shopping malls, was thoroughly homogenized, yet the population seemed more fragmented than ever along ethnic and ideological lines. In contradiction of basic socialization theories, ethnic fragmentation increased as everyday culture became unified. Behind this change lie economic and demographic shifts, and consequently a radical reinterpretation of the traditional American compromise between the individual, the group and the polity represented in the national motto *e pluribus unum*.

The tension in this motto runs between one *universal* political culture (protected by the Constitution and its amendments, as invoked in Chapter

3) and *many* ethnic cultures; between a concept of culture defined as the glorious project of Enlightenment which would lead mankind out of fear, darkness and discrimination and establish a universal bill of rights, and a *differentiating* concept of cultures which interprets the difference between, say, Chicanos and blacks not only as a human right to be different in cultural matters, but also as an entitlement to differential treatment in politics. 'Culture' has become thoroughly politicized since the 1960s and the two concepts (one culture vs many cultures) now mark the two extreme positions in a deep political conflict. It all began with racism.

'The trouble with American pluralism,' writes Stephen Steinberg, 'derives from the fact that it was built upon systematic inequalities . . . . This was the pitfall – the fatal flaw – that robbed ethnic pluralism of its cultural innocence.'[2] And class difference was compounded by racism. In the first immigration phase when ethnicity was associated with cultural inferiority, poverty and bad working conditions there was a powerful motive to assimilate to the mainstream culture. Even the ethnic groups themselves contributed to the demise of their own traditions if these stood in the way of economic betterment. The resulting 'melting pot' of former immigrants, however, remained 'encapsulated in white ethnocentrism'.[3] Whereas the allegedly 'colour-blind' American Creed swept many white ethnic groups into its fold, there remained the problem of racism and its baneful social consequences of open or tacit discrimination. Thus W.E.B. DuBois was prophetic when he wrote in 1903 that the problem of the twentieth century would be the colour line.

It is important to remember that the rise of ethnicity began as a fight against racism. It was the Civil Rights movement of black Americans that set in motion a rethinking of ethnicity, thus of culture and politics. After the 1954 Supreme Court decision *Brown* vs *Board of Education Topeka* established that separate facilities for blacks were 'inherently unequal', federal institutions were called upon to undo differential treatment and develop programmes in order to 'integrate' blacks into the mainstream. At the same time certain scholars were pointing out that black culture was not pathological or inferior but both 'beautiful' and 'different'. To erase the 'marks of oppression', the battle cry 'Black is Beautiful' of the black cultural nationalists called for a reversal of attitudes, and certain black ways of dressing, talking and dancing did indeed set a new agenda in the counter-culture. Under the Johnson administration affirmative steps were taken to undo the many barriers which kept blacks out of certain jobs or schools. But here, then, is the paradox: in order to achieve the promise of the colour-blind creed of one universal culture which would treat equally all Americans 'regardless of race, religion and national origin', the new legislation had to use anthropological criteria of cultural difference to determine who was entitled to 'affirmative action', to set-asides and to preferential treatment. The contradiction is that this desire to implement Civil Rights justice required a code of legislative criteria to establish where the colour line should be drawn or who was considered a minority.

The new appreciation for the legitimacy of black culture and the policy of affirmative action did much good; today there is a solid black upper-middle and middle class which penetrated into many professions that were classically white domains, and many blacks have embraced their own traditions with new appreciation. Yet there were unintended consequences. When other ethnic groups saw that 'ethnicity' could be turned into cultural, social and political advantage they cried 'me too'. Native Americans and Chicanos could also make strong claims, hence red and brown power movements followed in the wake of the black power movement. A particularly bitter reaction came from a white ethnic working class that – between 1830 and 1960 – had been socialized into the American racialist system, and who were puzzled that their understanding of the American creed (including its racial advantages) no longer held. The extreme swing of classical Democratic voters to the conservative independents (George Wallace) and to Nixon had a lot to do with this feeling of being ignored. The ensuing revival of white ethnicity may be seen as a conscious reaction to the new ethnic politics seeming to favour blacks, but it can also be seen as a depolarization movement. By taking the entitlements of white ethnic groups seriously, governmental institutions could deflect their anger over preferential treatment of blacks (and soon of Indians and Hispanics). All this led to a surprising revitalization of white ethnic consciousness and ethnic affirmation. Was it, as many ethnic lobbyists claim, a return of the repressed?

The claim by sociological writers Nathan Glazer and Daniel Moynihan that 'the melting pot did not happen' was often misunderstood to mean that the traditional original cultures had survived immigration. What they meant, however, was that the American ethnic group was not 'primordial', a 'survival from the age of mass immigration, but a new social form'. Milton Gordon argued along similar lines, namely that cultural pluralism would be replaced by a structural pluralism: although ethnic languages and cultural markers were fast disappearing, people from such groups interacted with their own members more frequently than with other groups. What we have then is not the old 'national', but a new 'ethnic' quality. As Frederick Barth has argued, we should focus on 'the ethnic boundary that defines the group, not the cultural stuff that it encloses'. Or in other words, the cultural stuff need not be 'genuine' or 'primordial' in order to shape an American ethnic group and define its boundaries.[4] 'Ethnicity', in other words, is a quality which emerges when several groups of different national origin are united in one political system, when, precisely, *many cultures* are united in *one culture*. But it is not only the rise of this new ethnicity, but also the failure of the American Creed that has to be taken into account.

The demise of the older ideological belief in universalist principles that would make Americans into *one people*, indeed that would turn all humankind into the *Family of Man*, as a much-visited exhibit of photography was called in the 1950s, had less to do with these new trends than with the loss of faith in America subsequent to the Vietnam War. The Vietnam trauma gave rise to a radical rejection of mainstream values and accelerated the rise of a counter-culture which fed on the riches of black culture. Then radical feminism defined power as masculine and white, and the Watergate scandal reduced executive authority. 'AmeriKKKa', it seemed, was a construct of pure repression, the American Creed was a sham, the American Dream a nightmare. There was, moreover, growing criticism of the urban capitalist Moloch that, with the help of the military–industrial complex, was set upon the destruction of our world. In this situation of American self-criticism and self-doubt the older ethnic memories acquired the glow of a pastoral alternative. Ethnic culture was seen as almost feminine, struggling against ruthless patriarchal power; small-is-beautiful was set against centralist homogeneity; and there was a veritable run for imagined communities. To sum up, in the ethnic revival of the 1960s there was a complex of motives at work.

To a certain degree, the more recent frictions described here are an outgrowth of new patterns of multicultural coexistence and self-conscious ethnic boundary-marking that increasingly replace melting-pot visions with images of 'salad bowls' or sinister 'boiling cauldrons'. While the neo-conservative backlash and the Reagan administration's social policy seem to have aimed at a reconsolidation of an 'American core', the 1980s also saw a scramble for public funds by interest groups rallying around rediscovered 'primordial ties', a rise in nativistic and racist agitation, concomitant eruptions of violence, and, ironically, an increase in cultural heterogeneity.

Then again, a crisis of national identity and social purpose is, of course, as old as the Republic. American identity may have started out as White Anglo-Saxon Protestant; but soon immigrant Catholics challenged the Protestant definition, then non-Anglo-Saxon groups from Europe questioned the Anglo-Saxon imperative; from the Civil War to the Civil Rights legislation there was a series of challenges to the adjective 'white'. The new debate over ethnicity belongs to this series of productive challenges, each of which has helped to transform American society. It is to be hoped that the politics of ethnicity will not result in a congeries of competing pockets of cultural nationalisms which imitate the worst excesses of a self-congratulatory American exceptionalism, and that ethnicity will continue to be defined under the incorporative motto: *e pluribus unum.*

NOTES

1. Federalist, No. 2; quotation taken from New American Library edition of *The Federalist Papers* (New York, 1961), p. 38.

2. Stephen Steinberg, *The Ethnic Myth: Race, Ethnicity and Class in America* (New York, 1981), pp. 254–5.

3. John Higham, quoted in Steinberg, p. 255.

4. Frederick Barth, *Ethnic Groups and Boundaries* (Bergen and Oslo, 1969), p. 15.

SUGGESTIONS FOR FURTHER READING

The history of Old and New Immigration is competently told by Leonard Dinnerstein and David M. Reimers, *Ethnic Americans: A History of Immigration and Assimilation* (New York, 1982), and Maldwyn Allen Jones, *American Immigration* (Chicago, 1960). Stanley Lieberson and Mary C. Waters in *From Many Strands: Ethnic and Racial Groups in Contemporary America* (New York, 1988) bring the story up to the 1980 census. Herbert Gutman's *Work, Culture and Society in Industrializing America* (New York, 1976) charts the interrelationship between immigration and industrialization, and Milton M. Gordon in *Assimilation in American Life: The Role of Race, Religion and National Origin* (New York, 1964) outlines models and choices of assimilation used by different groups.

A gold mine for the theory of ethnicity and the experience of ethnic groups is the *Harvard Encyclopedia of American Ethnic Groups* (Cambridge, MA, 1980) edited by Stephan Thernstrom and Ann Orlov; it contains 106 entries on ethnic groups and survey articles on a variety of topics, such as American identity, language maintenance, prejudice and race, and ethnic literature and arts. The last – barely mentioned in this essay because of space constraints – is also treated in Sollors, Ostendorf, and other titles below, as well as in a BAAS pamphlet by Edward A. Abramson, *The Immigrant Experience in American Literature* (Durham, 1981).

Stephen Steinberg in *The Ethnic Myth: Race, Ethnicity, and Class in America*, 2nd edn (Boston, 1989) argues that the discourse of and belief in ethnicity tends to obscure the class division of American society.

Richard Polenberg in One Nation Divisible: Class, Race, and Ethnicity in the United States since 1938 (New York, 1980) focuses on the intersections of race, class and ethnicity in American life; and Werner Sollors, *Beyond Ethnicity: Consent and Descent in American Culture* (New York, 1986), and Mary Waters, *Ethnic Options: Choosing Identities in America* (Berkeley, 1990), argue that ethnicity is not only a matter of descent but also of consent or free choice. Such arguments extend the debate as to whether immigrants were primarily uprooted, as in Oscar Handlin's classic title *The Uprooted* (Boston, 1951), or whether they were more 'transplanted', bringing, as has been suggested here, significant cultural resources with them – the position also advanced by John Bodnar's *The Transplanted: A History of Immigrants in Urban America* (Bloomington, IN, 1985). The anthropologist Frederick Barth helps define what separates ethnic groups from one another in *Ethnic Groups and Boundaries* (Oslo and Bergen, 1969), as does Berndt Ostendorf's 'Literary Acculturation: What Makes Ethnic Literature "Ethnic" ' in Monique Lecomte and Claudine Thomas (eds), *Le Facteur éthnique aux Etats-Unis et au Canada* (Lille, 1983). Julian Simon focuses on *The Economic Consequences of Immigration* (Oxford, 1989).

A useful resource for data and theory concerning the post-1965 immigration is Roy Simón Bryce-Laporte (ed.), *Sourcebook on the New Immigration* (New Brunswick, NJ, 1980), while David Reimers' *Still the Golden Door* (New York, 1985) presents a broad historical survey of American immigration patterns of the past thirty years that can serve as an introductory text. The collection of articles edited by Nancy Foner titled *New Immigrants in New York City* (New York, 1987) gives the best overview of recent immigration from an anthropological perspective. Contemporary migratory patterns from the Caribbean and parts of Latin America are surveyed in Barry B. Levine (ed.), *The Caribbean Exodus* (New York, 1987) and in Constance R. Sutton and Elsa M. Chaney (eds), *Caribbean Life in New York City: Sociocultural Dimensions* (New York, 1987), while Alejandro Portes and Robert L. Bach offer a penetrating comparative analysis of the various Latin-American cases in *Latin Journey* (Berkeley, 1985). Two special numbers of the *Annals of the American Academy of Political and Social Sciences*, Vols 485 and 487 of 1986, are devoted to issues of recent immigration and its policies. James P. Shenton, 'Ethnicity and Immigration', in Eric Foner (ed.), *The New American History* (Philadelphia, 1990), constitutes a helpful short guide to recent scholarship.

CHAPTER EIGHT

Industrialization, Business and Consumerism

David E. Nye

INTRODUCTION

In 1841 Solomon Northup, a free black man living in New York State, was kidnapped and sold into slavery. In the North he had acquired many skills, working at railroad construction, barge and canal work and farming, as well as performing extensively as a fiddle player. In the South Northup was considered an extremely clever slave. Because of his experience with barges and canals, he quickly saw that once local bayous were cleared of fallen trees they could be used to move cotton to market, instead of more costly wagon transport. He convinced his master to try the experiment, and it was successful. Similarly, he was able to fix a broken loom that belonged to his master's wife, and he constructed a fish trap that provided him with a steady protein supplement to the scanty slave rations. In short, Northup had the qualities that fostered the industrial revolution in the North. He was clever, inventive and self-reliant, and he found labour-saving short-cuts in his work. Unlike other slaves he could also read and write, but he kept these skills hidden from his owners. His fellow slaves had no education, had limited work experience, and had few examples to learn from. Northup represented everything that the South could never expect from its slaves and that the North got from its workers.

The industrialization of the North depended upon much more than having an educated and experienced work force, however. While popular wisdom maintains that America was built up by the hard work of individualists in a free-wheeling market economy, this is only a partial truth. In fact, American industrial development was assiduously fostered by the government. A high tariff wall – usually over 20 per cent – protected American manufactures from foreign competition throughout the nine-teenth century. Just as importantly, state and federal government helped to create the infrastructure of roads, canals, navigable rivers and railroads that was essential to establishing a national marketplace. Legislatures made large land grants to railway companies, giving them not only the right of way for their tracks but also other extensive land holdings, which they could sell to settlers. In this way the railroads not only built their tracks but determined where many towns would be. As they moved west, they did not so much serve a market as create one. Railroad building also stimulated the iron, steel and lumber industries that supplied thousands of miles of telegraph lines, steel rails and wooden cross beams, and they called into being extensive metal-working shops that furnished their rolling stock. Because the government gave away land in exchange for internal improvements, the United States rapidly created an industrial economy which by the 1850s could already challenge England in some areas of manufacturing. Government handouts to railroads helped to create a national marketplace, stimulated western settlement, and accelerated the development of heavy industry. The American transportation network became the most extensive in the world.

Northup knew first hand that urbanization and industrialization had proceeded more rapidly in the North than in the South. With the exception of Atlanta and New Orleans, all the major American cities were in the North, as were most of the factories. The divergence of the two regions is a striking reminder of the centrality of culture in determining which technologies will be adopted and how they will be used. Nevertheless, at mid-century there were many similarities between the regions. In both regions Americans still made many of their possessions, such as tables, quilts and simpler tools. Moreover, many of these home-made articles were quite durable and passed down to the next generation, which meant that people constructed much of their social identity through inheritance rather than through purchase. In both, small companies were still the norm, almost all of which were either partnerships or family owned. Most produced a limited range of goods, marketing primarily to local and regional markets. There were as yet few factories on a vast scale, the chief exception being textile mills. The world of work was still one where people knew one another personally, and where artisans instructed apprentices in their trade. The scale of production was small, and the artisan was often able to perform all of the tasks required to transform raw materials into finished products such as shoes or a farm wagon. This world would virtually disappear in half a century, to be replaced by the culture of consumption, dominated by large corporations.

CREATING THE LARGE CORPORATION

By the 1860s railroads were beginning to serve as the models for other large enterprises, which subdivided the work into more job categories. These enterprises often took advantage of new laws of incorporation that began to be passed after the Civil War. Before then corporations could be created only by special act of a state legislature; incorporation was deemed a special privilege that was usually granted for activities which clearly benefited the public, such as constructing bridges, harbour facilities, roads and canals. Amassing the necessary public support for entirely private ventures was difficult, not least because a corporation enjoyed special immunities compared with an ordinary business. The owner of a family firm was personally responsible for its financial obligations. If the business went bankrupt, so did the owner. In contrast, the liability of stock holders in a corporation was limited to their direct investment. Incorporation thus facilitated raising risk capital far larger than most individuals would or could invest. In addition, the corporation had another crucial advantage over the family firm: it facilitated the transfer of power from one generation to the next. Instead of faltering during the dotage of a patriarchal founder or floundering in the hands of an incompetent heir, the corporation selected its leadership at annual meetings. It could hire and fire managers at will, and was more likely to have competent leadership.

Yet these advantages had their price. Strangers could purchase shares in a company which they had never seen and whose employees they had never met, and they were interested only in its balance sheet, not employee welfare. Despite its diverse ownership and large size, however, the corporation was legally defined as though it were a person. As Mulford Sibley observed

> In historical perspective, the corporation represents an anomaly. While its activities obviously affect millions of persons, it is largely treated, in law and theory, as if it were simply a person with private objectives. Thus it can own and manipulate land, fix prices (in effect), and coerce individuals through its control of resources.[1]

It must be stressed, however, that the giant corporations of today did not come into existence simply because of a convenient legal fiction that facilitated investment while minimizing personal responsibility. Large corporations made economic sense only where there was a sizeable market, and in the United States the rapid growth of the population and of the transportation network in the nineteenth century together created an integrated internal market, with no trade restrictions, which was unmatched anywhere else in the world. The sheer size of this market invited new economies of production and distribution, making it feasible to create larger factories than ever before. When John D. Rockefeller entered the oil business in 1863, there were hundreds of small entrepreneurs in the field. It was relatively easy to drill a well, and oil did not seem to be a business ripe for monopoly. But Rockefeller realized that if he built very large refineries he could undersell rival companies with less efficient plants. He also had a policy of buying out well-run rivals, usually through exchange of stock. By 1872 he controlled one-quarter of all US oil shipments. To further his competitive advantage he also insisted on special low rates from freight railways in exchange for his shipping business. Rockefeller discovered that through large-scale manufacturing it was possible to gain control over an entire business. Only in later years did his companies move into oil exploration or marketing the product to consumers. In short, Rockefeller, like many others who created giant corporations, did not try to control raw materials, their extraction, or retail outlets. Rather, he emphasized efficient manufacturing at large facilities and control over wholesale marketing. Others, taking similar approaches, soon monopolized products such as whisky, sugar, cotton oil and lead.

Some companies, including Rockefeller's in its early years, tried to limit competition through joining cartels that controlled prices. They soon found, however, that price control agreements with rivals invariably broke down. A second alternative was buying out the competition, but that course proved ruinously expensive. By 1900 corporations had begun to learn that they could overwhelm most competition by out-performing them. The National Biscuit Company (Nabisco), for example, abandoned the policy of buying out competitors and, instead, focused on better internal management of its business. It saved through purchasing materials in huge quantities, it economized by manufacturing in a few large plants, it created a more systematic advertising programme, and it improved the quality of its goods. Within a few years its Uneeda Bisquit brands dominated the market. Similarly, the American Tobacco Company established itself as a monopoly by first obtaining exclusive rights to the new Bonsack machine, a largely automatic device that could produce huge quantities of cigarettes. With the problem of inexpensive production solved, marketing became the key to achieving monopoly control, and the company spent heavily on advertising. A similar combination of superior production technology and extensive advertising underlay the rapid growth of the Swift meat-packing company. It adopted refrigerated railway cars that enabled it to reach a national market from centralized slaughter houses in the Middle West.

In some industries financiers accelerated the process of consolidation, as was the case in the electrical manufacturing industry, which grew from a few telegraph supply firms in 1870 to a $200-million industry in 1900. The fifteen sizeable electrical corporations that had emerged by 1885 were merged into just two in 1892, General Electric and Westinghouse. These two giants were then rigorously rationalized, giving them a competitive advantage not merely because they were big but because they were efficient and provided comprehensive service. As a result, would-be competitors faced formidable barriers if they wished to enter the electrical field.

Too often industrial history is presented as an inevitable triumph of machines which inexorably change society. As these few examples suggest, however, technology in itself does not explain corporate development. The first large American corporations, such as Rockefeller's oil company, were created not by a technology but by entrepreneurs, whose companies grew not so much because they controlled patents but because they were shrewdly managed. By the end of the century, corporations were being created through complex mergers orchestrated on Wall Street. And because the great corporation was not the product of an inevitable historical process but of human design, the central question in 1900 became: how is it to be run?

THE TRANSFORMATION OF WORK

By 1890 corporations were no longer a novelty, but their proper management had become a central debate. Perhaps not surprisingly, by 1903 one of the first American investigative journalists, the 'muckraker' Ida M. Tarbell, who worked for *McClure's* magazine, could readily take Rockefeller's Standard Oil as her first target. Marxists saw corporations as a logical development in the history of capital that would soon lead to state-run monopolies, but Marxism never achieved a large following in the United States. Instead, millions did read utopian social fiction. Most notable was a novel also discussed in Chapter 14, Edward Bellamy's *Looking Backward* (1888). This depicted an ideal late-twentieth-century world where working hours had been drastically reduced, not only because of more efficient production but also because the wasteful duplication of services in many small businesses had been eliminated, and where goods were equally available to all from central warehouses. Progressives such as President Theodore Roosevelt proved to be the political mainstream, however, and they rejected such socialist visions in favour of government regulation and the break-up of absolute monopolies such as Standard Oil, to foster competition between a few large companies.

The public focused primarily on who should own the corporation and how large it should be permitted to be. Seen from the inside, however, the corporation faced two different problems: how best to manage it, and how to retain and motivate good workers. To solve the first problem, corporations relied increasingly on engineers, who rejected rule-of-thumb methods in favour of mathematical analysis and increased mechanization. Engineering schools expanded rapidly after 1880, and the engineer soon emerged as a new cultural hero. Corporations required other kinds of managerial expertise as well, and to meet them encouraged the Universities of Pennsylvania, Harvard, Chicago and New York to create the modern business school, whose mission was not to turn out commercial lawyers and accountants but to train managers with an overall grasp of the corporation. By the First World War they offered courses in such areas as railroad operation, industrial organization and marketing. By the 1920s a stream of university-trained managers entered the corporations, which they gradually transformed into their own professional world, with national societies, journals and other proofs of membership. During the early decades of the twentieth century, however, the wisdom of the business school was hardly well established, and the newly trained managers were still a minority. Corporate leadership often still lay in the hands of large stock-holders, inventors, engineers, lawyers, or clever men who had started on the shop floor. This mixture may have been untidy, but the presence of at least some men who had risen from the ranks helped companies deal with the other major internal problem: labour.

From the 1880s onwards, new ideas about how to deal with employees competed for managerial attention. Not only had the small shops in which workers and supervisors knew each other personally disappeared, but the new factories bristled with ethnic unrest, for they were full of immigrants from nations that were enemies: England and Ireland, Germany and France, Poland and Russia, Italy and Austria. Some managers exploited these rivalries to divide labour, but on the whole the problem was one of how to increase worker identification with their new country in general and with the factory itself. A few reformers called for sharing ownership with workers, in a variety of schemes ranging from stock ownership to a guaranteed percentage of profits. Others reintroduced the piece-rate system that had been common before industrialization but had largely disappeared in favour of set wages. Piece-work gave the labourer a direct incentive to produce more, although workers often worried that management might discharge slower workers, or that it would accumulate a surplus of manufactured goods and then lay people off. Partly to counter such fears, welfare capitalists argued that the corporation had to look after the health, safety and well-being of its workers, in part for humanitarian reasons but also on the grounds that welfare programmes increased loyalty and efficiency while diminishing labour unrest.

The sheer scale of the large corporations destroyed much of the intimacy and camaraderie once common among artisan labourers, who had long enjoyed an informal rhythm of intense work punctuated by periods of relaxation. Workers experienced a gulf opening up between them and the new engineer–managers, whose values were largely shaped not by working traditions but by scientific models. Rather than allow workers to determine how they wished to tackle a task such as shovelling, scientific managers such as Frederick Winslow Taylor designed specialized shovels and work routines that included when and how long a man should relax and how much work should be done in a set period. Taylor's efforts were probably less important, however, than the myriad changes in production brought about by the electrification of factories, where productivity more than doubled between 1900 and 1930. At the same time, workers lost much of their control over the flow of events on the shop floor, and they became increasingly restive. Indeed, in 1910 yearly worker turnover was over 100 per cent in many industries. Despite this, as the chapter here on racism has alerted us, blacks had an extremely hard time entering many employments. The turbulent labour force increased management's concern with the 'man' problem.

The difficulty might better be described as a 'job' problem, however. In a single generation workers had experienced an enormous upheaval in their daily lives, and many found that dull routines, a faster work pace and the deskilling of many jobs had largely destroyed the satisfactions of work. This was particularly true for those on the new assembly lines, pioneered at the Highland Park factory of the Ford Motor Company before the First World War. What made the assembly line somewhat palatable were the high wages that Henry Ford paid his workers, $5 a day, at a time when the going rate in most factories was only half that. At first this policy was sharply criticized by most businessmen, who feared that it would make their own labour force more demanding. The *Wall Street Journal* editorialized that the high wage 'may return to plague him and the industry he represents, as well as organized society'. Gradually, however, it became clear that Ford was able to pay the new wage because the assembly line had dramatically improved productivity. Chassis assembly time, which had required 700 minutes, was cut in half, and then gradually reduced to less than 100 minutes.

Ford was generous with the 'secret' of the assembly line, permitting journalists and other manufacturers to tour his plant, and displaying it at the 1915 Panama–Pacific Exposition in San Francisco. Within a decade assembly lines were common across the country, and it was found that new workers, many of them women, needed little time to learn how to perform the single task that they were to repeat endlessly on the line. Because workers needed little skill for this kind of production, they could easily be replaced, becoming nearly as interchangeable as the parts they assembled. Thus, during the First World War women were recruited into the war industries, and then just as quickly mustered out of the factories once the conflict was over. Radical critics of this mode of production soon coined the term 'Fordism'. This referred not only to the assembly line and the $5 day but also to the intense pressures of assembly-line production and to Ford's particular brand of welfare capitalism, that included a company sociological department which sought to shape the private lives of employees. They prohibited men from drinking or taking boarders into their homes, and strongly encouraged them to garden on company plots of land, buy Ford automobiles, avoid labour unions, and become American citizens if they were immigrants.

Aside from the assembly line itself, however, the Ford Motor Company was atypical of American industry as a whole. While a corporation in name, in fact Ford himself controlled virtually all of its stock and ran the company just as he pleased, with open contempt for accountants, bankers and new managers with Ivy League educations. More typical was General Motors, whose stock was actively traded on the stock market. In the 1920s its managers learned the lesson of diversification and decentralized administration from the Du Pont Chemical Corporation. Du Pont had to reinvest its large profits from the First World War, and invested a sizeable chunk of money in General Motors. Unlike Ford, GM produced and marketed several product lines in order to spread the risk of failure, since it was unlikely that every line of cars would falter at once. Where Ford centralized control in one man, GM decentralized power into separate divisions. Another important difference was also characteristic. Where Ford personally intervened in research and development, which was not administratively separated from manufacturing, GM treated research and development as a key function in corporate development.

By the 1930s corporate research had also begun to extend into the workplace. The Hawthorne experiments at an electrical assembly plant had demonstrated that output in routine work was less dependent on physical comfort than on psychological factors, particularly the relationship between experimenters and the workers. Corporations invested in industrial psychology, with the goal of raising output and creating contented labourers. A new administrative division, personnel management, became an important part of most companies. The impersonal attitude towards workers is suggested in the language of a standard textbook in the field: 'The goal of human behaviour is adjustment to need-stimulated tensions in a way that will bring satisfaction. When needs are frustrated, employee behaviour may be aggressive, regressive, fixated, or resigned . . . . Man is motivated by unsatisfied needs.'[2] Advertisers took a similar point of view.

CONSUMER CULTURE

As output soared, a flood of products poured into the society, spawning new institutions, such as the advertising agency, the department store and the mail-order catalogue, thus transforming the transaction between buyer and seller. In antebellum America commercial relations had been primarily face-to-face relations. But the sheer expanse of American space encouraged new forms of marketing that were no longer based on personal contact. The logic of the vast new marketplace based on the transcontinental railroad, with its far greater flows of goods and services, soon changed the dynamic of buying. In the enlarged marketplace the word 'customer' declined in usage in favour of 'consumer'. As Raymond Williams has noted, the word 'customer had always implied some degree of regular and continuing relationship to a supplier, whereas consumer indicates a more abstract figure in a more abstract market'.[3] In this more abstract market people encountered one another in increasingly impersonal ways, at first as an unknown clerk in a large department store and by the turn of the century in form letters from mail-order stores such as Sears, Roebuck and Company. As the human relation became anonymous, only the product itself was a known quantity, and as the variety of items available proliferated, brand names gradually became more necessary to manufacturers. The consumer could no longer rely on personal acquaintance with the storekeeper as a guarantee of quality, so he or she relied on knowledge of the product itself. Successful corporations such as Nabisco, Gillette or Swift offered standardized goods of proven quality, which they often backed with guarantees. Their products were immediately recognizable because of distinctive packaging.

But guarantees, brand names and packaging were themselves insufficient as marketing devices. National advertising, which had scarcely existed in 1880, became increasingly necessary, and was concentrated in newspapers and national magazines. Indeed, because of the surge of advertising dollars available in the 1890s, many new publications began to appear, including *The Saturday Evening Post*, *McClure's*, *The American* and *Pictorial Review*, each of which had a circulation twenty times that of the older literary monthlies, such as *Scribner's* or *The Atlantic Monthly*. The new magazines signalled the emergence of a mass print society that would last until the widespread adoption of television in the 1950s. They were not only considerably cheaper, but they also employed an entirely new layout that integrated advertising and articles in parallel columns. The older magazines at first persisted in isolating advertisements as end papers, but soon began to stretch articles over many pages. Thus the ostensible content had to compete for attention with the ads. These concentrated on 'reason why' copy, which provided information about products and attempted to persuade readers through rational argument. By the early 1920s, however, advertising agencies began to abandon rationality in favour of emotional appeals and better illustrations. New psychological theories and the success of pulp magazines seemed to demonstrate that consumers were irrational and 'feminine', responding more to fears, hopes and colourful design than to logic.

In the 1920s advertisers and the new profession of home economics together redefined the role of women. Proclaiming the ease of housework with new machines which eliminated the need to bake bread, can food or wash clothing by hand, women were invited to embrace a new role defined by consumption. Women were to protect their families and the economy as a whole from shoddy goods and to improve life in the home. In actuality, studies showed that although they had new appliances women had just as much housework as before, averaging over fifty hours a week. This is not to deny that some appliances made a particular task easier, but the workload remained excessive, in part because standards of cleanliness rose, in part because housewives acquired additional tasks which men had once performed, such as beating the rug, and in part because they re-acquired some tasks that had been on the way out of the house, notably laundry. Some feminists attempted to develop alternatives, such as collective appliance ownership or kitchenless apartments, but these did not appeal to the great middle class.

Home electrification illustrates well a process that Grant McCracken calls the 'Diderot effect', in which the acquisition of one new item calls into question a person's ensemble of objects, leading to the acquisition of a whole set of more expensive possessions that fit together. The term comes from Denis Diderot, the eighteenth-century philosopher, who described how he gradually refurbished his entire study because he had received a new dressing gown, which raised the standard for the room as a whole. Something similar occurred in most American homes during the 1920s, once the installation of electrical wiring opened up another level of acquisition. In 1905 less than one home in ten was wired for electricity, but on the eve of the Great Depression three out of four were, and most families had an iron, a toaster, a vacuum cleaner and many other devices that their ancestors had never even thought of owning. To instill a craving for electrical devices, General Electric not only sponsored campaigns for individual products, but also sought to create an 'electrical consciousness' in the public. By 1930 it circulated 5 billion messages a year through printed advertising. As one publicity man explained, 'It was not until people were told, emphatically and repeatedly, what the telegraph, the telephone, and the electric light could do for them, not until they had seen the possibilities of these strange new devices demonstrated before their eyes, that they began to develop a "want".'[4]

If advertising aroused the desire for products, department stores provided a new venue for their distribution. Just as the corporation embodied improved manufacturing at one central site, the department store offered improved purchasing at one central location. It gave consumers both wide selection and money-back assurance of quality. In doing so it reversed a trend towards specialized shops that had increasingly dominated trade in the first two-thirds of the nineteenth century. In 1850 the general store was found only in small towns, while speciality shops were common in cities. The department store in effect combined from fifty to a hundred such shops under one management, and had a competitive advantage over small businesses because of economies of scale in purchasing and inventory. Every customer brought in by one department was a potential customer in all the others, and managers soon realized that they could make more money with a high turnover of goods at a small profit than with a large profit margin on a slow turnover. Yet it was not competitive prices alone that brought the emerging middle class into Marshall Field's in Chicago or Filene's in Boston. These great stores offered spectacular architecture, dazzling lighting, free lectures, art exhibits, a fascinating group of shoppers, and of course alluring displays of the latest products. The department store was the palace of consumption, making shopping pleasurable, even theatrical, as the well-dressed crowds gazed at the chandeliers, rode in the new elevators, or looked at each other, measuring their position in this new world of fashion. At the turn of the century Thorstein Veblen coined the term 'conspicuous consumption' to describe the new symbolic uses that consumer goods had achieved, as the rich learned to display their wealth. Moreover, at all levels of society, Americans became obsessed with authenticity, paradoxically desiring both the genuine and the new, determined to possess 'the real thing'. Yet the very process of endlessly substituting new goods for old quickly made 'the real' obsolescent.

As people became more anonymous in commercial transactions, their sense of social class was complicated by the realization that they belonged to 'consumption communities'. As Daniel Boorstin has argued, 'The advertisers of nationally branded products constantly told their constituents that by buying their products they could join a special group, and millions of Americans were eager to join. These consumption communities, even while they became ever more significant in the daily life of the nation, were milder, less exclusive, and less serious than ... early New England Puritan village ... communities.' Instead of the intensity of such a religious community, 'Americans led more attenuated lives'.[5] People were being progressively detached from the local and immersed in ever larger contexts, and they learned to rely on abstract values determined by the marketplace. The next logical step was to measure one another using consumer goods, to make themselves 'known' through their products. As one businessman interviewed in the famous Middletown survey of the 1920s put it, this practice was 'perfectly natural. You see, they know money, and they don't know you.'[6]

The use of consumer goods as signs of the self had profound psychological implications. Because Willy Loman, the salesman in Arthur Miller's *Death of a Salesman* (discussed in Chapter 12), is unable to ensure the continual renewal of his family's consumer goods, he begins to feel unknown and 'kind of temporary about himself'. The personal marketplace that he had experienced as a young man, in which the salesman knew his clients, was giving way to an impersonal world. Mass production and mass consumption together created social conditions of alienation and deper-sonalization, with a sharp demarcation between work and pleasure. While these same generalizations can be made about any industrial country, they had particular force in the United States, for the enormous scale of the market made the individual just that much more insignificant, while the restless mobility of the work force weakened the bonds of community and family more than was the case in Europe. Writers living within such a society, including John Dos Passos, William Faulkner and William Carlos Williams, found it increasingly difficult to portray a coherent social world.

The ubiquity of consumer goods became a common feature of western economies, but the United States was unique in the way its citizens adopted them. They preferred individual rather than collective uses for most new devices. In the early twentieth century, Americans abandoned professional laundry service in favour of washing machines installed in the home; they ignored the efficiencies of cogenerating electricity and steam heat in favour of oil and coal furnaces in each home; they rejected the potential amenities of the central city to live in suburbia; and they cast aside a well-developed streetcar and inter-urban trolley system, not to mention what were once the world's best railways, in favour of the automobile. The automobile soon dictated land use, abetting the spread of suburban living. With the demise of most street railways in the 1930s, car ownership was essential to personal mobility. A person proclaimed adulthood by acquiring 'wheels', proved membership in the great middle class by owning a Ford or Chevrolet, and announced movement up the social scale by flaunting larger and more expensive cars. A car symbolized mobility for the individual and was used for exploration, self-gratification and escape as well as transportation. It became an icon displaying personal taste. Yet the automobile is a transient personal possession that cannot be transmitted through the generations. Its self-obsolescence implies the unstable sense of a personal identity that is maintained through consumption.

The motor car became the central consumer good after 1920, and it stimulated a wide range of subsidiary industries and suppliers, becoming the engine that ran the entire economy. Already at the end of the 1920s, automobiles contained 20 per cent of the nation's steel production, 80 per cent of its rubber and 75 per cent of its plate glass. The millions of new drivers demanded thousands of miles of improved roads, and patronized a wide range of popular institutions that grew up at the outskirts of towns. The strip, as it was soon called, contained miniature golf courses, fast-food restaurants, gas stations, motels, banks, the drive-in movie, and even drive-in churches.

These leisure activities were part of a vast popular culture that emerged between 1890 and 1920, and it appalled conservative and radical critics alike. To conservatives, the advent of radio, movies and other forms of mass-market leisure spelled the death of traditional community. To radicals, the same amusements signalled capitalism's invasion of private life, or the colonization of leisure. More recent critics, in contrast, have argued that such things as the amusement park, the romance novel or the Western film should be understood neither as threats to high culture nor as forms of false consciousness, but as experiences in which the consumer selects and defines much of the meaning. In this view, much of popular culture offers a necessary critique of, and psychic release from, the world of work, expressing utopian yearnings that subvert dominant cultural values.

Indeed, a host of other factors were dramatically reshaping the nature and distribution of the work. As output per man-hour in factories soared, more people worked in offices. By 1950 the majority of workers had shifted from manufacturing to the white-collar sector. Corporations became increasingly manager-intensive and had ever larger office staffs, and they demanded skilled teamwork. Sociologists noted that companies fostered an ethos, or corporate culture. Individualism, once considered a central virtue of capitalism, had become a secondary corporate virtue of less importance than cooperation and flexibility. The increasing conformity was symbolized in the 'organization man' who sacrificed himself for the company. This shift in values was paralleled by developments in leisure activities. After 1950 professional football, with its disciplined teamwork and technological complexity, became as popular as the more individualistic baseball. Likewise, the lone Western hero who had once dominated the Western film genre was gradually displaced by larger groups of professional gun-slingers, whose first loyalty was neither to abstract moral values nor to any community, but rather to their group.

INDUSTRIAL AND CONSUMER RESEARCH

To ensure long-term profits, corporations found it was not enough to produce and distribute familiar products efficiently. They also had to discover the popular products of tomorrow. As formal institutions, American industrial research laboratories date from 1900, when General Electric established its lab in Schenectady. Before then industries did not formally separate manufacturing and research, though they did recognize the importance of improving their machinery and often retained small numbers of skilled men to this end. In the last decades of the nineteenth century, a few independent inventors, notably Thomas Edison and Arthur D. Little, had their own research establishments. Edison began with less than a dozen employees but eventually controlled a work force of several hundred. Under his direction they invented the phonograph, the incandescent electric light (plus the generating and distribution system necessary to supply it), an improved telephone, the first practical movie camera, a poured-cement house, and much more, accumulating over one thousand patents.

Such independent operations were a transition to corporation research labs. Indeed, even Edison's electric light had been financed largely by J.P. Morgan and other bankers. By the First World War most corporations realized that they could maintain market dominance only if they owned patents for tomorrow's products as well as for those they already produced. Ford was the largest automotive manufacturer in 1920, but he refused to recognize the need for continual innovation. He resisted pressures from engineers in his company to develop new models and insisted on manufacturing the Model T from 1909 until 1927, albeit with small improvements. Meanwhile, General Motors lured customers away with a steady stream of innovations that were dramatized by yearly styling changes. Just as importantly, GM attracted customers to more expensive purchases by offering a finely graduated line of models. When Ford finally decided to create a new car, the Model A, he virtually stopped production for months in 1927 and in the process lost market share to GM, which had more expertise in gearing up to produce new models.

From the manager's point of view, the goal of industrial research was not only to enhance existing products but to create entirely new ones. Du Pont developed synthetic fibres; General Electric produced artificial diamonds; the pharmaceutical companies sought new drugs. The managerial drive for profitable innovations was not always congenial to company scientists, however, who were often primarily interested in basic research that was only tangentially related to commerce. Large research laboratories found it expedient to permit staff considerable freedom, in the hope that they would make breakthroughs into the unknown that would have commercial applications. In any case, what new products would sell? Some never did, such as the air-conditioned bed or the Edsel car, but others were widely adopted, including radio, paperback books, filter cigarettes, pet rocks, cabbage-patch dolls and the hoola-hoop, although the reasons for success were not always obvious. Companies invested in market research to determine what unrecognized needs might be lurking in the consumer, and they began to test-market products in order to fine-tune not only the innovation but the packaging.

In response to the proliferation of goods, a Consumer's League had already appeared in 1899, and provocative books periodically aroused the public to demand better quality, notably Upton Sinclair's attack on the meat-packing industry in *The Jungle* (1906) and later Stuart Chase and F.J. Schlink's *Your Money's Worth* (1927). In 1936 the Consumer's Union was founded, with the goal of systematically testing brand-name goods and publishing the results. While perceived as a radical group in its early years, after the Second World War it reached a broad public, not only through publications but also by word of mouth and library circulation. In 1970 its monthly magazine *Consumer Reports* had 1,800,000 subscribers, and it published books dealing with major areas of consumer interest. The Consumer's Union also regularly testifies before government commissions whose names reveal the growth of consumer issues in politics: the National Commission on Product Safety, the National Advisory Committee on Flammable Fabrics, and the National Motor Vehicle Safety Advisory Council. Nor was the Consumer's Union alone in this effort. In the 1960s activist Ralph Nader achieved national fame with his attack on automotive safety, *Unsafe at Any Speed* (1965), and built up a large student following whose contributions financed numerous studies and lobbying efforts on a wide range of issues.

While some government agencies responded to consumer complaints, far more federal money was spent on research and development. The national government had been only sporadically involved in funding research until the Second World War. It ran research stations for agriculture and forestry and occasionally funded defence-related projects.

After the Japanese attack on Pearl Harbor brought the nation into the Second World War, government-sponsored research increased dramatically. In response to a letter from Albert Einstein who suggested the feasibility of building an atom bomb, Franklin Roosevelt concluded that he had to surpass any German efforts to create such a weapon, and launched the vast secret project which produced the weapons dropped on Japan. Government money also poured into many other areas of military research, notably into code breaking, artificial languages and computers, creating a new relationship with universities, which often received the funds.

In the postwar years, according to an OECD economic survey, *The United States* (1989), Washington became the biggest single investor in research and development, supplying 48 per cent of all funds. In 1990 two-thirds of this support, as well as considerable corporate resources, went to defence work, rather than to developing new consumer products or to basic research. Some military or space research did result in spin-offs, such as various forms of miniaturization or Teflon, which found their way into the consumer market. Yet overall, military research distorted American development compared with that in Germany or Japan, since expensive weapons systems wasted human and physical resources and increased both taxes and the national debt. As Robert Sayre has noted, the Cold War inflicted almost as much damage as a military conflict: ' "cold" or not it has still done the economic, political, and social damage of a war. Americans have made wartime sacrifices – in diminished social programmes, deferred up-keep of their public facilities and services, over-allocation of wealth and resources to weaponry .... . The rusting bridges and run-down railroads have not been bombed by enemy planes. They have been knocked out by Cold-War neglect.'[7]

To be sure, the American economy continued to grow through the Cold War, and private companies did create a host of new goods, such as Xerox machines, polaroid cameras, portable air conditioners and the personal computer. Nevertheless, its progress was slower than that of Japan or Germany, neither of which was burdened with a large defence budget. Although the United States long devoted more resources to research and development than either country, and although it today publishes 38 per cent of the world's scientific literature, nevertheless it has lost the technological advantage it once had. Indeed, the Japanese have demonstrated a distinctive style of innovation, particularly in computer technologies, that coordinates private and public investments. By the late 1980s it became clear that, despite American efforts, Japan had taken the lead in developing the next generation of computer chips, just as it had earlier gained control of the production of televisions, cameras and many other products. Since computer research has long been supported both directly and indirectly by government, this development suggested a problem more fundamental than a distorted allocation of resources.

A decade earlier Americans had consoled themselves after defeats at the hands of Japanese corporations with the argument that cheaper labour costs in Japan combined with high tariff barriers explained the losses. By implication, the Japanese advantage was only temporary and would disappear once their wages rose to American levels. By the late 1980s, however, it became clear that Japan's corporations succeeded because they had another management style which gave more security and more decision-making power to workers and which insisted on stricter quality control. Indeed, Japanese corporations established some branch automotive plants in the United States that out-performed American factories. More ominous still from the American point of view, by 1990 the Japanese invested more in non-military R and D than the Americans.

ELECTRONIC CULTURE

National rivalry is probably not the best way to understand business, industrialization or consumption at the end of the twentieth century, however, as there is nothing inherently nation-bound in the nature of the corporation. Even before the First World War some companies had established branch plants abroad and, despite the disruptions of two world conflicts, most of them gradually expanded their operations. Where once foreign countries were attractive primarily as markets, it is now common to have manufacturing plants abroad as well. They may be inside the European Community, over the border in Mexico, or in the rapidly developing Asian countries. There are many reasons for this diversification, including not only lower wages but also avoidance of tariffs, access to new capital, and economies gained by manufacturing close to foreign markets. Because corporations are so multinational, their economic performance is harder to gauge. Unprofitable management activities may be located in the United States while high-profit manufacturing is abroad. A product could be designed in California, engineered in Japan, manufactured as components in several countries, and assembled in plants inside each market. Not only is the 'nationality' of the resulting product unclear, but the tax laws governing its manufacture and the profits reaped from its sale are exceedingly complex. Governments have a difficult time regulating the activities of multinationals or tracking the flow of money by electronic transfer from one continent to another.

While large corporations became international, retailing and smaller businesses increasingly abandoned the central city, relocating along the expressways and in suburbia. This trend towards urban deconcentration meant that after 1960 over half of all industrial jobs could be found outside central cities. In the same years the centre of consumption moved from downtown to the shopping malls. The first mall was founded already in the 1920s in Kansas City. At the end of the Second World War there were less than a dozen in the country, but in the following decade they mushroomed to more than 3,800. At the same time they grew in scale until they replicated the full range of stores once located on main street, contained in a vast interior without traffic or bad weather. Yet the mall was quite unlike main street, for it was a privately controlled space, without political or cultural institutions, and it was dedicated to the single purpose of sales. The department store in its heyday had offered not only products but exhibits, lectures and social uplift. At the shopping mall people met not as fellow citizens, neighbours, art lovers or aspirants to social distinction, but as consumers only. This development was the logical result of the increasing physical distance between people in the sprawling American suburbs and of the increasingly abstract nature of the jobs people held.

Since the 1950s more than half the population has worked in the service sector, producing things that are often intangible, invisible or arbitrarily valued: art, service, prestige, reputation, education, advice, security, information, protection, psychoanalysis, advertising and public relations. Even money itself seldom moves from hand to hand but is represented by plastic cards and registered in electronic impulses. The American increasingly exchanges only symbols without touching any tangible object, as can be clearly seen in the success of mail-order sales and tele-marketing. This development is the ultimate extension of the longer-term depersonalization of shopping. The nineteenth-century customer had relied on the reputation of a local business and personal acquaintance with its staff; the early-twentieth-century consumer relied little on the sales staff, trusting in the brand name and the ability to evaluate a product. But the post-industrial consumer has abandoned personal contact with the seller, the product or the money exchanged, and relies on visual representations and code numbers to complete a process that is distended over space and time. Perhaps as a result, Americans enjoy the unaccustomed immediacy of an outdoor market when travelling abroad. In contrast to their own abstract form of consumption, they are confronted with a human situation in which the contact is immediate, the price is uncertain, and the quality of the goods problematic.

Even as consumption has become an increasingly abstract and impersonal process, a symbolic system has developed, primarily through advertising, that many authors on the left, such as Jean Baudrillard, see as a solipsistic discourse detached from specific referents, where meaning in general is eroded. This floating empire of signs exists between truth and falsehood, proffering new intense experiences that nevertheless seem forever out of reach. The sense of displacement is further increased by a new set of miniaturized technologies which detach the consumer from fixed locations in space. The quantitative shrinkage in objects has resulted in a qualitative change in their use. Radios, once heavy wooden boxes that literally tied listeners down by their earphones, are now little larger than earphones that can be worn anywhere. The instantaneous access to music and information puts the consumer in touch with a larger, unseen world, but reduces contact with immediate surroundings. Similarly, a television that once was the size of a kitchen cabinet can now be scarcely larger than a cigarette packet. Telephones have become portable, and computers containing thousands of pages of information and complex programmes have been reduced to the size of a notebook. Such miniaturization has created a class of nomadic objects that permit people to work, communicate or consume anywhere, any time. This change, combined with jet air travel, has made the individual almost as hard to pin down as the corporation. Just as multinational companies no longer have a firm spatial or national definition, consumers likewise have become increasingly mobile and ubiquitous.

This mobility does not translate into invisibility, however, because technologies of surveillance have also improved dramatically. As a somewhat paranoid character in Don DeLillo's *Running Dog* (1978) put it

> Go into a bank, you're filmed . . . . Go into a department store, you're filmed. Increasingly, we see this. Try on a dress in the changing room, someone's watching you. Employees are watched too, spied on with hidden cameras. Drive your car anywhere. Radar, computer traffic scans. They're looking into the uterus, taking pictures. Everywhere. What circles the earth constantly? Spy satellites, weather balloons, U–2 aircraft. What are they doing? Taking pictures. Putting the whole world on film.[8]

The fear that no nook was free from surveillance was already powerfully articulated by George Orwell in *1984* (1948), a book dominated by the vision of totalitarian, centralized control which is the dark side of the culture of consumption.

These transformations suggest that the culture of consumption which emerged in the early twentieth century is being gradually replaced by another system, an emerging electronic culture that is defined by the convergence of television, the personal computer, the telefax machine and other electronic devices. The difference between these two systems can be measured by contrasting the automobile, central to the older culture of consumption, and the television/computer which has become the icon of the new order. The automobile was used to disperse the population into post-industrial cities, where housing, work and leisure were segregated from one another. The computer is dissolving these distinctions, permitting work and shopping to be done without leaving home. Americans used the automobile to escape from community into suburbs whose remoteness from the city centre was a measure of wealth and success. The computer permits the reinvention of communities which are not united in one location but which can communicate instantaneously. Unlike the culture of consumption with its monolithic system of advertising for standard brands, electronic culture builds upon two-way communication to create many distinct products tailored to the needs of subgroups. The culture of consumption required national magazines, and later shaped national radio and television networks that offered only a few choices. These communication systems defined Americans as a monolithic mass culture, targeting their fictions, programmes and advertisements at the lowest common denominator.

In contrast, electronic culture permits differential mailing to households based on zip codes, cable television stations that 'narrow-cast' to a well-defined public, radio stations that specialize in one musical form, and computer networks that foster ties between those with similar interests. The older 'consumption communities' were based on the purchase of a product, and the linkages between those who drove the same make of car or smoked the same brand of cigarettes were ephemeral at best. In contrast, the linkages in the emergent electronic culture are stronger, because increasingly they are based on two-way communication. The integration of the television, personal computer, fax machine and telephone allows self-conscious groups to form that are not a product of nation-wide advertising or public relations. The culture of consumption implied a centralized power visible in its national brands, mass marketing and national media networks. In contrast, the emergent electronic culture appears to be more dispersed yet global, more variegated yet uniformly available, more democratic yet technological, and more interactive, though on terms defined by computer software.

Nor are these characteristics confined to private life, as the electronic culture is already visible in many workplaces, in spite of corporate intentions to use computers as tools to strengthen centralization. When first introduced into business in the 1950s, computers were massive machines that only the central administrations of the largest corporations could afford. They were developed in part with funding by the military and the CIA, and soon became essential to banks, the Internal Revenue Service and credit agencies. They seemed to symbolize central control, systematic information gathering and the invasion of privacy. From the 1950s until the 1980s the computer was understood to be a powerful tool which managers could use to increase control over both production and human behaviour.

Yet as computers became more widespread and easier to operate, they soon turned out to be useful in undermining hierarchy, secrecy and centralization. By the 1980s on-site studies of computer networks in operation began to show that despite management's intention to use them to deskill workers and to increase its control over operatives, something quite different was taking place. Computers are two-way streets and they gave every operator access to all the information in the system. Previously, both workers and managers had withheld part of their working knowledge, whether intentionally or not. In contrast, at a fully computerized plant this working knowledge is transformed into text and figures, providing information that is far more detailed than that which previously existed, and covering all aspects of daily operations. Managers at sites ranging from saw mills to telephone companies have discovered that to realize the full potential of the computer they have to provide workers with wide access to the system's potential. Where management once had exclusive access to most information, computers take away this privilege, while they empower many who once had a narrow view of their job and did not understand the interconnections between their work and that of others. In short, the computer provides the opportunity to combine hands-on knowledge with detailed records generated from the computer system. The 'smart machine', which had been expected to concentrate power, can instead spread information through the company, weakening the position of managers and empowering workers. Moreover, personal computers mean that an increasing number of people no longer need to attend a workplace outside the home. On the one hand this may contribute to an increased sense of alienation, but on the other the obvious flexibility of such an arrangement could also help to redefine the very nature of both the 'home' and 'work', thus further eroding traditional gender roles.

Computers can be used to break down manager–worker divisions or they can be used as originally intended, to standardize and deskill many tasks. The choice occurs not in the abstract but in a competitive business environment, where the most efficient corporations will survive. It seems likely that given increasingly segmented markets, where demand shifts away from mass-produced goods to smaller batch production, computer-literate workers will prove more efficient than those performing rigid routines. The choice is not the same as that between slavery and freedom, but Solomon Northup knew in 1850 that the empowered, literate worker was more innovative and efficient than the illiterate slave.

186

NOTES

1. Mulford Sibley, *Political Ideas and Ideologies: A History of Political Thought* (New York, 1970), p. 526.

2. Edwin B. Flippo, *Principles of Personnel Management*, 2nd edn (New York, 1966), p. 365.

3. Raymond Williams, *Keywords* (New York, 1976), pp. 68–70.

4. John W. Hammond, 'The Psychology of a Nation's Wants', Hammond Papers L 5141, General Electric Company Library, Schenectady plant.

5. Daniel Boorstin, *The Americans: The Democratic Experience* (New York, 1973), p. 148.

6. Robert S. and Helen Merrell Lynd, *Middletown* (New York, 1956), p. 81.

7. Robert Sayre, 'Inventing Modern America: An Open University Project', *American Studies in Scandinavia* **21**:2 (1989): 95.

8. Don DeLillo, *Running Dog* (New York, 1978), pp. 149–50.

SUGGESTIONS FOR FURTHER READING

Solomon Northup's *Twelve Years a Slave* (Baton Rouge, LA, 1975) is a valuable source, providing the closest thing to a participant observer of antebellum slavery, since this author already knew freedom before he experienced slavery. A key work for understanding the emergence and evolving structure of the corporation in the nineteenth century is Alfred Chandler's *The Visible Hand* (Cambridge, MA, 1977). Alan Trachtenberg's *The Incorporation of America* (New York, 1982) uses the emergence of the corporation as the central cultural event between the Civil War and the 1893 Colombian Exhibition in Chicago. For the role of the engineers in corporate development, see David F. Noble, *America by Design* (New York, 1977). For labour history, Herbert Gutman's *Work, Culture, and Society* (New York, 1977) remains an essential work. On how electrification increased worker output and made possible the assembly line, and on the electrification of the home, see David E. Nye, *Electrifying America* (Cambridge, MA, 1990). The standard account of welfare capitalism is Stuart Brandes, *American Welfare Capitalism* (Chicago, 1976). Cecelia Tichi analyses how engineering values permeated cultural life in *Shifting Gears: Technology, Literature, Culture in Modernist America* (Chapel Hill, NC, 1987).

Thorstein Veblen's *Theory of the Leisure Class* (New York, 1979), first published in 1899, can still be read with profit. The term 'consumption communities' was coined by Daniel Boorstin in *The Americans: The*

Democratic Experience (New York, 1973), which remains an insightful book. Miles Orvell's *The Real Thing* (Chapel Hill, NC, 1989) is an exemplary interdisciplinary work that analyses imitation and authenticity between 1880 and 1940, and for some discussion of popular culture as critique and necessary relief, see David E. Nye, 'The Consumption of American Popular Culture', *Text and Context* **2**:1 (1988).

Studies of advertising have proliferated in recent years. Among the best works is Roland Marchand's *Advertising the American Dream: Making Way for Modernity, 1920–1940* (Berkeley, 1985), which analyses agencies, advertising campaigns and aesthetic strategies. Two older sociological works provide insight into the culture of consumption: Robert S. and Helen Merrell Lynd's *Middletown* (New York, 1956), first published in 1929, describes the full emergence of consumer culture in the 1920s, while David Riesman led a research group that produced *The Lonely Crowd* (New Haven, 1950), a searching analysis of conformist tendencies in 'American character'. Grant McCracken's *Culture and Consumption: New Approaches to the Symbolic Character of Consumer Goods and Activities* (Bloomington, IN, 1988) is innovative and stimulating. Ralph Gaedeke and Warren Etcheson's *Consumerism* (San Francisco, 1972) is a useful compendium on consumer activism, including documents from business, government and public interest groups. Ruth Schwartz Cowan's *More Work for Mother* (New York, 1983) analyses the often ironic consequences of new technologies in the home. Will Wright links transformations in the plot structure of Western films to transformations in the economy in *Sixguns and Society* (Berkeley, 1975).

Jackson Lears and Richard Wightman Fox contributed to and edited a clutch of important essays, *The Culture of Consumption* (New York, 1983). *American Studies and Consumption*, ed. David E. Nye and Carl Pedersen (Amsterdam, 1991), collects seventeen interdisciplinary essays, and Jean Baudrillard, *The Political Economy of the Sign* (St Louis, 1981), offers relevant and stimulating comments. Shoshana Zuboff's *In the Age of the Smart Machine* (New York, 1988) takes a moderately hopeful view of the computer in the workplace, in contrast to Barbara Garson, *The Electronic Sweatshop: How Computers are Transforming the Office of the Future into the Factory of the Past* (New York, 1989). Finally, Joshua Meyrowitz's *No Sense of Place* (New York, 1985) discusses the impact of electronic media on social behaviour.

Students looking for further materials should also consult the journals *Business History, Technology and Culture*, and *Harvard Business Review*.

CHAPTER NINE

Urbanization and Architecture

Glenn M. Andres

IN SEARCH OF AN AMERICAN ARCHITECTURE

At the beginning of the twentieth century architect Louis Sullivan observed: 'American architecture will mean, if it ever succeeds in meaning anything, American life.'[1] This would not necessarily posit a unique national style, for America is too varied; it has been too active a recipient and testing ground for the world's architectural tastes and dreams – transmitted via publication, importation, immigration, foreign education and travel. It would suggest, though, a national character, imparted to these received ideas and styles as they have been realized with American building materials and methods and under American attitudes and conditions. That character is particularly recognizable in several influential forms that have marked America's coming of age on the international scene: the dense, business-dominated city centre with its skyscrapers; the residential suburb with its single family homes; and the diffuse chaos of the automobile-oriented strip.

SUBURB AND SKYSCRAPER

In 1905 a nineteenth-century Henry Adams, the historian and novelist, confronted the twentieth-century high-rise city, as embodied in New York. As he wrote in *The Education of Henry Adams* (1907; 1917), he found it frantic and 'wonderful – unlike anything man had ever seen – and like nothing he had ever much cared to see'.[2] Adams's generation bridged two Americas – one of seemingly limitless land and exploitable resources, the other (since the official closing of the frontier in the 1890s) finite. The former had shaped tenacious national attitudes regarding open space, agrarian life, self-sufficiency, the independence of private ownership, and mobility. The latter confronted the nation with an industrial, urbanized reality at once exciting in its sublime power and repellent in its compaction and disorder.

A century earlier Thomas Jefferson had acknowledged the necessity of industrial/urban development for the prosperity of the country but expressed his distaste for it, preferring instead a nation dominated by citizen farmers. Open space and possession of land had been basic to American settlement patterns. Even in urban situations the ideal was that of Philadelphia – planned with individual houses centred on large plots to be a 'green country town which will never be burnt and always be wholesome'.[3] As nineteenth-century urban realities compromised this spacious image in favour of more European densities, the middle class espoused a scheme that provided them the best of both worlds – a compact, exclusively commercial city centre and more diffuse peripheral and suburban residential zones, socially and economically homogeneous, 'where every house could have a goodly expanse of ground about it filled with trees and shrubbery'.[4] The underclasses aspired to work their way from urban ghetto to white collar suburb.

Chicago, calling itself *Urbs in Hortus*, typified the pattern. The Congressional Land Ordinance of 1785 had mandated a unified survey of the entire country west of the Appalachians into a grid of one-mile squares oriented to the cardinal points, and Chicago, founded in 1830, was one of countless towns platted in a grid consistent with its coordinates. The system disregarded local topography and lacked aesthetic inspiration, but it was valued by most Americans for its convenience of layout and its utility for real estate transfer. By the end of the century Chicago was a booming metropolis. Rail lines radiated from its commercial centre, past neighbour-hoods of single family homes, to strings of suburbs, each focusing on its commuter station. Notable among the last was the speculative suburb of Riverside, designed in the late 1860s by Frederick Law Olmsted under the inspiration of the romantic landscape theories of Andrew Jackson Downing. Its irregularly curving roads, picturesque park strips and large building plots for individually constructed houses were conceived in purposeful contrast to the urban grid, 'to suggest and imply leisure, contemplativeness, and happy tranquility . . . secluded peacefulness'.[5]

The housing in these residential areas, in various of the picturesque styles adopted by nineteenth-century Americans to express material success and individuality, was mostly in wood. It used the balloon-framing technique that had developed in Chicago in the 1830s as a practical alternative to the heavy pegged timber frame of the East. This system of light, mill-dimensioned lumber joined with manufactured nails recommended itself for home-building by its economy of material, its ease of working, its adaptability to complex massing, and its suitability for mass production and shipment. Materials, details and entire houses could be prefabricated and shipped anywhere to shelter the rapidly growing population of the American Midwest and West. Since many middle-class homes had no domestic help, efficiency in planning was as desired as efficiency in construction – a need addressed in books both by professional architects and by women seeking to rationalize domestic management. Catherine Beecher and Harriet Beecher Stowe's *American Woman's Home* (1869) considered such topics as heating, ventilation, storage, sanitation, built-in furniture, the flexible and efficient use of rooms, kitchen design (which would be an ongoing American preoccupation) and verandahs (linking the house and its surrounding landscape).

Escalating land values at the head of the commuter lines and stringent building codes (stressing fireproof materials) had all but banished such single-family domestic construction from the business core of the cities. Here the conjunction of economics that favoured density, steel frames that made height feasible, and the elevator that rendered upper floors accessible and desirable made the skyscraper a virtual inevitability. Chicago provided conditions particularly conducive to the rapid evolution of the new building type. A fire in 1871 had destroyed the entire heart of the commercial metropolis. Its rebuilding drew numerous speculative investors and architects with common concerns for height, relatively light-weight construction, resistance to fire, and maximum natural illumination. William Le Baron Jenny's ten-storey Home Insurance Company (1883–85) – combining an all iron and steel frame with insulating masonry and a non-bearing façade – is considered to have been the world's first true skyscraper. Through the concerted work of Jenny's Chicago colleagues, the new type quickly matured as a tall rectilinear block drawing its proportions and order from its frame, characteristically filled with broad, three-part 'Chicago' windows.

The Chicago skyscraper is often represented as an invention of pure practicality – a mix of native common sense, hard-headed economic expediency and technical inventiveness. But it was not the product of naive provincials. Most of its principal authors had been educated in Boston, New York, London and Paris. For example, Henry Hobson Richardson, whose Marshall Field and Company wholesale store (1885–87) provided important lessons for the unified organization of tall and large façades, had attended the Ecole des Beaux Arts. They were also conversant with such European theories as those of Viollet-le-Duc, who had written in his *Entretiens* (1872): 'A practical architect might not unnaturally conceive the idea of erecting a vast edifice whose frame should be entirely of iron . . . preserving that frame by means of a casing of stone.' His ideas take material form in the likes of Burnham and Root's Reliance Building (begun 1889) and Louis Sullivan's Carson, Pirie, Scott department store (1899–1904), buildings that are virtually all skeleton and glass – the lightness of their steel frames emphasized by a minimal white terracotta sheathing.

Sullivan, the most famous of the Chicago skyscraper designers, drew inspiration from both European and American sources; included among the latter were not only other visual artists, such as sculptor Horatio Greenough and fellow architect Henry Hobson Richardson, but Transcendentalist philosopher Ralph Waldo Emerson and the American poet who most espoused organic form, Walt Whitman (see Chapter 15). His developed style of functional rationalism and distinctive geometric and vegetal decoration can be seen in the Auditorium Building (1886–90), built in partnership with Dankmar Adler. This was Chicago's immense opera house – a hall acclaimed for its sight lines and acoustics, wrapped by peripheral hotel and office spaces that generated income to underwrite the costs of operating the theatre. Within its appropriately businesslike exterior is a ravishing display of ahistoric decoration in iron, mosaic, stucco, stencilwork, stained glass and electric light bulbs. A democratic, private-enterprise counterpart to the likes of the aristocratic Paris Opéra, this building witnesses to the aesthetic as well as the functional sophistication of Chicago architecture.

Sullivan demonstrated aesthetic control over Adams's 'frantic' skyscrapers in his influential essay 'The Tall Office Building Artistically Considered' (*Lippincott's Magazine*, 1896), which drew upon his own experience designing the Wainwright Building (St Louis, MO, 1890–91), and the Guaranty Building (Buffalo, NY, 1895). Working from the premise that form follows function, he analysed the skyscraper façade into three zones: the commercial base, as open as possible and decorated with regard to the person on the street; the mid-section expressing its stacks of repetitive offices; and the mechanical attic serving as a visual cap for the building. Unlike his Chicago colleagues, Sullivan chose not to stress the horizontality of the steel structural bay, but rather emphasized the height of the building with a quick vertical rhythm of continuous masonry piers and stacks of windows. For him a skyscraper 'should be tall, every inch of it tall . . . a proud and soaring thing, rising in sheer exultation'.[6]

THE CHICAGO FAIR

In 1893 Chicago hosted the spectacular World's Columbian Exposition, visited by the equivalent of 40 per cent of the national population. Its fairgrounds provided them with an encyclopedic display of architectural and urban themes. There were the familiar grid, winding lanes with individual pavilions in varied styles, and a linear commercial 'Main Street'. This last was the unashamedly chaotic Midway, dedicated to the exposition's immensely popular rides, concessions and sideshows, housed in buildings that proclaimed their contents with symbolic forms and boldly painted messages. In sharp contrast, the natural lagoon with its wooded island revealed the English picturesque tastes of the fair's landscape designer, Olmsted, who with his British expatriate partner Calvert Vaux had created New York's Central Park (1858 ff) as relief from the city's bustling grid and had inspired similar park construction in major cities across the United States. It was the French-inspired Court of Honor, however, that established the dominant image of the fair.

This was a monumental basin surrounded by white-stuccoed classical buildings with uniform cornice heights, coordinated alignments and columnar porticoes conceived in competition with the formal court of the Paris Exposition of 1889. Instead of Paris's radical Eiffel Tower, though, the Chicago court had a baroque domed administration pavilion and referred as much to the Place de la Concorde as to the Champ de Mars. It was a surprising design for Chicago. Chicagoans had originally conceived of the fair as colourful and eclectic throughout; but as the planning evolved, director Daniel Burnham and a national team of architects decided to substitute a formally unified classical aesthetic for the Court of Honor. Not only were most of the architects adept with this style (by virtue of their training), but classical principles – horizontal cornice lines, symmetry, modularity – lent themselves to ensemble design while still permitting some individuality. The result was a revelation to an America where ensembles had not been designed for the better part of a century.

Henry Adams admired his compatriots' achievement in realizing such a complex but was troubled by the sense of borrowed forms and wondered whether the American people knew where they were driving. Critic Montgomery Schuyler praised it as scenic architecture but pondered what the public would make of it. A few years earlier architect Henry Van Brunt had observed about American taste that

> the natural desire of every citizen to own property of the best possible appearance at the lowest possible cost leads to what may be called an architecture of pretense – an architecture intended to appear better than it is. [It] has flattered the crude artistic aspirations of millions of intelligent and exceptionally ingenious and prosperous people . . . . Nowhere else in the civilized world can be found anything resembling it.[7]

Sensitive to this, Schuyler worried at the potential impact of the fair if people tried to replicate the lath and plaster vision in the real world.

THE CITY BEAUTIFUL

The fantasy of the Chicago Fair *was* reproduced – in other expositions (Buffalo, 1900; St Louis, 1904; San Francisco, 1915), in amusement parks and theatres, and also in the world of serious architecture. America at the turn of the century, with its rapidly consolidating mega-industries and its ever-growing wealth, sought an architectural image of suitable prestige in world estimation. Historicism, and particularly classicism, offered associations with culture and power that allayed the national cultural inferiority complex and indulged new American millionaires seeking social credentials. Unconstrained by specific iconographies, they pressed their architects to recreate historic forms, out of context and often on a larger scale. For the Vanderbilts (railroad money) the Beaux Arts-trained Richard Morris Hunt created limestone Francis I chateaux on New York's Fifth Avenue (1879–83) and outside of Asheville, North Carolina (Biltmore, 1895), a Genoese baroque villa (the Breakers, Newport, RI, 1892), and a Louis XV mansion (Marble House, Newport, RI, 1892–95). Besides reproducing old-world forms and details, such houses often used actual architectural fragments. Isabella Stewart Gardner's Boston residence (1903) incorporated the original façade of the Ca d'Oro from Venice. Others contained drawing rooms, fireplaces, libraries, art collections and suites of furniture acquired from impecunious aristocrats abroad.

The taste extended to public projects privately organized and financed by the same industrialists. Edward Bellamy's utopian *Looking Backward* (1888) had set the image for enlightened civic philanthropy. McKim, Mead, and White's Boston Public Library (1887–98) – essentially the Bibliothèque Ste Geneviève in Paris, enlarged and enriched – had set the standard. After the Chicago Fair, this Beaux Arts taste swept the country in projects ranging from grandiose art museums to small-town libraries built by the charitable foundation established by steel-maker Andrew Carnegie. The sense of formal ensemble demonstrated at the fair gave shape to monumental new campuses like that McKim, Mead, and White designed for Columbia University (New York, 1894 ff). It was applied to city design in the 1902 project of the MacMillan Commission to renew L'Enfant's grand but eroded baroque scheme for Washington DC. Their proposals established the programme for the monumental twentieth-century development of the capital, focusing on the redefined Mall lined with marble museums, memorials and bureaucratic palaces. Equally importantly, they captured the attention and imagination of the nation.

Private civic organizations commissioned similar schemes to enhance their cities. Along with designs for Cleveland and San Francisco, Burnham proposed in 1909 to overlay the Chicago grid with a radial and circumferential network of Parisian-like boulevards and parks. At its hub an avenue lined with cultural institutions would lead from a formal harbour to a civic plaza with a great domed city hall. Such visions spearheaded the City Beautiful Movement, inspiring hundreds of projects of varying scales across the country. Most involved civic buildings, magnificently exemplified in the San Francisco civic centre (City Hall, opera house, museum, city offices) begun by Bakewell and Brown in 1915. Some went beyond mere beautification. Burnham's Chicago plan also considered issues of regional growth, rail services, rapid transit, recreation, commerce and housing. The first comprehensive examination of American cities as integrated organisms, these private schemes helped to launch public civic planning in the United States (for example Hartford, CT, 1907; Chicago, 1909).

In their self-appointed role as national taste-makers, businessmen gave historical pretensions to banks, department stores and railroad stations. McKim, Mead, and White designed New York's colonnaded Pennsylvania Station (1902–10) as an enlarged version of the Baths of Caracalla in Rome. The rival New York Central responded with the colossal vaulted concourse of Grand Central Station (Warren and Wetmore, 1903–13), built as part of a City Beautiful scheme for Park Avenue. Privately developed over what had been an open railroad cut through the city, this broad street lined with uniformly massed apartment buildings boasted a central garden strip and terminated in a focal office tower adjacent to the station.

Skyscrapers, too, became gestures of cultural showmanship. The businessmen of New York and their architects wrapped the sublimely soaring frames in Beaux Arts skins of visually pleasing, easily accessible historical imagery. Such imagery had already appeared in the 1890s and early 1900s at New York's Coney Island amusement parks, combining the entertainment of Chicago's Midway with the sham architectural pretensions of the Court of Honor in an ever novel array of historical quotations, minarets, domes and towers (up to 375 feet in height) – all picked out at night by lights. It was as if Coney Island had moved to Manhattan when, in 1906–08, Ernest Flagg raised his fourteen-storey Singer Building of 1899 to a height of 600 feet, with a tower in Second Empire garb, and charged fifty cents for a ride to its top. In 1909 the Metropolitan Life Insurance Company followed with a 700-foot adaptation of the campanile of St Mark's in Venice. The ensuing race for the tallest or most singular skyscraper produced some of the most beloved architectural icons of the twentieth century. For his 792-foot Woolworth Building of 1911–13, Cass Gilbert created a gothicized terracotta sheathing with a crown of finials, gargoyles and buttresses that earned it the name 'the Cathedral of

Commerce'. In an international skyscraper competition sponsored by the Chicago *Tribune* in 1922, the judges passed over significant modernist proposals to select a design by Howells and Hood based on the late gothic Butter Tower of Rouen Cathedral.

Although some critics commented on the irrelevance of historic decoration to skyscraper design, as a whole they were less concerned with specific vocabulary than with issues of density, height, and relation to the rest of the city. As developers promoted buildings as complete worlds unto themselves and (as early as 1911) discussed pushing them to hundred-storey heights, others likened the skyscrapers to Frankenstein's monster, gone out of control, turning New York into a horribly jagged sierra, its streets into gloomy and windy canyons. In response, planners proposed height limits, and New York enacted the nation's first comprehensive zoning law (1916), mandating massing that steps back at prescribed elevations. The excitement over the showy skyscrapers was tempered by a definite discomfort.

Americans, historically accustomed to the luxury of moving away from things that gave them discomfort, fled in increasing numbers to suburbs of single family houses on individual plots. There they aspired to a lifestyle promoted by domestic arts programmes in the nation's land-grant universities and by popular crusading women's magazines – among them *House Beautiful* and *The Ladies' Home Journal* – dedicated to simplifying housework and improving family life. Their houses bore the mark, as well, of the Arts and Crafts movement, spearheaded by furniture-maker Gustave Stickley under the inspiration of William Morris in Britain. From 1901–11 Stickley published *The Craftsman*, a magazine dedicated to arts and crafts issues, that made available plans and construction drawings for houses and furnishings in the new domestic image. These designs advocated an open and informal plan, increased dependence on built-in furniture and fittings, and the use of natural materials and straightforward joinery.

A type ideally suited to these goals was the bungalow – a synthesis of Indian colonial and American domestic traditions. Of brick, or of frame construction sheathed in shingles or stucco, the bungalow had a broad front porch and a deeply overhanging, low-pitched roof that made it nestle and spread on its lot. The living room typically had exposed ceiling beams, built-in bookcases, sizeable windows, and a hearth – not so much for heat as a reference to the colonial hearth as the focus of American family life – and was integrated via an archway with a modest dining room. The kitchen, located as the control centre of the household, stressed compact efficiency (a 1902 article in *House Beautiful* advocated standards used for Pullman cars and yachts). Designed for self-sufficient nuclear-family life, bungalows were extolled as uniquely American. They were very popular in burgeoning California and came to be associated with its image of sunlight, youthfulness and renewal as the rest of the country adopted them as the everyman suburban ideal.

In Pasadena, California, the brothers Charles and Henry Greene built larger, more high-style versions of this ideal, like their Gamble House (1907–08), in which the wood-framed construction was articulated and finished inside and out with a Japanese-inspired care. Midwestern counterparts to the Greenes' houses were those of Frank Lloyd Wright (briefly mentioned in Chapter 5). Grounded in Ruskin, Viollet-le-Duc, the Arts and Crafts, and Japanese art, Wright had worked under Sullivan before beginning an independent career devoted largely to domestic architecture from his home and studio in the Chicago suburb of Oak Park. Between 1893 and 1900 he synthesized what he called the Prairie Style, publicized in a design entitled 'A House for a Prairie Town' in *The Ladies' Home Journal* in 1901. The style, exemplified by the Willitts House (Highland Park, IL, 1900–02) and the Robie House (Chicago, 1908–09), utilized cross-axial, open plans, with spaces pinwheeling outward from low, sheltered fireplace cores. The rooms were no longer boxes but volumes within a continuum, articulated by ceiling level, framing, and partial walls beneath extending roofs. Windows were not punched holes but continuous bands of leaded glazing, wrapping and dissolving corners, transparent screens between interior and exterior. Lighting and heating were integrated into the designs of the spaces; and furnishings, ideally, were designed by Wright in an Arts and Crafts mode. Exteriors were either frame, with pale stuccoed surfaces and dark wood trim, or exaggeratedly horizontal Roman brick. They grew as an interplay of rectilinear piers and parapets beneath a dramatically hovering, low-hipped roof, pinned down by a massive chimney. They expanded outward through wings, porches and terraces to the surrounding prairie landscape, echoing the horizontal character of the land.

The Prairie Style spread throughout the Chicago suburbs, across the Midwest, and abroad. In 1910 Wright was in Berlin to oversee the publication by Wasmuth of his early work in a book that would exert a potent influence on the European movements that gave rise to the International Style. In 1911 he relocated outside Spring Green, Wisconsin, where he built his home, drafting room and apprentices' quarters around the brow of a hill, naming it the Welsh 'Taliesin' (shining brow). In the late 1910s and early 1920s he received commissions in Japan (Imperial Hotel) and in the Los Angeles area (Hollyhock House, Storer and Freeman Houses), where he experimented in construction with patterned concrete blocks. Ultimately, though, middle-class taste followed that of the millionaires. While the Hearsts were erecting Julia Morgan's Spanish-style San Simeon (1920–37) in California, others of more moderate means were also building in historic styles – Tudor, French chateau, Spanish, and colonial revival. The last had evolved in the late nineteenth century with the realization that America was now old enough to have its own pedigree. Particularly popular and tenacious, it gained legitimacy from such prestigious projects as the Rockefeller family's reconstruction of eighteenth-century Williamsburg, Virginia (1920s ff). Various regions had their preferred 'colonial' modes, from Northeastern shingle and frame, to Southern brick Georgian, to Southwestern Spanish stucco. Sullivan, whose career had waned as the City Beautiful had waxed, likened this historicism to a spreading virus. Just before his death in 1924, he wrote in his important *The Autobiography of an Idea* (1924): 'The damage wrought by the World's Fair will last for half a century from its date, if not longer.'[8]

MODERNISM AND THE AUTOMOBILE

By the 1920s the majority of the American population was considered urban, and the cities were booming. So was the auto industry, the nation's largest, with 26 million cars on the road and Ford assembly lines alone producing a new one every ten seconds. Architecturally, historicism was still valid, speaking to most of legitimacy, wealth and success. The Cubist aesthetics, industrial character and proletarian associations of radical European modernism held little appeal for America's capitalistic patrons or for a generation of architects trained on the Beaux Arts model. What modernist urges the nation possessed seemed to be better satisfied by the visually glamorous Art Deco. More a symbolic than a functional expression of machine design, this decorative vocabulary, executed in manufactured and exotic materials, was that used to give a streamlined and forward-looking image to the rapid trains, automobiles and consumer products that epitomized the booming industrial economy of the 1920s. It offered architecture a fashionable alternative to Beaux Arts historicism – excitingly modern but less bald and less politically charged than European modernism. The ease with which it could be substituted for historic decoration is evident in William Van Alen's Chrysler Building (New York, 1926–30), where friezes of hub caps, hood ornaments as gargoyles, and an aluminium spire pierced by sunburst-like patterns of windows are suggestive of gothic skyscraper ideas translated into a vocabulary evocative of industrialism and energy.

The Art Deco entered American architecture significantly in the skyscrapers of the 1920s, often as stylized vegetal forms or geometric motifs (arcs, triangles, zigzags) repeated on varying scales and rhythms to impart a jazz-like embellishment to the surfaces of the great buildings. But it also reshaped their massing under the influence of two important models: Hugh Ferriss's visionary renderings exploring the formal implications of the New York setback laws, and Finnish-born Eliel Saarinen's vaguely gothic second-prize winner in the Chicago Tribune Tower competition. Both suggested a tapered, soaring ziggurat instead of the corniced block or capped tower. Raymond Hood used the type for his New York Daily News Building of 1930. Its sculptural, dramatically ascendant mass is in strong contrast to the more European elemental volumes, articulated skin and structure, horizontal bands of windows, and cantilevered office floors of the Philadelphia Savings Fund Society Building (1929–32) by George Howe and his Swiss-trained partner William Lescaze – the only tall American building of its day to qualify as mainstream International Style.

Stepped massing also appears in New York's streamlined, limestone-sheathed Empire State (Shreve, Lamb, and Harmon, 1929–31) and RCA Buildings (Hood, 1931–32). Rising from a block-square base, via coordinated setbacks and vertical patterns of windows, to a symbolic dirigible mast as its cap, the Empire State was for decades the world's tallest building. Visually it still expresses height and stability more successfully than do the usurpers to its title. The RCA is the centrepiece of Rockefeller Centre, twenty-one buildings occupying most of three city blocks, collaboratively designed between 1927 and 1935. Low base masses with focused decoration maintain a pedestrian scale at street level and create a formal pedestrian axis leading to a sunken fountain plaza at the core of the complex. Below ground a parking garage, service ramps, and passages lined with shops interconnect the various buildings. Above, slab-like office towers rise free in space, playing off of their neighbours with De Stijl-like dynamism. Altering the circulatory and land value systems of the New York grid, this ensemble demonstrates the positive potential of skyscraper urbanism to integrate pedestrian, vehicular and high-rise worlds and scales.

As the Depression tarnished the Beaux Arts historicism of the Robber Barons, the Art Deco modernism of these skyscrapers was embraced as a forward-looking, optimistic alternative. It appeared in simplified form on Works Progress Administration projects (post offices, court houses and bridges) across the country. It reigned colourfully at the next great fairs, Chicago in 1933 and New York in 1939. It was used for movie palaces, hotels and apartment buildings – in which guise it still dominates the well-preserved hotel district of Miami Beach, Florida. It lined the roadsides as the mass-produced glazed-tile and stainless-steel sheathing of streamlined service stations and diners.

American designers were cognizant of European modernism, even if they didn't use it verbatim. In 1929 Henry Russell Hitchcock and Philip

Johnson mounted an exhibition of avant-garde international architecture at the Museum of Modern Art in New York, followed in 1932 by their book *The International Style*, which identified the formal characteristics of the new architecture and gave it its name. The exhibition included works by Wright, though alongside the Europeans they looked old-fashioned, hand-crafted and decorated. Wright affected not to notice, but in the next decade his vocabulary signalled a recognition of more industrial materials and more international aesthetics. Notable is his Kaufmann House, 'Fallingwater', at Bear Run, Pennsylvania (1935), where hovering concrete planes cantilever from a stone masonry core that rises from a living ledge above a waterfall. Its De Stijl abstraction and metal-framed windows seem European inspired; yet its dramatic relation to its site, its emphasis on the hearth at its centre, and its incorporation of wood and stone in its interiors remain true to the principles of the Prairie Style.

Wright also recognized the economic advantages of prefabrication, but he used it to individualized rather than collective ends – to keep the single family home within the reach of the ordinary American. Wright's solution was the Usonian (from US) House of the 1930s, as realized in his Herbert Jacobs House (Madison, WI, 1936). These single-storey houses of modular, pre-fabricated wooden sandwich walls and flat roofs incorporated radiant-heated floor slabs, utility cores, storage walls, built-ins and carports in an infinite variety of configurations. A more radical solution was offered by technological visionary R. Buckminster Fuller with his Dymaxion House of 1929ff – a hexagonal two bedroom house with unitized kitchen and bathroom and built-in storage dividers that could be assembly-line produced for the cost of an average automobile. It never caught on, for its emphasis on compactness and machine production left Americans cold.

Nor did the collective urbanism advocated in Europe have much appeal. Rather than Walter Gropius's and Le Corbusier's uniform apartment blocks standing free in common green space, Americans preferred the turn-of-the-century Garden City of England's Ebenezer Howard – generally ignoring Howard's emphasis on density, urban self-sufficiency and communal space. In the late 1920s Clarence Stein and associates pursued the full garden-city programme for Radburn, New Jersey, adapting it for an automobile society. They divided the town into large superblocks, penetrated only by short peripheral cul-de-sacs with individual houses on very modest lots. The service areas of the houses faced the cul-de-sacs, while living areas looked towards footways leading to protected parks at the cores of blocks and linking blocks via underpasses. Parts of only two super-blocks had been constructed when this private venture was aborted by the Crash of 1929, but Radburn provided an internationally important prototype for automobile-oriented residential communities.

In the United States its principles, repeated in the WPA's modest Greenbelt Towns of the 1930s, were upstaged by the Depression-era urban planning of Frank Lloyd Wright. For Wright the compact city was the entrapper of the American citizen, and the automobile was the means for achieving a low-density alternative. In his Broadacre City, formulated between 1931 and 1935, he envisioned the entire country subdivided into one-acre sites with individualized Usonian houses surrounded by productive gardens. There would be scattered, small-scale industries, schools and marketing centres. The few activities that required more urban settings could be accommodated in county seats. Local transportation within this diffuse landscape would be by private automobile on limited-access highways. Long-distance travel would be by air. Wright's scheme was quintessentially American, offering withdrawal from a troubling urban/industrial world, and addressing deep-seated Jeffersonian feelings about freedom, self-sufficiency and the possession of land.

MODERNISM, AMERICAN STYLE

America emerged from the war years with renewed prosperity, industries ready to revert to peacetime production, patrons anxious to build after at least a decade of inactivity, and a new generation of architects prepared to introduce a new style. Masters fleeing an unstable Europe had brought the International Style with them. Walter Gropius, founder of the Bauhaus, and Ludwig Mies van der Rohe, its last director, settled respectively at Harvard University and the Illinois Institute of Technology (IIT), where they began to recast American architectural education in a Bauhaus mode. Their efforts gained critical support from Siegfried Giedion's *Space, Time, and Architecture* (1941), which established and celebrated a canonical 'mainstream' of modern architectural evolution – from nineteenth-century technological innovations through the Chicago School, to De Stijl and the International Style.

The great International Style masters provided important models. Gropius (with the Architects' Collaborative) built the Harvard Graduate centre in 1949–50, similar block-like units arranged in a space–time relationship. In Chicago Mies created a new campus for IIT (1939ff), where, half a century after the Columbian Exposition, he re-examined the premises of the Chicago School. He used the steel-framed box in a quasi-industrial vocabulary as a universal solution for classroom, power house and chapel alike, imparting distinction through his insistent modules, fine proportions and elegantly articulated detailing. Mies's doctrine of 'less is more' – the reduction of a building to its essence (frame, skin and neutral volume) and then the refinement of these components – is epitomized by his great, clear-span steel and glass pavilion of Crown Hall (1950–56), housing the architecture department at IIT, and his Lakeshore Drive Apartments (1948–51). The latter are two pristine rectilinear towers on pilotis standing free on the Chicago lake front, sheathed in glass curtain walls hung on an expressed steel frame. The purity of their forms depends upon the uniform expression of the facade membrane – and upon uniformly coloured draperies and mechanical climate control that accommodate non-uniform functions and exposures within.

A similar image appeared in New York with the construction of the United Nations complex. In 1947 an international commission adopted a scheme by Le Corbusier with a slab-like secretariat designed in purposeful contrast to America's skyscrapers (of which the French master had opined that there were too many and they were too small). Its execution (1949 ff) was entrusted to American Wallace Harrison, who interpreted the secretariat as a pristine, curtain-walled box. A climate-control nightmare, it nevertheless established a compellingly new and glamorous image for the skyscraper. In 1951–52 Gordon Bunshaft of Skidmore, Owings, and Merrill (SOM) utilized this image for New York's prestigious Lever House, introducing International Style rectilinear volumes, pilotis, roof terraces and curtain walls to Park Avenue. Across the street Mies built the Seagram Building (with Johnson, 1954–8), which rises in isolation from its extravagant plaza as a beautifully proportioned and detailed box of bronze and tinted glass.

In its wake, and encouraged by new zoning that waived setbacks in exchange for public-access plazas, the International Style became fashionable for business construction, exchanging its image of social and economic progressiveness for one of corporate power and wealth. SOM applied this neutral but slickly handsome vocabulary on all scales, from the small Manufacturers Hanover Trust Bank (New York, 1953–54) to the huge Chase Manhattan Bank (New York, 1957–60). It was a language that could be practised with competence by countless firms, much as Beaux Arts classicism had been. Achievable, however, through manufactured facade systems that could be applied to buildings of any scale, shape or budget, it was much more easily vulgarized.

The universal structure-and-skin architecture identified the patron and/or occupant of these buildings with the progressive corporate world of the man in the grey flannel suit; but it also risked an unwanted anonymity. Major practitioners of the style, therefore, rapidly evolved variants of the skin in terms of colour, material and detailing. Others emphasized virtuoso

structure. Bunshaft supported the shell of his Beineke Rare Book Library at
Yale University (1960–63) on only four corner points, its walls like bridge
trusses infilled with translucent marble slabs. SOM's hundred-storey John
Hancock Tower in Chicago (1965–70) is treated as a great rigidly framed
trapezoidal tube with bold diagonal wind bracing crossing its faces.

Eero Saarinen's Dulles Airport terminal outside Washington DC
(1958–63), with its sweeping cable-suspended roof carried on great angled
piers, demonstrated another way in which the inherently uniform
American International Style could be individualized – through identifiable
shapes. Conceived in isolation, International Style buildings worked as
huge, free-standing minimalist sculptures. As such, they were not
necessarily limited to rectilinear forms. Sculpturalism became a significant
antidote to the rectilinear uniformity of the dominant style. Wright had
provided a potent model in his Guggenheim Museum (New York,
constructed 1956–59), where he explored the implications of the circle and
the spiral. The museum winds its great introverted shell of reinforced
concrete around a skylighted central court, bearing little relationship to the
urban system around it. Saarinen explored such sculptural expressiveness in
his dynamic TWA terminal at New York's Kennedy Airport (1956–62),
where he manipulated the concrete shell roof to suggest an immense
swooping bird. The sculpturalist tendency also affected steel and glass
skyscraper design – I.M. Pei Associates' John Hancock Building (Boston,
1968–75), and Johnson and John Burgee's Pennzoil Place (Houston,
1972–76) becoming angled, featureless reflective glass objects.

Independent of setbacks and street frontages, individually shaped
buildings on plazas participated in the general dissolution of urban form
that typified the 1950s and 1960s. The Modernist ethic disdained the
historicism it had dislodged. Discounting the past, urban redevelopment
authorities eradicated and replaced ageing neighbourhoods. In Philadelphia
a mall cleared before Independence Hall left the eighteenth-century
landmark isolated from its context and dwarfed by new office blocks
proclaiming the city's progress. In St Louis, the nineteenth-century
riverfront cast-iron commercial district made way for Saarinen's Gateway
Arch (1948; constructed 1959–64) set in a sterile park along the Mississippi.
Inspired by European reconstruction projects and funded by the National
Housing Act of 1949, many cities cleared entire neighbourhoods of
deteriorating terraced houses and relocated their tenants to standardized
high-rise apartment blocks set amidst parking lots and paved play areas.
That housing types conceived for a European middle class were not a
universal solution for all is evidenced by the case of the Pruitt–Igoe
complex in St Louis, built by Minorou Yamasaki as model housing in
1952–55 and dynamited by the city as a social disaster in 1972.

The daytime inhabitants of the impersonal glass and steel towers felt little vested interest in such urban concerns, for they escaped the city by night in their cars, aided by the national highway programme. Modelled on the German autobahns of the 1930s, justified on grounds of defence, and financed by highway acts of 1944, 1956 and 1958, over 40,000 miles of limited-access, multi-laned interstate highways were built to link major urban areas. Multiple thoroughfares, ranging in scale up to the fourteen-lane Dan Ryan Expressway in Chicago, cut through the urban cores. Mass transit was ignored, and marginally profitable buildings were demolished for parking in the rush to accommodate the automobile. As much as one-third of the surface area of a city like Los Angeles came to be appropriated for the car, at the expense of urban coherency and pedestrian vitality.

Filling the landscape along these highways were a new generation of suburbs, built to house millions of returning military personnel and the ensuing baby boom that increased the national population by 33 per cent in the 1940s and 1950s. Except for a few notable examples – for instance the radical glass pavilions of Philip Johnson's own house (New Canaan, CT, 1949)´ and Mies's Farnsworth House (Plano, IL, 1949–50) – most of the new housing did not make high style statements. In general Americans were moving away from the historical styles, but they were not ready to replace them with a vocabulary primarily associated with the city centre.

The most popular image was one derived from Wright's Usonian designs of the 1930s and 1940s – the single-storey ranch house. The name and the casual, outdoors-oriented lifestyle the house was to serve give evidence of the strong pull exerted on the American imagination at this time by California, by 1963 the most populous state in the Union. Driveways were shortened, with garages (an increasingly integrated feature) on the street side of the house, giving easy access to both the front door and the kitchen. Spaces within were more open and multi-use, with storage walls and large areas of glass (picture windows). Bright, decorative kitchens frequently included informal eating areas and opened to the family (or recreation) room, often with its television set. Living spaces tended to orient to the back yard, where would be found the patio and barbecue. Its extended plan and outdoor orientation did not suit the ranch house ideally to all American climates. However, just as expenditures of energy could make the glass towers habitable anywhere, so too they could make California-type housing the universal mode. The nation's architecture became increasingly homogeneous.

Contributing to the homogeneity was mass production – of building components and of entire houses. In the late 1940s and 1950s developer William Levitt built some 40,000 houses on Long Island, New York, in New Jersey, and in Pennsylvania. He systematized construction to the point that his Levittown crews, using only 20 per cent skilled labour, produced the equivalent of a new house every fifteen minutes. In like fashion builders across the country pursued the economies of mass production, constructing large tracts of similar houses in particular price ranges. At lower ranges, the mobile-home industry produced assembly-line versions, Fuller's Dymaxion vision conventionalized in character and proportioned to move across the nation's highways to the individual's lot – often a mini-lot in a mobile-home park. Homogeneity in housing developments tended to extend beyond design and economic level to age grouping and race as well. Only 5 per cent of the nation's suburban population in 1960 was black. The blacks, on the whole, had been left behind in the cities.

The new suburban areas were less coherent than the old. Dormitory suburbs were scattered arbitrarily across unincorporated areas at the metropolitan fringes. As was pointed out in Chapter 8, commerce and services occupied unregulated strips along feeder highways or concentrated at strategic intersections in developer-built regional shopping malls surrounded by fields of parking. Open-air at first, by the mid-1950s the malls had become roofed, all-weather pedestrian main streets (for example Southdale in Minneapolis, MN, Gruen Associates, 1956). Typically they included one or two magnet stores, branches of large city-centre department stores that eventually became more significant to the retail business of the parent corporation than were their downtown operations. Corporations, lured by lower taxes and less dependent on specific location than on communication and air transportation, began to follow their officers and employees to the suburbs as well. There they built low-rise, International Style headquarters in park or campus-like settings, like SOM's Connecticut General Life Insurance Company outside Hartford, Connecticut (1957).

The new cities of Reston, Virginia (1961 ff) and Columbia, Maryland (1967 ff) attempted to assemble these pieces into comprehensive urban schemes. They were conceived as clusters of complete, picturesque neighbourhoods (or 'villages') – with residences in varying densities and price ranges, schools, recreational open space, pedestrian circulation and local commerce – tied to regional shopping, business and industrial zones that would provide significant local employment. However, the cost of their realization was discouragingly high; the financial returns were modest; and it became accepted that the building of similar complete new towns was beyond the realm of a profit-motivated private sector. Instead, economic, technological and social patterns moved the nation inexorably towards the looser pattern of Wright's Broadacre City – but with smaller lots, more crowded roads, poorer services, a lower quality of design and, ironically, less independence and individuality than Wright had envisioned for his semi-agrarian Americans.

POST-MODERN REACTIONS

In the 1960s and 1970s modern conventions of planning and building were challenged along with other aspects of the American experience. Critics Lewis Mumford (*The City in History*, 1961; *The Highway and the City*, 1963) and Jane Jacobs (*The Death and Life of the Great American Cities*, 1961) addressed the erosion and dehumanization of the city as it was recast for automobile convenience. Architect and author Peter Blake blasted what he saw as the hypocrisy of the International Style in his *Form Follows Fiasco* (1977), and Tom Wolfe popularized the message in *From Bauhaus to Our House* (1981). The oil crises of 1973 and 1979 dramatized the shortsightedness of auto-dominated planning and energy-wasteful building. The environmental movement of the late 1960s, climaxing in Earth Day (1970), decried the escalating violation of the natural environment. The preservation movement, undertaking an encyclopedic cataloguing of the nation's architectural heritage, encouraged recognition of the qualities of the existing built environment and the economic and social advantages of responding to rather than replacing it.

A new appreciation of neighbourhood values, urban vitality, and convenience of location to inner-city jobs led to reclamation programmes like Philadelphia's pioneering Society Hill project. Viable houses in this deteriorating historic residential district were restored, gaps were carefully infilled, and pedestrian greenways were constructed to provide a humane alternative circulation. Adaptive use schemes brought new life to outdated inner-city railroad stations, warehouses and factories. A chocolate factory overlooking San Francisco Bay and Boston's derelict but handsome Quincy wholesale markets (1820s) became the lively, multi-use pedestrian complexes of Ghirardelli Square (Lawrence Halprin Associates, 1965) and Fanueil Hall Marketplace (Ben Thompson Associates, 1973 ff). The latter served as a catalyst for residential and mixed use redevelopment of Boston's nearby waterfront. Such private-enterprise rehabilitation, though, was unable to re-accommodate the former, low-income occupants of these districts and confronted the cities with the new problem of displacement through gentrification.

New construction, reacting to the perceived impersonality of the International Style, found an antidote in the Brutalist movement inspired by the late work of Le Corbusier. Broken massing and expressively raw concrete and steel surfaces supplanted pure form and slick finishes. Internationally conceived as a new form of 'truth in architecture', Brutalism tended to operate in America more as an aesthetic (a built counterpart to painting's Abstract Expressionism, discussed in Chapter 13) than as a set of principles. It produced a string of massive buildings like Paul Rudolph's School of Art and Architecture at Yale University (1959–63) and Kallman, McKinnell and Knowles's Boston City Hall (1963–69), with their exaggeratedly complicated volumes and textured surfaces. Going beyond surface aesthetics, Louis Kahn combined Brutalism's underlying concepts of expressed function and construction with Beaux Arts conceptual and formal rigour. His Richards Medical laboratories (Philadelphia, 1957–61) and Salk laboratories (La Jolla, CA, 1959–65) used mass, materials, structure and scale to communicate such issues as hierarchy, privacy, community and services. In his library for Philips Academy (Exeter, NH, 1967–72) he added to brooding monumentality and specific functional expression a humane empathy and references to its specific setting.

From his example Kahn's students evolved a new critical approach to architectural design – dubbed Inclusivism. Proclaiming 'less is a bore', Inclusivism opposed the abstraction and remoteness (exclusivism) of the American International Style by taking into account the full range of factors that influence a building: its varied functions, its relation to its physical context, its communicated messages. The new outlook was potently articulated in Robert Venturi's *Complexity and Contradiction in Architecture* (1967) and Venturi, Izenour and Scott Brown's *Learning from Las Vegas* (1973), which argued for drawing lessons from all levels of the built environment and for adapting a building's design to its specific circumstances and uses.

Venturi's Guild House (Philadelphia, 1960–63) is a residence for the elderly with such complexity. It utilizes the ordinary vocabulary of its inner-city neighbourhood in sophisticated ways to relate to its setting, to express functions such as entry and television lounge, and to comment on constructive and decorative conventions in architecture. His approach is shared by Charles Moore (Citizen's Federal Savings and Loan, San Francisco, 1962; Hood Museum of Art, Hanover, NH, 1981–85), whose impure but distinctive buildings are generated from and expressive of a dynamic dialogue between architect, patrons and setting. Inclusive ideas are variously evident in the likes of Roche and Dinkeloo's Oakland Museums, California (1969), which are placed beneath a tiered civic garden; Romaldo Giurgola's INA Building (Philadelphia, 1976) with facades that vary in character dependent upon their neighbours and their solar orientation; and I.M. Pei's East Wing for the National Gallery of Art (Washington DC,

1973 ff), which derives its fascinating angles and white marble massing from its site and surroundings.

In their examination of the built environment, Venturi and his colleagues recognized the validity of the commercial strip as a response to the automobile and communication – forces that tended to diminish the significance of buildings as space definers and to increase their significance as *message*. There they identified 'Ducks', extraordinary buildings that favour communicative sculptural form over utility – a type used by restaurant chains like MacDonald's (golden arches) and Howard Johnson's (orange cupola) to achieve instant identifiability along the roadside – and 'Sheds', ordinary utilitarian buildings that have decorations appended to their faces. These vernacular types, extracted from their Pop environment, offered lessons for the return to a communicative, symbolic role for architecture. Venturi's house for his mother (Chestnut Hill, PA, 1962) assembles common American domestic symbols – a broad gabled silhouette, exaggerated central chimney, and stock window forms – to communicate the idea 'house'. The cartoon-like simplicity of its vocabulary is countered, however, by the wit with which these elements are distorted as chimney, stairs and entry compete to occupy the centre of the building.

In service of idea and communication, architecture has become an increasingly conceptual art, examining and manipulating vocabularies, systems and materials for intellectual rather than functional ends. Charles Moore's Piazza d'Italia (New Orleans, LA, 1976–79) uses a fountain-map of Italy and abstracted classical motifs executed in stucco, stainless steel, neon tubing and hot Pompeiian colours to make symbolic reference to the cultural origins of its patrons. Re-exploring themes of early modernism, Peter Eisenman's House II (Hardwick, VT, 1969) and House III (Lakeville, CT, 1970) shift white Corbusian grids out of phase or twist them on axis with each other in designs that have everything to do with system and little with function. Richard Meier makes this abstraction inclusive as he manipulates geometric volumes and rationalist grids in shining white, high-tech finishes in response to settings and functions, generating buildings of great sculptural fascination and complexity (Smith House, Darien, CT, 1965; High Museum of Art, Atlanta, GA, 1983). At the other end of the technological spectrum, Frank Gehry (own house, Santa Monica, CA, 1977–78; California Aerospace Museum, Los Angeles, 1982–84) has pursued the deconstruction and collision of vernacular building systems in such common materials as plywood, corrugated iron and chain-link fencing – making high art of their sculpturally juxtaposed forms and textures.

Issues of context, intellectual system and communication/allusion have led this architecture to depart from the dogma of modernism – to become postmodern. As architecture about the making of architecture, it addresses a narrow audience; but its disarming wit, its Pop connections and its accessible historicizing quotations have also given it a more popular message, opening the way for a less intellectually rigorous return to architectural communication and historic decoration. As the style has achieved fashionability in both commercial and domestic genres, it has come to embrace anything vaguely historical (pre-1950s), from neo-Vitruvian to Art Deco. Accuracy of form and context are not important, but the allusion to culturally elevated models is.

Commercial buildings have reassumed their role as monumental communicators, drawing variously upon the themes of the duck and the shed. Distinctive shapes bring notoriety and identifiability. Sometimes the forms are abstract, as in Caesar Pelli's Pacific Design centre (West Hollywood, CA, 1971–76), dubbed 'the blue whale' by locals and likened by others to a cash register or an extruded moulding. Other forms have specific historical associations, as with Johnson and Burgee's Flemish Renaissance Republic Bank centre (Houston, TX, 1984), and Helmut Jahn's Art Deco glass addition to the Chicago Board of Trade (1978–82). A statement of seminal importance to the skyscraper as allusive architecture is Johnson and Burgee's AT&T Building (New York, 1978-84). This conventionally planned office tower is veneered with references – from the Pazzi Chapel, to great New York skyscrapers of the 1930s, to Chippendale highboys – removed from context and reassembled at the architect's whim to convey a generic message of high culture and wealth. In its wake Jahn created a glazed piazza paved in emulation of the Campidoglio in Rome for his State of Illinois centre (Chicago, 1979–85). Michael Graves invented an iconographic programme to wrap the conventional box of his Portland Public Facilities Building (Portland, OR, 1979 ff) in a polychromed skin of abstracted columns, keystones, and garlands bespeaking civic monumentality.

As strip-generated ideas have reshaped the city centre, its modernist rectilinear uniformity has gained variety and, according to some critics, wit, or, according to others, the character of Van Brunt's 'best possible appearance at the lowest possible cost'. Strip types have not encouraged coherence. Developments like Detroit's Renaissance centre (John Portman, 1977) create the effect of self-contained shopping centres – reached by car from freeways, through parking garages, into spectacular introverted pedestrian concourses with shops, restaurants, hotels and offices. Inserted into the city in growing numbers (as in the core of Los Angeles), these destination complexes ignore the lessons of Rockefeller Centre to operate in complete isolation from neighbours and streetscape.

Meanwhile values generated by preservation, historicism and Inclusivism are influencing new planning at the suburban scale. Walt Disney World in Florida provides a compelling illustration of the new vision. Essentially another utopian fair, this much-visited 27,000-acre model community is a rare example of integrated urban planning in the 1970s and 1980s. Its progressive mass transit, power, communications, waste disposal and service systems support residential and commercial districts that recognize pedestrian and ecological concerns, dressing them all in what Montgomery Schuyler would have called scenic architecture – exotic, futuristic and historic. Its carefully planned mix is beginning to find parallels in small residential and vacation communities of the neo-traditional planning movement like Andres Duany and Elizabeth Plater-Zyberk's Seaside, Florida (1983 ff). With its narrow streets, planned vistas, footpaths, compact village centre, common spaces, individually designed houses on private building lots, and mandated massings, fenced yards and front porches, Seaside reinvokes ideas ranging from colonial Philadelphia to Burnham's Chicago, from Riverside to Radburn.

Throughout the variety that has marked the past century of American architecture and urbanism can be found important continuities in outlook. There is an ongoing sense of individualism, dynamism, material well-being, technical confidence, private initiative and popular accessibility; but these are accompanied by a striking recurrence of anti-urbanism, economic expediency, cultural insecurity, surface aesthetics and spatial incoherence. The results may often lack something of the poetry, fine art sensibility and high seriousness of much modernism abroad. They include, however, many of the century's most notable buildings and have had potent impact on the international scene. Perhaps more importantly, while they would still move Henry Adams to ask if American architecture knew where it was going, they would permit Louis Sullivan to affirm that it significantly mirrors the forces at work in American life.

NOTES

1. Louis H. Sullivan, 'Function and Form (1)', *Kindergarten Chats and other Writings* (New York, 1947), p. 44.

2. Henry Adams, *The Education of Henry Adams* (Boston, 1961), p. 499.

3. John Reps, *The Making of Urban America* (Princeton, 1965), p. 160.

4. An 1871 article in the New York *World* describing the ideal city of the nineteenth century; quoted in John Brinkerhoff Jackson, *American Space: The Centennial Years – 1865–1876* (New York, 1972), p. 21.

5. Reps, *Urban America*, p. 344.

6. Sullivan, *Kindergarten Chats*, p. 206.

7. Henry Van Brunt, 'Architecture in the West', *Inland Architect and News Record* XIV, 7 (1889–90), p. 78.

8. Louis Sullivan, *The Autobiography of an Idea* (New York, 1956), pp. 324–5.

SUGGESTIONS FOR FURTHER READING

The rich literature on late-nineteenth- and twentieth-century American architecture and urbanism includes excellent monographs on virtually every architect invoked in this discussion, significant theoretical publications by the architects themselves – most notably Louis Sullivan, Frank Lloyd Wright, R. Buckminster Fuller, Philip Johnson and Robert Venturi – and important critical commentaries by Montgomery Schuyler (1890s ff), Lewis Mumford (1920s–60s), Ada Louise Huxtable (1960s–70s), Wolfe von Eckardt (1960s ff) and Paul Goldberger (1970s ff). The following specific titles, supplementing those already mentioned in the text and notes, are recommended for their overviews of a cross-section of topics in American architecture, for their illustrations, and for their bibliographies.

Broad surveys include Leland Roth, *A Concise History of American Architecture* (New York, 1980); Vincent Scully, *American Architecture and Urbanism* (New York, 1969); Robert A.M. Stern, *Pride of Place* (Boston, 1986); Christopher Tunnard and Henry Hope Reed, *American Skyline* (New York 1953); and Marcus Whiffen and Frederick Koeper, *American Architecture, II: 1860–1976* (Cambridge, MA, 1981). Similarly broad compendia of major statements in theory and criticism are found in Lewis Mumford (ed.), *Roots of Contemporary American Architecture* (New York, 1952), and Leland M. Roth, *America Builds* (New York 1983).

Useful sources for particular periods or movements include H. Allen Brooks, *The Prairie School* (Toronto and Buffalo, NY, 1972); William H. Jordy, *American Buildings and their Architects, IV: Progressive and Academic Ideals at the Turn of the Twentieth Century* (New York, 1972) and *V: The Impact of European Modernism in the Mid-Twentieth Century* (New York, 1972); William B. Rhoads, *The Colonial Revival* (2 vols, New York and London, 1977); Cervin Robinson and Rosemarie Haag Bletter, *Skyscraper Style: Art Deco in New York* (New York, 1975); Robert A.M. Stern, *New Directions in American Architecture* (New York, 1969), particularly strong on Inclusivism; and Robert A.M. Stern (guest ed.), *American Architecture: After Modernism (A + U: Architecture and Urbanism*, March 1981).

For new town and suburban planning see: Carol Christensen, *The American Garden City and the New Towns Movement* (Ann Arbor, MI, 1986); Irving D. Fisher, *Frederick Law Olmsted and the City Planning Movement in the United States* (Ann Arbor, MI, 1986); Kenneth T. Jackson, *Crabgrass Frontier: The Suburbanization of America* (New York, 1985); David Popenoe, *The Suburban Environment* (Chicago, 1977); Clarence Stein, *Toward New Towns for America* (New York, 1957); and Frank Lloyd Wright, *The Living City* (New York, 1958).

Helpful surveys of domestic architecture include: Clifford E. Clark, Jr, *The American Family Home, 1800–1960* (Chapel Hill, NC, and London, 1986); Alan Gowans, *The Comfortable House: North American Suburban Architecture, 1890–1930* (Cambridge, MA, 1986); and Gwendolyn Wright, *Building the Dream: A Social History of Housing in America* (New York, 1981). Frank Lloyd Wright discusses his domestic ideas in *The Natural House* (New York, 1954). Dolores Hayden surveys the feminist reaction to domestic norms in *The Grand Domestic Revolution* (Cambridge, MA, 1981).

Significant discussions of the history and construction of skyscrapers can be found in Carl W. Condit, *American Building* (Chicago, 1968); Paul Goldberger, *The Skyscraper* (New York, 1982); William H. Jordy, volumes IV and V cited above; and Francisco Mujica, *History of the Skyscraper* (Paris, 1929; New York, 1977). Interpretive studies of the type are provided by Rem Koolhaas, *Delirious New York* (New York, 1978); and Thomas A.P. van Leeuwen, *The Skyward Trend of Thought: The Metaphysics of the American Skyscraper* (Cambridge, MA, 1988).

A comprehensive survey of roadside commercial architecture can be found in Chester H. Liebs, *Main Street to Miracle Mile* (Boston, 1985).

CHAPTER TEN
The Media

Ruth Vasey

The popular media of the United States have had such an extraordinary influence upon the nation's image of itself, and upon the face it has presented to the rest of the world, that it is has become virtually meaningless to attempt to distinguish between the creations of the media and 'reality' in contemporary America. Hollywood today, for example, is less a suburban locality than a mental realm, an over-the-rainbow world of emotional intensity and hair-breadth escapes. Yet Hollywood, California, is still a Mecca for real-life tourists (most of whom settle for the Universal Studios Tour and an excursion to Anaheim to visit Disneyland); and surely the whole world stumbled briefly into a Hollywood movie the day that Ronald Reagan pronounced the Soviet Union to be The Evil Empire. In America, agencies of popular entertainment have been allowed to define the nation's identity and values to an unparalleled extent. Indeed, historically most other countries have been dependent upon the United States for significant proportions of their media diet, with the result that even overseas the media themselves have often been synonymous with Americanism. The reasons for this state of affairs are intimately bound up with sweeping social and economic changes that transformed America's way of life in the nineteenth and twentieth centuries. The press, the movies, radio and TV, have literally 'mediated' between forces of conservatism and forces of change, to forge a shared iconographic vocabulary among the disparate communities of the United States.

THE PRESS

The popular press was the first medium to generate images of contemporary American life on a mass scale. The foundation of today's popular press was laid in the 1830s, specifically in New York City. Prior to this period, papers were sold at the relatively expensive price of six cents. They were produced more commonly on a weekly than a daily basis (in 1830 650 weeklies nationwide, compared to sixty-five dailies), and were marketed mainly by subscription. Some were published by commercial interests, and gave shipping details in addition to a short editorial and a couple of pages of advertisements; others were brought out by political interests, offering frankly partisan comment. In either case, they were aimed at known and clearly delimited readerships who were, moreover, associated with the ruling élite. The extent of their circulation reflected their limited appeal: in 1830 a daily paper sold an average of only 1,200.

The introduction of the penny press, beginning with the *New York Sun* in 1833, changed all that. This new style of journalism set out to capture the largest possible number of readers, not from the ranks of any specifically targeted group, but from across the social spectrum. Apart from making the papers six times more affordable than the old-style dailies, their proprietors proclaimed their political neutrality, and made them available to all and sundry by selling them through newsboys on street corners. By mid-1835 New York had three penny dailies, and their combined circulation was 44,000, compared with a combined circulation of 26,500 for eleven old-style papers in 1833. Boston, Philadelphia and Baltimore all soon followed New York's lead. The greatest departure of the penny press from the old style of paper was in the content: gazettes became *news*papers, reporting current events from court rooms, from the police beat, from high society functions, and from the street. The immediate, the fashionable, was marketed for the first time as having an intrinsic value; and local events with human interest, the chronicles of the everyday, were placed alongside reportage of political affairs. The fact that the papers were regionally rather than nationally based enabled them to stress their immediate relevance to the lives of their readers, while simultaneously acquainting them with news of nation-wide significance. Indeed, the American daily press was so much defined by its regional character that a truly national daily paper did not appear until the publication of *USA Today* in 1982.

The success of the mixture of regional and national content that characterized the penny press was related to a broader trend in America's consciousness in the mid-nineteenth century. Americans were beginning to participate more fully in the life of their nation, integrating their local, community-based concerns with a wider concept of society. In this climate the press provided an alternative sense of social relatedness, of shared information and experience. Now incidents and emergencies affecting complete strangers could enter the lives of the wider population, generating sympathy or scandal. Press reports of events in both the criminal underworld and high society enabled the middle-class reader to construct an imaginative picture of his or her entire social milieu. The papers competed with each other to be the first to press with the day's events, and by turning immediacy and topicality into matters of positive value they created a sense of the life of the metropolis as a constantly unfolding drama, in which anyone might suddenly be called upon to play a starring role – an impression that was heightened by the Civil War, which implicated so many families in its triumphs and reversals. Eventually newspaper reporters were themselves to become major players in starring roles, as when such correspondents as Sylvester Scovel and Richard Harding Davis were celebrated for their coverage of the Spanish–American War of 1898.

Alongside the daily press there also developed a mass circulation fiction industry. Known as 'steam literature', after the steam engines that drove the presses, these publications resembled the newspapers in format, consisting of several pages of closely-typed columns illustrated with lithographs. Some of their themes carried the stories of the corrupt metropolis which were featured in the daily press into more imaginative areas. Action stories in underworld settings warned of the dangers inherent in modern city life, while romances instructed young women in the ways to achieve true love in the modern world. These stories, which by the 1860s were generally termed 'dime novels' (see Chapter 14), also incorporated narratives set in more exotic locations, such as sea stories or frontier adventures. In their capacity to mythologize aspects of the American experience, their effect was complementary to that of the newspapers.

Towards the end of the nineteenth century the pace of social change accelerated markedly. The rise of large-scale corporate enterprise, and the growth of the culture of consumption that it implied, was fuelled by the immigrant influx of the 1880s and 1890s. Most of this disparate population settled in the cities, struggling to create coherent lives in chaotic conditions. Foreign language papers provided information about the worlds they had left behind (more than a thousand were in print in America at the turn of the century), while the American papers became authoritative interpreters of national and urban life, containing everything, from the tragic to the scandalous to the banal, within a reassuringly predictable format.

But the press not only encapsulated aspects of modern life: from the 1880s it often played a more active political role. While some proprietors, notably Adolph Ochs of the *New York Times*, eschewed sensationalism and soberly declared their dedication to 'clean, dignified and trustworthy' newsgathering, others promoted the power of their publications – and implicitly, the power of their readers – to make a difference, and actually to influence the life of the city. 'Muckraking' journalist Lincoln Steffens revealed political corruption in a series of articles for *Munsey's Magazine* called 'The Shame of the Cities' (also published as a book in 1904); and William Randolph Hearst waged vigorous campaigns against corruption in both big business and city administration in the *New York Journal*, claiming to champion the cause of 'the people'. Hearst effectively represented city life as a serialized melodrama, with villains, victims and Hearst and his collective readership as the heroes. These crusades and exposés demonstrated Hearst's belief that one of the primary functions of the popular press was to involve and entertain an audience. When he was not gunning for the enemies of the people, he was titillating them with sex and crime. The *New York Journal* and Joseph Pulitzer's *New York World*, which in the 1890s was the first to introduce comic strips and regularly use photographs, were the precursors of today's tabloids, and of their more eccentric cousins such as the *National Inquirer*, with its unrepentent partiality for 'reports' that vary from the outlandish to the ludicrous. The 'tabloids' were attacked for their opportunism and sensationalism by their more staid contemporaries, but the formulas they exploited resulted in their rapidly accumulating a readership that represented, for the first time, a wide cross-section of the American population.

By the turn of the century the major features of the nation's large-circulation newspapers were in place, including the status-related split of the dailies into one camp that perceived its function as primarily to impart information, and one camp that set out primarily to entertain. Their appeal transcended class boundaries, and by their selection and treatment of 'newsworthy' subjects they promoted a generalized sense of shared values and priorities. It is interesting that many influential American novelists – for example, Stephen Crane, Theodore Dreiser, Willa Cather and, a little later, Ernest Hemingway – got their start as writers in press journalism. The sheer dimensions of the popular press inevitably affected its social and commercial function, particularly in its relationship to advertising. In the 1880s ever more products were available in ever more venues, in exchange for an expanding pool of disposable private income. Department stores were expanding, and brand names, as we saw in Chapter 8, were emerging as a basis for product differentiation. Indeed, the explosion in the readership of the press itself, and its status as a disposable item with a transient life, is indicative of the rise of the culture of consumption. In this climate, the advertising space afforded by the newspapers was itself a valuable commodity, and graphic displays, increasingly aimed at women, replaced uniform columns of classified advertisements. Together with new features such as advice columns and fashion pages, the newspapers promoted a modern consumerist sensibility, and encouraged the adoption of new styles of dress and behaviour. The daily papers proposed an image of America to Americans, old and new, that they were literally willing to buy.

In the 1890s, colour-printing technology enabled the publication of a new class of mass literature in the form of popular magazines. *Collier's*, *The Saturday Evening Post* and other similar publications differed from the press not only because they were weekly, but also because they were distributed nationally, and carried national advertising (see Chapter 8). They offered a mixture of fiction and 'reportage', or reporting on current and human affairs; they thus extended the admixture of entertainment and information that characterized the daily press. Their circulation was enormous, both reflecting and promoting the rise of the middle class. In the 1920s *Time* introduced a new style of reporting orientated towards the presentation of information in a more condensed form, and in the 1930s *Life* set new standards for the art of photojournalism. In general, however, it was the weekly magazines designed simultaneously to enlighten and amuse the whole family that encapsulated the values of the American bourgeoisie until the Second World War.

In the 1950s, this broadly-based market fragmented, resolving itself into interest groups, each of which were targeted for their own specialist publications. Magazines appeared, for example, that were variously designed for teenagers, mothers with young babies, electronics buffs, jazz-lovers, classical music *aficionados*, and golfers. By the 1990s magazines appeared not just for users of personal computer technology, but for consumers of specific versions of specific brands of software. The majority of the daily press retained its regional emphasis; and the capacity to address 'middle America' as a whole devolved to other sections of the media.

EARLY DAYS OF THE MOVIES

At the same time as the popular press was achieving its first mass constituency, the motion picture business was finding its feet. Motion pictures were a peculiarly apt aesthetic consummation of the nineteenth century, combining the technology of the age of mechanical reproduction and the business methods of corporate capitalism: a single performative event could be replayed repeatedly, in virtually any venue, with little financial outlay beyond the initial investment in production. However, the economic or indeed the social consequences of the invention were not immediately apparent, in either Europe or the United States, where movies were developed virtually simultaneously in 1896. Certainly Thomas Edison had no inkling of what was to come when he invented his kinetoscope, a peep-show device for exhibiting a snatch of filmed action to individual viewers. In a misconception that he shared with those who first marketed radio, he regarded any potential profits as likely to arise from the machines, and not from the art they mediated. Nevertheless, before long a mode of projection was devised, and motion pictures, displayed first in music hall programmes and then in their own 'nickelodeon' venues (usually costing a dime for entry), became the entertainment craze of the moment. 'Actuality' footage, consisting of documentary-style reporting of newsworthy events, was early dominated by fictional narratives, which, because they could be filmed under relatively controlled conditions in a limited set of locations, were cheaper to produce on a regular basis.

Early nickelodeon programmes, always presented with musical accompaniment, consisted of a series of short films, ranging from sentimental dramas to westerns and comic sketches. They appealed greatly to the polyglot audiences of the big cities. For recent arrivals, both from overseas and from country areas, who found themselves cut off from their traditional communities and sources of amusement, the movies proved an ideal entertainment. Not only were they cheap, but for their enjoyment they also required no specific cultural qualifications. Many of the earliest films seen by American audiences were imported from Europe, especially France, but local film-makers soon began to exploit their own market, producing fast-paced films that depended upon graphic action more than written intertitles to communicate with their diverse audiences. The medium made rapid technical and aesthetic advances. At the beginning of the century movies were just a few minutes long, but by 1914 productions of over an hour were commonplace. The early achievements of cinematic art were perhaps most strikingly embodied in the work of director D.W. Griffith, whose racist epic *The Birth of a Nation* (1915) constituted a landmark in the development of spectacular feature productions.

The very popularity of motion pictures caused them to be viewed with suspicion by sections of the established middle class. Even more powerfully than the newspapers – which at least required a minimum level of literacy to be understood – the motion pictures advertised the modes of the modern era, and seemed to be at the forefront of a revolution in social norms. From its very beginnings, therefore, the motion picture business became a site of conflict between the conservative and the modern. For decades to come, conservative pressures would influence the treatment of subjects on the screen, while the box office would ensure that its underlying tendency was to satisfy the dreams and desires of the broadest mass of the population.

As with the newspaper business, in which magnates such as Hearst built publishing empires, the motion picture industry embodied the ethics of corporate capitalism; the business was both symptomatic of and contributory to the vast changes that were overtaking the American way of life. Throughout the first two decades of its existence, the relationships between the industry's branches of production, distribution and exhibition were in a process of flux, tending generally towards combination. Production companies, initially independent of exhibition interests, found that in order to guarantee their products a showing it was sound policy to acquire their own cinemas; conversely, exhibition chains built or acquired production facilities to assure their theatres of a regular supply of pictures. The result was that by the 1920s the industry was dominated by very large 'vertically integrated' companies – that is, with production, distribution and exhibition branches all under the one management. The development of the leading companies, notably Famous Players-Lasky and Loews, into giant corporations was characteristic of American big business in the 1910s and 1920s; and, like other corporate behemoths, they risked prosecution under anti-monopoly legislation, which made them vulnerable to attacks from hostile sections of the public. In 1914, 1916 and later in 1926 Congressional hearings were held into the state of the motion picture industry, with its critics arguing that it was in need of national regulation in terms of both its business practices and its output. At the heart of these complaints was anxiety about the influence of the medium upon children and other 'impressionable classes', which were taken to include adults of low intelligence and immigrants.

As early as 1909, prominent American producers answered criticism concerning the moral and social impact of their movies by voluntarily submitting all their products to the scrutiny of an independently constituted committee of respectable citizens, called the National Board of Censorship. The Board considered the effects of movies in terms of their treatment of such sensitive subjects as sex, violence, crime, drunkenness, vulgarity, moral outcome, etc.; but although it helped to ensure that movie narratives took place within approved moral frameworks, the major social impact of the movies was associated less with narrative outcomes than with the widespread dissemination of popular images. By 1916 several film companies were regularly distributing their most important features on a nation-wide basis. These days, when the whole planet can tune in simultaneously to the Academy Awards, it is hard to fathom the impact of showing the same personalities in the same action-packed or romantic scenarios across the United States; but at the time the results were sensational. Featured actors quickly became stars, and a whole industry

219

grew up around the celebration of both their public performances and their personal lives. Indeed, the level of the public's engagement with the movies can be judged by the success of such ancillary products as fan magazines and movie-inspired fashions. The centre of production had moved from New York to California during the early 1910s (although financial support of all the major companies remained in the hands of company directors in New York City), and by the end of the First World War Hollywood had become a national byword for glamour and extravagance. The lifestyles of such stars as Mary Pickford and Douglas Fairbanks seemed to embody the aspirations of a nation towards romantic love, physical well-being, and material success. Thousands of screen-struck teenagers made the trip to Hollywood in the routinely doomed attempt to emulate the careers of their idols.

CLASSICAL HOLLYWOOD

Due to the temporary demolition of film industries in Western Europe during the War, the late 1910s and early 1920s offered American companies a unique opportunity for foreign expansion. American movies were usually well received wherever they played, for the same reasons that made them popular at home: they combined quick-paced action with a fundamentally optimistic outlook, and were not difficult to decipher. By 1918 the major companies had managed to encircle the globe with a system of regional distribution networks. By 1920, despite the fact that the medium itself was barely twenty years old, the studios were routinely spending as much as $60,000 on average productions. For lavish spectaculars the figure was much higher: in 1922, Douglas Fairbanks's production of *Robin Hood* cost $1.5 million. For several reasons, it was in the interest of the established studios to peg their production budgets at these high levels. For one thing, its large-scale expenditure on sets, stars, and special effects helped to maintain the 'prestige' of the Hollywood product in the eyes of audiences overseas. More fundamentally, by setting up a high level of investment as the norm, the established companies sought to price fledgling competitors – both domestic and international – out of business.

If Hollywood represented a world of Utopian fantasy, the movie theatre itself represented an alternative world of fantasy for its audiences, concisely expressed in a 1925 Paramount advertisement which claimed that 'All the adventure, all the romance, all the excitement you lack in your daily life are in – Pictures.' The picture palaces of the 1920s, with their exotic designs, extravagant decor, and grandiose displays of luxury embodied the audience's sense of the movie theatre (and 'Hollywood') as an otherworldly place where wishes could come true. Even in the architecturally less impressive neighbourhood theatres, cinema separated audiences from the everyday world outside and propelled them into the more magical space of Hollywood. The picture palaces themselves were a phenomenon of the silent cinema: a city-centre theatre would employ a full-size orchestra as well as a phalanx of ushers.

In the 1930s, the combination of the sound film and depression economics spelt the end of the cycle of construction of major metropolitan picture palaces. In any case, by 1933 the five major vertically integrated companies – Paramount, Loew's, 20th Century-Fox, Warner Bros and RKO – had stabilized their theatre ownership. Between them, they owned or controlled the majority of the country's 'first-run' theatres – the biggest metropolitan cinemas where new releases were first screened, at the most expensive ticket prices, earning as much as 70 per cent of the industry's domestic box-office revenue.

By the late 1920s the major companies were each producing a movie a week. Columbia and Universal, which were somewhat smaller, were almost keeping pace. United Artists did not have production facilities of its own, so did not constitute a studio in the technical sense, but as a distributor it handled the work of independent production houses, and put movies into circulation at a rate that was comparable to the other companies. The sheer scale of film output necessitated the adoption of mass production techniques. Film-making was organized in a manner comparable to a factory production line, with different specialists within the studios being responsible for the various stages of scripting, production and post-production. The whole process was directed and coordinated by a 'production supervisor', who typically had several projects under his purview at once. Inevitably, films produced under this system tended to be 'formula' pictures, made up of comparatively standardized and predictable elements, both in terms of their representational style and their narrative development. Although their marketing usually promised novel sensations, in fact movie narratives functioned as convenient vehicles for the delivery of essentially repeatable ingredients: romantic scenes, spectacular chases, hairbreadth escapes, and so on.

Most movies offered something for everybody, but the particular mix of narrative ingredients depended broadly upon the genre of the film. For example, action sequences and spectacle were usually to the fore in Universal's westerns, at the expense of the love interest, while Paramount's sophisticated romantic comedies rewarded their audiences with witty intertitles and scenes of opulent luxury. The broad division of movies into generic types was recognized by the studios as a valuable marketing mechanism, as it enabled the public to identify the films that they found most attractive. By the same principle, movies were also differentiated according to their starring performers; the presence of stars enabled audiences to revisit the pleasures of previous movie experiences in a differently packaged form. Charlie Chaplin could be depended upon to perform some variation of his skilful clowning in each of his many films; Maurice Chevalier would unfailingly exude his sophisticated charm; Greta Garbo would be reliably erotic and mysterious. Elitist critics have found the predictability of Hollywood to be its most deplorable characteristic, but to the industry this predictability was an economically sound element in the standardization of its product, while to audiences it constituted a positive aid to pleasurable consumption.

The most substantial of Hollywood's genres, certainly in terms of the sheer number of films produced, was the western: until the 1960s, it consistently accounted for approximately a quarter of the industry's output. The great majority of westerns were low-budget movies aimed mainly at the rural market or, after the 1930s, as the second feature in double-bill programming. The western was also popular in sections of the foreign market, where action movies were frequently preferred to films that featured lengthy sections of dialogue. During the 1920s and 1930s a few large-budget spectacular westerns were produced, notably *The Covered Wagon* (1923), *The Iron Horse* (1924), and *Cimarron* (1930). However, the western as a staple of A-budget production was largely a phenomenon of the 1940s and 1950s, when the overwhelming majority of what are now regarded as 'classical' westerns were produced, including *Red River* (1948), *Shane* (1953), *The Searchers* (1956) and *Rio Bravo* (1959).

Like the earlier western dime novels, Hollywood westerns appealed predominantly to an adolescent male audience. The majority of Hollywood's genre cinema, however, was designed either to appeal to a female audience, or to couples. The industry's limited research into its audience indicated that although men and women attended as frequently as each other, women were opinion-leaders in choosing which films to attend. Largely in response to the perceived preferences of female spectators, nine movies out of ten featured a heterosexual romance. As fashion trends demonstrated, women also used the movies as fashion indicators. 'Society' dramas such as the 'Thin Man' series with William Powell and Myrna Loy, and musicals such as the Ginger Rogers and Fred Astaire series (see Chapter 12), combined romance and sophisticated fashion in their to appeal to the female audience.

The cooperative, oligopolistic approach of the major studios allowed them to formulate mutually acceptable standards for contractual agreements with labour and exhibitors, and standard specifications for technical apparatus (a standard width for film stock, for example). It also allowed producers to formulate acceptable standards for motion picture content. The producers were faced with the problem of making movies that pleased the largest number of people, or, at least, that avoided alienating any significant section of their audience. A cooperative approach to the problem was important because if any movie offended its audience it threatened to cause a wave of indignation against 'the movies', or 'Hollywood', rather than against the company directly responsible for the offence. Therefore, the major companies charged their trade association the MPPDA (Motion Picture Producers and Distributors of America, Inc.) with overseeing standards of content, so that each company could be protected from the actions of the others, as well as from any indiscretions it might be tempted to commit on its own behalf.

This 'self-regulation' of movie content was a process that evolved gradually throughout the 1920s and 1930s. It was tightened at the time of the introduction of sound technology at the end of the 1920s, because sound movies were not easily cut and rearranged to suit the predilections of particular audiences. At one level, self-regulation meant that every movie produced by the major studios was subject to scrutiny by an industry-appointed committee before being allowed to be released. However, this perspective can be misleading, as it seems to imply that the MPPDA was solely responsible for making the movies conform to industry guidelines. In fact, the process of tailoring movies to an agreed set of parameters involved each company's overseer inspecting every stage of production. This did not affect the range of subjects that could be represented in the movies so much as the way in which those subjects were handled. For example, sexual explicitness was not permitted, and nor was gruesomeness or detailed depictions of criminal methods; but sex, brutality and crime continued to feature in movie narratives, on the implicit condition that their detailed elaboration was left to the imagination of the audience.

While some themes, such as those dealing with homosexuality, were considered to be unsuitable for representation under any circumstances, many other controversial issues, notably prostitution and adultery, were considered valid, and could be represented as long as the story came to a suitably moral conclusion. For example, Marlene Dietrich in *Blonde Venus* (1932) and Barbara Stanwyck in *Baby Face* (1933) renounced their wild ways at the end of the movies to find fulfillment in the role of wife and/or mother. Similarly, the depiction of the life of a criminal was not taboo so long as it was contained within a suitable framework, to the effect that

Crime Does Not Pay: James Cagney dying ingloriously at the end of *The Roaring Twenties* (1939) typified the outcome of a criminal career. In an effort to avoid alienating the rich and powerful, Hollywood also attempted to treat the representation of political and industrial interests with some delicacy. *Mr Smith Goes to Washington* (1939) was unusual in that it tackled the matter of political corruption, but in the end it affirmed the integrity of the American political process. Names of existing corporations were rarely used outright, and foreign locations were given names such as Ruritania to avoid direct offence to actual political entities.

Representations of ethnic groups were also typically pragmatic. The social mingling of blacks and whites was impossible on the screen because of the probable adverse reaction from Southern states. The political powerlessness of Native Americans was clearly illustrated by Hollywood's free appropriation of their screen identity as a loosely defined symbol of savagery; on the other hand, care was taken to avoid offence to ethnic communities with powerful domestic constituencies, or with the capacity to impose reprisals at the level of international trade and diplomacy. For example, in the 1920s the MPPDA took steps to stamp out a rash of villainous Mexican roles, and following Paul Muni's performance in *Scarface* (1932), they pleaded with producers to make their gangsters 'less obviously Italian'. However, the results were often little improvement upon the original causes of offence, with the new 'friendly' Mexicans transformed into comic stereotypes, and the 'less Italian' gangsters merely seeming to be inaccurately portrayed.

These practices had important consequences for the nature of the universe represented by Hollywood pictures by the late 1930s. They developed a remarkable consistency, with movies from all the major studios, and representing all genres, being contained within the same over-arching moral framework. Self-regulation significantly affected the image of the United States that was elaborated in the movies, and that helped to define the nation both to its own people and to the world. Like the press, but to an even greater extent, the movies created a shared vocabulary and cultural consciousness. Stars such as Clark Gable, Bette Davis, Cary Grant and Marlene Dietrich were more widely known and celebrated than America's political leaders. Hollywood's audience was remarkable for its diversity, and was drawn from all geographical areas, every social class, and every age group. Yet the American nation it described had little ethnic diversity. It derived its values from the patriarchal family unit and from corporate enterprise. Its government and business agencies were benign, or at least not corrupt. Blacks and whites invariably moved in separate circles. Poverty could be overcome with sufficient individual initiative, and indeed, material acquisition was a personal objective that carried considerable moral force. Dancing girls and hostesses substituted for prostitutes.

THE MOVIES AFTER THE SECOND WORLD WAR

Hollywood's stable system of representation was significantly disrupted by its overt recruitment by the government in the service of the war effort during the Second World War. The State Department enlisted Hollywood's assistance, collaborating over the preparation of ideologically useful projects and guaranteeing their producers against loss. Hollywood enthusiastically joined in the battle, and proved how effective it could be as a generator of propaganda. The conditions the studios faced after the war were in many respects drastically altered, and not to their benefit. In 1948, as a result of a long-standing government investigation into the industry's monopolistic structure, the big corporations were ordered to break up their operations. The Supreme Court ruled that, amongst other changes, they should divorce the management of their production/distribution arms from their exhibition chains. With the loss of direct control over their sources of revenue, the major studios faced an uncertain future.

Hollywood also faced a new public relations emergency. The very effectiveness of its propaganda effort during the war had managed to make the nation aware of its capacity to influence opinion, and now new questions were being raised about the fitness of the studio heads to control such a powerful medium. Some projects undertaken early in the war in support of the Russians – *Mission to Moscow* (1943), for example – came back to haunt them in the climate of the Cold War, and a finger-pointing public began to identify Communist affiliations at every level of the industry. The result was that actors, directors and writers were summoned to appear before the infamous House Committee on Un-American Activities. They were to 'name names' of their supposedly Un-American associates, leading to the blacklisting of dozens of personnel alleged to be guilty. Until 1954, the industry operated in an atmosphere clouded by paranoia.

At the same time, the movies faced increasing competition for their audiences from television. Enthusiasm for the small screen broke over the country like a wave after the Second World War: in 1947, 7,000 sets were sold, but in 1950 the number had rocketed to seven million. The major producers fought back with innovations that offered more spectacle and more expense: colour, widescreen formats, exorbitant production values. But because there was a higher investment in each product fewer movies were produced, and the overheads associated with studio operation rendered the old production structures increasingly obsolete. Smaller independent companies, often producing low-budget 'exploitation' pictures aimed at the teenage market, literally defied regulation. The cinema – and now the drive-in – became public spaces that were less reassuring than sensational, and formerly taboo subjects vied for public attention on the screen. Those who wanted a pleasant and affordable evening's entertainment with the family stayed home and watched TV.

Before the dismantling of the 'Classical' studio system of production in the 1950s, the majority of Hollywood movies had made small profits. By the late 1960s, however, only about 10 per cent of movies earned profits, but these were large enough to cover the losses of the other 90 per cent. *The Sound of Music* (1965), for example, cost $8 million to produce, but grossed $78 million in the United States and Canada alone. The 'blockbuster' success became the cornerstone of industry accounting: *The Graduate* (1967), *Bonnie and Clyde* (1967), and *Easy Rider* (1969) all returned phenomenal profits in the 1960s, to be followed by *Jaws* (1975) and *Star Wars* (1977) in the 1970s, and the Indiana Jones films in the 1980s. Instead of being assembled on a creative production line, movies were financed as individual 'packages', including video rights and profits from spin-off sales of associated merchandise such as toys and T-shirts. The essential ingredients for the package were stars and/or spectacle. Actors such as Paul Newman, Meryl Streep and Jack Nicholson could guarantee that virtually any project would receive financial backing. Since the late 1960s, the identity of the director has also become a marketable factor, with the names of George Lucas, Steven Spielberg, and Martin Scorcese featuring prominently in the films with which they have been associated.

Economic factors have transformed the nature of exhibition as thoroughly as they have changed the nature of production. 'Multiplex' cinemas, containing a number of mini-auditoria, enable exhibitors to rationalize their use of screen time. If an exhibitor is contractually obliged to screen a movie for a minimum number of weeks but the film turns out to be a flop, its run can be played out in a minor theatrette, while the larger screens are devoted to more profitable entertainment. Distribution and film financing is still largely in the hands of the old Hollywood studios and through this means they have managed, despite the Supreme Court's best efforts, to retain a large measure of control over the American industry. In the meantime, however, those studios have themselves been either taken over or merged with other corporations; for example, in 1959 Universal was absorbed by MCA (The Music Corporation of America), and in 1981 MGM acquired United Artists to form a new company, MGM/UA Entertainment Company. The movement towards combination, which was evident from the first years of the motion picture business, still determines the fortunes of the industry.

RADIO

Like the press and the movies, radio was not originally orientated towards mass consumption. The medium was the result of turn-of-the-century military research in both Britain and America. Since it was aimed at facilitating communications with ships at sea, its potential for widespread reception was first regarded as less of an asset than a liability, although the navy was forced to accept that enthusiastic amateurs could not very well be prevented from listening in on their home-made radios. Slowly, however, receiving sets began to appear in the stores. In 1916 David Sarnoff (then an assistant manager of the Marconi Company, but to become one of the most powerful executives in broadcasting) proposed the development of a 'Radio Music Box' that he hoped would make radio a 'household utility' in the same sense as the piano or the phonograph. An early manufacturer was Westinghouse, which in 1920 came up with a simple and innovative promotional scheme: it opened a radio station. Within just two years, 570 licensed stations had opened in the United States, and by 1924 two million radios had been sold.

An initial difficulty was to work out how to maintain the medium's economic viability once the market for receivers had been saturated. There was no obvious way to charge for radio waves which rained down indiscriminately on the population. In other countries the question was resolved by establishing broadcasting as a state-run institution: in Britain, for example, radio was organized as a public utility, funded through licence fees as well as through general taxation. In the United States, on the other hand, a more commercially-orientated model prevailed. Some early American radio stations functioned as public service facilities – particularly those that were run by universities – and in 1922 Herbert Hoover, then Secretary of Commerce, went so far as to declare that 'it is inconceivable that we should allow so great a possibility for service . . . to be drowned in advertising matter'. However, radio advertising began in the same year and by 1927 it was firmly established as the dominant means of financing the medium. Instead of selling receivers to listeners, American broadcasters sold listeners to advertisers, holding the listeners' attention by providing them with free entertainment. Sponsorship usually extended to an entire programme; 'spot advertising', such as characterizes commercial stations today, was only gradually introduced from the end of the 1930s.

In 1926, largely on the initiative of Sarnoff, the National Broadcasting Company (NBC) was formed as a subsidiary of RCA (itself a monopolistic shelter corporation for General Electric, Westinghouse, AT&T and United Fruit). In the next year NBC set up two national networks. Meanwhile, cigar manufacturer Sam Paley established a third network of stations under his Columbia Phonograph Broadcasting System (CBS), soon turning it over to his son William. A form of government regulation over the industry was established in 1927, with the creation of the Federal Radio Commission (from 1934, the Federal Communications Commission). The Commission was charged with regulating the broadcasting system 'in the public interest, convenience and necessity'; however, far from challenging the power of the networks, in practice this meant upholding the status quo by limiting the destabilizing effects of competition.

The range and format of America's radio entertainment had been established by the early 1930s, and it did not alter much over the next fifteen years. The network schedules were dominated by musical variety programmes and comedy, while the rest of the nation's airtime was made up with news, sports, serials, talk shows, game shows and the occasional serious drama or religious programme. The most popular format was the variety programme derived from vaudeville, with the personality of the master of ceremonies dominating proceedings and giving them coherence. Compere comedians such as Jack Benny, George Burns, Gracie Allen and Bing Crosby, played 'themselves', constructing personae that became nationally beloved. Serials were also popular, and the protagonists of *The Shadow*, *The Whistler* and *Sherlock Holmes* became household names. Often the programmes ran for years: *The Lone Ranger*, for example, was incarnated in 2,956 episodes from 1933 to 1954, before gaining a new lease of life on television; and, as we saw in Chapter 6, radio's version of comic blackface minstrels, *Amos'n'Andy*, played continuously from 1929 to 1954.

Many radio serial characters, like Dick Tracy and Little Orphan Annie, first appeared in newspaper comic strips, or, like Superman, in comic books; radio evinced an impressive capacity to absorb the material of popular culture, just as the movies, and later television, frequently 'borrowed' the creations of radio. Indeed, although motion picture studios at first tried to prevent their stars from appearing on radio, there was considerable cross-over from one medium to another: *Lux Radio Theatre* was one of several shows tied closely to Hollywood, in that it regularly used movie stars in its productions, and also staged radio adaptations of current movies in promotional campaigns. The genres of radio drama broadly corresponded to those of the movies, and the cowboy hero Tom Mix, for example, had a career in radio as well as on film.

Daytime soap operas (so-called after the companies that usually sponsored them), such as *The Goldbergs, Just Plain Bill* and *The Romance of Helen Trent* ('can a woman over thirty-five find romance?'), constituted a variation on the form of the serial, in that instead of presenting characters in new situations every episode, the same story evolved from week to week. The number of these soap operas expanded until in the 1939–40 season over sixty were broadcast nationally, all produced in a fifteen-minute format, five times a week. Evening programming tended to favour 'serious' drama, with plays being presented on such programmes as *Lux Radio Theatre, Inner Sanctum, Suspense,* and *The Mercury Theatre.* In 1938 the latter demonstrated the power of the radio medium in spectacular style when *The War of the Worlds*, a radio play about a Martian invasion produced by Orson Welles, was taken for actual reporting by many Americans, causing instances of panic across the country.

Non-dramatic shows, including music, sport and current affairs, also made up a significant part of radio programming. Popular music was featured on such shows as *The Hit Parade* and *The Voice of Firestone*, while classical music was broadcast on NBC's *Music Appreciation Hour*, introduced by Walter Damrosch, and on *The Standard Music Hour*, sponsored by Standard Oil from 1926 to 1956. News and public affairs coverage was always well served by the immediacy of radio. CBS's *March of Time* series set a standard for current affairs reporting in the early 1930s, and President Roosevelt himself used the medium for a series of 'fireside chats'. Radio news coverage expanded gradually throughout the decade, and came fully into its own during the Second World War.

The function of radio in the United States during the first two decades of its operation in some ways resembled the function of the popular press. Radios themselves became mass-produced consumer items – by 1930 more than thirteen million sets were in use, in 40 per cent of households – and, as was the case with newspapers, the consumer culture was also promulgated by the advertisements that financed broadcasts. Again like the press, radio supplied a variety of different needs, with an emphasis on information and entertainment. Just as the newspapers presented a collage of modern life to their readers, the radio stations juxtaposed items with similarly diverse flavours and intentions, in a constant stream of sound. Many programmes reached a national audience through the three networks; other programmes catered for regional constituencies, contributing to the same mixture of regional and national content that characterized the press.

At the same time, radio, like the movies, was more closely related to the concept of 'leisure time' that was a by-product of the industrial revolution. It could not, before the development of the transistor, be consulted on the run, and specific time periods needed to be set aside for listening in to favourite programmes. In addition, listening to the radio was clearly a less isolating experience than reading a newspaper, and this was true on two levels. Families could, and did, orientate their leisure hours towards listening to the radio together; and individual listeners were constituted by the medium as part of a vast collective audience, simultaneously responding to the amusements and dramas that unfolded on the air. The medium implied a significant level of consensus among those thousands of people listening in. The immediacy of the radio made it a living presence in people's homes, turning the events of the public arena into integral components of their private and domestic lives (a phenomenon fondly evoked in Woody Allen's 1989 film *Radio Days*).

At the end of the Second World War the networks were in a sufficiently powerful position to turn their energies to the development of television. As television began to permeate the culture, radio lost audiences and, consequently, advertising revenue. Instead of large networked shows, radio broadcasting began to take on a more regional character, dominated by the economical combination of music and talk that had always been the mainstay of small independent stations. At the same time, increasingly sophisticated market research techniques led to a more precise notion of intended audiences for advertisements and their vehicle programmes. In particular, the growth of the consumer power of youth made the specialist programming for the younger generation a matter of good economic sense, and some programmes – even the whole output of some stations – were orientated to the requirements of the young. In the larger cities, which could potentially offer as many as fifteen or twenty channels, this fragmentation of the market continued. The development of FM radio in the 1960s encouraged this trend, by creating a space for non-commercial channels with minority appeal, such as university and Christian fundamentalist stations, or those playing innovatory rock, classical music, or programmes orientated to particular ethnic groups. In 1967 a Public Broadcasting Act established a National Public Radio which, although given minimal public funding (relying instead on public subscription for support) nevertheless officially established a niche for public service broadcasting. The majority of channels were, however, still run along firmly commercial lines, with programmes carefully orientated to their target audiences. After the 1950s an urban American radio listener could choose between different channels offering rock, classical music, country and western, soul, talk shows, all-news, and many others. Responsibility for providing programmes for the whole family was still in the hands of the networks, but they were now exercising it through the medium of television.

TELEVISION

American television combined the iconographic power of movies with the advertising methods of radio and the authority of the press. And, more completely than any other medium, it blurred the boundaries between the public and the private. The 'talking heads' so typical of television infiltrated the living rooms, the play rooms, and even the bedrooms of the American home. The admixture of entertainment, news and salesmanship that had characterized radio and the press was re-presented on television in a new, compelling, almost hypnotic form, which was now effectively interactive with the minutiae of domestic life. If the press had encouraged its readers to think more globally, and the movies had created elaborate public fantasies, television contained both the world and the fantasy in a small box, which sat in the alcoves of the average family home. It could be switched on and off as convenient; or it could be allowed to run without interruption, its images constituting the psychic wallpaper of the domestic environment.

Television was invented in the 1920s but few people took much interest in it until after the Second World War. It was a medium that seemed perfectly designed for the suburbs, the growth of which was described in Chapter 9. At the end of the 1950s suburban areas housed a quarter of the entire population. Unlike city life, where families took their leisure in public spaces such as parks and cinemas, suburban culture placed a primary emphasis upon the home itself, and the self-contained domestic drama enacted within it. Television offered a level of entertainment comparable to the movies in a form which could be privately consumed within the comfort and privacy of one's own home. For many suburbanites, whose young children were part of the post-war baby boom, television had the advantage of sparing them the trouble and expense of organizing a baby-sitter.

As a broadcast medium, television shared many of its characteristics with radio – a condition that was exaggerated in the United States by the fact that the medium was controlled by networks that had originated in radio broadcasting. The dominant companies continued to operate as an oligopoly: NBC and CBS had been joined in 1941 by ABC, as a result of a Federal Communications Commission ruling requiring NBC to divest itself of one of its two networks. From the beginning of large-scale TV broadcasting, the commercial models of sponsorship and advertising that had been developed to fund radio were adopted as the economic basis of the American TV industry. Moreover, the TV networks adopted much the same approach to programming as had characterized radio. News and current affairs shows alternated with comedy, music and drama, with individual productions contributing to the wider continuous programming of the day's entertainment, linked by a continuous thread of advertising. Just as the characters and catch-phrases created by radio 'personalities' had been an American lingua franca in the 1930s, their television counterparts created a shared cultural vocabulary in the 1950s. Indeed, the television shows of the 1950s echoed the early days of radio, featuring variety and acts with popular comperes, such as Ed Sullivan in *Toast of the Town*, Milton Berle in the *Texaco Star Theatre* and Sid Caesar and Imogene Coca in *Your Show of Shows*. Cultural institutions such as the baseball World Series could now be brought directly into the home, the visual image creating a fuller sense of 'being there' than could be achieved through descriptions on the radio. There was an abstract sense in which, by simply switching on the television set, Americans were committing themselves to an act of cultural participation. By 1960 over 90 per cent of American homes had television.

Because television attracted the mass audience that was lost to the movies after the War, it found itself with the movies' burden of trying to keep everybody happy at once. Motion pictures, targeted now towards more specific audiences, were slowly divesting themselves of the inhibitions associated with 'self-regulation'. Television, however, was received indiscriminately in households across the nation, and so risked a public backlash if it was politically incautious. In the early 1950s, the conservatism inherent in the system was exaggerated by the influence of the same anti-Communist zealotry that was dogging the movie industry, with black-listing a frequent fact of life. Nevertheless, network-produced television drama managed to achieve a surprising degree of licence in New York shows like *Kraft Television Theatre* and *Philco Television Playhouse*, *Studio One* and *Playhouse 90*, which employed Broadway figures to stage single plays with a broadly social realist ethic, such as *Marty* and *Requiem for a Heavyweight*. Although these dramas constituted a 'Golden Age' of TV drama in the opinion of many critics, they could not compete in the ratings with more formulaic shows produced in Los Angeles. By the end of the 1950s the centre of production had moved to the West Coast.

The principle of repeatable pleasures that had informed genre movies and the radio serial was a governing aesthetic practice of West Coast production, and Westerns such as *Cheyenne* and *Gunsmoke* allowed viewers to revisit familiar characters and contexts, and promised a predictable measure of action and incident. As in the radio series, narrative closure was also assured, with the implied caveat that a new problem would complicate matters in the next episode. Lucille Ball's *I Love Lucy* constituted a model for the 'situation comedy', an endlessly reworkable format that combined familiar characters with novel incidents within a stable context. Jack Webb's *Dragnet*, which revolved around a sergeant in the Los Angeles

Police Department, used location shooting and a strongly defined central character to set a standard for an action series in a contemporary setting. It created a precedent for countless imitators, to the extent that the police action series now constitutes an established television genre comparable to the western. On the other hand, *Dr Kildare*, which was built around the professional experiences of a young doctor, constituted an example of a series that concentrated less on action and more on emotional and ethical crises: a kind of 'professional drama' that could feature lawyers, teachers or social workers as easily as doctors and nurses. The formulas involved were not just popular within the United States. The networks pioneered global syndication, distributing television properties worldwide and allowing the American dramas to reach scores of millions of viewers. Concern in many customer countries about American cultural imperialism was not sufficient to counter the basic economic facts: it was many times cheaper for a foreign television station to buy packages of American entertainment than to generate programmes of its own.

By the 1960s, the daily format of television programming had fallen into a conventional pattern, with the half-hour action or drama series and the half-hour comedy occupying 'prime time' in the early to mid-evening. 'Classical' network TV consisted of a programming formula not necessarily tied to the individual programmes, but to the continuous flow of programming in a designated time slot. Day-time programming consisted of talk shows, game shows, and soap operas; reruns of old Hollywood movies were also common after 1955, when several of the major studios released their older films for broadcast. Programmes for children were often featured in the afternoons and on Saturday mornings.

Although prime-time shows were typically purchased from independent producers, the networks continued to make their own chat shows and sports programmes. They also produced their own news and current events shows, which were useful in promoting their recognition and credibility. Television anchormen themselves became 'personalities', mixing an informal style of address with 'objective' news presentations. Although Walter Cronkite, the anchorman of *CBS News*, was reputed to be 'the most trusted man in America' in the 1960s, the nightly news broadcasts of all the networks regularly included visually dramatic footage and emotionally loaded human interest stories, which blurred the distinction between the news and the programming that surrounded it. Only the implacable coverage of the Vietnam War, which denied its audience the expectation of a satisfactory narrative resolution, was sufficiently disturbing to make the function and responsibility of television news a matter of public debate.

By the late 1960s television had been a participant in American culture long enough to begin to parody itself. *Rowan and Martin's Laugh-In* and *The Smothers Brothers Comedy Hour* rebelled against the conventional structures of programme presentation and presented topical humour in a zany, anarchic format. It was not accidental that their humour was directed at a young, urban audience: at this time the networks were beginning to cater less for the broadly based population of 'Middle America', and more for an 'upmarket' audience with greater education and a relatively large disposable income. This trend has also contributed to the success of 'quality' American television, such as the relatively complex police series *Hill Street Blues*, the expensively produced *LA Law*, and even the self-proclaimed élitist soap opera parody *Twin Peaks*.

The mini-series, with increasingly costly production values and advertising budgets, became a feature of American TV following the spectacular success in 1977 of Alex Haley's *Roots*, the dramatic recreation of the genealogy of a black family from the slave trade to the present. Meanwhile, quality television from Britain was introduced to American audiences following the institution in 1969 of the Public Broadcasting Service (PBS), consisting of a loosely linked chain of educational stations. The 1970s also saw the innovation of a new style of topical comedy, with the production of *The Mary Tyler Moore Show*, and *All in the Family*, based on the English series *Till Death Do Us Part*. Both presented subjects that had previously been considered out of bounds for comedy, including the problems faced by single women, racial prejudice, and class divisions in American society. They were sufficiently popular to generate at least twelve 'spin-off' series and imitations between them within the next five years, including *Lou Grant*, *Rhoda* and *Phyllis* from *Mary Tyler Moore*, and *The Jeffersons*, *Maude*, and *Gloria* from *All in the Family*. Spin-offs, copies and 'recombinant' programmes, which attempt to fuse together the most popular aspects of popular productions, constitute television's peculiar variation of the concept of genre. Like the western movie that reliably delivered a familiar combination of entertainment values, the imitative series offers a package of elements that achieved popularity under a different title, with a modicum of variation. In a spin-off, at least one of the characters carries over from the original series – for example the eponymous hero of *Trapper John, MD*, who originated in *M★A★S★H* – while in the copy the characters are different, but the basic situation remains the same, as it did from *LA Law* to *Equal Justice*. The sense of *déjà vu* that is characteristic of the experience of consuming American TV is even more pronounced as a result of the phenomenon of 're-runs'; re-releasing a popular series is an even cheaper option than making one exactly like it.

Historically, the television networks have exercised control over portrayals of sex, the occult and other sensitive matters, resulting in an overall consistency of representational conventions similar to those that prevailed in Classical Hollywood. Since the late 1980s, however, a change has come about in the enforcement of these representational conventions. Pay or Cable television and satellite broadcasting have constituted the first serious threat to the power of the networks, by offering audiences different modes of programme delivery. Viewers subscribing to these services can choose between specialized services offering, for example, all-news, all-weather, all-sports or all-movies. Moreover, the new technologies, by allowing subscribers to nominate their own television fare, have been able to avoid the restrictions that have applied to universally available entertainment. Consequently the networks, no longer fully responsible for the character of television programming, have allowed their guard to relax somewhat, effectively dismantling much of their broadcast standards and practices departments. Although they remain likely to reject seriously transgressive programmes, they have allowed much of the responsibility for content to devolve to individual producers. Nevertheless, compared to the fragmentation of reception that has occurred in radio, movies and magazines, and the comparative regionality of the daily press, television is still the medium that is closest to maintaining responsibility for addressing an undifferentiated mass audience.

CONCLUSION

The mass media in the United States have been interdependent throughout the twentieth century. For example, the radio network RCA also owned a major Hollywood movie studio (RKO); and the two other networks, NBC and CBS, have had control of the television networks since their inception. Today, media conglomerates extend and diversify their holdings across the range of media, to the limits of the law.

The substance of the media has often coincided as well. The sale to television of movie holdings has meant that subsequent generations have gained their knowledge of 'Classical' Hollywood cinema almost entirely from the small screen. The popularity of video rentals, and the importance of video and television rights in modern film financing, has helped to muddy the distinction between film and television. The forthcoming High Definition Television (HDTV), which promises a picture quality and size comparable to a projected image, will exacerbate this trend.

Meanwhile, the 'personalities' created on TV and film are continually elaborated in the press and on radio, and it is increasingly common for soap-opera stars to try their talents in a recording studio. At the same time, events that are headline news one minute are Major Motion Pictures the next. For example, the Watergate revelations began with the 'factual' investigations of newspaper reporters (see Chapter 14) and wound up on the silver screen with Robert Redford and Dustin Hoffman in *All the President's Men* (1976). The inverted terminology of 'faction', or 'infotainment' that has been used in reference to contemporary film and television encapsulates something that has always been a dominant media activity: the process of turning the incoherent data of daily life into conventionalized dramatic modes. Through the constant juxtaposition of banal and significant items, the media have anticipated and helped to form the postmodernist sensibility that characterizes contemporary America. In particular television's practice of recycling its own history in an inexhaustible stream of reruns, and the increasing number of shows *about* television (*TV Bloopers*, for example, and quiz shows testing the contestants' recall of TV trivia) feeds a self-reflexive and ironic spectator position.

The factor that has united the American media more thoroughly than any other has been their appeal to the mass of the population. The press, the cinema, radio and TV have all, at different times, served to bring together people from disparate backgrounds, uniting the culture in the recognition of, if not actually in devotion to, new sets of cultural norms. The particular forms that the media have taken have been determined by their essentially capitalistic enterprise of trying to make as many sales as possible. Critical comment surrounding the American media has often found it to be devoid of substance and 'artistic' merit. Since the birth of the movies, an argument has been waged over the effects of mass entertainments – particularly representations of sex and violence – on the nation's moral fibre. However, for better or for worse, the media have formed the quintessential aesthetic summation of American popular culture in the twentieth century.

SUGGESTIONS FOR FURTHER READING

There are several thought-provoking commentaries on the subject of the American media which place them in the context of their wider social and cultural developments in modern American history. Stewart Ewan's *Captains of Consciousness* (New York, 1976) and his *Channels of Desire: Mass Images and the Shaping of American Consciousness* (New York, 1982) are highly recommended. Other useful publications with a broad cultural emphasis include Richard Wightman Fox and T.J. Lears (eds), *The Culture of Consumption: Critical Essays in American History, 1880–1890* (New York, 1983); Richard Maltby (ed.), *Dreams for Sale: Popular Culture in the Twentieth Century* (London, 1989); and, more specifically, Jeremy Tunstall, *The Media Are American: Anglo-American Media in the World* (New York, 1978). Roland Marchand's *Advertising the American Dream: Making Way for Modernity, 1920–1940* (Berkeley, 1985) suggests the centrality of the ethics and aesthetics of advertising across all American media – a subject which also features in Michael Schudson's *Advertising, the Uneasy Persuasion* (New York, 1984). Lary May's *Screening Out the Past: The Birth of Mass Culture and the Motion Picture Industry* (New York, 1980) is an excellent sociological study of the beginnings of America's mass media.

An historical account of the development of the press that is both scholarly and readable is constituted by Michael Schudson's *Discovering the News: A Social History of American Newspapers* (New York, 1984). Literature on radio is surprisingly sparse, but Eric Barnouw has written several useful commentaries: *A Tower in Babel* (New York, 1966), *The Golden Web* (New York, 1968) and *The Image Empire* (New York, 1970).

Literature on Hollywood movies constitutes a considerable subsection of commercial publishing, but much of it is long on anecdote and short on analysis. However, in the last fifteen years an increasing number of publications have appeared that provide penetrating insights into Hollywood's history and industrial organization. Robert Sklar broke new ground with *Movie-made America: A Cultural History of the Movies* (New York, 1976) in which he examined the routine output of the studios in their cultural and industrial context, rather than concentrating on specific texts as if they were products of individual genius. *The American Film Industry* (New York, 1976), ed. Tino Balio, contains essays similarly cognizant of the industrial realities of film production; a revised edition was published in 1985. Thomas Schatz lays bare the operations of individual studios in *The Genius of the System: Hollywood Filmmaking in the Studio Era* (New York, 1988); and Richard Maltby's *Harmless Entertainment: Hollywood and the Ideology of Consensus* (Metuchen, NJ, 1983) is an excellent historical and cultural overview of the workings of the industry. David Bordwell, Janet Staiger and Kristin Thompson carry the discussion of systematic studio production into the realms of narrative construction and *mise-en-scène* in their indispensable book *The Classical Hollywood Cinema: Film Style and Mode of Production to 1960* (New York, 1985). A useful extension of the publications on Hollywood industry has been made by *Hollywood in the Age of Television* (New York, 1990), ed. Tino Balio, which considers the contemporary implications of the media's tendency towards combination.

A standard work on the genres of American television is Horace Newcomb, *TV: The Most Popular Art* (New York, 1974). David Buxton,

From the Avengers to Miami Vice: Form and Ideology in Television Series (Manchester, 1990) provides an interesting alternative perspective. Eric Barnouw, *Tube of Plenty: The Evolution of American Television* (Oxford, 1975) is a reliable history of American television. A history more orientated towards TV's sociological aspects can be found in George Comstock, *The Evolution of American Television* (Newbury Park, CA, 1989). *MTM: 'Quality Television'* ed. Jane Feuer, Paul Kerr and Tise Vahimagi (London, 1984) is a valuable study of one influential production company. Finally, the phenomenon of 're-combinant' television, with its spin-offs and copies, is discussed in Todd Gitlin, *Inside Prime Time* (New York, 1983).

CHAPTER ELEVEN
Musical America

David Horn

One of the hallmarks of America's music is the richness and subtlety of its relationships, and this offers a key to understanding. These relationships can be found within musical practice itself – for example, between voice and instruments, or between melody and rhythm. Or they can occur in the interdependence of musical practice and other activities – social, economic, technological. This chapter offers an introduction to the relationships that underpin musical America in the late nineteenth and twentieth centuries. It uses two alternating approaches. The first involves the selection of certain key periods and the attempt to explore them both topographically and historically, looking 'laterally' across their activity as well as 'vertically' into past and future. The periods chosen are the early 1900s, the 1920s and the late 1940s/mid-1950s. The second approach is to focus on particular genres or groups of genres, considering their origins, development, conventions and publics.

THE TURN-OF-THE-CENTURY

In the early years of the twentieth century the relationship between music and changes taking place in technology, commerce and society was strikingly close. By the mid-1890s sound recording had become a commercial enterprise, building on Edison's 1877 invention of the cylinder 'phonograph'. It was the flat disc with the spiral groove, however, developed by Emil Berliner, that proved best suited to the growing consumer market, since it lent itself well to multiple reproduction and was marketed deliberately for entertainment purposes. Then, in 1901,

239

Marconi's transatlantic wireless telegraph message from Cape Cod confirmed the arrival of radio.

In allowing the musical moment to be captured and released later at will, technology bequeathed an unprecedented flexibility, but one tied in with a growing preference for passive reproduction over personal involvement. In 1900, however, most music was still made known and heard at live performances: from the concert halls, opera houses and theatres of large towns to the churches, dance halls, restaurants, bars and streets of almost any locality, and to the interior of the home. With particular help from German immigrants, concert life had blossomed among the urban white middle classes, but if any large-scale contemporary music could be said to be commonly known it was that of the 'March King', John Philip Sousa.

For many Americans, the home was still where music was most likely to be heard. In providing music for this growing middle-class market, publishers had already been moving towards mass production. Some of Sousa's marches – for example, 'The Washington Post' – were sold by the thousands in piano reductions for home performance. The 1890s saw an acceleration of this process, epitomized by songwriter–publisher Charles K. Harris. Harris may not have invented 'songplugging' or musical mass production, but he was their most successful early exponent. The inclusion – and promotion – of his 1892 song 'After the Ball' in a vaudeville show led to sales which eventually topped five million copies. The link between promotion and mass production created a new situation. Up to now, musical styles had coexisted in a structured diversity, sometimes unfamiliar with each other's existence. Now, in theory anyway, the means existed to make one idiom dominant, as the effects of mass production looked set to reach into all sections of society.

In economic terms, the music scene was indeed dominated from about 1900 by the New York publishers, many now located in 28th Street (where the noise of songpluggers promoting songs to performers on battered pianos earned the street the name of 'Tin Pan Alley'). Bolstered by copyright protection, publishers were developing a system which would make them and their products an integral part of a new economic and social order. Songplugging, first in shows, then in restaurants and shops, was music's contribution to the rapid rise of advertising. Advertising itself was helping to engender a more widespread consumer mentality, part of a fundamental conflict in social ethos between the older tradition of hard work and self-denial and the emerging, leisure-centred 'culture of abundance' (see Chapter 8). Music was involved in these changes. Secular music, with its obvious links to pleasure, had been argued over before but had maintained an important role, especially in more marginalized social groups. The middle classes, for their part, had successfully accommodated it by considering music itself marginal (or, which was sometimes the same thing, the province of women), but now it began a move to centre stage.

These key developments occurred in music's social, technical and economic relations. The songs themselves, with their simple, memorable melodies and frequent hints of pathos, showed features discernible in the mid-century songs of Stephen Foster. The most obvious influence upon Foster was that of the European parlour music that had been developed in the late eighteenth century for the expanding middle class. Some scholars have noted the presence of the folk song tradition of the British Isles, and of doctored 'Irish melodies'. They also point out that the Foster songs purporting to depict the lifestyle of black slaves contain no obvious Afro-American elements. Fascination with the culture of black America resulted, here as elsewhere, in caricature.

The song form we see evolving in early 'Tin Pan Alley' was to be a constant presence in America's music. During the nineteenth century simple strophic form had given way to a verse–chorus structure. Now the chorus became the location of the most interesting melody, reducing the importance of the narrative element (in the verses) in favour of more static descriptive statements. Linking the strongest melody to the repetitive element was also an effective marketing technique.

The music of ethnic and racial groups

These examples of musical and socio-economic evidence only tell part of the story. Linked together they may make us think that key musical developments always take place on a macro-level, involving and affecting large numbers of people in much the same way. Some developments did indeed work that way in America's music. But more often the opposite was true: that the wellspring of musical change was to be found in what made people different. Differences did not necessarily activate change. African music did not influence America by remaining African music. Change was generally brought about by dialogue between positions of difference, and/or the development of tension between whatever made any music different, and what threatened that difference.

With immigration rising to unprecedented levels, the country was now home to many different ethnic groups, all undergoing the shock of dispossession, but all with their own heritage (see Chapter 7). Many neither had nor acquired any fluency in the dominant language and were excluded from much of its culture. To some extent – and despite the 'melting pot' ethos – America allowed differences to be preserved (in the 1920s, for example, record companies recorded music in many different European languages). But more important was the response of the second generation, which was often uneasy about its cultural inheritance but, equally, confused about America's. Popular culture offered a space where they could begin to work out a relationship between the two. This relationship was founded on cultural difference, but what made it productive was dialogue – between individuals from different groups, and between any one individual and what constituted popular culture at the time. In some cases the results could be far-reaching.

The songwriter Irving Berlin is a good case in point. Born Israel Baline in Russia in 1888, the son of a cantor who emigrated to America in 1893, Berlin was brought up with a deep knowledge of Russian–Jewish culture, but 'he was at home in the streets, that marginal land between his own culture and the culture of his new society . . . where choices and sights could provide feelings of constant experience of the self uprooted from a stable past'. The young Berlin began writing songs in the early 1900s. His long-lasting success as a songwriter was based in part on his enthusiastic early mastery of the system (by 1919 he had formed his own publishing company), but also on his ability to take 'his speech and rhythm from the city streets, from Yiddish intonations, and from Italian, Yiddish, black and Irish voices and caricatures he found around him.'[1]

In no area of America's music is the importance of difference and the productivity of its relationships so marked as in the music of black Americans. The new musical genres at various stages of emergence as the century turned – ragtime, jazz, blues – had at least part of their roots in differences going back to Africa (for example, the close connections between music and movement, and between speech and melody), but what had provided the motor of change was contact and dialogue – between black and black, black and white – over more than two centuries.

The diversity of European cultures entering America is acknowledged, but a similar recognition is not automatically accorded to African cultures arriving on the slave ships. Yet even the areas from which most slaves were taken demonstrate musical diversity – in scales, instruments, intonation. Contact between different musical cultures was an ongoing phenomenon in Africa as elsewhere. This continued in the New World (including the Caribbean), but under very different circumstances. Particularly important was the contact between Africans from the Muslim-dominated savannah regions, with their nasal intonation, string instruments and griot tradition, and those from the coastal areas, which strongly featured percussion. String players fared better during slavery, since the potential of drummers to incite rebellion made owners nervous. But even without drums, the percussive approach to music remained an important component in the dialogue.

The process of contact was paralleled in the long history of musical dialogue between black and white in America. This occurred across a range of musical activities: vocal and instrumental techniques, song forms, body movement. Out of the complex story, one particular set of contacts stands out: that between Africans and Celts. The first influx of Celtic people had taken place in the eighteenth century. The nineteenth century saw further arrivals, fleeing Ireland's social difficulties. Both groups had a lowly status, and contact, though not evenly spread, was frequent. Despite many differences, aspects of their musical culture sometimes ran remarkably parallel: in intonation, in embellishment, in the practice of answering one musical phrase with another. These similarities may have had their roots in the distant period of Arabic influence on Europe and Africa, influence indirectly received in Scotland and Ireland, but persistent because of those countries' remoteness. It is at least possible that the dialogue which took place in the New World had a special power because it incorporated a reconnecting, under circumstances of not identical, but comparable dispossession.

Contacts continued after Emancipation, but the changed circumstances had other consequences for music. Hitherto substantially excluded from participating in the white-run commercial entertainment system of which music was a part, (except when caricaturing themselves as minstrels), black Americans now began to explore new opportunities. They did so from a position of extreme disadvantage, but contact with the system provided a considerable stimulus to the growth of new musical genres.

Ragtime

By 1900 ragtime had become a craze among white Americans, thanks largely to dissemination of piano 'rags' by music publishers who had scented the commercial possibilities of the music's low-life associations and its links with new, risqué dance steps. Fascination with another culture was again an important ingredient, but this time much – though by no means all – of the music was indeed the creation of black Americans.

Though not the first black musician to have 'rags' published, Scott Joplin became the best known. His 'Maple Leaf Rag', published in 1899, sold half a million copies in the next decade. Joplin is a good example of the opportunities and frustrations faced by a black musician at the time. Ragtime itself was forged from the encounter, after the Civil War, between syncopated black dance rhythms, the pulse and more mildly syncopated inclinations of the march and the harmony of European 'light' music. As heard in a bar-room, ragtime piano was a performer's music, with scope for varying the interplay between the more regular left hand

and the more syncopated right. Joplin, however, was classically trained and sought to 'raise' this music to the aesthetic status accorded to classical piano music – pre-composed, played as written. This aesthetic opportunity was matched by the commercial one which publication now seemed to offer certain types of black or black-derived music. Joplin's frustration when his second ragtime opera, 'Treemonisha', could not be properly staged, was due mainly to his failure to abide by the constraints of commercial music – and to recognize the strictly observed frontiers of cultural racism.

Ragtime had a novel sound, but in its piano form it was also part of a continuity of music for the home. The early 1900s craze for ragtime-related dances such as the Bunny Hug was a more obvious break with custom. The growth of dance halls brought dancing into the public arena, engendering a new fierce debate about shifting standards of behaviour, particularly new attitudes to physical expression (see also Chapter 12).

Charles Ives

At the time 'Maple Leaf Rag' was published, Charles Ives, a twenty-five-year-old Yale University music graduate and composer, was finding his way in business in New York – not in music, but in insurance. The music Ives wrote in his spare time was much later to secure its sceptical creator the accolade of 'first American composer'. Whereas, in 28th Street, music and business were inextricably entangled, up near Central Park Ives appeared to keep the two distinct (though he maintained his business and his music helped each other). Nor was he influenced by what an audience might think, since his work received scarcely any public performances until after he had stopped composing in the 1920s. Whether this encouraged the pioneering experimentation for which he is famous, or whether his experimentation discouraged his desire to seek an audience, is still open to debate. But in other ways Ives's music (mainly orchestral works, chamber and piano music, and songs) displays, particularly in his way of handling apparently opposing tendencies, a number of features which run intriguingly parallel to aspects of popular styles.

Ives is often portrayed as the first composer to break the stranglehold of European tradition, and it is true that his experiments with such things as dissonance and polyrhythms were counter to the prevailing fashion, in advance of that fashion's decline in Europe itself, and subsequently in America. But much of Ives's music is cast in conventional European forms – sonatas, symphonies, string quartets. He seems to have been more interested in re-examining these than in subverting them; but – crucially – in doing so through the filter of a different (American) tradition.

This is especially evident in his extensive use of quotations from 'all types of music dear to an American town' – hymns, marches, Foster songs.[2] Never used as mere local colour, these tunes often constitute part of the music's raw material. They work by taking the collective memory of the small-town America in which Ives grew up (a 'real', known world), right into the heart of the (distant) European tradition. In the process both are re-explored. Not once, but repeatedly – many tunes recur, but in different contexts, as if memory was being continually questioned from different viewpoints. In Ives's orchestral work 'Central Park in the Dark', foreground music and background music move separately throughout, producing various 'polytemporal' effects. Ives revelled in coexistence, in simultaneity, because they demonstrated difference. He was, however, strongly influenced by Transcendentalism, as discussed in Chapter 4, and difference was, ultimately, a symbol of unity: 'the fabric of existence weaves itself whole'.[3]

The blues

The blues' first appearance in the context of commercial music occurred when numerous songs called 'blues' were published in the 1910s. The year 1920 is more significant, however, for it was then that Mamie Smith recorded 'Crazy Blues', becoming the first black singer to record a blues (it was actually a vaudeville song) and, even more important, to see it marketed exclusively to black America. Because sheet music had only limited sales to this audience, music publishers had made few efforts in their direction, but the fast-growing record companies discovered – to their surprise – a large, untapped market for what they called 'race records'. The early years of recording were dominated by women – the 'classic' blues singers whose strong voices performed a variety of popular songs to a backing, usually, of jazz musicians. Most famous of these was Bessie Smith, the 'deep, unhappy, surging quality' of whose voice singled her out.[4] In Bessie's performances – which spoke especially powerfully to black women – an assertive strength sat alongside experience of suffering.

The urban commercial world of the 'classic' singers was a long way from the roots of the blues in nineteenth-century Southern black culture, though in its diversity of style and mood it pointed to a feature which was to remain constant. In the intricate story of the blues' origins two major influences stand out: the work song and the field holler. The work song, with its strong reminders of Africa, was a functional music with a 'call-and-response' pattern (a leader calls, the group responds). With the postbellum decline of the plantation economy, group work songs also declined and the holler, a solo form sometimes passed from one individual to another, took its place. Already present before the war the holler, with its highly individualistic, lonely-sounding vocal line, was more expressive of the mood brought about by the economic and social changes of Reconstruction, as well as more suited to changed work patterns.

By itself, and as segregation increased, the holler might have been a cul-de-sac. But 'freedom', however tarnished, allowed a growth in social gatherings at which making music and dancing were central. Slowly, too, opportunities for professional entertainers expanded and here instrumental techniques began to come into their own. The music which developed in the 1880s/1890s was as diverse as the complexity of its history would suggest, and what would later be recognized as 'blues' was probably one idiom among many. But, in seeking to understand the rise of the blues, three related points are helpful:

(1) Music was important in helping to create the awareness of identity which was a vital part of black communities' response to their social situation.

(2) That identity drew heavily on the collective experiences of the past (including the long history of black–white relations) and engaged them with the problems of the present. In doing so, it placed particular emphasis on the relationship between self and other (whether 'other' was individual or collective).

(3) Musical idioms which best expressed the sense of the past and which provided the clearest space for exploration of self–other relationships in the daily world of the present would eventually predominate. One of those was the blues.

Documentary evidence for the early history of the blues is scanty. By contrast, it is extremely rich from around 1925, when record companies diversified their 'race record' catalogues and began recording the music of the 'downhome' (Southern rural and small town) bluesmen. By then the blues, while immensely varied regionally, was demonstrating a preference for certain forms, topics and styles. Recording may have encouraged this tendency, but the music of many of the musicians recorded in the 1920s had probably changed little over the years.

In musical terms, the most common blues form is one which uses a repeated twelve-bar unit, in the course of which shifts in the underlying harmony twice give a sense of moving away from 'base', only to return 'home'. Words are fitted into this cyclical pattern in various ways, but one way is particularly common: the twelve-bar unit is divided into three units of four bars; for all three four-bar units there is a complete line of verse, but for the second four bars the first line is repeated, giving an overall

three-line stanza in an 'aab' form. The individual lines of verse rarely
occupy all the bars of musical time. In many blues with this stanza form the
singer will give equal space to the instrument(s), which emerge from the
role of accompanist and fashion a response to the voice. In these
instrumental spaces the solo guitarists in particular demonstrate their various
levels of skill, some, like Blind Lemon Jefferson from Texas, developing
single-string melody lines which behave like another individual, and others,
like Tommy Johnson from Mississippi, using heavier, more insistent
chording, with more of a 'group' sound. Blues melody frequently employs
so-called 'blue notes', the practice of introducing slight dissonance at
certain points in the scale by 'bending' the note. Vocal and instrumental
lines are both likely to be highly rhythmic. The scope for internal
variation, within the elasticity of the overall structure, is almost endless.

The reputation of blues lyrics for mournfulness is only partly deserved.
Particularly in the early recordings the richness of subject matter is
remarkable, encompassing a great many aspects of daily life. If one theme
predominates it is dislocation – and if one problem predominates it is
control, especially in personal relationships. Blues also had a major function
in providing dance music, and these lyrics (usually employing a different fit
of words to the twelve-bar pattern, one allowing less time for reflection)
were characteristically assertive, often earthy. This form later provided the
basic material for rock'n'roll. But however depressed a blues performer
might seem, he/she frequently stands to be revitalized, not just by the
catharsis of self-expression, but from the energizing power of the rhythm
and the instrumental responses, and, if performing live, by the feedback
from the audience. There are exceptions to this, and one reason why the
legendary 1930s bluesman Robert Johnson has appealed, years later, to
white audiences may be that his extraordinary instrumental skill seems
designed to intensify the sense of alienation and isolation in his lyrics, not
relieve it.

Blues musicians were part of the migration to the Northern cities,
where their styles changed. The city blues of the 1930s was a less intense,
more dispassionate music. But the experience of Chicago in particular bred
new responses, culminating in the 1940s in the amplified blues of musicians
such as Muddy Waters, who drew inspiration from the harsher Mississippi
style in particular and, using the opportunities offered by technology,
forged an intensely personalized sound that could be both physically and
mentally overpowering.

Jazz

The blues has remained an intensely subjective music; equally, it has constantly demonstrated its ability to explore the paradoxes of self–other relationships, whether at an intimate personal level, within a community (as between performer and audience), or in a wider, even national, social arena. Jazz shares the ability to express subtleties of relationships and it, too, often places the individual in a context where subjectivity is explored, though without the explicitness of blues. But jazz differs from blues in that, despite its reputation as a showcase for individual prowess, it has a strong collective base, and this allows it flexibility in choice of vantage points.

The wider public life of jazz dates from 1916–17, when the Original Dixieland Jass Band from New Orleans played to enthusiastic audiences in Chicago and New York, making the first jazz recording in 1917. The fact that the 'ODJB' was a white band has led to contradictory interpretations of early jazz history (the argument over whether white musicians 'stole' the music, then and later, has been particularly bitter), but it at least suggests that black and white have both been involved in some way from the start. Mamie Smith's 'Crazy Blues' was significant for jazz also, as the revelation of a market for black music prepared the way for black jazz musicians themselves to begin recording. But whereas blues and gospel performers had been segregated to the race record catalogues, some companies recorded both white and black jazz musicians and promoted the records on general lists, thus giving black jazz a slightly wider currency in the country as a whole. Nevertheless, the phenomenon of the white-owned industry marketing black music back to black America was present in jazz also.

Numerous attempts have been made to dent, if not demolish, New Orleans's claim to be the birthplace of jazz. Such iconoclasm is based on evidence of widespread musical activity in the black subculture in the late nineteenth century. 'Yet', says one historian, 'in truth, the old legend is almost certainly correct.'[5] The majority of early jazz musicians, black and white, hailed from the city or its environs; its musical history was unique in its high level of activity and musical literacy, and in the interaction of concert and leisure music; it was influenced by its proximity to the Caribbean islands; its Franco-Hispanic culture was less repressive; and it had a long-established brass band tradition. The role of the city's black Creole population may have been crucial. When the Jim Crow laws of the 1890s forced this group, with its strong, proud ties to the culture of the French and Spanish settlers, down to the social level of the rest of the black population, they looked to music to try to maintain their sense of difference. At the same time, their musical practices came fully into contact with those of other parts of black society.

The first recordings of black New Orleans jazz musicians were made not in New Orleans but in Chicago. Jazz history holds the 1923 recordings by King Oliver's Creole Jazz Band in high regard, as being the first coherent musical statement of the tradition in the context of the music industry. The recordings are characterized by an integrated ensemble approach, in which each musician has a carefully defined role: melody on trumpet, clarinet adding ornamentation, trombone providing harmonic support, plus rhythm section. (Oliver's band was unusual in adding a second trumpet, embellishing the melody.) Some limited space was provided for improvised solos, within a tight structure. This ensemble style, with its relaxed 'swing', perhaps reached its peak with the 1926–27 recordings by Jelly Roll Morton's Red Hot Peppers, but what distinguishes them above all was that they were 'carefully organized structures in which all the details . . . were realized as integral compositional elements'.[6]

Providing the second trumpet for Oliver was the young Louis Armstrong, whom Oliver had summoned from New Orleans to follow a much-travelled migratory route to join him in Chicago. Oliver's collective style soon cramped his protégé's talent. In 1925–27, following a spell in New York, Armstrong made an outstanding series of studio recordings with his Hot Five and Hot Seven, in which he matched an unheard-of technical ability to a highly imaginative approach to phrasing and rhythm. The recordings exuded a sense of risk-taking successfully negotiated, as, for example in his 'stop-time' solo on 'Potato Head Blues'. This is also a persuasive illustration of writer Ralph Ellison's contention that something basic to the 'Negro-American style . . . reminds us that the world is ever unexplored'.[7] Much of the richness of jazz after Armstrong relates to a desire to explore the alternatives, without a corresponding one to impose solutions. In the 1930s Armstrong obtained considerable commercial success, an achievement which opened doors for many other black musicians. For many (mainly white) commentators, however, this tied him too closely into a career as an entertainer, while his style of entertaining left him open to criticism from later generations of black musicians. What a contemporary assessment can say is that Armstrong occupied an ambiguous position between cultures and that this both freed and constrained him.

Although Armstrong and others pointed the way forward for the soloist, jazz did not immediately move in that direction. New York in particular was the breeding ground for an ensemble approach which made possible the existence of the 'big band'. In New Orleans ensembles each instrument's musical line preserved its identity within the group sound, and solos seemed to arise naturally out of this approach. However ideal as a social symbol, the style had limitations as soon as it became necessary to increase the size of the band (for example, to make more noise in a bigger venue). More individual instrumental lines would have meant the texture becoming too thick, and improvisation within bigger ensembles risked undermining cohesion. In the dance band style, by contrast, the instruments forfeited sustained individuality in favour of 'vertical' integration into an overall sound. In the music of Fletcher Henderson, Duke Ellington and others from the late 1920s on, the advantages of this harmonic approach were wedded to the New Orleans approach to rhythm and phrasing to produce a flexible, often dynamic ensemble style, in which it was the job of the arranger to introduce contrast (for example, by playing off homogeneous groups within the orchestra against each other). Solos became another tool in the overall design, and here Ellington in particular was able to incorporate the distinctive qualities of each soloist with great effect.

The big band approach to ensemble playing subdued individuality, but offset this loss by switching the focus from group to soloist in the way the music was organized. These often improvised solo spots came to be filled by outstanding soloists such as Coleman Hawkins or Lester Young, but the constraints of the format became too much for advancing technique and individual aspiration to bear. A link between the media, commerce and racial factors was also important in provoking change. Radio promotion had enabled the late 1930s 'swing' bands to give jazz its first era of nation-wide commercial success, but although bands began to be mixed racially, the spoils were not always evenly shared. Radio also encouraged an unadventurous approach. As a result, younger black musicians such as Charlie Parker and Dizzy Gillespie began to fashion a new style, which responded to both musical and non-musical problems. Spawned in after-hours 'jam' sessions, especially in New York, in the early 1940s, 'bebop' returned to small group jazz, but with an added emphasis on improvisation, of a technical standard too far advanced for would-be imitators among the commercially-minded. There was a cultural price to pay, as the more 'difficult' music, despite the increased presence of the blues, began to lose the broad receptivity black America had accorded to earlier styles. An increasing musical adventurousness and virtuosity characterized much jazz after bebop, as in the music of John Coltrane and Ornette Coleman. Miles Davis, by contrast, continually found ways to develop new approaches without stretching technical skill to its limits.

The big band tradition did not die out, but from bebop on, the prevailing approach has remained one in which the small group format provides the opportunity for (sometimes extensive) self-expression. Even so, jazz musicians are rarely able to be wholly autonomous. Any one performance can be affected by a number of interconnecting relationships: with the other musicians on the session; with the underlying rhythmic patterns; with the pre-existing tune; with others who have also conversed with it. Sensing these relationships may help us to see what is some-times perceived as the musician's continuous search for originality as actually a complex form of negotiation between the expected and the unexpected.

THE 1920s

In the image of Twenties America music is regularly identified with enjoyment. But the 'Jazz Age' also marked the culmination of a controversy over profound changes taking place in social and moral behaviour, and in this public schism nothing was so likely to provoke argument as innocent-seeming 'jazz' and its associated dances. The music known as 'jazz' was usually the jazz-inflected sound of dance bands such as Paul Whiteman's, but its roots were common knowledge – and there is no doubting the racism behind such accounts of the origins of jazz as 'the accompaniment of the voodoo dancer . . . stimulating the half-crazed barbarian to the vilest deeds'.[8] Fear engendered by the prominence of immigrant ethnic groups in disseminating the music was also evident, as was disquiet over the 'generation gap' and the potential of dance to liberalize the role of women – a process hastened in the 1910s by dancers such as Irene Castle.

Partly in response to moral outrage, some bandleaders attempted to synthesize the rhythmic subtlety of jazz with the less threatening harmonies and structures of classical music. The outstanding example of this was performed by Whiteman's orchestra in 1924: Gershwin's 'Rhapsody in Blue' was intended to show how jazz had 'progressed', though the work's subsequent durability may have had more to do with Gershwin's individual skills than with the virtues of 'symphonic jazz'.

Two from Brooklyn

George Gershwin, like Irving Berlin the child of Russian–Jewish immigrants, was similarly attracted to popular culture as a way forward for those starting with little. (See also Chapter 12.) His early employment as a songplugger familiarized him with the constraints and opportunities of the popular song form and its commercial milieu. His subsequent songwriting remains his major achievement. Gershwin's songs are often harmonically sophisticated, but what distinguishes them from those of his contemporaries is the way that rhythmic individuality – Gershwin's profound feeling for African–American rhythm seems to have been exceptional – is wedded to melodic shape and phrasing. Unlike his peers, Gershwin also fashioned a successful career as a composer. The success of his concert music provided a rare bridge between 'classical' and 'popular' – something the musical estab lishment has not always been ready to forgive.

Although deplored with equal frequency for aesthetic reasons by cultural guardians, jazz exerted a fascination on younger composers such as Aaron Copland. Copland's background was similar to Gershwin's, but his early training led him not to Tin Pan Alley but to study in Paris. There, however, the closeness of French music to French life produced 'the conviction . . . that the two things that seemed always to have been so separate in America – music and the life about me – must be made to touch'.[9] Without Gershwin's intimacy with contemporary popular idioms, Copland's approach to integrating jazz – for example, in 'Music For the Theater' (1925) – seems studied. But the underlying determination to 'find an American solution' remained. During the early 1930s awareness of the gap between 'art' and 'life' struck Copland with new force, but, ironically, his most cerebral music comes from this period. Then, as America tried to pull out of the Depression, composers such as Copland and Virgil Thomson were enlisted to help in the process by producing music evoking the unique resources of the country – its landscapes, its communities, its energy. Copland responded with numerous works with a folk theme, such as 'El Salon Mexico' (1936). In these, and in his Hollywood scores, such as *The City* (1939), he achieved what he had failed to do before: he fashioned an orchestral style which matched, indeed appeared to derive from, the vernacular material which was its base. It was an echo of Ives, with the major difference that, in this instance at least, Copland's style was market-conscious.

The music industry, the media and 'hillbilly' music

The liberalization processes of the 1920s produced a heightened sense of individual difference and this was apparent in music also, as stars and songwriters began to proliferate, aided by the burgeoning music and media industry. Yet the same industry also looked to create and profit from greater homogeneity and legal control.

By 1921 the record industry had overtaken sheet music in production levels and earnings. Records were sold on the basis of distinctions, not only between songs, but between performers – but, as with sheet music, such distinctions could not be too prominent. This ambivalence was even more marked when, by the mid-1920s, commercial radio began to replace records as the main provider of entertainment. Under the network system, radio companies sold the same entertainment to stations across the country (see Chapter 10). By 1930 live transmissions of dance-band music accounted for three-quarters of all programmes, and band-leaders such as Guy Lombardo became household names. But radio's ability to deliver a huge audience to commercial sponsors encouraged a cautious approach to interpretation, even of Broadway hits. Songwriters were more highly valued than before, but power still lay with a relatively small group of publishers. All were members of the performing rights organization ASCAP, which collected revenue on live performances of their music, including broadcasts, and through its catalogues effectively controlled most of what was performed on air.

Network radio-programming did much to disguise the diversity of America's music. A black jazz musician had very limited access to the airwaves, and a blues musician virtually none at all. In parts of the South, however, local radio stations began picking up on rural white folk performers, especially fiddlers. By 1925 radio barn dances were a popular local feature, particularly round Nashville. But the prime mover in bringing this music into full contact with the commercial world was the record industry. Its involvement began in June 1923, when the Okeh label's Ralph Peer (who also recorded Mamie Smith) recorded Fiddlin' John Carson in Atlanta and inaugurated another marketing category: 'hillbilly music'. Here again, the industry was a surprised participant in the profitable process of selling back musical culture to a marginalized section of society. Centred on fiddle, banjo and guitar, the hillbilly music recorded in the 1920s was no Appalachian museum piece, but a rich, constantly evolving mixture of British (especially Celtic) and black American secular and religious song, already reflecting considerable exposure to the world of commercial music (all these elements can be seen in the repertoire of a performer like 'Uncle Dave' Macon). Nevertheless, the mountains which were the music's principal home no doubt contributed to the strength and longevity of the British input.

The coming of radio and the record industry was but one manifestation of the social and economic 'modernization' affecting the South. These processes had two principal effects on the music. One was to introduce (or reinforce) a sense of tradition-at-risk. This was epitomized by the Carter Family, whose records, beginning in 1927, responded to threats to the sense of unified communities by maintaining a dialogue with old ways and old virtues. The other effect was a more positive response to the forces and symbols of change. First to follow this path was Mississippi-born Jimmie Rodgers, the start of whose recording career coincided precisely with that of the Carter Family, but whose songs, drawing on and adapting the more individualistic, this-worldy aspects of the repertoire, began to propel the music into the urbane world of commercial entertainment. Country music, the later term for the profusion of styles, has continued to demonstrate the creative potential of both these basic trends.

THE LATE 1940s/EARLY 1950s

America's musical scene in the late 1940s was remarkably varied. Black music, collectively termed 'rhythm & blues' in 1949 by the magazine *Billboard*, embraced numerous separable, though overlapping styles of blues, jazz and gospel music – not forgetting the gospel-influenced 'doo-wop' male vocal quartets. Some, like bebop and the Chicago blues, tended towards separatism, while others, such as the infectious 'jump' blues of Louis Jordan, were beginning to appeal across racial divides. 'Country and western' (another *Billboard* term) included hillbilly, bluegrass, cowboy, Nashville and white gospel. One style in particular, the 'western swing' typified by Bob Wills, demonstrated the continuing process of contact between styles and races in its use of jazz-like improvisation and blues riffs.

Few listeners were fully aware of this variety since, for the most part, the availability of these musics was still restricted. By 1950, however, developments were taking place in the entertainment industry, and in society as a whole, which would help bring about a significant change. The most important of these occurred in the broadcasting and record industries. The growing commercial importance of television reduced the networks' opposition to the granting of new radio station licences. Unlike the stations affiliated to the networks, these new, independent stations relied heavily on records for their programming. While some used 'mainstream' music, most used rhythm & blues and country records, tailoring their output to the particular make-up of their audiences, and ignoring the protests of the American Federation of Musicians against the decline (precipitated by juke-boxes in the 1930s) of live music. The reason this variety of recordings was available was that the 1940s also saw a dramatic growth in small record companies, many based in Los Angeles (a major recipient of black and white migrant labour during the war). These independent companies had a sense of musical developments and audience preferences the major companies now lacked. Aided by the arrival of magnetic recording tape, which increased flexibility in recording and reduced reliance on big studios, they emerged to challenge the majors for a share of the market, using radio play on the new stations as a powerful means of achieving this.

In this new situation, songplugging continued unabated, but in a different guise. Record companies targeted their promotional activities at another new arrival, the disc-jockey. The advent of the lightweight 45 rpm vinyl disc, developed by major company RCA in the late 1940s to rival CBS's $33\frac{1}{3}$ rpm LP, helped them by allowing cheaper mail-shots. The greater variety of music on the air soon began to reach a wider audience, particularly among teenagers, who then began purchasing the records and, not infrequently, involving themselves in performance.

Teenagers' tastes had influenced the musical market in the 'swing era' of the late 1930s. Their emergence as a recognizable group, however, belongs to the postwar years, when a growth in their spending power and leisure time increased not only their visibility but their potential as an identifiable – and profitable – market. The context in which this took place was that of a 'polyglot, urban working-class culture', where 'the social meanings previously conveyed in isolation by blues, country, polka, zydeco and Latin musics found new expression as they blended in an urban setting . . . .' Rock'n'roll helped devise a common musical language for people previously divided by ethnicity.'[10]

John Cage

Among American composers experimentalism was gathering pace, building on the 1920s compositions of Edgard Varèse and others. Its new momentum was due substantially to John Cage. In the late 1940s, influenced by Henry Cowell, Cage developed the 'prepared piano'. Pieces of wood, paper, metal, etc. were inserted into a grand piano, converting it into an unusual percussion instrument, with enhanced pitch and rhythmic possibilities. In exploring these, Cage drew on Eastern music. Audiences were mystified.

The 1950s saw Cage at his most radical, as ideas from Oriental philosophy interacted with his long-felt iconoclasm. 'Music of Changes' (1951) was the first of many works in which compositional control was yielded to an element of chance, with pitch, duration, succession governed by I Ching, the ancient Chinese Book of Changes. Underlying this was the tenet that composition should be process-centred, not object-centred. In nature (according to Jung's comment on I Ching), 'every process is partially or totally interfered with by chance', and music, said Cage, should not attempt to 'bring order out of chaos'.[11] Similar sentiments lay behind his famous piece '4'33"', in which the pianist remains silent, the 'music' being whatever sounds occur in that space of time. Cage's experiments gained him considerable notoriety. His influence extended beyond the avant-garde to jazz and, later, to areas of rock. Paradoxically, perhaps, while his ideas related music closely to the natural condition of the world, his music seemed to some to be 'dehumanized'.

Rock'n'roll, rock and soul

Important as industrial, social and other changes were in the emergence of rock'n'roll, they do not fully explain it. The music, too, had an evolutionary history, in which a major role was played by trends apparent in the 1940s. Much can be traced to a renewed *rapprochement* between blues and country music, in urban surroundings. Many rhythm & blues and western swing numbers of the 1940s 'sound very like' rock'n'roll, particularly in their use of 'boogie' rhythms (strong, repeated bass-line patterns, with off-beat accents and a fondness for turning major chords into 'walking' motions up and down the scale). Bill Haley's 'Rock Around the Clock' (1954) shows a clear debt to a 'blues–boogie' tradition. Haley was also following the practice of 'covering' songs first recorded by rhythm & blues performers (as did Elvis Presley with his first recordings in 1954). But evolution was also revolution, not so much in the dramatic sense (though Haley, to his embarrassment, caused some rioting, and Presley's physicality was unprecedented in a white singer), as in the biggest shift yet in music's movement to a central position, socially, culturally and economically. It may have been this, more than youthful rebellion, that engendered a fresh wave of moral panic. Many of the same arguments – and fears – are evident as in the 1920s, but 'what was so shocking was the fact that this music was now being taken seriously by a rising generation' – seriously, because it offered a relationship between art and life.[12]

One result was an increasing democratization of music. Not fully realized till the 1960s – and then, as now, a site for struggle between the different interest groups involved in musical production (musicians, managers, engineers, executives, etc.) – it is seen, for example, in the emergence of Buddy Holly as the first young white songwriter–performer. Presley's career, by comparison, is in one sense an illustration of 'cooptation' – the continuing power of the industry to turn 'one of us', with apparent independence but limited earning potential, into a remote, but commercially luxuriant and artistically pliant 'star'. But Presley's music also illustrates 'that rock'n'roll was internally contradictory from the start: not just boogie rhythms, rough sound, blues shouts and physical involvement, but also sentimental ballads, melodies and forms, "angelic" backing vocal effects and "novelty" gimmicks'.[13]

By the late 1950s, following some recovery of lost ground by major companies and compromising gestures towards concerned parents by radio stations, the more sentimental side of the repertoire was in the ascendant. The innovations of the 1960s – when rock'n'roll sheds the ephemerality of the 'roll', to emphasize the durability of the 'rock' – came from two main quarters: the folk revival and British 'beat'. The commitment shown to the concerns and expressive means of folk music by an urban musical left wing in the 1940s and 1950s (including Woody Guthrie and Pete Seeger) and their involvement in political causes, attracted a younger generation to the folk world. Bob Dylan and others, however, were not content to preserve and adapt, but drew on these resources as a source of technique and style, and also of 'authenticity', to fashion their own expression. The apparent non-commercialism of the music was an important factor in its spread, as was its ability to incorporate intellectual ideas, thanks to the more prominent role given to lyrics.

Although interest in rock'n'roll and rhythm & blues declined in late 1950s America, in Britain rhythm & blues in particular increased in popularity, due to American forces' radio and the presence of US troops. Records by performers such as Chuck Berry, who had never garnered the same rewards as white rock'n'rollers, provided the impetus for British 'beat' music. When the success of groups such as the Beatles and the Rolling Stones crossed the Atlantic in the mid-1960s, America began to re-awaken to the rhythmic vitality of its musical traditions. The British 'invasion' and the American response, produced a musical scene of unprecedented vitality. Central to this was the abandonment of the practice of thinking of songwriters and performers as separate. From the Beatles' 'A Hard Day's Night' album on, rock musicians were expected to be creators and performers of their music. This implied notions of freedom, something the West Coast lifestyle was well suited to developing – in the leisure music of the Beach Boys, or the psychedelia of the Byrds and Jefferson Airplane.

In this context, and with the added ingredient of the 'counter-culture' and its opposition to convention, the music of the later 1960s seems to mark a decided shift in the relationship between autonomy and constraint. Helped by the metamorphosis of the LP from compilation to concept, musicians and audiences alike began to see the music as authentic, independent expression. Technology played its part: improved amplification made possible the outdoor concert, unrestrained by bricks and mortar. For those concerned about commerce, the Beatles had shown that artistic freedom without compromise was a possibility – and a revitalized and grateful industry could even find a way of seeming to join the conspiracy.

Nevertheless, significant tensions existed in the relationship: musically, between working innovatively within the conventions of form and seeking to replace them with opportunities for more extended development (as in 'progressive rock'); technologically, between the possibilities for manipulating sound offered by multi-tracking and the increasing importance of producers and engineers; commercially, between notions of 'art' and the commercial pressure to make a living. What the Beatles appeared to have achieved in reconciling independence, shared control of production and commercial success, was not open to all to copy, especially since the rewards involved were now so huge. Rock's potential to articulate political ideology was inevitably paradoxical, given the wealth of many protagonists. When political issues re-emerged in the 1980s, in the context of the global media festivals for charity such as 'Live Aid', similar paradoxes were still there.

All these and similar tensions have continued to characterize the music. As the process of producing music becomes increasingly collective the notion of individual artistic expression has become more problematic. Meanwhile, technological developments involving computers have thrown the entire notions of creativity and performance into some confusion. Nevertheless, the idea of the independent creator–performer persists, especially among 'singer-songwriters' (many of them women – for example, Michelle Shocked). Meanwhile – and, again, with a debt to Britain – the emergence of 'pop' as an antidote to the inflated ideas of rock has continued to provoke discussion about the role and nature of music in popular culture.

With the exception of Jimi Hendrix, few black musicians played any part in rock. The failure of rock'n'roll to offer equal fruits of success to rhythm & blues performers was an important factor in encouraging black businessmen to seek a greater measure of independent control. One of them, Berry Gordy, set up the Motown label in 1960, the first black-owned and run record company to achieve success. In contrast to the direction of much rock, the essence of the Motown style was formed by its songwriter-producers (Holland–Dozier–Holland and Smokey Robinson), blending the more emotional side of rhythm & blues with the immediacy of late 1950s Top Forty popular song. Later in the 1960s, under producers such as Norman Whitfield, the Motown sound grew more 'soulful', in response to developments elsewhere in black music.

Soul itself is no easier to define than rhythm & blues, but the change of name reflects a change of style that began in the late 1950s, with the increasing emotional fervour of performers such as James Brown and Ray Charles, whose singing showed the influence of gospel intensity. The confidence on display in the gospel inflections and heightened involvement was to prove better able to articulate the changing aspirations of black America than music with its roots in the blues. While rock and jazz, in their different ways, were drawing particular attention to instrumental technique, soul continued to explore the singing voice. Later developments in the music of black America – disco, hip-hop – have been inclined to turn their backs on this particular phenomenon. Seekers after continuity point to the ongoing importance of dance – from ragtime to rap.

CONCLUSION

We noted at the outset the importance of understanding music's relationships. We can see now that these are seldom marked by equilibrium – for example, music's reputation for independence has never rested easily alongside the commercial impulse driving much musical activity. Other tensions frequently occur – between the musics of subordinate groups and centres of power, between self and other, autonomy and control. Diversity itself has rarely remained a 'neutral' phenomenon in America's music: as styles have come into contact they have seldom interacted, or even coexisted, as equals.

NOTES

1. Lewis Erenberg, *Steppin' Out: New York Nightlife and the Transformation of American Culture, 1890–1930* (Westport, CT, 1981), p. 74.

2. John Kirkpatrick, 'Charles Ives', in *The New Grove Dictionary of American Music*, ed. H.W. Hitchcock and S. Sadie (London, 1986), II, p. 503.

3. Quoted in Henry Bellamann, 'Charles Ives and his Music', *Musical Quarterly*, XIX (1938): p. 47.

4. Philip Larkin, *All What Jazz: a Record Diary 1961–1971* (London, 1985 edn), p. 272.

5. James Lincoln Collier, *The Making of Jazz* (New York, 1979), p. 57.

6. Gunther Schuller, *Early Jazz* (New York, 1969), p. 136.

7. Ralph Ellison, 'What America Would Be Without Blacks', *Time*, 6 April 1970: pp. 54–5.

8. Neil Leonard, *Jazz and the White Americans* (Chicago, 1962), pp. 35, 39.

9. Aaron Copland, *Music and Imagination* (Cambridge, MA, 1952) p. 99.

10. George Lipsitz, *Class and Culture in Cold War America* (South Hadley, MA, 1982), p. 214.

11. John Cage, 'Experimental Music', in *The American Composer Speaks*, ed. Gilbert Chase (Baton Rouge, 1966), p. 233.

12. Peter Wicke, *Rock Music: Culture, Aesthetics and Sociology* (Cambridge, 1990), p. 11.

13. Richard Middleton, *Studying Popular Music* (Milton Keynes, 1990), p. 18.

SUGGESTIONS FOR FURTHER READING

The New Grove Dictionary of American Music (London, 1986) and *The New Grove Dictionary of Jazz* (1988) provide detailed reference information. For bibliographical support see D.W. Krummel's *Bibliographic Handbook of American Music* (Urbana, IL, 1987) and David Horn's *The Literature of American Music in Books and Folk Song Collections* (Metuchen, NJ, 1977) and its *First Supplement* (with Richard Jackson, 1988). The best general history is Gilbert Chase's *America's Music: from the Pilgrims to the Present* (3rd edn, Urbana, IL, 1987), though Daniel Kingman's *American Music: A Panorama* (New York, 1979) offers a more thorough treatment of popular styles. The music industry is exhaustively chronicled in Russell Sanjek's *American Popular Music and its Business* (New York, 1988). Sanjek's earlier overview *From Print to Plastic* (Brooklyn, 1983) is a useful introduction. Sound recording lacks a modern history to succeed Oliver Read and Walter L. Welch's *From Tinfoil to Stereo* (2nd edn, Indianapolis, 1976) and Ronald Gelatt's *The Fabulous Phonograph* (rev. edn, New York, 1965), though Evan Eisenberg's *The Recording Angel: Explorations in Phonography* (New York, 1987) is an original contribution to the issues.

Two exceptional musicological histories of popular music are Charles Hamm's *Yesterdays: Popular Song in America* (New York, 1979) and Peter Van der Merwe's *Origins of the Popular Style* (Oxford, 1989). *Ethnicity and Popular Music*, by Berndt Ostendorf (Exeter, 1983) is a short but telling essay. The major, all-round history of black music is Eileen Southern's *The Music of Black Americans* (2nd edn, New York, 1983). Documentary accounts of early developments are found in Dena J. Epstein's *Sinful Tunes and Spirituals* (Urbana, IL, 1977), while Leroi Jones's *Blues People: Negro Music in White America* (New York, 1963) and Ben Sidran's *Black Talk* (New York, 1971) provide more speculative insights.

The music of ragtime is well covered by Edward A. Berlin's *Ragtime* (Berkeley, 1980). Paul Oliver's richly illustrated *The Story of the Blues* (London, 1969) and Giles Oakley's *The Devil's Music* (rev. edn, London, 1983) are good histories, complemented by more specific considerations in Oliver's *Blues Fell This Morning* (2nd edn, Cambridge, 1990). His *Songsters and Saints: Vocal Traditions on Race Records* (Cambridge, 1984) explores the breadth of the recorded black music repertoire. For a musicological study see Jeff Todd Titon's *Early Downhome Blues* (Urbana, IL, 1977) and for a classic anthropological account of male performers see Charles Keil's *Urban Blues* (Chicago, 1966). From the huge jazz literature should be singled out James Lincoln Collier's rewarding, if uneven, *The Making of Jazz: A Comprehensive History* (Boston, 1978). *Jazz Styles*, by Mark C. Gridley (rev. edn, Englewood Cliffs, NJ, 1990) is a useful introduction to the postwar period. Gunther Schuller's seminal musicological study, *Early Jazz: its Roots and Musical Development* (New York, 1969) is complemented by his *The Swing Era* (New York, 1990).

Country music history is well served by *Country Music, USA* by Bill C. Malone (rev. edn, Austin, 1985). *The Death of Rhythm and Blues*, by Nelson George (New York, 1988) and Charlie Gillett's *The Sound of the City: The Rise of Rock and Roll* (rev. edn, London, 1983) are essential reading, as are the essays in Greil Marcus's *Mystery Train: Images of America in Rock'n'Roll Music* (3rd edn, London, 1982). *Rock of Ages: the Rolling Stone History of Rock & Roll*, ed. Ed Ward (New York, 1983) is the basic rock history. Less definitive, but often more interesting is David Hatch and Stephen Millward's *From Blues to Rock: an Analytical History of Pop Music* (Manchester, 1987). For soul, *The Soul Book*, ed. Ian Hoare (London, 1975) remains an excellent place to begin.

CHAPTER TWELVE
Performance Arts

Robert Lawson-Peebles

THE PERFORMANCE ARTS AND THE MELTING POT

The sun is setting over Manhattan. The scene is a roof-garden of an immigrant settlement house, from which can be seen the New York skyline and the Statue of Liberty. It symbolizes the reconciliation of the hero and heroine; as they embrace the sunset transfigures the sky into a 'glory of burning flame'. Understandably, the hero is 'prophetically exalted by the spectacle'. He calls Manhattan 'the great Melting-Pot' where ships 'come from the ends of the world to pour in their human freight'. He lists the origins, races and religions of the 'freight', and concludes:

> Here shall they all unite to build the Republic of Man and the Kingdom of God ... what is the glory of Rome and Jerusalem where all races and nations come to worship and look back, compared with the glory of America, where all races and nations come to labour and look forward! ... Peace, peace to all ye unborn millions, fated to fill the giant continent – the God of our *children* give you Peace!

This is the final speech in Israel Zangwill's play *The Melting-Pot*. Reviewing the first Broadway production in 1909, the *New York Times* called it 'sentimental trash masquerading as a human document', yet the play ran for a respectable 136 performances.[1]

The play brought issues about Americanization into sharp focus. The image of the melting-pot, truly apt or not, has been a common one in American culture, particularly at the beginning of the twentieth century, with its massive waves of immigrants (see Chapter 7). Nativists feared the influx, and introduced a quota system. Zangwill felt differently. An English Jew, he had been brought up in the poor conditions of London's East End, and the promise of America came to him like a revelation. *The Melting-Pot* reflects that revelation. It concerns a love-affair between David Quixano, a

Jewish boy orphaned in a Russian pogrom, and a Russian aristocrat. Both families place obstacles in their path, but love conquers all in time for the closing apotheosis, with its optimism in an American future where unity will be forged out of diversity.

The Melting-Pot made a deep impact. It influenced a graduation ritual acted by immigrants studying at the Ford Motor Company's English School. Dressed in their national costumes, they descended ladders into an enormous cauldron, to emerge dressed in everyday American clothes and waving little American flags. *The Melting-Pot* also influenced one of the longest-running plays on Broadway. *Abie's Irish Rose*, by Anne Nichols, was first staged in 1922, ran for 2,327 performances and has often been revived. It concerns a Jewish–American soldier, Abraham Levy, who marries an Irish–American entertainer, Rosemary Murphy, during the First World War. To escape his father's wrath, Abie introduces her as Rosie Murphyski, but his subterfuge is discovered when Rosie's father, Patrick, appears. A comic war ensues, forcing the couple to get married twice more, by a Rabbi and a Catholic priest. It finally ends when Rosie providentially produces twins, naming one Rebecca and the other Patrick Joseph. The germ of this comedy is to be found in the character of Kathleen O'Reilly, the maid in Zangwill's play. She at first dislikes the Quixanos, but eventually identifies with them so closely that she slips between Irish–American English and Yiddish, often within the same sentence: '*Wo geht Ihr*, bedad? . . . Houly Moses, *komm' zurick!*' Will Rebecca and Patrick Joseph Levy become similarly interlinguistic? Unfortunately, we will never know.

A central theme of *The Melting-Pot* is music. Quixano is a composer. His moment of triumph occurs when his *Sinfonia Americana* is performed at the settlement house before the immigrants. Its final movement is a vision of 'the real American . . . the fusion of all races'. The freedom that David enjoys to pursue his art in America is contrasted with the fate of his father, a cantor in a Russian synagogue. During the pogrom his tongue was cut out, and he was murdered. The theme recurs in Samson Raphaelson's 1925 play *The Jazz Singer*, which concerns Jakie Rabinowitz, a cantor's son who leaves home to sing 'jazz songs' rather than succeed his father. He is about to make his debut on Broadway when he learns that his father is dying. Unable to deny his father's final wishes, he quits the show to take up the post occupied by five generations of Rabinowitzes. He rejects the beliefs of Quixano in favour of ethnic separatism. This view, too, was popular. *The Jazz Singer* ran on Broadway for 303 performances and in 1927 was made into the first commercially successful sound film.

Al Jolson was cast as Jakie in the film. Although elements of Jolson's early life resemble Jakie's, he did not reject his stage career. Indeed, his career bears a closer resemblance to that of the fictional Quixano. Born in Russia, Jolson escaped the pogroms to come to America, embracing his adopted home and his audiences with intensity. Americans responded in kind. The critic Gilbert Seldes praised Jolson as a 'galvanic little figure' upon whom rested 'our national health and gaiety'.[2] Jolson appeared in 'blackface' (see Chapter 6) and several of his popular blackface songs had been written by the Irish–American composer Stephen Foster. Foster influenced many songwriters, including George Gershwin, whose song 'Swanee' Jolson made into a big hit, Gershwin's first, in 1920. The song is an early example of the imaginative leaps that Gershwin made, for he was born in Brooklyn, far away spatially, temporally and ethnically from the black South that the song celebrated. Sung by a Jewish immigrant, written by a Jewish–American drawing on songs by an Irish–American who was adapting a black–white tradition, 'Swanee' is one of the most molten songs in American culture.

I have begun with *The Melting-Pot* and its influence for two reasons. First, it can be seen that the performance arts address significant issues in American culture. *The Melting-Pot*, *Abie's Irish Rose*, *The Jazz Singer* and 'Swanee' are unperformed today, but they are nevertheless important cultural artefacts. They help us to understand the relation that must exist between composers, writers, performers and their audiences. Second, these artefacts state my theme in bold outline. The American performance arts attained their vitality and significance by playing variations on a complex dynamic between past and present, old and new, Europe and America, the imported and the vernacular. Their central theme is often family life, for the dynamic achieved its clearest focus there. It cut across the artificial divisions made between highbrow and lowbrow, amateur and professional, commerce and art, 'showbiz' and 'legitimate theatre', Broadway and the rest of America.

THE THEATRE ON BROADWAY AND ELSEWHERE

Broadway has always been distinctive. On the map it looks like the drunk man of Manhattan, weaving diagonally across the rational street grid of the island. By the mid-nineteenth century it had become an important theatre district, but it reached its peak in the 1920s. In 1925 Broadway boasted eighty theatres, and its record season was in 1927–28, when it put on 280 new productions. The Wall Street Crash began a decline which was furthered by competition from film and, later, television. Yet in 1980

Broadway still had forty theatres, most of them now in the side streets. In its heyday it was a sensation, and if any one person was responsible it was George M. Cohan, who made his reputation as a song-and-dance man, comedian, song-writer and playwright. One critic called him 'a vulgar, cheap, blatant, ill-mannered, flashily-dressed, insolent smart Aleck'.[3] To these virtues he added a keen awareness of his audience, for whom he put on slick, punchy productions full of sentiment, patriotism and verve. Cohan's first great success was *Little Johnny Jones* (1904) which, with its two hit songs, 'Yankee Doodle Boy' and 'Give My Regards to Broadway', set the tone of his future work. Broadway became Cohan's favourite subject. He wrote several plays about it, including *Forty-Five Minutes from Broadway* (1906) and *The Man Who Owns Broadway* (1909), creating a standard of self-celebration continued in shows like *Broadway* (1926), *Forty-Second Street* (1933) and *A Chorus Line* (1975).

The complacency and commercialism of Broadway provoked a number of responses. The best-known is Off-Broadway. It is said to have begun in 1915, when the Washington Square Players and the Provincetown Players first staged productions in New York. The first group amateur and the second professional, they had only vague ideas about what they wanted to do. They were clear about what they *didn't* want to do; Broadway was doing that already. In rejecting Broadway they rejected Cohan's Americanism, looking for inspiration instead to European avant-garde dramatists like Chekhov, Ibsen and Shaw. The Provincetown Players are the better known. Several of their members, like the radical journalist John Reed and the playwright Eugene O'Neill, became famous. They first performed at the Cape Cod town from which they took their name, in a building on a wharf. Photographs reveal a structure so rickety that it might shortly become Off-America, but it survived many productions. In their twelve seasons the Provincetown Players performed European plays, a Mozart opera and Gilbert and Sullivan's *Patience*; but their emphasis was on new American plays, by such writers as Djuna Barnes, Theodore Dreiser, Edna Ferber and Wallace Stevens.

Some sense of the Players' work is given by a bill of three one-act plays staged in 1916. Two of them, Louise Bryant's *The Game* and Floyd Dell's *King Arthur's Socks*, are insipid pieces haunted by the ghosts of Chekhov and Ibsen, seeing contemporary American life as dull and pointless. They serve to emphasize the merits of Broadway: nothing happened on Broadway too, but at least it happened quickly. They also highlight the virtues of the third play in the collection. *Bound East for Cardiff* was the first of O'Neill's plays to be staged. This is its opening speech, as acted at the Wharf Theatre on 28 July 1916: 'Maikin' love to me, she was! It's Gawd's truth! A bloomin' nigger! Greased all over with coconut oil, she was.

Gawd blimey, I couldn't stand 'er. Bloody old cow, I says; and with that I fetched 'er a biff on the ear wot knocked 'er silly . . .'. This is a long way from the Broadway of Cohan and Jolson. The melting-pot is transformed into a cauldron of hatred. Spoken by a vicious Cockney appropriately called Cocky, this is just the first of many speeches replete with racism, sexism and profanity. The setting is the forecastle of a tramp steamer, and the action gradually focuses on two characters, Yank and the Irishman Driscoll. Yank has been fatally injured in a fall, and while Driscoll sits with him they recall old times, discovering that both wished to buy a farm. Cocky re-enters to find Driscoll praying over the corpse. The closing speech of the play echoes the opening one but, spoken by Cocky in a hushed whisper, indicates the distance that even he has travelled in this short, static drama. It is just two words: 'Gawd blimey'.[4]

The Provincetown Players staged sixteen more of O'Neill's plays. They were both exhilarated and stretched by his constant experiments, pushing dramatic form to its limits. Two examples will suffice. *Strange Interlude* (1928) has nine acts and, in its first production, lasted from 5.30 to 11 p.m., with an hour's break for dinner. Its length is due to the complex interrelation of thought and action, requiring the audience to distinguish two levels, one an intelligible account of social and sexual relationships, the other a series of interior monologues which modify and sometimes undermine the overt action. *Mourning Becomes Electra* (1931) has a simpler structure but also makes great demands. A trilogy of thirteen acts, it lasts almost an hour longer than *Strange Interlude*, provoking one critic into heading his review 'Evening becomes intolerable'.[5]

O'Neill's experiments would indeed be intolerable were they not closely related to his theme. I use the singular deliberately, for with one exception O'Neill's plays may be regarded as variations on a plot that is succinctly stated in *More Stately Mansions* (posth., 1967): 'human life is a silly disappointment, a liar's promise . . . a daily appointment in which we wait day after day, hoping against hope, listening to each footstep, and when finally the bride or bridegroom cometh, we discover we are kissing Death'.[6] Again, the influence of the modern European dramatists is evident, but O'Neill's technical virtuosity prompts him to move from under their shadow. *Bound East for Cardiff* is a case in point. The use of Cockney vernacular is an innovation on the serious American stage, presenting a character that is distinctive yet just as boorish as the others, setting in context the fleeting pastoral dreams of Yank and Driscoll. Anything other than barbarity is a liar's promise, a veneer which, when stripped away, reveals the frightened savage beneath. In just one respect is *Bound East for Cardiff* at odds with all but one of O'Neill's plays. Its conclusion, that friendship is finally achieved in death, is unusually cheerful. Most of O'Neill's work is more in tune with Cocky's raucous, opening 'gawd blimey' than with his reverential, closing 'gawd blimey'. The profanity, moreover, is aptly chosen, for in O'Neill's view God blinds indiscriminately, with hatred. Family life, in particular, is hell, even when the family is all-male and afloat, for like Melville's seafarers in *Moby-Dick*, O'Neill's present a metaphor of the family.

O'Neill trades in the most basic emotions, filtered through a reading of some of the most sophisticated European thinkers: Nietzsche, Schopenhauer, Freud and Jung. He is also deeply indebted to classical tragedy. Yet, in what are arguably his two finest plays, he achieves an integration of European sources with American material. This occurs more obviously in *Mourning Becomes Electra*. The play is a reworking of the *Oresteia*, with the American Civil War replacing the Trojan War. The setting is New England. A fratricidal war and an environment of Puritan repression provide appropriate contexts for the events in the Mannon family. Visions of happiness appear briefly, to be lost in a maelstrom of devouring passions, causing two murders and two suicides before Lavinia (Electra), alone, shuts the door on the rest of her life and brings the play to an end. In *Long Day's Journey Into Night* (hereafter *Journey*) the focus is closer to home. O'Neill's own family is examined, in a lightly fictionalized form. The father is modelled on O'Neill's father, James, who became a matinee idol playing in *The Count of Monte Cristo* more than six thousand times. The play's touching and much-quoted dedication, to O'Neill's wife Carlotta, is misleading. These people have failed in love, and for each of them the failure has its counterpart in another frailty. The father is a miser; his wife is a junkie; the elder son is a drunkard and wastrel; the younger is a tubercular dreamer. As the play moves into night the three men tear each other to shreds while the mother, in her lonely pursuit of happiness, is transformed by her addiction into a living ghost. *Mourning Becomes Electra* and *Journey* can be regarded as complementary. Together, they provide a comment on national and theatrical history through the prism of American family life, and in doing so they establish O'Neill's claim to be the foremost tragedian of the twentieth century.

At first sight, *Journey* seems to emphasize the antipathy between Broadway and Off-Broadway. The reality is more complex. *Ah, Wilderness!*, the exception noted above, is O'Neill's only comedy. It is an exercise in small-town nostalgia and a homage to rather than a criticism of the American family. In its first, 1933, production, it starred Mr Broadway, George M. Cohan. O'Neill was no stranger to Broadway. From 1920 onwards, his plays often appeared there. Occasionally they were transformed by it. *Anna Christie* (1921), about a sick prostitute, was made into a musical called *New Girl in Town* (1957). Yet Broadway was also flexible and tough enough to be able to take O'Neill unadulterated. *Strange Interlude*, though banned in Boston, did well on Broadway, running for 428 performances and winning O'Neill his third Pulitzer Prize in eight years. It is fitting, therefore, that *Journey* should receive its American premiere on Broadway in 1956. It ran for 390 performances.

Nevertheless, Off-Broadway theatre companies had an uneasy relationship with Broadway. They rejected its frank commercialism yet needed to attract an audience to maintain financial viability. They also found that Broadway and Hollywood enticed some of their most talented members. The history of modern American theatre is therefore characterized by the rise and fall of Off-Broadway companies. The Theatre Guild rose out of the ashes of the Washington Square Players. It put on many enterprising productions, including several O'Neill plays, Dorothy and DuBose Heyward's all-black *Porgy* (1927) and the Gershwin brothers' adaptation, *Porgy and Bess* (1935). The Guild's attitude to Broadway is summed up by its treatment of that quintessential Broadway product, the musical. In 1925 it put on a revue, *The Garrick Gaieties*, merely to raise money. It did so well that new editions were produced in 1926 and 1930. Yet they received only one mention in the book celebrating the tenth anniversary of the Guild, when their director honestly recalled them as 'a forbidden liqueur'.[7] In the early 1940s the Guild was again saved from extinction by a musical, *Oklahoma!*. Much of the Guild's innovative edge had already been blunted by a series of disagreements which prompted two breakaway companies, the Group Theatre and the Playwrights' Company. The Group Theatre was founded in 1931 and disbanded in 1940. The dates are significant, for the company was the creation of the Great Depression, and its most notable productions, like Clifford Odets's *Waiting for Lefty* (1935), reflected that decade's social concerns. The Playwrights' Company lasted longer, from 1938 to 1960, mounting productions like the musical *Knickerbocker Holiday* (1938), Tennessee Williams's *Cat On A Hot Tin Roof* (1955), and Gore Vidal's political drama, *The Best Man* (1960).

After the Second World War many other groups sprung up Off-Broadway. Their variety is best illustrated by Joseph Papp's New York Shakespeare Festival and the Living Theatre, founded by Judith Malina and Julian Beck. The New York Shakespeare Festival celebrates the Bard, free, in Central Park, but has done much more, including *A Chorus Line*, which opened in 1975 and by 1983 had become the longest-running musical. Some of the Shakespeare Festival productions ended up behind the proscenium arches of Broadway. In contrast, those of the Living Theatre threatened to gyrate off stage entirely, and eventually led to their demise. Their attempts to erode the conventional distance between performer and viewer made them descendants of Jolson but involved methods which he never tried. On several occasions they physically attacked their audience. Consequently they underwent a series of critical, legal and financial battles which finally made them close their theatre and go on tour perpetually.

The tensions between Broadway and Off-Broadway provided a creative environment for the three most prominent playwrights to emerge since the Second World War: Tennessee Williams, Arthur Miller and Edward Albee. The work of all three has appeared on both arenas; all have written about the American family; and all tread in the footsteps of O'Neill. Of the three, Albee most clearly follows O'Neill, partly perhaps because he too came from a theatrical family, but more importantly because he experimented with one-act plays before writing a large-scale drama about the family. *The American Dream*, first staged Off-Broadway in 1961, is a case-study in cartoon malevolence. Mommy – we never know her name – has a bad shopping disorder, henpecks her husband, dismembers her adopted child, makes advances to his long-lost twin brother, and packs Grandma off to an asylum. *Who's Afraid of Virginia Woolf?*, first staged on Broadway in 1962, spreads the evil more widely. The play bears a close resemblance to O'Neill's posthumously-staged masterpiece, to the extent that some have retitled it *Long Night's Journey Into Day*, which it certainly is. Both plays are lengthy chamber works involving four major parts. Both observe the classical unities of time and place within the tradition of conventional living-room drama. Both employ their settings ironically, for they are hardly homages to family piety. George and Martha, named after the nation's first First Family, are the heavyweights in this extended bout of tag-wrestling. Nick and Honey have not yet achieved full combat readiness, but a parallel between the two couples suggests they may. Honey has had a phantom pregnancy, while George and Martha have created and now kill a palliative fiction, the son they never had.

Williams has a view of the past that is similar to O'Neill's. His first successful play, *The Glass Menagerie*, which opened in Chicago in 1944, is another chamber work for four players, identified in the cast list merely as the Mother, her Son, her Daughter, and the Gentleman Caller. There is an absent but important fifth character, their father, whose 'larger-than-life-size photograph' hangs over the mantle. His wife dreams about the marriages she might have had with seventeen Gentleman Callers she supposedly received one Sunday afternoon. Now she arranges a Gentleman Caller for her daughter Laura. The meeting is not a success. Laura's own dreams are shattered and her favourite glass figure, a unicorn, is broken. Tom leaves home in his 'father's footsteps', but he cannot escape the memory of Laura. The plot is slight, but has great power and poignancy, held in place by the firm structure. The meeting with the Gentleman Caller dooms daughter to follow mother, and son father. They are trapped in the past, their hopes as transient and insubstantial as the light shining through the glass animals that act as symbols for their frozen lives.[8]

The Gentleman Caller is an insensitive oaf, but he is delicacy itself compared with Stanley Kowalski in *A Streetcar Named Desire*, first staged on Broadway in 1947. From that moment in the first scene when Stanley heaves a package of bloody meat to his wife Stella, we know we are in for strong stuff. Indeed, one critic travestied the play by calling it the 'story of a girl of good family reduced by rape to destitution, degradation, insult and madness in New Orleans'. On the other hand, the novelist Mary McCarthy dismissed the play as a dispute over bathroom rights. The truth is that it confirms and transcends these apparently opposing criticisms which, together, have the virtue of revealing the structural link between *A Streetcar Named Desire* and *The Glass Menagerie*. Both show the traumas consequent upon minor setbacks. Certainly, Stanley is (in McCarthy's unforgettable words) 'the man who wants to pee, the realist of the bladder'. He is also a man who knows the moral value of good sex. It follows from this that Stella produces a child and the enlarged family is finally reunited. It follows, too, that Blanche must be destroyed, for Blanche is bad sex; the hints at her unsavoury past have to be masked by scent and shaded lights. The destruction is brutal, for Stanley is a brute; but he can recognize the enemy when it arrives under the pretext of a sisterly visit. In her own way, Blanche is just as destructive. Her husband committed suicide, and she is variously described as 'a moth' (in a stage direction) and a 'tarantula' (by herself, in a moment of drunken honesty). The strength of the play is that it displays a struggle between principles of life and death within the dimensions of a domestic dispute.[9]

The work of Miller is less tortured than that of Williams. He too is interested in family life, but sets it more firmly in a national context. His most famous play, *Death of a Salesman*, which opened on Broadway in 1949, owes something to the innovations of O'Neill. The set is occupied by a house whose furnishings are sparse but solid enough. The house, however, has transparent walls. They are almost overwhelmed by the expressionist backdrop of 'towering, angular shapes' bathed in 'an angry glow of orange'. They also allow an easy transition between past and present. The salesman, Willy Loman, is haunted by the voices of the past. Now, in some professions, history certainly and perhaps banking, this is an advantage. Not in selling. A salesman is a transient figure, 'a man way out there in the blue, riding on a smile and a shoeshine'. Now there's little blue left; but rather the angry orange of the backdrop. So Willy dreams his way from day to day, reciting the list of Great Salesmen I Have Known, complaining to his wife Linda about his 'goddam arch supports', and causing traffic problems in Yonkers.

Do we need to know all this? Do we have to agree with Linda when she asserts that 'attention must finally be paid to such a person'? I think we do. In the first place, there is a close link between Willy's dreams and the popularized American Dream. Willy's failure to realize the myth of rags-to-riches turns the play into an American Tragedy, and one that is made all the more poignant by the meretriciousness of the gadgets which he both praises and denigrates. A similarity with *The Great Gatsby* is clear and, like Fitzgerald's novel, the play is extremely popular with American audiences, for it touches an American nerve. Secondly, it touches a more general nerve. Although less tightly structured than *The Glass Menagerie*, the play shares its concern with the consequences of the sins of the father. The names in *Death of a Salesman* are significant. Willy is a low man though not an unusual man, and he affects his two sons differently. Biff, the potential all-American sportsman, is knocked out by discovering Willy's unfaithfulness. The other son, Happy, is happy to continue Willy's predilections. He is a make-out king with, he admits, 'an overdeveloped sense of competition'. The link between commercial and sexual behaviour is confirmed, and it is a poor omen for the future that, in the play's penultimate speech, Happy repeats Willy's platitudes.[10]

The Price (1968) is possibly Miller's other most accomplished work. It is, again, a chamber work with a cast of four and a single set. This time it is not a sitting-room, but an attic cluttered with the detritus of a family life that is long past. Gregory Solomon, the eighty-nine-year-old dealer who comes to buy the furniture, makes the point vividly: 'A man sits down to such a table he knows not only he's married, he's got to stay married . . . the main thing today is – shopping . . . . With this kind of furniture the shopping is over . . . .' Times and furniture change, and morals change with them. But the rich and heavy furniture of Miller's precise stage direction remains as mute testimony to the inability to escape the past. The play aches with the tensions between the major characters, two brothers who carry the burden of old animosities. This time the burden is created not by a myth but by a specific historical moment, the Great Depression. It negated the American Dream – and also the message of *The Melting-Pot*. Zangwill's play celebrated those who came 'to labour and look forward', integrating the races in the great American family. *The Price*, like the other plays discussed here, shows a family in crisis looking back at past sins.[11]

The three playwrights all benefited from the love–hate relation of Broadway and Off-Broadway. Other kinds of theatre tried to avoid Broadway altogether. One, appropriately enough, is called Off-Off-Broadway. It shared the anti-establishment ethos of the Living Theatre, but not its (semi-)permanent premises. Off-Off-Broadway theatre companies performed wherever they could find a space: in theatres, certainly, but also in cafes, lofts, churches, garages, parks and in the street. Their work encompasses an enormous range, from updated, politically-orientated versions of Shakespeare to communal improvisation to dramas by and about minority groups. Off-Off-Broadway is prolific, inventive and transient. If anything unites its multifarious groups it is, in Papp's words, 'a commitment to theatre as an art form and to theatre as a vehicle for responding to that which is contemporary'.[12]

Similar views had inspired the Federal Theatre Project more than forty-five years earlier. It represented the first attempt by the Federal Government to fund the arts. In the three years (1936–39) of its existence the Project founded many semi-autonomous groups which together produced more than one thousand plays. They ranged from a black version of Gilbert and Sullivan, *The Swing Mikado*, to the simultaneous opening, in twenty-one cities across seventeen states, of a dramatization of Sinclair Lewis's attack on Fascism, *It Can't Happen Here*. The Federal Theatre Project sponsored much lively and innovative theatre, including documentary 'living newspapers' based on significant current events, but because the nation had no tradition of public support for the arts it was highly controversial. It was eventually closed down, but the first step in public support had been taken. It would be followed by the National Endowment for the Arts, founded by Congress in 1965, and the Theatre Development Fund, which from 1967 onwards has made reduced-price tickets for selected plays, on Broadway and off, available to the public. The TKTS booth on Times Square is familiar to many visitors to Manhattan, and the service has spread to other major cities.

A third kind of theatre consists of the art and non-profit theatres that exist, in Cohan's words, more than forty-five minutes from Broadway. They include the Hedgerow Theatre near Philadelphia, founded by Jasper Deeter, who left the Provincetown Players when they became too commercial for him; and the Actors' Workshop, which lasted from 1952 to 1966 in San Francisco. Such theatres are too many and various to sum up with ease; one will have to stand as their representative. The Pasadena Playhouse is in Southern California, ten miles north-east of Los Angeles. It was built in 1925, and in its sometimes uncertain history has put on a wide range of productions, from Shakespeare to Lorca; has run its own acting school and workshop; and produced a series of nineteen summer festivals devoted, among other things, to Shaw, California Playwrights and Cohan. Actors who came up through its ranks included Jean Arthur, Raymond Burr, Lee J. Cobb, William Holden and Elaine May. It mounted the first production of *Lazarus Laughed* (1926), another of O'Neill's challenges to dramatic form, in this instance with casting. The play has more than 420 roles. Inevitably, it is rarely performed. The Pasadena Playhouse managed its run of twenty-eight performances by using 159 actors doubling roles.

All the non-Broadway kinds of theatre described here found it difficult to dissociate themselves entirely from the commercial arena. Techniques first tried in avant-garde theatres became more widely used. The plot as well as the form of *A Chorus Line* came from a series of group improvisations that were pioneered by Joseph Chaikin's Off-Off-Broadway Open Theatre. Productions, too, moved to Broadway. The New York Shakespeare Festival contributed the 'tribal love-rock musical' *Hair* (1967) as well as *A Chorus Line*. In the years 1968–69, Washington's Arena Stage provided Arthur Kopit's *Indians* and *The Great White Hope*, Howard Sackler's play about the black boxer Jack Johnson. Seattle Rep contributed Richard Greenberg's *Eastern Standard* (1988). The traffic, moreover, has not been one-way. Provincial theatres have hired a 'star' to enhance a production's draw, and many companies have financed experimental plays by staging a Broadway hit. The result is a varied and vibrant arena for American drama, which now ranges from Neil Simon's white middle-class comedies to Adrienne Kennedy's examinations of black feminist conscious-ness. Playwrights who have become prominent include James Baldwin, Lorraine Hansberry, David Mamet, Murray Schisgall, Sam Shepard and Megan Terry. Not everyone reaches Broadway. Many do not seek it. But the existence of Broadway means that they have a better chance of being seen somewhere. In 1939 the critic Joseph Wood Krutch remarked that 'the history of the American drama during the past twenty years is almost as much a part of the history of regular commercial productions as it is the history of any art theater'.[13] The same is true of the subsequent fifty years.

DANCE

Of the three performance arts discussed here, dance perhaps comes closest to the melting-pot image. Contemporary dance companies are often voraciously eclectic. The American Dance Machine, for instance, includes in its repertoire excerpts from Agnes de Mille's *Carousel*, Michael Kidd's *Can-Can*, and tap dancing from *Bubbling Brown Sugar*. Japanese Butoh and German Tanzteater influenced modern American dance in the 1980s; and, in return, American choreographers such as Glen Tetley, Merce Cunningham and Twyla Tharp have produced work for European dance companies. The eclecticism of dance may be due to the circumstances of its evolution. It has always been controversial in America, even denounced as sacrilegious by generations of Christian writers, from Increase Mather in *An Arrow Against Profane and Promiscuous Dancing* (1685) to Don Humphreys in *What Makes Dancing Wrong* (1963). That made dancing all the more fascinating, as Mark Twain revealed when he first saw the Parisian Can-Can: 'I placed my hands before my face for very shame. But I looked through my fingers.' Havelock Ellis, a leading psychologist, celebrated dance as the most 'primary and essential' of the arts, and perhaps its central attraction is that it is inherently dangerous.[14] It treads a fine line between grace and wildness, order and chaos, civility and barbarity. I shall discuss it as a series of counterpoints between these opposing qualities.

At the beginning of this century, two forms of professional dancing were to be seen in America: the tutus and toe shoes of the European-influenced ballet companies, and the bump and grind of the vaudeville houses. This mould was broken by three young dancers who, significantly, first became famous in Europe: Maude Allan, Loie Fuller and Isadora Duncan. Duncan is the most famous. Indeed, she is notorious. Two years after her death, William Bolitho remarked that 'she, above all women of our time, in scale, in courage, in the spirit, made the purest attempt at the life of adventure'.[15] She regarded dancing as a romantic expression of the soul. She took some ballet lessons, but the style she evolved was the antithesis of ballet, relying on inner propulsion and stamina rather than discipline and conventionalized steps. Often barefoot, dressed only in a simple, light, flowing robe, her dancing alternated dramatic poses with scampering circuits of the bare stage. In some respects her work has dated badly. It seems overblown, and the nickname given to her six eldest followers, 'the Isadorables', suggests that her art was interlaced with wide streaks of ham. The purple prose of those who saw her indicate that it was sustaining ham. She seemed like a force of nature, a gust of New World air in a claustrophobic Old World art form, a stamping return of the dionysiac after years of appollonian restraint.

If Duncan was a force of nature, popular dances in the early years of the century tried to return to nature by imitating animals. Examples are the Turkey Trot, the Bunny Hug and the Grizzly Bear. Fortunately, perhaps, humans can go only so far in copying animals. This may well account in part for the popularity of Walt Disney cartoons. From *Oswald the Lucky Rabbit* (1928) to *Bambi* (1943) mice, monkeys, pigs and ducks leaped, spun and hoofed their way across the nation's screens. It is now generally agreed that *Fantasia* (1940) marks the high-point of Disney's career. It was produced with the assistance of a number of leading dancers and choreographers, but thanks to animation it achieved results beyond their wildest dreams. 'The Dance of the Hours', performed by a corps of swaying hippopotami and lecherous alligators, is probably the closest that human imagination will get to Terpsichore, the muse of the dance. When the prima hipporina makes a *grand jeté* of several hundred feet, to land precisely in the flexible but (as it turns out) formidable arms of her lantern-jawed consort, we know that we are witnessing the ultimate union of danger and delight.

Outside the confines of the Disney Studio, the most dangerous and delightful dance form is probably tap. Originally a black vernacular dance, tap was developed by Bert Williams and Bill (Bojangles) Robinson, among others, on Broadway; and by a wide range of dancers in Hollywood film, including Shirley Temple (Bojangles's pupil), Ruby Keeler and Eleanor Powell. The contexts of tap ranged from amateur street-corner contests to the massed, machine-like choruses of Busby Berkeley's 1930s musical films. The most dangerous tap dancers were almost certainly the Nicholas Brothers, Harold and Fayard. Their routines combined acrobatics with tap, including flying full splits over each other down a flight of stairs and, in the stage version of *Babes in Arms* (1937, choreographed by Balanchine), sliding splits through the legs of eight girls. Fortunately, some of their best work can be seen on film: the all-black *Stormy Weather* (1943) and *Orchestra Wives* (1942), in which Harold defies gravity and threatens his masculinity by running up a pillar and going into a backward flip to land in a full split on the floor.

The turn that dance had taken towards sensuality and violence produced books like *Thirty-Four Reasons Why Christians Should Not Dance* (1928), and attempts to reassert its potential for decorum and order. In 1928 Henry Ford published a manual giving steps for the Quadrille, the Lancers and the Waltz, which he believed were best fitted for 'the American temperament', insisting above all that 'modesty' was essential. Another manual, *Modern Dancing*, published in 1914 by the ballroom dancers Vernon and Irene Castle, promoted such dances as the One-Step and Maxixe, but also disapproved of close bodily contact, contrasting what it called 'real dancing' with 'gymnastic contortions' and 'hoydenish romping'. It particularly recommended the Tango, which it described – quite inaccurately – as 'an evolution of the eighteenth-century minuet'.[16]

We all know that Ford and the Castles were fighting a lost cause. Yet if one person delayed the victory of Dionysus it was Fred Astaire. He did it by unifying tap with ballroom dancing, thereby transforming tap from a percussive acrobatics to a nimble form of levitation. Astaire came as close as possible to denying the heft, and thus the mortality, of the body. He is best remembered in the garb celebrated by the song 'Top Hat, White Tie, and Tails', written for him by Irving Berlin (see Chapter 11). The series of nine films he made with Ginger Rogers for RKO from 1933 to 1940 show the Astaire style at its most elegant. The complex rococo figures they spun around each other, and the cool grace of their bodily contact, established dance as extended and lightly erotic foreplay, substituting romance for sex. It is entirely appropriate that the final film of their RKO series should be

The Story of Vernon and Irene Castle (1940). Ironically, as Astaire grew older his style grew more butch. This was in part due to an understandable broadening of style, which included slapstick comedy in *Easter Parade* (1948). It was also due to his choice of partners, from the animal exuberance of Rita Hayworth (particularly in *You Were Never Lovelier*, 1942) to the explosive Betty Hutton (*Let's Dance*, 1950) to the threateningly long-legged Cyd Charisse (particularly in *The Band Wagon*, 1953). It may have been due, as well, to the growing popularity of Gene Kelly. Kelly never masked his mortality; hence the always-visible scar on his cheek. Neither did he defuse his masculinity. Kelly's style was rooted in acrobatics rather than ballroom dancing. It was earthy, although certainly not earth-bound. It was more eclectic and pretentious than Astaire's. Kelly was at his best in everyday roles (a sailor in *On the Town*, 1949) or in comedy (*Singin' in the Rain*, 1952). His ballets in *An American in Paris* (1951) and *Invitation to the Dance* (1956) are notable mainly for their brilliant technical effects. Yet in general his work was an appropriate antidote to the ethereal dancing of Astaire. It is fitting that Kelly should have danced with a cartoon mouse (in *Anchors Aweigh*, 1945), and that one of his films (*The Pirate*, 1948) should have included the Nicholas Brothers.

The most famous modern dance company was founded by Martha Graham. Her religious belief in the primacy of dance led her to create a form which treated the body as a breathing, highly disciplined force of nature rather than just a beautiful object. It is, above all, this organicism, which parallels certain American developments in poetry (see Chapter 15), that is her legacy. For all their varied styles, Merce Cunningham, Paul Taylor (both Graham pupils), Alvin Ailey and Twyla Tharp were deeply influenced by her. The Russian choreographer Michel Fokine called Graham's work 'ugly'. Strip the word of its pejorative connotations, and there is a germ of truth in this. The dancing of Graham and her company contained harsh, striking attitudes and austere, angular lines, emphasized by crisp shadows and by extensive use of the floor. While Astaire seemed to deny the earth's surface, Graham insisted on relating closely to it. She also insisted on relating closely to the concerns of its human inhabitants. Her most famous dance, *Appalachian Spring* (1944), celebrates the pioneer woman. The set is stark: no more than a frame suggesting the house in which the Husbandman and his Bride will live and raise their family. The sexuality of the couple is counterpointed against the steadying influences of an older woman and a revivalist (danced in the first performances by Cunningham), and against the innocence of four younger women. Celebrating one American myth, *Appalachian Spring* realized another. The set was by Isamu Noguchi, a Japanese American. Graham herself was by upbringing a Californian; her family could be traced on one side to the

Pilgrim Fathers, and on the other to Irish immigrants. The music was by Aaron Copland, another Brooklyn Jewish composer (see Chapter 11), and the closing melody of the score is a Shaker hymn, 'Simple Gifts'. *Appalachian Spring* is another exemplar of the melting-pot, and it is appropriate that it should celebrate the family.

Three choreographers have taken Graham's American enterprise further, and in doing so have moved between ballet and Broadway. The work of Agnes de Mille invites the closest comparison with Graham. Like Graham she believes in the primacy of dance. She too commissioned music from Copland for a cowboy ballet, *Rodeo* (1942). Together with *Billy the Kid* (commissioned in 1938 by the choreographer Eugene Loring) and *Appalachian Spring*, *Rodeo* makes up Copland's so-called 'trio' of Wild West Ballets. The term is somewhat inaccurate. *Appalachian Spring* may be about a frontier, but it is hardly wild. *Rodeo* certainly is, and this accounts for much of its popularity. Perhaps de Mille was aware of 'The Cowboy's Dance Song' by James Barton Adams, quoted by the critic and promoter Lincoln Kirstein when in 1938 he attacked Russian ballet:

> You can't expect a cowboy to agitate his shanks
> In etiquettish manner in aristocratic ranks
> When he's always been accustomed to shake the heel and toe
> At rattling rancher dances where much etiquet don't go.[17]

Certainly, the shanks of de Mille's dancers are agitated with a minimum of etiquette. She depicts such everyday ranching activities as bronco-busting, and the gossiping and flirting common to young people everywhere – although the context, a square-dance, is western enough. The plot now seems quaint: it concerns a cowgirl who vainly competes with the cowboys, but gets her man once she changes into a dress. But the informality of the choreography and the simple spontaneity of the dancers forges a unity of theme and form. *Fall River Legend* (1948), with music by Morton Gould, is another de Mille investigation of American folklore. It deals with a famous nineteenth-century murder:

> Lizzie Borden took an axe
> And gave her mother forty whacks
> When she saw what she had done
> She gave her father forty-one.

The prim New England setting and grim home life of young Lizzie serve both to explain the murders and place them firmly in an American setting. The ballet's strong narrative line links it with the work of O'Neill and his successors, while its blend of dance forms links it with *Rodeo* and *Oklahoma!* (to be discussed shortly).

George Balanchine worked with Diaghilev before emigrating to the United States to form, with the support of Kirstein, the School of

American Ballet in 1935 and the New York City Ballet in 1948. Balanchine's work falls fairly cleanly into two parts: traditional and contemporary ballets, and a wide range of Broadway shows. He even produced an elephant ballet for the Ringling Brothers' circus. It would be difficult to escape the impression of a journeyman choreographer, were it not for two major achievements. One was to create an American dance company to equal the Russians. The other was to choreograph a ballet, *Slaughter on Tenth Avenue*, as an integral part of a Broadway show, *On Your Toes* (1936). While it hasn't aged well, it did open the way for the more adventurous work of Jerome Robbins.

Robbins was the first important choreographer to emerge from the American Ballet Theatre, founded in 1940. The title of the company is important: Ballet Theatre never lost sight of drama. It prompted Robbins to make an easy transition between ballet and Broadway. Indeed, at its best, the division between the two disappeared in Robbins's work, which for some twenty years (1944–64) appeared in both arenas. On Broadway he recalled aspects of American history, with an affectionate look back at the 1920s (*Billion Dollar Baby*, 1946), biographies of the stripper Gypsy Rose Lee (*Gypsy*, 1959) and the comedienne Fanny Brice (*Funny Girl*, 1964), and, in his last musical, the story of a Russian shtetl on the eve of emigration to America (*Fiddler on the Roof*, 1964). The compilation he made of his Broadway work (*Jerome Robbins' Broadway*, 1989) shows how much was lost by the decision to work exclusively for the New York City Ballet from 1965 to 1988, sometimes in collaboration with Balanchine. For it is clear that his work in one arena fertilized the work in the other. In part it was thematic, with one musical on ballet (*Look, Ma, I'm Dancin'*, 1948) and one ballet on Jazz (*N.Y. Export: Opus Jazz*, 1958). More importantly, it was technical. In a series of collaborations with the composer Leonard Bernstein, Robbins developed a choreography that reflected the cares and joys of ordinary people. *Facsimile* (1946) dealt with the problem of loneliness, while *The Age of Anxiety* (1951) examined the despair of modern urban life. The line between ballet and musical was eroded when Robbins' first ballet, *Fancy Free* (1944), about three sailors on shore leave, was developed into *On the Town* (1945). It disappeared completely in *West Side Story* (1957), to be discussed in the next section.

THE MUSICAL

It is sometimes claimed that the musical is the one original American contribution to western culture. The claim is overstated in two respects: it devalues Jazz, and it ignores the precedent European forms, particularly operetta, from which the musical developed. Operetta moved to America with three *émigrés*: the Dubliner Victor Herbert, the Bohemian Rudolf Friml and the Hungarian Sigmund Romberg. Although written and performed in America, their operettas could have taken place anywhere. Even Friml's *Rose Marie*, claimed as the first operetta with a believable North American setting, exists in never-never land. With its chorus of redcoated Mounties in the Canadian Rockies it was scarcely a relevant experience for the Broadway audience of 1924. Not that never-never land isn't vitally important to the American musical; it is a significant element of the melting-pot mythology which is central to the most interesting musicals. Other elements are the use of the vernacular, the theme of intermarriage and a sense of contemporary relevance. With its love-affair between a white fur-trapper and a part-Indian woman whose English is charmingly colloquial, *Rose Marie* certainly scores on the first two counts, but not on the third.

Contemporary relevance was supplied by the other contributory genre to the American musical, the musical comedy or revue. Revues were not strong on plot. They were a hotch-potch of songs, leg shows, and a great comedian like Bert Lahr (the cowardly lion in *The Wizard of Oz*). The titles of some revues indicate their reason for existence: *The Ziegfeld Follies of 1907*, *George White's Scandals of 1928*, *Blackbirds of 1939*. They were as fresh as paint, and when the paint flaked they died – with the exception of their songs. The years of the revues were also the years of songwriters such as Irving Berlin, Jerome Kern, Cole Porter, George Gershwin and Richard Rodgers, and lyricists like Lorenz Hart, Oscar Hammerstein II and Ira Gershwin (George's brother). They produced a body of song to rival the best works of Schubert and Wolf. It is said that in the 1930s, particularly with such musicals as the Gershwins' *Of Thee I Sing* (1931) and the English version of the Brecht–Weill *Threepenny Opera* (1933), the form became socially conscious. For instance, *Pins and Needles* (1937), was sponsored by the International Ladies' Garment Workers' Union and included such songs as 'It's Better with a Union Man' and 'Sing Me a Song with Social Significance'. This argument should not be taken too far. Songs in the revues always had elements of social significance in them. Their social awareness and use of vernacular transformed operetta into the American musical. I shall plot its growth by discussing four examples: *Show Boat* (1927), *Porgy and Bess* (1935), *Oklahoma!* (1943), and *West Side Story* (1957).

The action of *Show Boat* ignores Broadway in favour of middle America, sweeping from Twain's Mississippi to Chicago at an important period of modernization, and back to the New South. In adapting Edna Ferber's novel, Hammerstein emphasized three themes germane to the 1920s:

279

unstable marriages, mixed marriages and race relations. The uneasy yet ultimately happy marriage of Magnolia, the daughter of the showboat's owner, Captain Andy Hawks, to a genteel Southern rake, Gaylord Ravenal, is counterpointed against the marriage of Julie La Verne, the showboat's leading actress to its leading man. Julie and her husband are forced to flee the South when it is discovered that Julie has mixed blood. Miscegenation is condoned in the North, but she is deserted there by her husband. In this case there is no happy ending. Julie, now an alcoholic, is last seen leaving a Chicago theatre without a job. The contrasted marriages are reflected in Kern's contrasted songs. 'You Are Love' is deliberately old-fashioned. It would fit in an operetta and celebrates the love affair and reunion of Magnolia and Gaylord. Two songs are associated with Julie. 'Bill' deals with the realities of love with a flawed, ordinary man; while 'Can't Help Lovin' Dat Man' uses a version of black vernacular to suggest her racial background. Together, the songs provide an answer to the romantic 'You Are Love', and to Cap'n Andy's repeated assertion that showboat people are 'jest one big happy family'. Families do not always survive the tests of economics and race, everyday realities underlined by the musical's most famous song, 'Ol' Man River':

> Niggers all work on de Mississippi,
> Niggers all work while de white folks play,
> Pullin' dem boats from de dawn to sunset,
> Gittin' no rest till de Judgement Day.

Magnificently sung by Paul Robeson in the 1936 film version, the song, despite its ironic accommodation to racist vocabulary, exposes the speciousness of Gaylord's Southern pretensions and reveals the appropriately unstable foundations on which the showboat rests.[18]

The temporal and spatial dimensions of *Show Boat* are large. Those of *Porgy and Bess* (hereafter *Porgy*) are confined to a few days in the gaunt tenements of Catfish Row, Charleston, with one fateful excursion to Kittiwake Island, off the South Carolina coast. The consequence is a greater power and concentration than *Show Boat*. Yet the two musicals have the use of black vernacular and the theme of racial oppression in common. The latter is emphasized in *Porgy* by its setting within the black community. The arrival of whites is always an intrusion and usually means trouble. Not that Catfish Row is trouble-free. Although there are suggestions that this could be an Eden, emotional relationships are marked by instability, for which gambling is the metaphor. The Edenic theme of the opening lullaby, 'Summertime', is therefore promptly superseded by a crap game. It causes a fight in which the brutal Crown kills Robbins. The murder prompts Serena, Robbins's wife, to express her loss in the most movingly everyday terms:

My man's gone now,
Ain't no use alistenin'
For his tired foot-steps,
Climbin' up de stairs.

It also forces Crown to flee to Kittiwake Island, deserting his girlfriend Bess.

The other rivals for Bess's affections represent two further themes: religion and economics. To an extent, Porgy is a Christ-figure, in but not of the world, a crippled beggar separated from others by his disability and by his rejection of the economic process with the song 'I got plenty o' nuthin' '. His opponent, the drug dealer Sportin' Life, represents the underside of American capitalism, and he preaches a pastiche sermon using some of Ira Gershwin's most inspired vernacular couplets and reinterpreting the Bible in terms of sex and gambling. Sportin' Life eventually takes Bess to New York, which he depicts as a shoppers' heaven. Ironically, Porgy sees it in more directly religious terms. Setting off in hopeless pursuit in his goat-cart, he casts it as 'a Heav'nly lan'' in the closing spiritual. The curtain falls with that irreconcilably mixed note of hope and despair that, as we saw in Chapter 6, figures so prominently in black history.[19]

Porgy has a thematic unity and complex characterization which make it a more mature work than *Show Boat*. *Oklahoma!*, which has the same lyricist as *Show Boat*, is also a more mature work. Hammerstein provides two love-triangles. The counterpointed female characters – an element in *Show Boat* – are therefore placed in the position of Bess, pulled from one man to another. Female sexuality is thus again recognized, most clearly in Ado Annie's song, 'I Cain't Say No'. So is the question of intermarriage. It occurs in each triangle: comically with a Persian pedlar and a cowboy competing for Ado Annie, and more seriously with those traditional western enemies, a farmhand and another cowboy, rivals for the hand of Laurey Williams. Intermarriage was a subject that fascinated Hammerstein, and with his new collaborator Richard Rodgers he investigated it further in *South Pacific* (1949), *The King and I* (1951) and *The Flower Drum Song* (1958). Written during the Second World War, *Oklahoma!* is in part an assertion of Americanism. Set just before the admission of Oklahoma to statehood, its title song presents a vision unrecognizable to the poor Okies of Steinbeck's *The Grapes of Wrath*:

We know we belong to the land,
And the land we belong to is grand.

Oklahoma is a microcosm of the nation. Its maturation is accompanied, and perhaps made acceptable, by that typical comic resolution, a marriage. Like *The Melting-Pot*, *Oklahoma!* looks forward in an Edenic vision of racial

and social unity. *Oklahoma!* opens with 'Oh, What a Beautiful Mornin'',
employing an imagery similar to that of the lullaby which opens *Porgy*. But
while *Porgy* ends with a spiritual hoping for better things in another world,
the finale of *Oklahoma!* reprises that opening song.

While *Porgy* looks back to the dramatic form of European opera,
particularly Puccini, *Oklahoma!* looks back to European dances like the
waltz and mixes them with vernacular forms like the square-dance. Dance
is central to *Oklahoma!*, just as its social gathering provides its denouement.
Choreographed by de Mille, the various forms of dance mirror the feelings
of the protagonists and at one point, in Laurey's 'Dream Ballet', carry the
plot forward. George Gershwin called *Porgy* 'a folk opera'; the critic Cecil
Smith called *Oklahoma!* 'a people's opera'. The latter is perhaps a more
satisfactory phrase to apply to both works. It allows us to see that, for all
their differences, *Porgy* and *Oklahoma!* are united in giving voice to the
hopes and fears of people hitherto neglected on the operatic stage.[20]

The three musicals discussed so far take place more than forty-five
minutes from Broadway. In *West Side Story* we are thrust back into modern
New York City. The set is dominated by the defaced walls and mesh
fences of an urban slum. A tenement fire-escape becomes the balcony on
which the lovers Tony and Maria meet, for this is an updated version of
Romeo and Juliet. It is a proletarian version, too, with the aristocratic
Montagues and Capulets replaced by two gangs: the Jets, whose native
Upper West Side 'turf' (the term is deeply ironic, for there isn't a blade of
grass anywhere) is being threatened by the immigrant Puerto Rican Sharks.
The opening 'Jet Song' sets the tone, presenting violence in terms of
technology and, perversely, in the milieu of a family:

> When you're a Jet,
> If the spit hits the fan,
> You got brothers around,
> You're a family man!

Love, the initial impulse if not the staying-power of the modern family,
does not stand a chance in these circumstances. The individual members of
the gang are not evil, but simply helpless. The gang is the only family they
have, with disastrous consequences. The Sharks have the additional
disadvantage of being newcomers. This is apparent in their song, the
dystopian 'America'. Most of them regard Puerto Rico as hell, but they are
cynically self-aware enough to know that discrimination makes Manhattan
only marginally better (see Chapter 7 on Puerto Rican immigration). It is
both deeply ironic and poignant that the lyrics are set to the most
exuberant music and high-spirited dancing in the work, powered by an
infectious Latin-American rhythm.

The love-affair of Tony and Maria blooms temporarily, only to be crushed by the inevitable violence. The soaring melodies of 'Maria' and 'One Hand, One Heart' are therefore overwhelmed by 'The Rumble', where Bernstein draws on the violently declamatory moments of Stravinsky's *Rite of Spring*; and by the frighteningly neurotic 'Cool', where the lyrics fragment under the pressure of a relentless 4/4 beat and fortissimo swing-inspired tuttis from the orchestra, reducing the Jets to shouting 'Crazy', 'Cool' and 'Go' against screaming trumpets and thunderous drums. In this environment there is almost no hope. A comparison with *Oklahoma!* is helpful. The sets in the earlier work were highly stylized suggestions of optimistic open spaces. In *West Side Story* the gritty urban scenes tend towards realism. The dances in *Oklahoma!* were celebrations of community and realizations of a dream. In *West Side Story* Robbins's choreography employs such everyday actions as walking and running. Jeans and sneakers replace gingham dresses and cowboy boots. The dances are not celebrations of community but expressions of violence. *Oklahoma!*'s first song is a waltz. The 'Jet Song' uses a frenetic 6/8 beat.

However, in just two ways *West Side Story* could be said to resemble *Oklahoma!* First, Stephen Sondheim's lyrics persuasively employ ethnic vernacular; he learned the technique from his mentor Oscar Hammerstein II. It is fortunate for the genre that Sondheim has continued to write musicals, giving evidence in works like *Pacific Overtures* (1976) and *Sweeney Todd* (1979) that the genre can still comment on such contemporary concerns as race relations and class oppression. Second, muted expressions of hope may still be found in *West Side Story*. 'A Boy Like That', Anita's song of hatred after Tony has killed her lover Bernardo, modulates into Maria's 'I Have A Love', with Anita singing the closing lines in harmony with her. Tony, in turn, is killed, but his dying words repeat the Edenic theme that 'Somewhere' there is 'a place for us'. The song is taken up by Maria and the two gangs in a moment of reconciliation. But the message is clear. Eden is not here, not now. Manhattan, and by extension America, will not provide 'a new way of living'. With its eclecticism *West Side Story* could be regarded as a realization of David Quixano's *Sinfonia Americana*; but its message that love does not conquer all provides a decisive answer to the optimism of *The Melting-Pot*.[21]

NOTES

1. Israel Zangwill, *The Melting-Pot* (New York, 1909), pp. 198–9.
2. Gilbert Seldes, *The Seven Lively Arts* (New York, 1924), pp. 192–5.

3. James S. Metcalfe, in John McCabe, *George M. Cohan: The Man Who Owned Broadway* (New York, 1973), p. 77.

4. Eugene G. O'Neill, *Bound East for Cardiff*, with the Louise Bryant and Floyd Dell plays, is in *The Provincetown Plays: First Series* (New York, 1916). *Bound East for Cardiff*, with slightly different spelling and punctuation, is also in the Library of America collection, O'Neill, *Complete Plays* (3 vols, New York, 1988) I, pp. 185–99.

5. J. George Frederick, 'Evening Becomes Intolerable', *Vanity Fair*, **37** (January, 1932): pp. 46–7.

6. O'Neill, *More Stately Mansions*, Act IV, Scene ii, *Complete Plays*, III, p. 528.

7. Walter P. Eaton, *The Theatre Guild: The First Ten Years* (New York, 1929), p. 165.

8. Tennessee Williams, *The Glass Menagerie* (New York, 1945), pp. 5–6, 123.

9. Harold Hobson, *The Sunday Times*, 27 February 1983, quoted in Bigsby, *A Critical Introduction to Twentieth-Century American Drama* (3 vols, Cambridge, 1982–5), II, p. 18. Mary McCarthy, *Sights and Spectacles, 1937–1956* (New York, 1956), pp. 131–5. Williams, *A Streetcar Named Desire* (New York, 1947), pp. 42–3, 139–40, 12.

10. Arthur Miller, *Death of a Salesman*, in *Collected Plays* (2 vols, New York, 1957, 1982) I, pp. 130, 141, 157, 162, 180–1, 189, 221–2.

11. Miller, *The Price*, in *Collected Plays* II, pp. 323, 298–9, 373.

12. Joseph Papp, quoted in Bigsby, *A Critical Introduction*, III, p. 28.

13. Joseph Wood Krutch, *American Drama Since 1918* (Rev. edn, New York, 1957), p. 7.

14. Mark Twain, *Innocents Abroad* (1869; reprinted New York, 1984), p. 108. Havelock Ellis, *The Dance of Life* (Boston, 1923), pp. 36–7.

15. William Bolitho, *Twelve Against the Gods: The Story of Adventure* (London, 1930), p. 334.

16. Henry Ford, *'Good Morning': After a Sleep of Twenty-Five Years, Old-Fashioned Dancing is Being Revived by Mr and Mrs Henry Ford* (Dearborn, MI, 1926), pp. 8–17. Mr and Mrs Vernon Castle, *Modern Dancing* (New York, 1914), pp. 146, 37, 20.

17. Lincoln Kirstein, *Blast at Ballet: A Corrective for the American Audience* (New York: Lincoln Kirstein, 1938), p. 45.

18. *Show Boat* (1927; reprinted London, 1988), p.66.

19. George and Ira Gershwin, *Porgy and Bess* (1935; reprinted London, 1976), p.19.

20. Richard Rodgers–Oscar Hammerstein II, *Oklahoma!* Cecil Smith, quoted in Gerald Bordman, *American Operetta: From HMS Pinafore to Sweeney Todd* (New York, 1981), p. 150.

21. Arthur Laurents–Leonard Bernstein-Stephen Sondheim, *West Side Story* (1956; reprinted London, 1972), pp. 20, 98.

SUGGESTIONS FOR FURTHER READING

Werner Sollors, *Beyond Ethnicity: Consent and Descent in American Culture* (New York, 1986) contains a sophisticated discussion of the melting-pot idea. Joseph Wood Krutch's *The American Drama Since 1918* (rev. edn, New York, 1957) is still valuable, but the standard survey is now CWE Bigsby's *A Critical Introduction to Twentieth-Century American Drama* (3 vols, Cambridge, 1982–85). This can be supplemented by texts from the Macmillan Modern Dramatists series: *Eugene O'Neill*, Normand Berlin (1982); *Edward Albee*, Gerry McCarthy (1987); *Tennessee Williams*, Roger Boxhill (1987); *Arthur Miller*, Neil Carson (1982); *American Alternative Theatre*, Theodore Shank (1982); *New American Dramatists*, Ruby Cohn (1982). Diane Alexander, *Playhouse* (Los Angeles, 1984) is an amusing, anecdotal account of the Pasadena Playhouse. Gerald Bordman, *The Oxford Companion to American Theatre* (New York, 1984) and Glenn Loney, *Twentieth Century Theatre* (2 vols, New York, 1983) are essential reference works.

Mary Kerner, *Barefoot to Balanchine: How to Watch Dance* (New York, 1990) is a helpful introduction to the field, while Susan Au, *Ballet and Modern Dance* (London, 1988) is more detailed and finely illustrated. Walter Terry and Arlene Croce are perceptive dance critics whose work is always worth reading; particularly relevant are Terry, *Frontiers of Dance: The Life of Martha Graham* (New York, 1975) and Croce, *The Fred Astaire and Ginger Rogers Book* (New York, 1977), while John Mueller, *Astaire Dancing: The Musical Films* (New York, 1985) is more wide-ranging. Marshall and Jean Stearns, *Jazz Dance: The Development of American Vernacular Dance* (1964; reprinted, New York, 1979) and Rusty E. Frank, *Tap!: The Greatest Tap Dance Stars and Their Stories, 1900–1955* (New York, 1990) are the best books on tap.

In the past the musical has suffered from what might be called the fanzine approach. This has now been altered by the prolific Gerald Bordman, who has produced an important reference work, *American Musical Theatre* (expanded edn, New York, 1986) and surveys of American operetta, musical revues and Jerome Kern. Lehman Engel, *The American Musical Theatre* (New York, 1975) is valuable because the author conducted many famous productions from the pit, while Rick Altman (ed.), *Genre: The Musical* (London, 1981) is a good collection of essays about film. Recordings of musicals, too, are benefiting from a more scholarly approach. The 1988 EMI recording of *Show Boat* gives all the music of the 1927 production, plus unused and subsequent material. Miles Kreuger, *Show Boat: The Story of an American Classic Musical* (rev. edn, New York, 1990) is an important companion, lavishly illustrated. The 1976 Decca recording of

Porgy and Bess, with Lorin Maazel conducting, first made the full reach and weight of this work apparent. A good history is Hollis Alpert, *The Life and Times of Porgy and Bess* (London, 1990). Bernstein's own 1984 recording of *West Side Story* is a more controversial example of the use of opera stars in a musical. There is as yet no fully adequate recording of *Oklahoma!*, but the 1955 film, directed by Fred Zinnemann in Technicolor and Todd-AO, is a joy to behold.

CHAPTER THIRTEEN
Visual America

Paul Oliver

A former military stores would seem an unlikely locale for an artistic event. Yet the International Exhibition of Modern Art, which opened in February 1913 in the vast premises of New York's 69th Regiment Armory on 25th Street was of major importance in the history of American art. Some 1,600 works introduced modern painting to tens of thousands of Americans. Impressionist and Post-Impressionist, Cubist and Fauve works were well represented and if the Italian Futurists refused to exhibit, and the show was weak on sculpture, the Armory Show was still a revelation of the dynamic changes that had taken place in art since the turn of the century. Later, the Show went on to Chicago and Boston, to be seen by 300,000 visitors. The press had a field day, the works were ridiculed and the artists vilified as 'anarchists'. But perceptive galleries and private collectors bought many of the works, and young artists were stimulated by the energy, colour and freedom expressed in many of the paintings by the symbolist Odilon Redon, the Cubist works of Pablo Picasso, the lyrical Fauvism of Henri Matisse and the Cubo-Futurist work of Marcel Duchamp.

The revolution in painting that had taken place in the first decade of the century stemmed from the visual explorations of the Post-Impressionists. They were not a unified group, but a number of individuals whose work inspired a younger generation of Parisian artists. Matisse and the Fauves, and the German artists of Die Brucke were excited by the expressive colour and gestural brushwork of Van Gogh and Edvard Munch; Picasso and the Cubists were to follow the investigations into the analysis of structure of Paul Cézanne; while Paul Gauguin's delineation of shape and sense of design was a source for both groups. Such artists revealed that the world of visual appearances need not be replicated to create art, as had been the case with naturalistic painting, though it remained a source of inspiration. Paintings were visual phenomena on their own account, composed on the picture plane. Artists abstracted from their visual experience to create a new reality which was charged by their own emotional responses and expressive abilities.

One of the intentions of the organizers of the Armory Show, who included several artists, was to place modern American painters in the context of contemporary artistic movements. It was hoped that this would gain them a new respect. In particular there was the group, mostly from Philadelphia, who called themselves 'The Eight'. Led by Robert Henri, this generation of artists included John Sloan and George Bellows. They were realists, artists who drew their inspiration from the everyday world of the Bowery and the boxing ring, a predilection which earned them the name of the 'Ash Can School'. They painted in a meaty technique with dark tones broken by the highlights of street lamps and footlights, as in Henri's *Snow in New York*, or the chiaroscuro of Bellows's *Stag at Sharkey's*, with its unleashed power.

The Eight had exhibited in 1908, the year that the photographer Alfred Stieglitz opened a gallery at 291 Fifth Avenue. Here he showed many paintings by the Cubists and gave exhibitions to young Americans such as John Marin, with his translucent, shattered watercolours of the city, and Georgia O'Keeffe, whose abstract use of natural forms carried an erotic charge. But his exhibitions were seen only by a small circle; it was the achievement of the Armory Show that, ridiculed or not, it made modern art widely known in America, though it had the less welcome outcome of emphasizing the creative supremacy of the so-called 'School of Paris'.

AMPOULES OF PARIS AIR

American artists, critics and collectors had long been active in Paris. Mary Cassatt, James McNeill Whistler and, later, Maurice Prendergast had made significant contributions to the Impressionist and Post-Impressionist movements; the painter Max Weber had been one of the first Cubists, and the writer Gertrude Stein, together with her collector brother Leo, had been an early champion of the new developments. American artists often chose to serve a European apprenticeship, and many stayed. Morgan Russell and Stanton Macdonald Wright developed a form of geometric abstraction: Synchronism. Another expatriate American, Lyonel Feininger, developed a crystalline style which incorporated Italian Futurist 'lines of force'. When the German architect Walter Gropius founded the Bauhaus school of design in the postwar Weimar Republic, Feininger was one of his first appointees to the faculty.

With these expatriates in mind it is reasonable at this stage to ask what is an 'American' artist? One born in the United States, or one who has spent a substantial amount of a working life there? And what is American art? Art by American-born artists, irrespective of where they lived and worked? Art by those with American nationality? Art created on American soil? The questions are far from irrelevant for, with the advent of the Great War and, again, with the Second World War, many European artists moved to the United States, some to take temporary refuge, some to emigrate for good. There is no simple answer to these questions, but for the purposes of this chapter an 'American artist' is one who has claimed United States nationality as a birthright or by adoption, augmented by artists of other nationalities who have significantly contributed to the art of America while living on US soil. But this is a post-rationalization; at the time of the Paris revolution American artists were those who came to Europe from the United States.

Numerous problems confronted them as they sought to establish themselves in the fermenting world of art. How could they participate in the new developments in modern art which emanated from Europe, and yet remain American? Could an American modern movement be developed which could stand on its own terms? If modernist painters and sculptors were to be in the 'avant-garde', as the term was, to what extent would they separate themselves from the American public? With whom were they communicating? Who would buy their work? Who would be their supporters and their patrons? Faced with the dilemma of disassociating themselves from the prevalent naturalism of art in the United States to participate in the exciting events then focused in Paris, aspiring artists had to confront the overriding problem of their identity. With shifts of emphasis, the issues that faced them persisted over several decades and, in certain respects, face some of their successors still.

A year after the Armory Show, war broke out in Europe. Many artists returned home where, in New York, the Dadaists were creating havoc. It could be argued that the irrational 'art anti-art' movement, Dada, arose in many cities as a reaction to the senselessness of the Great War. But it also raucously confronted the persisting conventions of nineteenth-century art, and it was this radicalism that appealed to some young New York artists. Their response to European Dada illustrates the problem of identifying what is essentially American. New York Dada developed under the meteoric influence of the Parisian painter Francis Picabia, a close friend of Stieglitz, who was exhilarated by Manhattan when he came to the Armory Show and who made witty comments on New York socialites with his machine-orientated aesthetic.

Later on, the brilliant Duchamp (whose *Nude Descending a Staircase* was the scandal of the Armory Show) arrived in New York, carrying an ampoule of 'Paris air' for the millionaire collector Walter Arensberg. He collaborated with the young American painter and photographer Man Ray, whose blanket-covered and roped sewing machine, *The Enigma of Isadora Duncan* was quintessentially Dadaist. Duchamp resigned from his position as vice-president of the Society of American Artists on the eve of the opening of its 1917 exhibition when his 'ready-made' urinal entitled *Fountain*, signed by 'R. Mutt', was rejected by the committee. He stayed on to 'incomplete' his 'Large Glass', *The Bride Stripped Bare by Her Bachelors, Even*. If New York Dadaists were never as totally anarchic as the Zurich Dadaists still they were challenging and satirical. Marsden Hartley's *Portrait of a German Officer*, who was depicted solely by his medals and insignia, was one of several works which made their points with vigour.

Yet Dadaist nihilism was too subversive to have provided a secure basis for a new American approach to painting; an alternative was stimulated by the 1915 Panama–Pacific show, held in San Francisco, which introduced the dynamic mechanicism of the Futurists. Their successor, Italian-born Joseph Stella, translated their hard, urban imagery to the USA, with restless but glittering interpretations of Brooklyn Bridge in his polyptich *The Voice of the City of New York Interpreted*, while Charles Demuth projected the momentum of the subway train with *I Saw the Figure 5 in Gold*, the numeral echoing against a red sign. The title was drawn from a poem by William Carlos Williams (see Chapter 15), and many connections can be traced between the artists and writers of the period. In *My Egypt* Demuth both stabilized his imagery with a new monumentalism and drew an explicit classical parallel with the forms of a grain silo.

Demuth's fellow 'Precisionist' Charles Sheeler confirmed the trends towards an essentially American content and a neo-Cubist, sharply delineated classicism. His paintings of cityscapes and urban hardware were uncompromising and unsentimental, if dehumanized. A skilled photographer, his series of the Ford Motor Company's River Rouge Plant in 1927 was a landmark in industrial photography. In later years Sheeler adapted the effects of multiple exposures to his clear-toned painting. He admired Stieglitz's photographs for their poetic quality and was a champion of photography as art.

THE AMERICAN SCENE

In its urban documentary form, modern American photography came of age largely in the powerful reporting of Lewis W. Hine. He was not a disinterested observer; he used photography to reveal social injustices and the exploitation of labour. A trained sociologist, he had an attachment to the nobility of men at work, particularly in his breathtaking shots of derrick men and riveters assembling the Empire State Building. While drawing his subjects from everyday American life, his sense of composition showed the influence of abstract art.

With the development of the 291 Gallery circle, painters and photographers met and influenced each other more overtly. Early photographs by Stieglitz's disciple Edward Steichen had the soft, painterly impressionism that was also evident in many of Edward S. Curtis's photographs of Native Americans, but the critical clarity demanded of him in his capacity as a war photographer changed his approach. He mastered light and his camera with painful discipline, taking literally hundreds of photographs of the same subjects: a cup and saucer, a tree in a yard. The same emphasis on sharp definition and ascetic abstraction was evident in the peppers, nudes and sand dunes of Edward Weston, or the etched details of fences, trees and rockfaces of Ansel Adams, or, especially, the flower studies of Imogen Cunningham. In these f.64 Group camera artists the Precisionists, too, had their counterparts.

It was the Depression and Roosevelt's New Deal which gave photographers both a new patronage and an undeniably American focus. In 1935 Roy E. Stryker was invited to head a project for the Farm Security Administration, an agency whose chief aim was the resettlement of farmers of limited means, through low interest loans, on more productive, viable farms. He selected a (changing) team of young photographers and sought a documentary record not just of the FSA itself but of the nation which emphasized, but did not romanticize, the plight of the 'submerged third'. Arthur Rothstein's dust-bowl shots, the portraits of migrants by Dorothea Lange, Walker Evans's Southern streets and barber shops have left an indelible imprint on the national memory. Indirectly the photographers may have prepared the American audience for some aspects of modernism. The two-dimensionality and face-on parallelism of many FSA photographs, especially those of Evans, perhaps derived from the modernist emphasis on the picture plane, while the cacophony of signs and lettering seen in others echoes Cubo-Futurist use of typography.

But however abstract the organization of the photographs might be, their sturdy realism appealed to a large audience. FSA photographs were disseminated through brochures put out by the FSA and other government agencies, in exhibitions, as magazine illustrations, and in such publications as *Land of the Free* (1938), in which poems by Archibald MacLeish serve as a 'sound track', and Richard Wright's photographic book on the black experience, *12 Million Black Voices* (1941). The FSA photographic unit aroused some disquiet in Congress, and the charge of Communist sympathizing was levelled at the unit whose record was considered by some to be politically motivated. One of the photographers, Ben Shahn, was already noted as the painter of *The Passion of Sacco and Vanzetti*, based on the trial and execution of the suspected anarchists. An assistant at one stage to the Communist Mexican artist Diego Rivera, his shrewd and sympathetic perceptions of the poor were heightened in those years, and expressed in paintings like *Scott's Run, West Virginia*.

'I paint the American Scene', claimed a contemporary of these photographers, Stuart Davis. Recalling Matisse's cut-paper collages, his brilliantly coloured abstractions, like *Rapt at Rappaport's*, drew on advertisements, packaging and jazz for inspiration. Davis's work was American in content, but it was essentially European in approach, and failed to satisfy those who demanded a return to American values in art – values that were based on verisimilitude, representationalism. Indeed, many painters reflected the violent populist opposition to the Armory Show and its aftermath. Reginald Marsh followed the lead of the Ash Can School into the 1930s with realist Depression paintings like *The Bowery*. More lasting in the impact of his bleak, city locations, seen in evening or very early morning light, were the paintings of Edward Hopper. He had affinities with Sloan, but his work soon assumed an airless, torpid character which captured the loneliness of the apartment and the street. Hopper's rendition of an all-night café in *Nighthawks* was evocative of urban anomie.

Other painters turned their backs on the city and looked to the rural regions for inspiration, among them John Steuart Curry. His landscapes were often windswept and disturbed, but they captured the feeling of the wide open spaces of the Midwest; less successful were his fiery, mythical portraits of the abolitionist John Brown. Thomas Hart Benton was an even more outspoken opponent of Modernism and advocate of Regionalism (see Chapter 5). Benton painted sweeping, agitated scenes of farm workers, cowhands and country musicians but with a certain vigorous romanticism. In contrast to his restless compositions, the works of Grant Wood were still and minutely crafted; his double portrait of a pitchfork-holding farmer and his daughter seen against their boarded frame house, *American Gothic*, was the most popular of all Regionalist pictures.

In the early 1930s the Mexican painters Rivera, José Clemente Orozco and David Siquieros all worked in the United States. These forceful and politically committed artists brought a breadth of scale to their work which was a revelation to some of the young American painters who were apprenticed to them. 'I want to use my art as a weapon', declared Rivera, and when he attacked capitalism in his murals for the Rockefeller Center they were destroyed, amid a seething reaction among supporters and opponents alike.[1] Rivera had demonstrated the power of mural paintings to communicate, and when the Works Progress Administration's Federal Art Project (WPA/FAP) was initiated in 1935 murals figured prominently. Under the directorship of Holger Cahill – once a Dadaist himself – the project gave employment to some 5,000 artists, who painted 2,500 murals in post offices, banks, hospitals and other civil buildings. Over 100,000 easel paintings, nearly 20,000 sculptures, over 20,000 plates for the Index of American Design, some 200,000 graphic prints and approximately two million screen prints from 35,000 poster designs were produced in the seven years or so of the project.

As a social achievement the WPA/FAP undertaking was quite remarkable; as an aesthetic achievement it was, at best, little above mediocre. Although Cahill favoured abstraction, it found no support with other administrators. Far too many of the works were parochial rather than regional, enfeebling rather than ennobling in the posturing compositions of workers, which figured prominently in the paintings and prints. The inferior quality of much of the artwork was commented upon at the time by many critics. To the Director of the Whitney Museum, Julianna Force, 'there can be no true selectivity when the basic reason for choosing an artist is his poverty'.[2] But others regarded the failure of much WPA art as the result of administrative interference and lack of nerve. The choice of parochial subject matter, the attitudinizing of the figures, and the often unadventurous approach of the WPA artists to their media can be related to many factors, including the desire to instill pride of place and country in the Depression years, the conservatism of small-town America, the immaturity of many of the painters. But the project also reflected the isolation, and isolationism, of millions of Americans. The artists had the opportunity, the patronage, and the outlets to the public which could have laid the foundations for an accessible, modern American art. Whatever the reasons, which must always be a subject of debate, the outcome was a disappointing compromise.

BROADWAY BOOGIE WOOGIE

If American isolationism during the interwar period was reflected in thousands of WPA works, total insulation from European influence was impossible. In fact, a number of the WPA artists, including Mark Rothko, Willem de Kooning and Arshile Gorky, had emigrated, with their parents, from Europe to the United States. They were joined by an influx of refugee artists from the Nazi repression of the 1930s, to settle in an unfamiliar world but bringing with them the ideas that had continued to ferment in Europe. In spite of the attempts of its last director, Mies van der Rohe, to keep the Bauhaus alive, the school was closed by the Nazis in 1933. Many of its most brilliant architects and artists moved to the United States (see also Chapter 9). Among the ex-Bauhaus faculty and students who took prominent positions in art and design education in the United States were its first director, Gropius, and van der Rohe. Laszlo Moholy-Nagy founded the New Bauhaus in Chicago, Marcel Breuer joined Gropius at Harvard, and Josef Albers became Head of the Art Department at the innovatory Black Mountain College. The influence of these figures was incalculable, for they substantially shaped the policies and the staffing of the institutions where they taught. Their impact was particularly felt by the generation of artists who came to prominence after the War.

More immediate in their influence were the abstract artists who emigrated to the United States to escape the repressive dictatorships. Hans Hofmann opened his 8th Street School in New York in 1934. Amadee Ozenfant, who, with architect Le Corbusier had founded the Purist movement, also taught in New York. Their presence gave heart to an expanding group of American abstractionists, among them the young sculptor David Smith and the most significant female abstractionist, Lee Krasner. In 1936 several of them formed an association of American Abstract Artists, from which they defended their patch against the prevailing trend of romantic realism. They were given a considerable boost by the arrival in 1940 of Piet Mondrian, the founder of the Dutch constructivist movement De Stijl, whose *Broadway Boogie Woogie* was a paean to city rhythms.

In 1935 the Whitney Museum showed an exhibition of American Abstract Art and the following year Alfred Barr Jr, the director of the Museum of Modern Art (MOMA), mounted an important show of 'Cubism and Abstract Art'. These pioneering exhibitions endorsed the work of modernists, though they also attracted popular hostility. When the Solomon Guggenheim Museum of Non-Objective Art was opened in 1937 it fixed a term for abstraction that was to be widely adopted in the United States. 'Non-Objective art' was nonetheless ambiguous, implying the *subjective*, which abstract art in general was not. Such confusing terminology only added to public uncertainty about modern American art, which was further provoked by the Surrealists.

Barr also mounted 'Fantastic Art, Dada and Surrealism' at MOMA in 1936, and some young artists experimented with the dream-world that the Surrealists evoked in their paintings. But it was the arrival of Matta Echauren in 1939, and, soon after, André Masson, with his 'automatic' techniques of undirected subconscious drawing, that opened up new possibilities. The ingenious German-born artist Max Ernst devised 'grattage' and 'frottage' techniques – combed and grained textures which served to inspire images of primeval landscapes. More obvious in his use of Freudian symbolism, the flamboyant Spanish painter Salvador Dali employed startling visual puns. Under the leadership of the poet André Breton, many European Surrealists made their home in New York as war broke out once more. Like Dada in the First World War, the irrationality of international conflict seemed both echoed and satirized in Surrealism. Their penetration of the subconscious and exposure of sexual fantasies and bizarre juxtapositions attracted the attention of the millionaire Peggy Guggenheim; she showed their work, as well as that of the abstractionists, in her 'Art of This Century' gallery, which opened in 1942.

Quite the most original of the American artists associated with Surrealism was Robert Motherwell. A graduate of both philosophy and archaeology, he wrote and lectured extensively. 'Art is not national', he said, dismissing the concerns of his contemporaries; 'to be merely an American or a French artist is to be nothing; to fail to overcome one's initial environment is never to reach the human'.[3] Motherwell tapped subconscious fears with his child-like, but not childish, treatment of a Mexican revolutionary, *Pancho Villa, Dead or Alive*. The plight of Spain, torn apart by Civil War, he paralleled to the bullfight, symbolized in compelling abstractions like *Five in the Afternoon*, with its black, crushed, genital shapes.

Turning their attention to the East, the Seattle artists Morris Graves and Mark Tobey wove paintings of a mystic intricacy. Tobey invented what he termed 'white writing', a fluid, automatic, cursive style which owed a great deal to Japanese calligraphy. Typically, an intricate white web engulfed a dark plain in *Edge of Autumn*. But if they were captivated by Eastern culture, the influence of Europe on progressive art in the United States was overwhelming; only the regional realism of the WPA painters maintained an essentially American, if totally conservative, perception. Nevertheless, during the Depression the WPA did give employment to abstractionists like Hartley and Davis, as well as to Benton. And the young artists whose abilities were tested by the Project included Adolph Gottlieb, Gorky, de Kooning, Jackson Pollock, Ad Reinhardt and Rothko – all names which were to revolutionize American painting in the years after the Second World War.

SONGS OF THE BLACKSMITHS

It is tempting to relate the flowering of American abstract expressionism in the period after the Second World War to the new role as world power that the United States assumed. International stature and the spirit of expansionism imbued a confidence in the nation which the breadth and scale of the new art may seem to reflect. One of the principal features of postwar painting was the freedom expressed by the artists in their approach to paint; instead of the tight, boundary-constrained work that was characteristic of the Precisionists as well as the WPA muralists, the new painting rejoiced in the fluidity of the medium. The New Art could be seen as a metaphor for the new America.

But the changes that took place were more an outcome of earlier aesthetic struggles than of recent national achievement. There were forerunners to the approach: Arthur Dove, for instance, who painted abstracts as early as 1910 and whose *Flour Mill* (1938), with its loose, shimmering brushwork and shapes, was a remarkable precursor of later trends. But if there was one artist who heralded the postwar triumph of American art it was surely the tormented spirit of Arshile Gorky. Gorky's merging of Cubism and Surrealism culminated in a succession of remarkable works created by the use of 'automatic' line and strained or poured colour. The shapes bore a subliminal sexuality, the colours were hot, the painting impassioned, and the titles evoked irrational juxtapositions, as in *The Liver is the Cock's Comb*. A tortured figure, he committed suicide in 1948 at the age of forty-three. Gorky's influence was considerable, though it had nothing to do with American power; rather the contrary. His liberated brushwork was evident in the paintings of his friend de Kooning, whose series *Woman* attacked classic poses and glamorous stereotypes with obsessional, perhaps misogynistic, ferocity. And his impact on the restless young man from Wyoming, and assistant to Benton on the WPA, Jackson Pollock, was greater still.

Pollock was introduced to Peggy Guggenheim by Motherwell; she encouraged him for some five years while Pollock emerged as the most precocious talent among the new generation of painters. From expressive paintings like *The She-Wolf* – derived from Picasso in spite of his declared dislike of European artists – he began to use Gorky's automatic line techniques. Then he experimented with paint trickled on horizontal canvasses laid on the floor, weaving lines and shapes in sweeping arabesques. 'When I am in my painting, I'm not aware of what I'm doing', he wrote in 1947, 'there is pure harmony, an easy give and take, and the painting comes out well' – a harmony exemplified in *Full Fathom Five* of that year.[4] Many of Pollock's paintings were of great size: *One* was seventeen feet by nine. 'Action painting', as the critic Harold Rosenberg termed it, 'Abstract Expressionism', as others preferred to call it, was not restricted to Pollock: the New York School of the 1940s and 1950s abounded with painters using free, expressive, calligraphic brushwork. Among the most impressive was Clyfford Still, whose fields of sombre colour appeared to be attacked by flickering tongues of white flame. Dramatic contrast was exploited by Franz Kline, who painted immense black hieroglyphs broadly brushed against a glaring white ground.

Still and Pollock were exhibited by Peggy Guggenheim, Kline and de Kooning showed at the Egan Gallery, while others were to be seen at the Betty Parsons and other galleries. Private gallery-owners with their wealthy clienteles ensured that many artists had the patronage they sought and were able to work out their ideas with a new-found freedom. Many of the works by these painters were of mural scale; their consciousness of the wall expressed their awareness of the essential nature of all painting – that three-dimensional space is always an illusion and that the essence of the painting is the surface plane itself.

Now the action painters who synthesized expressive brushwork, surrealist automatic gestures, abstract design and WPA mural scale together created an art that was uncompromisingly American. British artists of the St Ives school who were working contemporaneously have since claimed that their approach was appropriated by the New York painters. But their easel-paintings had neither the freedom nor the intensity of the American works. To the Americans the two-dimensional plane was liberating rather than constraining, and some, like Gottlieb or Rothko, experimented with vibrant areas of colour. While Gottlieb contrasted black suns with exploding splash-stars, Rothko slid translucent fields of red, purple or orange over each other. He regarded his later works as mandalas for contemplation.

Abstract art was dividing between the spontaneous and emotionally charged action painting championed by Rosenberg and the 'post-painterly abstraction' advocated by Clement Greenberg. Once a colleague of Albers at Black Mountain, Greenberg argued that the expressive brush-stroke was a distraction from the pure harmonies of chromatic planes, painted with a cool and unemotional control. Barnett Newman and Ad Reinhardt explored the tension of an etiolated vertical line splitting the colour field, but both moved towards a more severe and controlled design and a progressively restricted range of tone and hue. Their later canvasses, though large and sometimes shaped, moved towards an ultimate reductionism. Newman even produced slender, vertical, linear sculptures in polished and eroded metals.

Surprisingly perhaps, in a country where transcontinental migrants had continually sought to leave their mark upon the land, sculpture had been the least developed of the visual arts in America. In the first half of the twentieth century there were few sculptors who were not of European origin. 'The interplay of form must function ... according to the perfection of the working relation of its parts', declared William Zorach, but his own Maillolesque figures had none of the mechanism of his image.[5] Several modern European sculptors, such as the Cubist Jacques Lipschitz, moved to the United States, but their influence on American sculptors was not comparable to that of European immigrants on American painters.

Though the American-born sculptors were few, two at least were exceptional. Witty and original, Alexander Calder was attracted by the shapes employed by the Surrealist Joan Miró and created unique wire and metal constructions. 'How fine it would be if everything there moved', he is said to have remarked after visiting Mondrian's studio; the thought inspired his celebrated 'mobiles', air-blown detached bodies floating in space. Calder's mobiles rapidly became a popular success, their progeny eventually to hang over every baby's crib, but he continued creating bold, arching structures in welded steel plates, vividly painted.

David Smith was well-named, a sculptor in raw welded metal whose early works of the mid-1930s were forged in Brooklyn's Terminal Iron Works. He had a natural affinity with his material, chosen largely because it had little aesthetic precedent. He turned to Eskimo art for inspiration, hanging symbolic shapes in twisted frames, like *Blackburn – Song of an Irish Blacksmith*. In the 1950s his linear technique was replaced by monumental structures made from industrial parts, presaging the thirty days he spent at Spoleto, Italy. In a period of demonic energy he created his *Voltri-Bolton* series, works of unprecedented power largely constructed from found metal objects. They were the inspiration for many of his subsequent works.

Several American sculptors followed the lead of Calder and Smith. More significantly, for the first time, European artists turned to America for inspiration. They had been exposed to the new developments by the shows that Peggy Guggenheim had mounted in several countries, though it was the stunning touring exhibition 'New American Painting' which, in the late 1950s, amazed European artists and public alike with the bravura of their skills, the strength of their works and the scale that they employed with such confidence. If the content and style of American art of that time was not much affected by America's status as a superpower, the ability of its patrons to market it ultimately was. The torch of visual creativity had been wrested from the grip of Paris. American artists of the New York school had not only found their identity: they rejoiced in it.

BETWEEN LIFE AND ART

For the Abstract Expressionists their limited audiences at home remained a problem. The kinds of aesthetic issues with which they were concerned were debated among an intellectual, and largely New York-based, élite. They had better opportunities to reach a larger audience with graphics which had also undergone a renaissance. Credit for this was largely due to Louis Schanker, director of the WPA's graphic arts programme. He introduced new techniques in cutting and printing, motivating younger artists born after the First World War, such as the Uruguayan-born Antonio Frasconi, who chose mining and other working-class themes in the manner of Shahn, or Leonard Baskin, whose powerful woodcuts, like *Man of Peace* (of a concentration camp victim holding a dead dove), were printed on an unprecedented scale. Most of the Abstract Expressionists also produced prints, and reached a somewhat larger audience by doing so.

Yet artists were making few direct links with the culture at large; art was insulated, obsessed with its own exciting revolution. At Black Mountain College, however, the composer John Cage (see Chapter 11) gave a series of lectures which challenged the exclusiveness of art and advanced the aesthetics of the banal and the accidental. One artist there who responded was Robert Rauschenberg, who exploited the techniques of Abstract Expressionism, while attacking its aesthetic by incorporating in his works unexpected objects from everyday experience. By using the separation sheets of incomplete colour prints, coke bottles, even a stuffed hen or a kitchen chair, his 'combine paintings' sought to fill, he said, 'the gap between art and life'.[6]

He was not the first to draw inspiration from familiar objects: in the 1920s Dove had made complete compositions of accoutrements, such as the angler's kit of *Goin' Fishin'*. Assemblage, or art made from the juxtaposed objects of the 'junk culture', rapidly became an international movement, 'The Art of Assemblage', as an exhibition of 'the collage environment' organized at MOMA in 1961, clearly demonstrated. Assemblage produced one sculptor of note, Louise Nevelson, who collected off-cuts and objects of turned wood, incorporating them in clustered boxes and unifying them with a single colour – gunmetal grey in the case of *Cathedral–Moon Garden + One*. There was an element of nostalgia in the use of cast-off objects, as Jim Dine, a leading member of the generation born in the 1930s, soon realized. He had used discarded frocks and wire coat-hangers in some of his works, but they contained, he quipped, 'too much of other people's mystery'. Jasper Johns did not use actual objects in his works; instead he remodelled them, casting a tooth brush in his satirical *The Critic Smiles*. He shocked with his paintings of the sacrosanct national flag 'Old Glory', laying one upon another till they drained meaning and colour. But even this was a shade too 'painterly' for the 'Pop' artists.

Pop Art dominated the 1960s. Previous art movements had drawn visual inspiration from scenes of popular culture, but Pop Art went much further, deriving its very forms from the artefacts of popular culture themselves, and much of its techniques from them too. In his painting of a cigarette packet, *Lucky Strike*, Stuart Davis had been almost alone in recognizing the painting potential of commercial packaging. Once despised, 'commercial art' was now a source for motifs and methods alike. Spray-gun textures, block-printed ads, poster art, colour diagrams, comic 'funny papers', with all their mismatches, provided new ways of expressing the brash, commercial world. American consumerism (discussed in Chapter 8), once abhorred by the artists, was now the form and the content of their work. The doyen of Pop Art, Andy Warhol, exploited both the slipped registers of poor printing and the fading image of popular idols with his multi-image *Marilyn Monroe*, and hammered home the message of the supermarket with his multiple Campbell soup cans and Brillo boxes. They were almost facsimiles. Roy Lichtenstein got across his ideas with magnification. Employing the 'Ben Day dots' of contemporary screen-printed advertisements and cartoons he painted mural-scale works, like *Wham!*, which simulated a strip from a combat comic.

Magnification and the contradictory use of materials were clues to the sculpture of Claes Oldenburg. He enlarged everyday articles, like a garden trowel or a hamburger with pickles, to gargantuan proportions and made interpretations of hard objects, such as a typewriter or a *Giant Soft Swedish Light Switch*, in deflated plastic. 'I am for the art that a kid licks, after peeling away the wrapper', Oldenburg claimed.[7] He conceived witty, if unrealized monuments for the world's cities: a pair of legs standing in the Seine or Nelson's column replaced by a gear-shift – one suspects in bottom gear. Though at first confined to exhibitions in the Martha Jackson Gallery or the Sidney Janis Gallery, where they were proclaimed as 'the New Realists', popular taste swiftly swung in the pop artists' favour, with some getting commissions to design record sleeves or billboards. Yet the public's involvement was passive and some artists sought a more active participation in the creative process.

Oldenburg, like Rauschenberg, was a pioneer of the 'Happening', which was distinguished by its extempore nature. Oldenburg's *Store Days* was a loosely structured pattern of events which took place in his 'Ray-Gun Theatre', in which the bedroom was likened to a jail and the kitchen to a butcher's shop. Audience participation in Happenings was customary, and though certain elements were controlled, chance, accident and non-

sequential events were fundamental. Principal exponent of Happenings was
Alan Kaprow, who presented his *18 Happenings in 6 Parts* at the Reuben
Gallery, New York, in a succession of scripted events; his later works were
less pre-planned and freed from the gallery milieu. Kaprow came to
Happenings by way of Action painting and assemblage, as did Dine, who
briefly experimented with them – most notably with *Car Crash*. Visceral,
messy, charged with the *frisson* of released sexuality and potential danger,
Happenings challenged the concept of the work of art as static or lasting,
and bridged the space between music, drama and the visual arts. But the
improvisatory, impermanent nature of the Happening contributed to its
decline, if not its demise. It could not be described or convincingly filmed;
it was exciting, often rewarding for the participants, but excluded all but
those present from the experiences that it offered.

Somewhere between Assemblage, Pop Art sculpture and Happenings
was situated the 'environment' or 'installation'. George Segal recreated
lonely but unwalled rooms, shop window displays or cinema foyers
peopled with life-sized figures. Modelled and clothed in white plaster, as in
Costume Party or *Cinema*, their ghostly, impassive presence seemed
encapsulated in a moment of time. In contrast, Ed Kienholz devised part-
Realist, part-Surrealist tableaux, loaded with sexual metaphor, irony and
painful observation. Politically motivated, *The Portable War Memorial*
combined a reduced-scale Iwo Jima flag-raising memorial sculpture with a
hot dog and chilli bar, including working coke vendor. *The Beanery*
replicated a Los Angeles café, reduced in scale though occupied with life-
size figures. While music played and cooking smells percolated, the
spectator could squeeze past them in the cramped space.

Such works pushed back the frontiers of sculpture, but they were still
installed in a gallery space, still purchasable as commodities. Some sculptors
sought a somewhat more durable art which was subject to natural processes
rather than induced ones, which yet required sponsorship rather than
conceding to the gallery system. Born in Bulgaria, Christo settled in New
York in his late twenties. Mysterious and disquieting, his wrapped objects
were the descendants of Man Ray's *Isadora Duncan*. From first wrapping
such objects as a supermarket trolley Christo wrapped whole buildings, and
even attempted the conceptually impossible in a *Wrapped Floor*.

Christo's plastic sheeted *Running Fence*, which undulated eighteen miles
across California valleys, was a popular success as it slowly succumbed to
the tearing of the winds. Other artists worked with landscape itself, Robert
Smithson being the most influential of these. With mechanical earth-
movers he extended his *Spiral Jetty* into the Great Salt Lake in Utah. His
assistant Michael Heizer moved nearly a quarter of a million tons of rock to
entrench his *Double Negative* at Mormon Mesa, Nevada, while Dennis

Oppenheim left a cattleman's brand on a mountainside at San Pablo, California. Such works both reshaped the earth and commented on humanity's use of it. Often they appeared to be the abstract successors to Gutzon Borglum's notorious 1930s sculpting (with rock-drill and dynamite) of presidential heads at Mount Rushmore in the Black Hills of Dakota, but with social criticism replacing patriotism. Like Happenings, Land Art could not be bought or sold; it was there to be encountered. In exploring – literally – these artists were declaring their dissatisfaction with the commercial world of the galleries and their desire to create a purely experiential art.

TIME TO REFLECT

With Pop Art, Assemblages, Happenings and Land Art, the gaps between art and life, between élite culture and popular culture, between commercial and fine art, between dreams and consciousness, between media hype and hyper-reality had been closed. School-kids and easel painters alike could share the same sources, experiment with the same means and explore the same world of images. Pop Art and its related idioms tapped popular resources and fed back into them. Experientially rather than aesthetically based, they heightened awareness of the urban, suburban and, in Land Art, even wilderness environments without reference to classical tenets of design. Only photography among art forms had been so readily accepted in the popular domain.

Photography had not been unaffected by the revolution in painting and sculpture. A number of photographers turned to abstraction, among them Aaron Siskind and Gyorgy Kepes, who found parallels with abstract expressionism in their photographs of peeling paintwork and decaying materials. Even fashion photography was not wholly impervious to the new wave of image-making; Richard Avedon was able to match his striking portraits of Stravinsky or Ezra Pound with his commissions for *Vogue*. Yet the work of these photographers seemed self-conscious in its artistic selectivity and more interesting achievements were to be found in the history of the rightly named 'straight tradition' of American photography, especially in the field of reportage.

With the development of high-speed films, fast processing and ever-more efficient cameras the photograph pervaded the newspapers and magazines. Outstanding reporters such as Robert Capa or Margaret Bourke-White, whose war-time courage earned her the affection of the forces, became household names. Succeeded by Gordon Parks, Eliot

Elisofon and the teams of the Condé-Nast publications or photographic consortia such as Magnum, the new generation of photographers explored fresh dimensions of space and imagery, breaking conventions in camerawork and subject matter. New talents were apparent in Danny Lyon's penetrating exposés of racism and the Civil Rights campaign in the South, in Dennis Stock's revelation of the world of jazz musicians, and in the candid camera spontaneity of William Klein's portrait of New York street-life.

To some extent Klein tapped the veins that fed popular art, but this was most uncomfortably evident in the photographs of Diane Arbus, with her disturbing portraits of twins, dress-alike couples, mental hospital patients, transvestites and circus performers. The remarkable posthumous success of the exhibition of her work indicated that the American public recognized itself in what Susan Sontag termed the 'idiot village' she depicted. A fine art photographer like Cindy Sherman, with her self-portraits in various guises, such as the starlet or the bobbysoxer, introduced a subtle vein of social comment. By graphically exploring American visual conventions in so far as they applied to women she also quietly pilloried conventional America. That same public was shocked by Robert Mapplethorpe's beautiful and overtly homosexual studies of the male form, especially when their representatives railed against the fact that they were exhibited under the patronage of the National Endowment for the Arts.

While photography remained in black and white there was bound to be a strong element of abstraction in its images, whatever their subject matter, and at first colour film presented a challenge to those who wished to retain a primary sense of design in the newer medium. One cameraman able to meet it was Ernst Haas, who in fact had a feeling for the expansion of design potential that colour offered. It was photographs like Haas's *Window Reflections on Third Avenue* that appear to have influenced the Hyper-Realist painters. In the 1970s painting was at the crossroads. Though some Pop painters, including Dine and Lichtenstein, had clearly developed their interpretations of the means and messages of popular culture with a view to expanding their range as artists, there was a suspicion that the 'anything goes' philosophy was self-destructive. Unexpectedly, many artists turned to the photograph for direction. 'The trouble with Pop Art is that it made too much comment. Once you get the message you lose interest', declared Richard Estes.[8] (It was an observation that some would apply to his own work.)

Hyper-Realism depended heavily on the use of the camera. Combining the pin-sharp clarity of the Precisionists with the unemotional detail of the lens, the Hyper-Realist depicted the modern American scene with a cool eye. Estes, a leading figure in the new trend, shared Haas's fascination with the reflections in shop windows. *Helenes Florist* played skilfully with multiple images. While Noel Mahaffey painted high-level views of St Louis or Phoenix with painstaking attention to detail and perspective, portrait-painter Chuck Close scrutinized the photographs of his sitters and inflated them to a scale which exposed every pore and facial hair. Others were obsessed — not too strong a word — with the glitter of chromium-plated motor cycles, or, in the case of John Cacere, with female underwear. Sculptors in the photographic vein were understandably few, but Duane Hanson was an exception. His *Woman with a Shopping Cart* was cruelly accurate, modelled, dressed and painted from hair curlers to towelling slippers with remorseless detail. Yet his life-like sculptures of a race riot or a motor-cycle accident conveyed their vivid messages with a concern which was not shared by the painters.

If Hyper-Realism indicated one way at the crossroads, the alternative route lead to a more disciplined abstraction. The 'painterly' approach of the Abstract Expressionists had been questioned by Newman and Reinhardt and their deliberate works, which left nothing to chance, had their followers. Among them were Ellsworth Kelly and Kenneth Noland. Kelly's *Manhattan* recalled Kline in its stark use of black and white, but his clever manipulation of the letters NY revealed a combination of wit and stark simplicity. The 'Hard Edge' definition of colour fields was picked up by Frank Stella, who used bands of Art Deco colours on shaped canvasses of deceptive complexity, such as *Tahkt-1-Suluyman 1*. Such Hard-Edge works with their self-evident modernism but subject-free design were bold and colourful without being distracting. As such they fitted the context of the board-room and the office of the progressive business executive. Corporate patronage, which had been little in evidence since Sheeler's work for the Ford Motor Company three decades before, regained its place in the 1960s. Eventually a quarter of the entire art market was to be taken by the purchases of commercial corporations.

The cool methodology of the Hard-Edge painters was more than matched by the Minimalism of the sculptors. Illusionism in painting was, for Donald Judd, 'one of the salient and most objectionable relics of European art'.[9] His own work in polished metal sheeting was uncompromisingly formal, repetitive, seemingly endless, and without titles — all allusion and illusion dispelled. Later he employed coloured and plastic materials, though with the same classical control. Judd's boxes had their linear complement in the constructions of Sol LeWitt, whose *7 Part Variation of 2 Different Cubes* summarized the formal problems and solutions of the Minimalist sculptors. Such reductionism found many supporters among artists who were dissatisfied with the spontaneity of the 'creative accident'. One was Dan Flavin, who exploited the potential of fluorescent tubes while succeeding in draining from them all their sensual connotations.

Large-scale sculpture is expensive to construct and install, but it is usually durable and suited to exposure in open locations where it can be appreciated three-dimensionally. More to the taste of many artists than the exclusivity of much corporate sponsorship was the introduction in some cities of a percentage levy on all building contracts for the public purchase of art. In Washington State, for example, the Seattle Arts Commission administered 1 per cent of the costs of all county and city construction projects for the purchase and installation of artworks in public places. Over 300 works of art are now on view in parks and buildings, including rock sculpture by Heizer.

Commercial and civic patronage ensured increasing support for American artists in the 1970s and 1980s, but a number literally turned in on themselves fearing perhaps, that patronage also implied a measure of control. Some, like Vito Acconci and Bruce Nauman, moved into the fields of 'Body Art', where the artist's own physical attributes and secretions became the basis of creativity; others, such as Hans Haacke, chose the rarified realms of Conceptual Art, where the idea and the activity took precedence over the making of a product. Conversely, computers and the electronic technologies opened up new possibilities for a number of artists, while video art was capable of synthesizing within one product a variety of means and techniques. Doris Chase is just one of a number of artists whose use of video combines movement, time and sculptural form, as in her 'filmdance', *Circles II*. The nature of their media and the rapidity of communications facilitated links with artists of similar inclinations all over the world.

In the 1980s the pluralism that was detectable in all aspects of society was evident in the diverse directions which artists felt free to pursue. While the veterans of the early postwar era like de Kooning or Reinhardt were still producing with the conviction of their maturity, younger artists like John Alexander and David Reed carried abstraction and expressionism in to a new era. A revived delight in the physical act of painting was to be seen in the work of many – even beneath the broken ceramics of Julian Schnabel's collages. Ceramics, in the form of personally ritualized dinner plates each devoted to a distinguished woman and place set as if for a meal, figured prominently in *The Dinner Party* installation of the feminist artist Judy Chicago, while Terry Allen mixed media and technology and pop imagery with perplexing wit. Through the greater use of media and the installation of public art, immediate communication with an ever more sophisticated audience was possible, and patronage was provided to an unprecedented level. With the confidence gained by autonomy and the awareness that the creative torch had been wrested from Parisian fingers, the question of national and personal identity was, it seemed, no longer an issue.

Not, at any rate, for the artist of the American mainstream. But for the artists of the nation's racial and ethnic minorities there were battles still to be won.

SOLDIERS ON THE FRONTIER

For black Americans, Hispanics and Indians, groups continually viewed as 'others' by the dominant culture, as earlier contributions here, especially Chapter 6, have emphasized, access to means of expression and the issue of identity have always been fraught with tensions beyond the control of the individual. While by the mid-twentieth century Jewish artists, for example, including several figures treated here, could declare their Jewishness and decide whether or not to exhibit at New York's Jewish Museum almost at will, for members of the three groups mentioned above the position was different. Racism and economic disparities meant that for a very long time there were proportionately fewer trained artists – though there were singular naive artists, most notably Horace Pippin, the black painter whose *John Brown* series constituted a moving tribute to the firebrand Abolitionist. And when racial minority artists were permitted to participate in the general art movements of their times, they had to determine, not always wholly for themselves, the degree to which they would represent their group.

Aaron Douglas and Charles Alston were WPA muralists who used the stylized mannerisms of the time to document rural and urban ghetto scenes, while Richmond Barthe sculpted powerful bronze nudes in a manner akin to Jacob Epstein. The most celebrated African American painter of the first half of the century, invited by Albers to join the faculty at Black Mountain, was Jacob Lawrence, who used the semi-abstract Cubist-derived shapes of the 1940s Modernism to make forceful statements of black life in his *Migration of the Negro* and *Harlem* series. Acclaim came later to Romare Bearden who used biblical themes for his expressive, Picasso-inspired paintings, before using collage in such works as *The Prevalence of Ritual: Baptism*.

After the Second World War, many black artists participated in the new movements, among them Charles White whose *Wanted Poster* series used Pop Art techniques to make sober indictments of racist victimization. More pointed than those by Jasper Johns, the 'Flag' paintings of Faith Ringgold delivered angry messages; none more so than the stars and stripes that spelled the title of *Die Nigger*. Pop design and techniques were particularly suited to activist propaganda and the Black Arts Movement, with its declared allegiance to Black Power, had many adherents. 'I'm not trying to be aesthetically pleasing. I'm trying to be relevant', declared Dana Chandler; *Fred Hampton's Door*, his moving memorial to the violent death of the Black Panther leader, with its bullet-riddled detail, was effectively both.[10]

Some artists, among them Barbara Chase-Riboud, found inspiration in their African heritage rather than in the American black experience. Her early bronze *The Last Supper* was supported by Senufo-derived masks made by the African lost-wax casting process. In the immense public sculptures executed in sheet aluminium, stained glass, stone and canvas, paint-bespattered and brilliantly animated, Sam Gilliam explored, as he termed it, 'a different kind of jazz'.[11] Increasingly, a number of black artists have participated in the main currents of contemporary American art, secure perhaps in the recognition they have attained. But for others, working and living in the ghettos of Washington and a score of other cities, art, and particularly external mural painting, has become a vehicle for the finding and assertion of African American identity.

This has been the case to some extent with the Hispanic artists whose numbers have multiplied in recent years as the Latin-American minority has grown (see Chapter 7). Their artistic presence has been felt since the early 1960s in the challenging murals of East Los Angeles proclaiming the solidarity of 'La Raza', or those painted by Los Artes Guadalupanos de Aztlan in Santa Fe, New Mexico. During the 1970s and 1980s many artists, supported by local networks, were emerging in the Hispanic *barrios* of the cities. Their sources were various: the popular culture of Mexican Roman Catholicism and The Day of the Dead, the exhilaration of carnival, the wall art of the streets, the tradition of Mexican muralists. The masked figures and half-menacing revellers in the paintings of Gilbert Sanchez Lujan and Carlos Almaraz, born in the war years, reveal many of these characteristics, if not influences. In the violent *Discussion at the Table* by the Texan artist Rolando Briseno and the grotesque sophisticates in *Cabin Fever* by the Los Angeles artist Gronk, Expressionist Realism regains its power for social comment. Yet it was not until 1988 that a major national exhibition of Hispanic painters was held. Under the significant title 'Resistance and Affirmation' more than eighty Chicano artists exhibited at the Wight Art Gallery, on the campus of the University of California, Los Angeles, in 1990, indication enough of the burgeoning art that stems from this minority.

And the first Americans, the descendants of the aboriginal peoples that inhabited the continent? What part have they played in modern art in the United States? Native American art has flourished on the Reservations, often in symbolist forms that relate to traditional functions, such as pueblo and tipi painting, though sometimes bearing the evidence of the stylization introduced by 'Anglo' teachers. Many Navajo, Apache, Hopi, Sioux and Kiowa painters, often working in water-colour, contributed to this extension of tradition. 'Every tribe has as a life style this way of art, not a self-conscious thing, but a way of beauty', stated Fritz Scholder.[12] In Europe, Scholder saw the work of the English artist Francis Bacon, whose influence on his portraits, such as *Indian With Beer Can*, was releasing rather than limiting. Scholder's later paintings and prints are as impressive as any by contemporary American artists. And mention of the commercially successful R.C. Gorman, or Dan Naningha, painter of vibrant South-western landscapes, or Michael Kabotie, one of the founders of Artists Hopid, a pueblo painters' collaborative, should show that the Indian contribution to American modern art is not just token, but varied, becoming institutionalized and vigorous.

Soldiers, a painting by T.C. Cannon, a Kiowa and one of Scholder's influential students, depicted a spread-eagled figure, half Indian, half American cavalryman, at once a symbol of opposition and of one nation. For Native American artists, as for African and Hispanic Americans, theirs is less a problem of finding their identity than of recovering their pride in it, and of making that identity known and respected by Americans as a whole. There are still many battles to be fought in the revolution that began with the Armory Show.

Over the century American artists of the mainstream have not only liberated themselves from the ties of Europe but have dominated Western art. Exhibitions in national public collections and the private galleries of So-Ho, and the patronage of collectors, corporations and civic authorities have been secured for innumerable artists over several years. Access to the American public, through Federal Art Projects, the borrowing of idioms in Pop Art, the invention of participatory art forms, and the use of modern communication media has been achieved on a considerable scale. The question of American identity, on which at one time every mainstream artist was likely to pronounce, is also no longer an issue. Except, that is, for the ethnic minorities. Observing the energetic, sometimes somewhat crude and polemical but always vibrant and challenging art of identifiably proud black Americans, Hispanics and Native Americans, one cannot but be aware of the contrast with the cool asceticism of Minimalism, the narcissism of Hyper-Realism, the cerebral games of Conceptual Art or the affluent media manipulation of Video Art. Was the identity of the American mainstream artist bought at too high a price?

NOTES

1. Diego Rivera, 'The Revolution in Painting', *Creative Art*, IV (1929), pp. 298–30.

2. Quoted in Marlene Park and Gerald E. Markowitz, *New Deal for Art* (New York, 1977), p. 12.

3. Robert Motherwell, Statement in TV interview with Bryan Robertson in 'Art, N.Y.', 15 December 1964.

4. Jackson Pollock, 'My Painting', *Possibilities* **1** (Winter, 1947–48): 78–82.

5. William Zorach, 'New Tendencies in Art', *Arts* **4** (1923): p. 179.

6. Quoted in Lucy Lippard, *Pop Art* (London, 1966), p. 23.

7. Quoted in John Russell and Suzi Gablick, *Pop Art Redefined* (London, 1969), p. 97.

8. Quoted in Linda Chase, *Hyperrealism* (London, 1975), p. 12.

9. Donald Judd, 'Specific Objects' (Statement), *Arts Yearbook*, No. 8 (New York, 1965), p. 82.

10. Quoted in Elsa Honig Fine, *The Afro-American Artist* (New York, 1973), p. 203.

11. This was the title of Sam Gilliam's 1987 one-person show; see 'Sam Gilliam's Art for Public Places', *Dialogue* **79**, No. 1 (1988), p. 64.

12. Fritz Scholder, quoted in C.R. Wenzell, *Artists of Santa Fé* (Boston, 1969), p. 42.

SUGGESTIONS FOR FURTHER READING

There is a considerable literature on modern American art. Much is in the form of monographs on individual artists and, to a lesser extent, on schools, groups or movements. Many of these books have excellent illustrations in full colour. They can be found in library catalogues under the proper nouns used in this chapter; many are cited in Bernard Karpel (ed.), *Arts in America: A Bibliography*, 4 vols (Washington, DC, 1979) and *The Britannica Encyclopedia of American Art* (New York, 1973). Nevertheless, books are no substitute for seeing the original art works. Most of the major cities of Europe and the United States have public galleries with collections of modern art, frequently with good representation of American works.

The following books are general works which develop at length some of the aspects of American art broached in this chapter. For a reasonably comprehensive overview, *American Art Since 1900: A Critical*

History (London, 1967) by Barbara Rose is useful. A larger work is Sam Hunter's *American Art of the Twentieth Century* (London, 1973). *Masterworks of American Photography* (Birmingham, AL, 1982) by Martha A. Sandweiss is an illustrated history of its subject, and American photographers figure prominently in both Beaumont Newhall's standard *The History of Photography* (rev. edn, London, 1982) and Susan Sontag's important critique *On Photography* (Harmondsworth, 1979). Alan Trachtenberg, *Reading American Photographs* (New York, 1989) is a major study and Mick Gidley provides a clear pamphlet–length treatment in *American Photography* (Durham, 1983).

The first twenty years of American modernism is surveyed in Milton W. Brown, *American Painting: From the Armory Show to the Depression* (Princeton, NJ, 1955), and *Alfred Stieglitz and the American Avant-Garde* (London, 1977) by William Innes Homer shows how the New York art world took shape, a topic extended almost to the present by Peter Conrad's *The Art of the City: Views and Versions of New York* (New York, 1984). A book written closer in time to the developments it describes, and still refreshing, is John J.H. Bauer, *Revolution and Tradition in Modern American Art* (Cambridge, MA, 1951).

Art in the 1930s was not well reviewed until recently, but Francis V. O'Connor edited a useful collection of papers in *Art for the Millions* (Boston, 1973), Park and Markowitz wrote the more localized study cited in the Notes, and Richard D. McKenzie produced *The New Deal for Artists* (Princeton, 1973). The political commitments of the artists themselves are frequently stated in David Shapiro (ed.), *Social Realism: Art as a Weapon* (New York, 1973). Important histories include Belisario R. Contreras, *Tradition and Innovation in New Deal Art* (Lewisburg, PA, 1983), Karal Ann Marling, *Wall-to-Wall America: A Cultural History of Post Office Murals in the Great Depression* (Minneapolis, 1982) and Philip S. Foner and Reinhard Schultz, *The Other America: Art and the Labour Movement in the United States* (London, 1985). FSA photography is treated in F. Jack Hurley, *Portrait of a Decade: Roy E. Stryker and the Development of Documentary Photography in the Thirties* (Baton Rouge, LA, 1972) and Carl Fleischhauer and Beverly W. Brannan (eds), *Documenting America 1935–1943* (Berkeley, 1988).

Postwar art developments are surveyed by various authors: Henry Geldzahler, *New York Painting and Sculpture, 1940–1970* (London, 1969); Lawrence Alloway, *Topics in American Art Since 1945* (New York, 1975); Dore Ashton, *American Art Since 1945* (London, 1982); and William Seitz, *Abstract Expressionism in America* (Cambridge, MA, 1983). A provocative view is Serge Guilbert's *How New York Stole the Idea of Modern Art* (Chicago, 1983), which stresses the Cold War as a context. Important specific movements are covered in: *Black Mountain: An Exploration in*

Community (London, 1972) by Martin Duberman; *Happenings: An illustrated Anthology* (London, 1965) by Michael Kirby; and *Pop Art* (London, 1966) by Lucy R. Lippard. The most influential contemporary critics were Clement Greenberg, *Art and Culture* (Boston, 1961) and Harold Rosenberg, *The Anxious Object* (New York, 1964). For additional material on photography, Marianne Fulton, *Photojournalism in America* (Boston, 1988) is helpful, and for this particular period, see Helen Gee, *Photography of the Fifties: An American Perspective* (Tucson, AZ, 1980).

More recent art phenomena are discussed in Calvin Tomkins, *The Scene: Reports on Post-Modern Art* (New York, 1976) and evoked in S. Nairne, *State of the Art: Ideas and Images in the 1980s* (London, 1987) and the catalogue of a show at the Ceolfrith Gallery, Sunderland: *Who Chicago: Contemporary Images* (1981). Policy, patronage and commercial support are documented in such works as James M. Rupp and Mary Radlett, *Art in Seattle's Public Places* (Seattle, 1991) and Rosanna Martorella, *Corporate Art* (Newark, NJ, 1991).

A pioneering study of African American art, first published in 1943, is James A. Porter's *Modern Negro Art* (New York, 1969), and Elsa Honig Fine's book, cited in the Notes, expands on the theme. The evolution of a tradition in Native American art is discussed by Clara Lee Tanner in *Southwest Indian Painting: A Changing Art* (Tucson, AZ, 1973), and later trends are illustrated in Jaymake Highwater, *The Sweet Grass Lives On: Fifty Contemporary North American Indian Artists* (New York, 1980). We have to wait for a comprehensive study of Hispanic American art, but some is illustrated in 'Hispanic Art in America', *Dialogue* **81** (Autumn, 1988): 64–71, available in many libraries.

CHAPTER FOURTEEN
American Genre Fiction

Cynthia Hamilton

The figure in faded denims packs a six-shooter on his hip. His eyes are shaded by his broad-brimmed hat as he strides alone down the middle of a dusty street. The spaceship hurtles through space to a destination light years away. The mansion is isolated, surrounded by perpetual dusk. Its endless rooms, dim corridors, threatening shadowy nooks, and dark cellars perpetually disorientate and threaten the hapless visitor. Such are the stock figures and settings of American genre fiction which spark immediate recognition. American genre fiction has clearly come of age, for it can count on an audience aware of its conventional elements. This awareness is not the result of reading only. Radio, film, television and the comics – each with its tendency towards genre construction for economic reasons, as we saw in Chapter 10 – have all played their part in building a vocabulary of stock images.

Robert Coover's *A Night at the Movies or, You Must Remember This* (1987) illustrates the way fiction can draw very directly on the images from an assortment of genres. Here Coover explores the different weight and treatment given to death in various genre films. We are introduced to this programme of coming attractions by an old projectionist who tries a variety of techniques to see beyond the mere image on the screen, for as both he and Rick (from the book's version of *Casablanca*) realize, 'it is not so much about the frames, their useless dated content, as the gaps between: infinitesimally small when looked at two-dimensionally, yet in their third dimension as deep and mysterious as the cosmos'. The most interesting works of genre fiction are those in which the writer, like the old projectionist, attempts to see beyond the common structuring elements which give a genre its particular identity, exploring the gaps and hidden assumptions in the formula. As Coover realizes, the playful author can count on the strength of the associational power of conventional images, and so can use them in unusual ways since he and his audience share a common awareness of generic structures and images. Ishmael Reed's *Yellow Back Radio Broke-Down* (1969) adapts many of the familiar images of the western. Richard Brautigan's *Willard and his Bowling Trophies: A Perverse Mystery* (1975) plays with the conventions of the crime novel. And Kurt Vonnegut's *Slaughterhouse 5* (1969), though it treats the bombing of Dresden in the Second World War, makes use of familiar scenarios from science fiction. All of these authors employ images in a way which calls on their readers to recognize the contrast between the conventional use of the images they import and the deliberately inappropriate use to which they put them.

The clarity of the generic identity of certain images and the extent to which they can survive transplantation into unusual contexts while retaining their generic resonance may seem to imply a discreteness of generic identity which is not, in fact, the case. It is easy to point to works which exemplify a generic formula in all its aspects, but such showpieces do not evidence the more problematic ground where genres blend together. Nonetheless, definitions of generic archetypes are extremely useful if they are not used as Procrustean beds for individual works. Defining typical structures and elements allows one to follow developments, identify blends, and discover the source of philosophical or ideological rifts which are otherwise difficult to explain. Still, defining genres is problematic, for they are extremely malleable. Authors using genre open up possibilities, shift the focus, change one element, and blend elements from different genres together to produce ever new variations, some of which become the starting point for whole new generic groupings.

CATEGORIES: WHAT CATEGORIES?

If one looks at the chameleon nature of science fiction, some of the problems of generic definition become apparent. All works of science fiction share a family resemblance, for they are all works of speculative fiction which extrapolate from social or climatic trends or from technological advances or possibilities. But the range of possibilities which such extrapolation allows is enormous, and science fiction displays that variety: adventure fiction such as Alan Dean Foster's *Icerigger* (1974); crime stories like Ray Bradbury's *Fahrenheit 451* (1953); and utopian novels like

Ursula LeGuin's *The Dispossessed* (1974). As Isaac Asimov comments in the Introduction to a collection of his mysteries:

> There is a tendency for many people who don't know any better to classify
> science fiction as just one more member of the group of specialized
> literatures that include mysteries, westerns, adventures, sports stories, love
> stories, and so on. This has always seemed odd to those who know science
> fiction well, for s.f. is a literary response to scientific change, and that
> response can run the entire gamut of the human experience. Science fiction,
> in other words, includes everything.[1]

The thriller, with its many subgenres – the classical mystery, the hard-boiled detective novel, the crime novel, the police procedural, and the spy story – poses similar problems in a less extreme form. As a group thrillers deal with crime, be it personal, social or international. Their plots involve a quest for victim or criminal. Grouping works together as thrillers highlights one set of common elements, allowing comparisons among subgenres despite the highly distinctive features each has. For example, the recognition of family resemblances behind the differences invites comparisons between the way 'crime' is conceived in these various subgenres.

In the context of American culture, adventure writing and its different subgenres, including its relationships to other major generic strands, such as the gothic and the sentimental novel, provide the most useful points of departure, and will do so here. There are many subgenres of American adventure writing: the Indian captivity narrative, the slave narrative, the frontier romance, the novel of frontier adventure, the western, the adventure detective novel, the hard-boiled detective novel, the crime novel, the police procedural, the historical romance, and the space opera. All these subgenres feature a hero or heroine trapped in a hostile environment who must use all his/her resources to survive and to achieve whatever success is possible.

GOTHIC, HORROR AND THE FRONTIER

The first American novels drew on genres which had been popular in Britain and were to have a significant and lasting influence on American literature: the sentimental novel and the gothic romance. Imports such as Horace Walpole's *The Castle of Otranto* (1764) found favour with the American reading public, as did American reprints beginning with an edition of Richardson's *Pamela* in 1744. Popularity provided a strong motive for imitation, and by the end of the century American offerings had appeared: William Hill Brown's sentimental novel *The Power of Sympathy* (1789) and Charles Brockden Brown's gothic novel *Wieland* (1798). The uniqueness – or, at least, the special nature – of the American wilderness experience left its mark on both genres very quickly, as Susannah Rowson's *Reuben and Rachel* (1798) and Brockden Brown's *Edgar Huntly* (1799) show. While the wilderness experience provided the sentimental novelist with fresh costuming and a new set of trials for the heroine and hero, the gothic novelist found material which amplified the characteristic themes of that genre: 'The oldest and strongest emotion of mankind is fear', comments H.P. Lovecraft, 'and the oldest and strongest fear is fear of the unknown'.[2] In his Preface to *Edgar Huntly*, Brockden Brown compared the 'incidents of Indian hostility and the perils of the Western wilderness' to the 'Gothic castles and chimeras' used by British writers to excite such passions and sympathies.

The gothic potential of the wilderness consisted in its ability to shatter expectations and beliefs about 'normal' experience. Both Edgar Allan Poe's *The Narrative of Arthur Gordon Pym* (1838) and H.P. Lovecraft's *At the Mountains of Madness* (1931), a work inspired by Poe's *Narrative*, depict the psychological impact of a new world so beyond normal expectations that it shatters all preconceptions and introduces a new threatening reality, an apocalyptic quality. Traditionally, the gothic had dealt with threats on a more directly personal level. With its haunted castles, pursued maidens, monsters and gothic villains, it depicted threatened innocence and tortured, shameful guilt. On this personal level, the motifs of the gothic were, as Kate Ferguson Ellis argues, closely related to the domestic concerns of the sentimental novel:

> Focusing on crumbling castles as sites of terror, and on homeless protagonists who wander the face of the earth, the Gothic, too, is preoccupied with the home . . . . Either the home has lost its prelapsarian purity and is in need of rectification, or else the wandering protagonist has been driven from the home in a grotesque reenactment of God's punishment of Satan, Adam, and Eve.[3]

The gothic castle, the nightmare home, where guilt and shame rather than innocence hold sway and where feminine virtue is threatened rather than preserved, has long been a set piece of gothic fiction. Recognizable versions of the gothic castle feature in such diverse works as George Lippard's *The Quaker City* (1844–45), Nathaniel Hawthorne's *The House of the Seven Gables* (1851), William Faulkner's *Sanctuary* (1931) and Stephen King's *The Shining* (1977). Perhaps the most interesting recent reincarnation of the gothic castle is to be found in the high-technology, high-security intensive care hospital in Robin Cook's *Coma* (1977), with its unethical trade in human organs for transplants.

The gothic novel and the horror fiction which is its descendent derive much of their power from the threat of violation. The threat may be physical, intellectual, spiritual or psychological, but is most acute when it comes not only from external forces, but from the recognition of kinship or complicity with those forces. Although the book as a whole provides a rather shallow reading experience, the dynamics of Bret Easton Ellis's *American Psycho* (1991) are revealing. The horror exists on several levels. The reader is presented with sickening descriptions of physical violence, and with a more covert hostility toward women which is deeply disturbing. On these levels, repulsion and (for the female reader) fear preclude identification. But on the more profound level of shared social values, where some identification is unavoidable, the social criticism of 1980s hedonism and conspicuous consumption is powerful and pointed. As an arbiter of tasteful dress to his friends and a child of conspicuous consumption, mass murderer Patrick Bateman is a model being: his materialistic value system is frighteningly 'normal'; it also enables Bateman to operate within society, for he is judged on his appearance rather than his character. Bateman literally embodies the terrifying closeness of the ordinary and the perverse.

CONTINUITY AND CHANGE: THE CASE OF FRONTIER FICTION

The development of frontier literature shows a range of strategies employed by writers to deal with a subject which has altered with time, with the most interesting developments occurring since the extinction of the actual frontier. Chapter 5 contains a discussion of some of the ideological factors at work in the creation of both the West and the western. The setting and focus of frontier fiction changed, and key concepts were redefined, as the tradition developed. Continuity has nevertheless been maintained, for all frontier literature, as John Cawelti has pointed out, examines the nature of the civilized in relation to some concept of the savage. However, the notion of savagery changes as the tradition develops. By the twentieth century, savagery is projected onto the Native Americans less often. Instead, it is used to explore the self-destructive forces emanating from the dominant society itself.

The first accounts of frontier adventure were the Indian captivity narratives. Following in the footsteps of Mary Rowlandson's extremely popular *A Narrative of the Captivity and Restoration of Mrs Mary Rowlandson*

(1682), the captivity narratives were autobiographical accounts of being taken and held prisoner by Native Americans until some form of ransom or rescue could be arranged. Louise Barnett has argued that the move from captivity narrative to frontier romance was characterized by a change in focus. Where the earlier captivity narrative focused on the trials and travels of the helpless captive, the frontier romance focused on the attempts of a hero to rescue the captives – a move from passive victim to active adventurer. James Fenimore Cooper's Leatherstocking tales, especially *The Last of the Mohicans* (1826) and *The Deerslayer* (1841), illustrate the outcome of this shift. Cooper's backwoodsman hero, Natty Bumppo, is the prototype for all the western heroes who follow. He is the restless, staunchly individualistic hero who acts in accordance with his own inbuilt sense of morality, and so can exist, because he carries within himself the civilizing force, and often must exist, due to his temperament as much as to practical necessity, outside society.

As the tradition of frontier literature develops, the nature of the frontier itself changes, mirroring, for a time, the spread of the nation across the continent. Owen Wister's *The Virginian* (1902) features a cowboy rather than a backwoodsman as hero, and its setting is much further west than any of the Leatherstocking tales. By Wister's time, the sense of the vastness and plenitude of the West had diminished markedly. The works of Rowlandson, Cooper, and Wister also reveal a changing attitude to nature, not only within the tradition, but within American society as well. For Rowlandson, the frontier is a 'vast and desolate wilderness', an attitude typical of her time, and one which imbued 'wilderness' with biblical echoes. Natty Bumppo, we are told in *The Deerslayer*, 'loved the woods for their freshness, their sublime solitudes, their vastness, and the impress that they everywhere bore of the divine hand of their Creator'; he has an appreciation of their significance and beauty typical of the Transcendentalists. Wister echoes his contemporary, Frederick Jackson Turner, whose views were evoked in Chapters 1 and 5, in seeing the Western frontier as a revitalizing force which trains and tests men liable to become soft from overmuch civilization.

When the frontier ceased to be a recent memory, frontier fiction, as a genre, risked becoming – and to some extent has become – a decadent form. One glimpses the anachronistic and nostalgic quality of the genre in Zane Grey's *The Code of the West* (1934), where the West has been invaded by flappers and automobiles. The transitory nature of the frontier meant that it was always threatened with incorporation into society. A nostalgic sense of impending loss, as well as a more forward-looking sense of progress were incorporated into the tradition as early as Cooper's *The Pioneers* (1823). There is a sense, of course, in which whatever the 'reality' of its actual settlement by whites, the frontier was *always* an imaginative projection and incorporation by the dominant society. Louis L'Amour's painstaking historical reconstructions are a logical progression from Wister's attempts to preserve for posterity 'a vanished world'.

If one frontier was closed, others beckoned. E.E. 'Doc' Smith and other writers of the space opera projected the frontier outward into space. Smith's Lensman series, with *Galactic Patrol* (serialized 1937–38) and *Grey Lensman* (serialized 1939–40), pits a western-style hero, with spaceship and blaster instead of horse and six gun, against a dangerous universe dominated by an evil alien conspiracy of awe-inspiring proportions. The best man wins, of course. But the link between speculative fiction and frontier literature is far deeper than the relocation of cowboys and Indians in space. In so far as the experience of the frontier shatters old assumptions and reveals new possibilities, it is closely associated with the apocalyptic imagination, as David Ketterer has pointed out:

> The discovery of America did in fact what the best science fiction stories attempt to do in imagination; the American perspective provided a radical re-orientation of man's perceptions and his understanding, and it placed man in a new context, with the result that a previously accepted, stable reality was cast abruptly into question.[4]

This is the ground on which science fiction, the gothic tradition, and frontier literature meet. Generic frontier literature has never fully explored its apocalyptic possibilities, though the progressive revelations in Smith's series move in that direction.

Inverted forms of the western formula, such as E.L. Doctorow's *Welcome to Hard Times* (1975) – in which the 'bad man from Bodie', far from being confronted by a virtuous opponent, is fawned upon – or Thomas Berger's *Little Big Man* (1964), attempt to reinterpret the meaning of the frontier from a different perspective. This was an endeavour which paralleled historical reassessments during the 1960s and 1970s of the contributions of disenfranchised groups to American social and cultural development. Like the hippie subculture of the 1960s, Berger's novel gives priority to an alternative *Weltanschauung*. *Little Big Man* reverses traditional hegemonic notions of savagery, and places its allegiance with the Native Americans, the Cheyennes (who, tellingly, call themselves 'the human beings') and their civilization, rather than with the marauding Army of the United States. The novel's boastful hero, Jack Crabb, who claims to have taken part in every significant event during the so-called taming of the frontier, is actually unconscious as many a battle rages. He is a travesty of the conventional hero, a wimpish braggart. Such inversions have considerable subversive potential, for they undermine traditional justifications for the conquest of the West. This is especially so when handled by Native

American authors, such as Gerald Vizenor, and Carter Revard and, in their extraordinary return to the conquest's beginning in *The Crown of Columbus* (1991), Louise Erdrich and Michael Dorris.

Discussion may shift from frontier experience to the genre itself, exposing the outmoded quality of conventional elements, and exploring discontinuities and absurdities in the formula itself, as well as in the ideology encoded within it. Readers have come to associate such self-reflexive genre fiction with postmodernist writers, but as Christine Bold has pointed out, novels like Robert Ward's *Cattle Annie and Little Britches* (1977) actually hark back to the work of self-conscious nineteenth-century dime novelists such as Edward S. Ellis and Edward Wheeler. The competing discourses of popular fiction achieve greatest visibility in fiction of this type. Reed's *Yellow Back Radio Broke-Down* is an extreme example. Reed's book resembles a jigsaw puzzle which has been put together without reference to the original design. The structural unity which gives coherence to the conventional elements in genre fiction is destroyed, leaving the individual elements fragmented and exposed. This makes it easy for Reed to highlight the racial bias of the traditional western. He does so explicitly through direct commentary, and implicitly through the incorporation of a noticeably 'inappropriate' colloquial style, jive talk, and an 'alien' voodoo tradition distinctly at odds with the nominally Christian base of the genre.

Though much more extreme, the subversive potential of Reed's novel is comparable with *Larramee's Ranch* (1924) by George Owen Baxter (Frederick Faust), for both are written from the perspective of an underclass and attack the dominant ideology which equates success with worth. Both draw on folk traditions which offer alternative value sets. Both provide their heroes with magical powers which allow them to triumph over those in entrenched positions of power. And both self-consciously draw attention to the fantastical nature of their stories, undermining the apparent naturalness of the formulaic discourse. But the differences between the two novels are significant. While Faust attacks the class bias of the western, Reed wreaks havoc in every sphere. Including Benjamin Franklin and John Wesley Hardin in a world where an Indian flies between Video Junction and Yellow Back Radio in a helicopter destroys the historical costuming of the traditional western and discounts the idea of progress so central to both frontier fiction and the culture which produced and consumed it. In *Yellow Back Radio Broke-Down*, the often coy treatment of sex in the genre is replaced by an overabundance of kinky sex mixed with violence. Reed's novel is a smash grab raid on the western which destroys its associational power without extending the possibilities of the formula; it is a very clever dead end work in which the rage directed at a genre which valorizes

WASP (White Anglo-Saxon Protestant) traditions and values is all-consuming.

AN INTERMITTENT TRADITION: THE CLASSICAL MYSTERY

Poe's ratiocinative tales, especially 'The Murders in the Rue Morgue' (1841), 'The Purloined Letter' (1845), and 'The Mystery of Marie Roget' (1842–43) are generally acknowledged as the origins of the classical mystery. Poe set the pattern with a detective whose extraordinary mental powers enabled him to solve crimes which baffled the police, and with his implicit definition of crime as an aberrant phenomenon traceable through the disruption left behind in the form of 'clues'. As Dorothy Sayers noted in her introductory essay to *The Omnibus of Crime* (1929), Poe developed many of the standard ploys of the classical mystery: the story narrated by a not-so-clever friend of the detective, the locked room and the wrongly suspected man. Poe's ratiocinative tales drew on a number of popular genres which had achieved a wide following in the United States, such as the gothic, exposés of crime, and pamphlets recounting the trials of famous criminals. Vidocq's *Memoires*, published in Paris in 1829, which purported to give details of real-life detection, undoubtedly influenced Poe as well.

Although he drew on popular traditions, Poe's particular blends did not immediately attract imitators. B.J. Rahn has identified the first American classical mystery novel as *The Dead Letter* (1867) by Seeley Regester (Metta Victoria Fuller Victor). The second is arguably Anna Katharine Green's *The Leavenworth Case* (1878). The gaps in time are significant; it was not until after the immense popularity of the Sherlock Holmes stories, and the rash of imitations they inspired, that the classical mystery achieved a critical mass sufficient to be recognizable as a genre. Mark Twain's *Tom Sawyer, Detective* (1896) was one of the many works which attempted to exploit Arthur Conan Doyle's popularity. By the 1940s, when Raymond Chandler complained of the sterility of the classical mystery, and expressed the desire to return murder to the people who really knew something about it, far from stately homes and country vicarages, publishers were successfully marketing mystery sets, and such writers as Ellery Queen and S.S. Van Dine had achieved enormous popularity. There was scant generic development, however, for the relative rigidity of the formula made it unproductive of diverse generic progeny. In contrast to frontier literature, the conventional elements proved to be difficult to redefine in ways which kept them freshly relevant to changing social preoccupations. It would be left to Chandler's breed of tough-guy writing to confront the vitality, aggression and sleaze of the modern American city.

Furthermore, the particular combination of elements conspired together to keep the focus of the genre narrow. Asimov's science-fiction mysteries *Caves of Steel* (1954) and its sequel *The Naked Sun* (1957) serve as the extensions which prove the case. Asimov questions the nature of the intellectual powers needed by the detective: could a robot, unimpeded by emotion and capable of gathering, sorting and storing information far more efficiently and completely than a human ever achieve intellectual superiority? Asimov's answer is negative. Like Poe, he argues that one must be a mathematician *and* a poet to reason well. The classical mystery allows Asimov, writing more than a century after Poe, to explore in a new context an old issue of fresh relevance.

LIMITLESS POSSIBILITIES: THE TOUGH GUYS

The roots of the tough-guy tradition of crime and detection are to be found in the episodic city novel, which laid bare the abuses of power within the city, depicted the flesh-pots of urban life, and gave vivid representation to the misery of the city poor. Eugene Sue's *The Mysteries of Paris* (1842) was undoubtedly influential in the development of this type of novel, as was the popularity, especially in America, of exposés of sensational crime in the popular press, the development of which was described in Chapter 10. The most important early example of a city novel is George Lippard's *The Quaker City*, a romp through the seamy underworld of Philadelphia. As David Reynolds has noted in *Beneath the American Renaissance* (1988), the city novels of the mid-nineteenth century justify their exposés as pleas for reform while taking a voyeuristic interest in scenes of crime and violence. It is this milieu and this tension which give rise to the adventure-detective of the 1880s, and eventually to the hard-boiled detective stories of the interwar years. Frontier adventure stories also had an impact. Most notably, the tradition of crime and detection appropriated the lawless world and individualistic hero of frontier fiction. Old Sleuth, who first made his appearance in 1872, and Old Captain Collier, who came on the scene a decade later, were two of the most popular early fictional detective heroes who battled with crime rather than detecting it. Fictionalized accounts of the exploits of the Pinkerton detective agency began appearing in the 1870s, and they too played a part.

The adventure detective novel came of age in the 1920s with the development of the hard-boiled, tough-guy detective formula by Dashiell Hammett, himself an ex-Pinkerton operative, and Carroll John Daly. The formula that emerged dealt with crime, like the earlier adventure detective story, and had a hero who, like the hero of frontier adventure, existed on the margins of society. The hard-boiled hero, however, is more conscious of his marginality and vulnerability. The toughness displayed when reacting to abuse with tight-lipped stoicism or wise-cracking rejoinders shows the hero's defiant acceptance of his potential victimization. His attitude toward society is also different: despite working within society, his code separates and protects him from the corruption which involvement, seemingly necessarily, invites. Nonetheless, the links between the western and tough-guy writing remain strong. Indeed, the hard-boiled detective novel has been called an urban western; both William Rhuehlmann and George Grella see it in this light. The closeness of these two subgenres of the American adventure formula can be appreciated in novels like Zane Grey's *The Lone Star Ranger* (1936) and Raymond Chandler's *The Lady in the Lake* (1944), which blend the two, as well as in Elmore Leonard's police procedural *City Primeval: High Noon in Detroit* (1980), which shows the continuing strength of the bond in further developments of the tough detective tradition.

The hard-boiled detective story is easily transformed into the police procedural, which uses a member of the official police force as hero, and focuses on the inadequacy of the routine investigative procedures and on the legal restraints which, in the name of civil liberty, are shown to give criminals the advantage. Making the hero a low-ranking police detective allows some degree of reintegration in society; he may even marry. But the detective's ability to solve the crime and bring the criminal to justice is often even more equivocal in the police procedural than in the hard-boiled detective novel. Ed McBain's 87th Precinct stories and Chester Himes's Harlem novels are good examples. Himes's *Blind Man With a Pistol* (1969) is particularly interesting because its attempts to portray a full canvas of social disorder and racial tension give it an episodic quality which harks back very strongly to the city novel as described by Reynolds. Since Himes fully exploits the formula's potential for pointed social criticism, in his work a popular form is used to offer voyeuristic – perhaps transgressive – pleasure *while* subverting the values of the dominant society. The procedural may voice the anxieties of those interested in the status quo or those who would challenge it; in either case it speaks of the flashpoints of a society where professed 'liberal' values sit uneasily upon real inequalities.

The detective figure in this tough school may be neither private eye nor policeman; he may be a journalist bent on exposing corruption in high places, as in Horace McCoy's *No Pockets in a Shroud* (1937), where the investigation – and book – end with the death of the hero. Even more interesting is Carl Bernstein and Bob Woodward's *All the President's Men* (1974), the title of which ironically recalls Robert Penn Warren's *All the King's Men* (1946), an account of the ascent and precipitous fall of a Southern demagogue, which was loosely based on the career of Huey Long, Governor of Louisiana in the 1930s. *All the President's Men* uses the hard-boiled detective formula to structure a 'New Journalistic' account of the unmasking of the Watergate Scandal which ultimately dethroned President Nixon. The criminal conspiracy, which in the hard-boiled detective novels of the interwar years often involved city officials, has found a larger focus. In *All The President's Men*, the President of the United States is at the centre of a web of corruption, coercive practices and deceit.

The hard-boiled detective story may move in the direction of exploring the psychological dynamics and effects of crime rather than its social consequences, as is the case with Ross MacDonald's Lew Archer stories. In these stories Archer is the observer and assessor of psychological disorder. Both Elmore Leonard and Paul Auster explore the bond between pursuer and pursued, recalling William Godwin's *Caleb Williams* (1794), Poe's detective's comments on the necessity of the detective's duplicating the thought processes of the criminal, and more generally, the gothic's preoccupation with the double. It is Auster who follows the psychological consequences of this process of identification to its logical conclusion in 'The New York Trilogy' (1985–86). Auster slows the action down to the point where, in *Ghosts*, the middle novella of the trilogy, the detective spends most of his time in one room watching his adversary sitting writing in a room across the street. The detective becomes aware that his quarry's mundane, pointless life is dominating his own, and that he has become nothing more than his quarry's shadow; that he has lost himself and faces psychic death.

The closeness of the detective mentality to that of the criminal is also a running theme in Don DeLillo's *Libra* (1988), a fictionalized account of the assassination of President Kennedy. It is at this point that one glimpses the close links between the crime novel and the hard-boiled detective story. James M. Cain's *The Postman Always Rings Twice* (1934), Truman Capote's *In Cold Blood* (1965), solidly based on an actual horrific murder and its perpetrators in a manner Capote called 'the non-fiction novel', and Elmore Leonard's *Glitz* (1985) show the shifting focus as one moves away from the pure crime novel toward the police procedural. While the crime novel follows the criminal as he moves toward his victim and attempts to evade arrest, the detective novel attempts to discover and apprehend the criminal; both are variants of the chase. Blends of the two are capable of heightened suspense, for the reader is aware of what must happen, but does not know when it will happen, or how. Leonard is particularly skilful at using and increasing this kind of suspense.

The versatility of the tough school of crime and detection is a result of its focus on the social dynamics of crime rather than on the detection of crime, a difference which W.H. Auden recognized when he praised the work of Chandler, who he said, 'is interested in writing, not detective stories, but serious studies of a criminal milieu, the Great Wrong Place'.[5] With such a focus, it is possible to vary the skills and attributes of the hero to cover a wide range of issues, and to vary the setting to depict a variety of types of social breakdown and lawlessness.

THE IMPERFECT MIRROR OF GENRE FICTION

The way crime is portrayed in the classical mystery is indicative of the focus of the genre on intellectual rather than social issues. However, the difference in focus does not mirror a difference in the perceived social realities of crime more generally at the time the two genres emerged, as is demonstrated by the city novel, which developed alongside of the classical mystery. With its strong sense of social corruption, conspiracy and the corrupting power of money, the city novel depicts crime in a manner much closer to the hard-boiled detective stories of a century later than to the contemporary ratiocinative tales of Poe. Genre literature, like all other forms of representation, is not an exact mirror of its time, especially if one focuses on a single development in genre literature, but it does reflect important concerns and preoccupations of the society which produces and consumes it. The interest in criminal conspiracy which one finds in the hard-boiled detective novel during the interwar years is a case in point. The Teapot Dome scandal of 1923 had unmasked corruption over the lease of oil rights within the federal government. The Pecora Committee exposed the dishonest practices at the heart of the financial world. And the growth of organized crime, based on sales of illegal alcohol during these same Prohibition years further stimulated public concern. When, in his highly acclaimed essay 'The Simple Art of Murder' (1944), Chandler criticized the classical mystery as a static, outdated, and implausible form, he was obviously voicing his distance from it. Nonetheless, one could argue that the enormous popularity of the classical mystery during the interwar years reflected the nostalgia of those years; that, like the hard-boiled detective story, it addressed, albeit in a different manner, the same sense of lost innocence.

The difference between the qualities assigned to the detective in the classical mystery and in the hard-boiled detective story is also indicative. Poe shared his interest in the power of rationality and in humankind's ability to assign definitive meaning to things and events with the other writers of the American Renaissance. The problematic process through which his detective distills meaning from evidence in 'The Murders in the Rue Morgue' is explored in a more complex manner by Hawthorne in *The Scarlet Letter* (1850). Hester Prynne attempts to understand, from the evidence of her child's behaviour, the nature of her child, and reading further backwards, the nature and meaning of her adultery. Like Dupin, Hester finds the evidence contradictory, but in contrast to Dupin's case, neither Hester nor the narrator present a formulation which accounts for all the contradictions. Legrand's attempts to decipher a code he has happened upon in another of Poe's ratiocinative tales, 'The Gold Bug' (1843), anticipate the more profound and equivocal decoding of the doubloon – or, indeed, of the White Whale himself – in *Moby Dick* (1851). And the impatience Dupin shows in 'The Purloined Letter' with those who cannot go beyond a mechanical level of analysis echoes some of the sentiments expressed in Emerson's essays (see Chapter 4).

The toughness of the hard-boiled detective reflects a sense of the diminishing power and significance of the individual. Henry Ford's introduction of the assembly line in 1914 made the individual attendant to the productive machinery, and the increasing rationalization of corporate structures, described in Chapter 8, made employees keenly aware of their subordination. Politically, the power of the party machine dwarfed the individual voter. And on the battlefields of the First World War, the individual soldier was made vividly aware of his vulnerability and individual insignificance. Heroes in books as different as F. Scott Fitzgerald's *The Great Gatsby* (1925) and John Dos Passos's *USA* (1937) share the tough hero's sense of the individual's loss of control over his own future. They also share the tough hero's sense of lost innocence. Unable to trust a society which appeared morally bankrupt, these heroes had to find alternative guidance for their lives. The code of Hammett's Op, which protects him from the meaninglessness and disorder that surround him, is closely related to the code of Ernest Hemingway's heroes which allows them to exhibit the necessary famous 'grace under pressure'. The weary cynicism of Hammett's heroes, like the careful self control of Hemingway's, reflects the isolation, uncertainty, and disillusionment of the 1920s.

One also finds an important shift in mood between the 1920s and 1930s in both the hard-boiled detective fiction and other literature of the period. The difference between the attitudes of Hammett's detectives and Chandler's reflects a more general shift from the cynicism of the Roaring Twenties to the activism of the New Deal years, as John Paterson has pointed out. The moral outrage and commitment to righting wrongs which one finds in *Farewell, My Lovely* (1940) is much closer to the attitude of John Steinbeck's *The Grapes of Wrath* (1939) than it is to that of Hemingway's *The Sun Also Rises* (1926). Genre fiction certainly reflects the changing moods, interests, and preoccupations of the society which produces and consumes it, but it is always a partial, imperfect reflection. If one were to derive a picture of society during the interwar years from the hard-boiled detective novel alone, one would miss both the continuing sympathies and influence of small-town America, as represented in such novels as Sinclair Lewis' *Main Street* (1920), and the importance of ethnic communities within the city, as represented in, for example, Mike Gold's *Jews Without Money* (1935) or James T. Farrell's Irish–American Studs Lonigan trilogy (1932–35).

Genre fiction distorts while reflecting society, for the depiction of society in formula fiction is by no means disinterested. Indeed, the metaphor of the mirror may be less than fully apt; genre fiction may best be viewed not as a reflection of society but as a site of *negotiation* of complex relationships – among readers, the 'culture industries' which market the fiction, overt political positions, the material institutions of class, race and gender, and more. The American adventure formula is, for example, dominated by male writers, male heroes, and a male perspective. Within this tradition, women have generally been viewed as prizes to be won, weak beings to be protected, civilizers whose presence in dangerous territory is inappropriate and inconvenient, or as temptresses dangerous to the hero. In novels of frontier adventure, women provide justification for the violence, as the hero rescues, or makes the world safe for them. In the hard-boiled detective novel, women precipitate much of the violence, either doing the killing themselves after disarming or weakening their prey, or using their sexuality to manipulate men into fighting for them. Both subgenres reinforce the notion of separate spheres for men and women. In the hard-boiled detective novel of the interwar years, the jaundiced view of women reflects a deep resentment toward those women who had, in increasing numbers, invaded traditionally male spheres in their attempt to achieve greater equality and personal fulfillment politically, occupationally and socially.

DOMESTICITY AND ADVENTURE

A tension has long existed in American genre writing between the domestic world and the world of adventure. Viewed from a male perspective conditioned by the idea of separate spheres, the ideal domestic world was one of tranquil stability, a haven from the world of commerce and adventure. One sees the sanctification of the domestic feminine sphere set against an active world of male adventure in Brown's *Edgar Huntly*, Cooper's *The Pioneers*, Wister's *The Virginian*, and Chandler's *Farewell, My Lovely*. A more complex portrayal of women's role is found in the sentimental novel. In *Reuben and Rachel*, Susannah Rowson makes it plain that the home can not be isolated from the outside world. Both the political situation in England and the insecurity of a home in the wilderness demonstrate the need for women to prepare themselves to meet the demands of a wider world. Furthermore, Rowson recreates a historical period when women are shown to rule effectively as monarchs.

In *Hope Leslie* (1827), Catherine Marie Sedgwick sets up a contrast between a young lady who is passive and retiring, exemplary in virtue and obedient to her elders, and one who is active in the community, outspoken and opinionated. Rewards are bestowed on the heroine who takes her life into her own hands and who defies the law of the community when it is used unjustly. Here again, a separate sphere of feminine virtue is denied as the heroine participates in the world beyond the home. As in Rowson's novel, a love plot is interwoven with an adventure, but, in contrast to the situation in novels by male writers which blend adventure with sentiment, such as William Alexander Caruthers's *The Cavaliers of Virginia* (1834), in Sedgwick's adventure interludes, the heroine is not left at home to brood. Mrs E.D.E.N. Southworth's *The Deserted Wife* (1850) contains a savage critique of the subjugation of women within the domestic sphere. When Hagar's husband sells the horse and dogs with which she has been accustomed to ride freely, he tells her, 'Come, love, you are a spirited little thing, but you will be docile by and by, and then – '. 'I wish you joy of your automaton!', Hagar responds. Later, Charlotte Perkins Gilman's 'The Yellow Wallpaper' (1892) depicts domestic tranquillity as a nightmare of isolated imprisonment, and Kate Chopin's 'Charlie' (1900) explores the impossible choice posed by separate spheres for a woman of spirit and enterprise.

One does find strong heroines in the tradition of frontier literature. Surveying the Amazonian heroines of the dime novels of the late 1870s, and more particularly the 1880s, Henry Nash Smith finds little difference between the behaviour and accomplishments of such strong female heroines as Hurricane Nell and Calamity Jane, both the creations of Edward Wheeler, and the traditional male hero. As Smith also points out, however, such heroines are treated as exceptional within the stories themselves, and their behaviour is often motivated and justified by some wrong done to them by a man in their past. Jenni Calder argues that there

327

are basically two types of western heroine: 'the decorative heroine, who is associated with civilization, domesticity, the schoolhouse and the church, and the spunky heroine, who is not averse to riding the range and encountering man-sized dangers but who is almost always sufficiently tamed to provide a suitable mate for the hero'.[6] The spunky heroine, as the many examples in Grey's westerns show, is apt to discover that her true nature yearns to yield to the protective arms of a strong and worthy man. Not surprisingly, given this essentially male viewpoint of American adventure fiction, full-blown westerns by women writers, such as B.M. Bower's *Chip of the Flying U* (1906), are scarce. Women have found other forms more serviceable in writing about their frontier experiences. In addition to sentimental novels, journals and diaries, we have Willa Cather's compelling accounts of life on the remote farms of the Midwest in *O Pioneers!* (1913) and *My Antonia* (1918), and the much earlier descriptions of life in the backwoods of Tennessee, *In the Tennessee Mountains* (1884) and *The Prophet of the Great Smoky Mountains* (1885), both by George Egbert Craddock (Mary N. Murfree).

Female sleuths within the tradition of adventure detectives are also rare. Indeed, Kathleen Klein has estimated that only fifteen of the some 500 detective novels put out by dime-novel publishers Beadle and Adams featured female investigators. Nonetheless, Harlan P. Halsey, creator of Old Sleuth, also introduced Kate Goelet in *The Lady Detective* (1880). Although Goelet is a formidable adversary, she quickly succumbs to matrimonial inclinations. Edward L. Wheeler, the creator of Calamity Jane, also gave his readers *New York Nell, the Boy–Girl Detective* (1886), a figure he married off at the end of a single novel. At a later date, we have the decidedly unsympathetic Bertha Cool, created by A.A. Fair (Erle Stanley Gardner), who first appeared in *The Bigger They Come* (1939) and the bumbling Dol Bonner of Rex Stout's *The Hand in the Glove* (1937). Given such an ancestry and the jaundiced view of women in the hard-boiled tradition, the introduction of Sue Grafton's Kinsey Millhone and Sara Paretsky's V.I. Warshawski is highly significant. The female detectives of these female writers are well aware of the incongruity of their position, for they are constantly reminded that they are women doing 'men's work'. Such novels as Paretsky's *Killing Orders* (1985) and Grafton's *D is for Deadbeat* (1987) show women who are well-balanced, competent and realistically aware of their vulnerability. Paretsky's work is especially noteworthy, for she works to expose the male bias of the formula.

The male domination of the American adventure formula raises the issue of gender specific interpretations, and, as was hinted above, of readership. Are novels of frontier and detective adventure written by men for men? Much of the criticism of these genres certainly implies that this is the case. Discussion tends to focus on the hero, assuming that the reader identifies with this male figure fully. John G. Cawelti discusses the appeal of the western in terms of the Oedipal conflict and in terms of the western's strong reinforcement of male dominance. When Jerry Palmer discusses the treatment of sexuality in the thriller, he focuses on the male hero's needs, and sees sexual encounters as confrontations in which the male must demonstrate control. Daryl E. Jones sees Calamity Jane not as strong female heroine, but as the victim of male violation. The question of the actual readership of American adventure fiction is one that is very difficult to answer.

Michael Denning states the case succinctly: 'Recent accounts of the readers of dime novels by literary critics and cultural historians tend to be rather vague.'[7] His own attempts to piece together some picture of readership from the contemporary accounts of nineteenth-century observers and reformers as well as from workers' autobiographies and memoirs, though emphasizing class rather than gender, are noteworthy. Similarly, not enough work has been done on the actual readership of the western and hard-boiled detective novel in the twentieth century to define the audience with certainty. Still, the serialization of many of Grey's westerns in leading women's magazines, and the number of letters from women published in *Western Story Magazine* should keep one from jumping to easy conclusions. The question of how female readers handle male-centred genres like the western and hard-boiled detective fiction cannot be answered simply. Clearly, for the female reader there is always a double awareness, of identification and separation. But even those aspects of the genre which at first glance would appear to make it most off-putting may be capable of alternative readings. It is possible, for example, to see the fear of sexuality which one finds in the hard-boiled detective novel as a tribute to the power of female sexuality.

EXPLOITING THE POLEMICAL POTENTIAL OF GENRE FICTION

During the first half of the nineteenth century, genre fiction was made to service the needs of reform very directly. The temperance novel, a variant of the sentimental novel, developed in conjunction with the temperance crusade which flourished in the years after 1820. T.S. Arthur's *Ten Nights in a Bar Room* (1854) and Sarah Josepha Hale's *My Cousin Mary; or, The Inebriate* (1839) are crudely managed cautionary tales which chronicle the descent into misery, penury and degradation which visited the abuser of alcohol and his family. Also during this period, the slave narrative was appropriated by the abolitionist cause to document the case against slavery. Slave narratives such as those by William Grimes (1825) and Henry Box Brown (1849) chronicled the abuses and miseries of slavery, and charted the slave's attempts to secure freedom. Frederick Douglass's enormously popular *Narrative of the Life of an American Slave* (1845) shows the genre at its sophisticated best. Novelistic accounts such as Richard Hildreth's *The Slave* (1836) and Harriet Beecher Stowe's *Dred* (1856) develop the potential links between the slave narrative and the adventure story.

Whereas both the temperance novel and the slave narrative became vehicles for a single perspective on a single social issue, the relationship between the utopian novels of the 1890s and the social debates of those years is more complicated. The outpouring of utopian, anti-utopian, and dystopian fiction sparked off by the publication of Edward Bellamy's *Looking Backward* (1888) is remarkable. Kenneth Roemer's study of the utopian novels published between 1888 and 1900 is based on over 150 works, many of which show the influence of Bellamy's work. Bellamy's achievement was the successful blending of conventional elements drawn from the tradition of the sentimental novel with elements drawn from the tradition of speculative fiction within the overriding pattern of the utopian novel. The synthesis which Bellamy achieved had already been anticipated in some measure. There was a long association of the sentimental novel with reform causes. Bellamy combined his futuristic setting, complete with technological wonders, with characters drawn from the sentimental tradition. His characters, despite their novel surroundings, brought with them values which were reassuringly familiar, and involved themselves in domestic situations which were commonplace.

Looking Backward, as is usual in the utopian novel, transports its hero to an alternative society. Typically, the new society is compared to the society left behind, enabling an analysis of the ills of that homeland. The alternative society which Bellamy depicts traces the logic of trends within late nineteenth-century society to their natural conclusions, however. The increasing horizontal and vertical integration practised by industry has led to a centrally controlled economy, and the unions have become an industrial army. Because Bellamy's utopia was a vision of what could develop, it had tremendous emotive power, a power which is demon-strated by the outpouring of literary responses to that novel. Richard C. Michaelis's *Looking Further Forward, An Answer to Looking Backward by Edward Bellamy* (1890) and Ludwig Geissler's *Looking Beyond; A Sequel to 'Looking Backward', by Edward Bellamy, and An Answer to 'Looking Further Forward', by Richard Michaelis* (1891) give some indication of the furore raised by Bellamy's work.

GENRE FICTION AND LITERATURE

Much genre fiction is classified as popular culture rather than as literature, but this apparent binary divide is no more absolute than the generic categories themselves. While it is certainly true that genre fiction relies on conventional elements and structural formulas, these conventional attributes need not restrict its range or depth. Such postmodernist writers as Thomas Pynchon, DeLillo and Doctorow show their awareness that one of the widest, richest referential systems which they and their audience share is that of genre literature and its media spin-offs.

When, in Pynchon's *The Crying of Lot 49* (1966), Oedipa squints into the sunlight as she takes her Impala down a slope which overlooks San Narciso, or when she walks the almost deserted streets of San Francisco late at night – 'that optimistic baby [who] had come on so like the private eye in any long-ago radio drama' – typical scenarios from the western and the hard-boiled detective genres spring immediately to mind. Pynchon plays with the joke of Oedipa as private eye, as anyone familiar with the genre will recognize. Pynchon's borrowings are not superficial, however. He uses the basic plot pattern of the hard-boiled detective novel, with Oedipa initially unaware of what the job she takes on will involve. As she proceeds, she must uncover the extent and nature of a conspiracy, if it exists, and her task becomes inexplicably more dangerous, and more complex. This could act as a plot summary for any number of hard-boiled detective novels. Not surprisingly, in Pynchon's work there are strong echoes of Hammett's, for both explore the cosmic chaos which is a magnification of the essential lawlessness of the private eye's world. Even the term 'private eye' is exploited by Pynchon, who uses it to emphasize the solipsistic nature of Oedipa's quest.

It is easy to recognize borrowings by contemporary authors from generic traditions which are still vital components of our popular culture. The problem comes when one deals with contemporary authors who borrow from more distant popular genres, as is the case with Toni Morrison's *Beloved* (1987), a novel described in Chapter 6, which draws on the tradition of the slave narrative. It is even more difficult to spot borrowings by major authors of the last century from popular traditions which are either no longer flourishing or have undergone evolutionary transformations. This is a further reason why the study by David Reynolds mentioned above is noteworthy: it discusses the way canonical authors – such as Hawthorne, Melville, Dickinson and Whitman – drew on the conventions of popular genre fiction of their time, thus restoring what has become a lost dimension of their work. That lost dimension is often one 'closer' to the rest of their culture – its specific anxieties as much as its specific ordinary concerns – than the general, even universal, truths that have sometimes been claimed as the only true province of art. It is actually the same dimension that we see in genre fiction itself.

NOTES

1. Isaac Asimov, 'Introduction', *Asimov's Mysteries* (London, 1969), p. 9.

2. H.P. Lovecraft, 'Supernatural Horror in Literature', *H.P. Lovecraft Omnibus 2: Dagon and Other Macabre Tales* (London, 1985), p. 423.

3. Kate Ferguson Ellis, *The Contested Castle: Gothic Novels and the Subversion of Domestic Ideology* (Urbana, IL, 1989), p. ix.

4. David Ketterer, *New Worlds For Old: The Apocalyptic Imagination, Science Fiction and American Literature* (Bloomington, IN, 1974), p. 26.

5. W.H. Auden, 'The Guilty Vicarage', *The Dyer's Hand* (London, 1962), p. 151.

6. Jenni Calder, *There Must Be a Lone Ranger: The Myth and Reality of the American Wild West* (London, 1974), p. 170.

7. Michael Denning, *Mechanic Accents: Dime Novels and Working Class Culture* (London, 1987), p. 27.

SUGGESTIONS FOR FURTHER READING

M. Thomas Inge's *Handbook of American Popular Culture*, vol. 1 (Westport, CT, 1981) is a good bibliographic source. James D. Hart, *The Popular Book* (New York, 1950) and Alice Payne Hackett, *Seventy Years of Best Sellers, 1895–1965* (New York, 1967) are useful on bestsellers. A number of works place American genre fiction within an international context, including: David Punter, *The Literature of Terror* (London, 1980); Brian W. Aldiss with David Wingrove, *Trillion Year Spree: The History of Science Fiction* (London, 1986); Jerry Palmer, *Thrillers* (London, 1978); and Julian Symons, *Bloody Murder* (London, 1972). An important context is that of American fiction in general; the book by Reynolds titled in the text (New York, 1988); Brian Lee, *American Fiction 1865–1940* (London, 1987); Malcolm Bradbury, *Modern American Fiction* (Oxford, 1983); and Tony Tanner, *City of Words: American Fiction 1950–1970* (London, 1971) are useful studies.

Andrew Ross, *No Respect* (New York, 1989) and Michael Denning's book cited above provide a fuller discussion of reader orientation within competing discourses. Annette Kolodny, *The Land Before Her* (Chapel Hill, NC, 1984); Kathleen Klein, *The Woman Detective* (Urbana, IL, 1988); and B.J. Rahn, 'Seeley Regester: America's First Detective Novelist', in Barbara A. Rader and Howard G. Zettler (eds), *The Sleuth and the Scholar: Origins, Evolution, and Current Trends in Detective Fiction* (New York, 1988) recover women's contributions to genre literature and reassess the gender politics of genre. Mary V. Dearborn, *Pocahontas's Daughters* (New York, 1986) and Hazel V. Carby, *Reconstructing Womanhood* (New York, 1987) deal with ethnicity as well as gender. Henry Louis Gates, *The Signifying Monkey* (New York, 1988) reasserts the authority of the Afro-American tradition.

A more detailed look at the interrelationship between different subgenres at a specific time within a historical context is contained in Cynthia S. Hamilton, *Western and Hardboiled Detective Fiction in America* (London, 1987). See Leslie Fiedler, *Love and Death in the American Novel* (New York, 1960) on relationships between the gothic and the sentimental novel. On the sentimental novel itself, see Herbert Ross Brown, *The Sentimental Novel in America* (1940, New York, 1975); Cathy N. Davidson, *Revolution and the Word* (New York, 1986); Jane Tompkins, *Sensational Designs* (New York, 1985); Helen Waite Papashvily, *All the Happy Endings* (New York, 1956); and Janice Radway, *Reading the Romance* (Chapel Hill, NC, 1984). For information on gothic and horror fiction, see Donald Ringe, *American Gothic* (Lexington, KY, 1982); H.P. Lovecraft, 'Supernatural Horror in Literature', originally published in 1927 and reprinted in the collection cited in the Notes; and Stephen King, *Danse Macabre* (London, 1981).

See Louise K. Barnett, *The Ignoble Savage* (Westport, CT, 1975), and Richard Slotkin, *Regeneration Through Violence* (Middletown, CT, 1973) on the Indian captivity narrative. On the western, see John G. Cawelti, *The Six-Gun Mystique* (Bowling Green, OH, 1975); Henry Nash Smith, *Virgin Land* (New York, 1957); and Christine Bold, *Selling the Wild West* (Bloomington, IN, 1987). A short treatment of dime-novel westerns may be found in Daryl E. Jones, 'Blood 'n Thunder: Virgins, Villains, and Violence in the Dime Novel Western', *Journal of Popular Culture*, **4** (1970): 507–17. For more on women's diaries of frontier experience, see Lillian Schlissel, *Women's Diaries of the Westward Journey* (New York, 1982). On the hard-boiled detective novel, see John G. Cawelti, *Adventure, Mystery and Romance* (Chicago, 1976) and William Rhuehlmann, *Saint With a Gun* (New York, 1974), as well as two important essays: George Grella, 'Murder and the Mean Streets: The Hard-boiled Detective Novel', *Contempora*, **1** (1970): 6–15, and John Paterson, 'A Cosmic View of the Private Eye', *Saturday Review*, **45** (22 August 1953): 7–8, 31–3. On the slave narrative, including the various discourses which impinge upon it, see Marion Starling, *The Slave Narrative* (Washington, DC, 1988), and Stephen Butterfield, *Black Autobiography in America* (Amherst, MA, 1974). For utopian writing, see Vernon Louis Parrington, *American Dreams* (New York, 1964); Kenneth Roemer, *The Obsolete Necessity* (1976); and Mary Jean Pfaelzer, *The Utopian Novel in America, 1886–1896* (Pittsburgh, 1984). On science fiction, see David Ketterer, *New Worlds for Old* (Bloomington, IN, 1974); J.O. Bailey, *Pilgrims Through Space and Time* (New York, 1947); and H. Bruce Franklin, *Future Perfect* (New York, 1966).

CHAPTER FIFTEEN
Poetry and Poetics

David Murray

Any attempt to represent American poetry in a short essay inevitably comes up against the issue of what exactly is representative. Is it the one-of-everything approach, which attempts to include the huge range and diversity of poetry and poetic positions, or is it the singling out of a tradition of poetry based on some idea of what has been and remains most typical, most characteristic, most American? In many ways, of course, this question echoes a crucial political debate about pluralism and unity, and in choosing to take the second option here, by pursuing Walt Whitman's idea of an inclusive American vision, I want to show that this poetic tradition is itself closely related to a political vision of an inclusive America. Opting to follow this tradition entails concentrating on only one nineteenth-century poet, Whitman, and mainly on those twentieth-century poets who continue, in their very different ways, his concerns.

The dangers of invoking an American essence or tradition, however loose, which expresses a national and cultural unity and identity, but which can obscure awareness of class, gender and ethnic groupings and conflicts are, of course, fully discussed in the opening chapters of this book. The immediate and important objection to such a 'Great Tradition' approach is that it actually excludes or marginalizes that very diversity which it is supposed to be celebrating, by taking upon itself the power to speak *for* it. The argument would be that it is no more acceptable for white males (or any other group) to claim to speak *for* everyone else in poetry than it is in politics. Aspirations to the universal are therefore to be viewed with suspicion, and the personal and the specific can be a resource to be used *against* such claims. But in following through the ways in which the idea of poetic vision has interacted with a pervasive idea of America itself as an inclusive and utopian project, I hope to show that it does manage to include the local and particular, rather than effacing them in some general idea of culture or nation.

In the name of this vision of America, of course, can come profound criticism of the actual America, which falls short of the ideal. This tradition does not *have* to act as a comfortable orthodoxy, and I want to explore the idea of a literary canon which, far from limiting invention by establishing norms, insists on nothing less than a permanent revolution, and on its ability to include and express new elements. This tradition has itself engaged with those issues of diversity and unity, specificity and representativeness which have such urgency today.

By common consent, the major poets of the nineteenth century, and those which mark off American poetry from its English antecedents, are Whitman and Emily Dickinson. From Whitman, as I shall show, runs a line which goes through William Carlos Williams and the Objectivists to Charles Olson, Allen Ginsberg, and Denise Levertov today. By the 1920s the impact of Ezra Pound and T.S. Eliot with their modernist stress on impersonality, pessimism about modern life and their polyglot internationalism, had influentially challenged aspects of the Whitman tradition. My argument concentrates on the Whitman line and on the modernist reactions to it.

Anyone reading contemporary poetry will notice the very *personal* quality of a great deal of the writing, and the way that this is often connected with finding a voice and a place for otherwise underheard or marginalized groups. Neither Whitman, with his use of a public, even bardic self, nor Eliot, with his rejection of any directly personal elements, may seem to offer a model for the whole range of personal poetry which has developed. It is here that we can acknowledge that other nineteenth-century founding figure, Emily Dickinson, whose short, brilliant poems, almost entirely unpublished and unknown in her lifetime, offer an example of the use of an utterly distinctive personal voice, expressing an astonishing range of emotions with a disturbing clarity and intelligence. The fact that Dickinson has not founded a tradition is due partly of course to that widespread condescension towards women's writing which sees it as 'merely' personal, and which has concentrated on Dickinson as recluse, or frustrated woman rather than self-conscious artist, but there are also problems in relating her sort of writing to the Whitman tradition in general. If the influx of poetic power and vision was an enabling one for Whitman, which allowed him to take upon himself a central and centralizing role, the same poetic power for a woman at the time could find no appropriate social or personal expression. As the present-day poet Adrienne Rich points out, Dickinson had to find indirect means of expression. She had to 'retranslate her own unorthodox subversive, sometimes volcanic propensities into a dialect called metaphor: her native language. "Tell all the Truth – but tell it Slant – ".[1]

This points to the possibility of poetry as an expression of whole areas of experience not included either in the prevailing norms or even in Whitman's claim ('through me many long dumb voices') to be able to speak for all, and we can point to the large range of poetry, particularly by women but also by other groups, who have felt deprived of a public voice, and have operated obliquely, telling it 'slant' , often exploiting precisely those personal and localized areas to which they felt confined or relegated.

Such arguments against the idea of a centralizing tradition or canon have certainly been influential, judging by the greatly increased range and variety of writing now included in American college textbooks and anthologies. They relate to a wider paradox in the idea of America concerned with the rival claims of change and continuity, of diversity and unity, and my chosen poets are useful in clarifying the issues. The very idea of America summons up on the one hand a seemingly unbounded natural landscape, timeless, sublime and inspiring, and on the other the breathtaking speed of industrial and technological development, which has made American cities the very symbols of modernity and change. The appeal to nature can be used as a way of invoking a permanent, and unchanging essence. This can be nature itself, with its cyclic renewals, or nature seen as an expression of a divine presence which can be read in and through it. This view of nature can be used to dismiss the world of human social activity, represented by the city and history, in which case nature can become a retreat and a refuge. More commonly, though, within American poetry this awareness of nature is used as a critical tool, a yardstick by which to measure human society and its achievements. This is perhaps the most distinctive aspect of American poetry in one of its major strains, and can be called visionary or prophetic. Jerome Rothenberg borrowed from William Blake in calling his brilliant anthology of American writing *America, A Prophecy* (1974), underlining the curious way in which, in being new, in being original, America is also a working-out of something original, an origin which lies before it as well as in its future.

If we extend the idea of Nature to include the idea of human nature, the idea, that is, of a self which is more fundamental or primordial than the social self, then we find the same potential critical and political implications. Instead of the self being a bounded and known domain which is our own, and which can fit quite well within the dominant property-owning values of American society, it is possible to find within the nineteenth-century traditions of American Transcendentalism a much more radical version of the self. This self is fundamentally at odds with social consensus, and, as we saw in Chapter 4, takes its authority from powers and intuitions more fundamental than those taught by society. This idea of self can, of course, be used as a way of opting out of a coercive social consensus, in the traditions of the isolated and unworldly artist, but of more fundamental importance in American poetry is its use as a critical and political resource. By appealing to a primordial self the poet's vision can be presented as not eccentric but central, more representative than the commonsensical; it is in touch with a greater totality or 'incorporation', and validated and justified by it. This prophetic and bardic stance comes and goes with differing degrees of explicitness in American poetry, and with different political orientations, but one of the most distinctive aspects of American poetry is the way that this Transcendental sense of self can be operative even when least visible.

WHITMAN

We can trace the different stages of this Transcendental faith most easily in just one section from Whitman. 'Walt Whitman, an American, one of the roughs, a cosmos', as he describes himself in 'Song of Myself', the poem produced in successive editions of his *Leaves of Grass* (1855 onwards), in which the New York journalist and printer presented a changing and developing persona by which he could represent America, through its rapid expansion, change and democratic optimism, but also through the traumas of its Civil War. In section 5 of 'Song of Myself' he describes a sort of union of body and soul, evoked in strangely diffused sexual terms. Addressing his soul, Walt says,

> I mind how we lay in June, such a transparent summer morning;
> You settled your head upon my hips and gently turned over upon me
> And parted the shirt from my bosom-bone, and plunged your tongue to my
> bare-stript heart.
> And reached till you felt my beard, and reached till you felt my feet.

This leads to a peace and knowledge which surpasses 'all the art and argument of the earth', but it is the sequence of assertions which this faith allows him which is so striking.

> And I know that the hand of God is the elderhand of my own,
> And I know that the spirit of God is the elder brother of my own
> And that all the men ever born are also my brothers . . . and
> the women my sisters and lovers,
> And that a kelson of the creation is love;
> And limitless are leaves stiff and drooping in the fields,

And brown ants in the little wells beneath them,
And mossy scabs of the wormfence, and heaped stones, and elder, and
mullen, and pokeweed.[2]

The parallelism operating at the beginning of these lines keeps a rhetorical momentum but the subject matter and language is changing, from 'the spirit of God' to 'mossy scabs' and 'pokeweed'. When we look at the syntactical structure which is binding it all together we discover a steady process of elision in which 'I know that' becomes 'And that' and then merely 'And'. It could be said that the presence of Walt, knowing, is there throughout, but the effect at the end is surely of objects themselves, almost as if at 'And limitless are leaves' we have come upon a new main clause, not subordinate to Walt's knowing. To put it another way, 'I' disappears in the knowing, in the radiance of the vision of the detail and multiplicity of the physical world.

The two parts of the poem, religious affirmation and concrete impersonal detail are separate and yet absolutely interdependent, as the ambiguity of syntax within its last sentence suggests. For Whitman the philosophical faith in a unity binding together all the elements of the universe, and the rejection of a duality of mind and matter,can involve a confidence which does not feel the need to *assert* this unity and interrelatedness, but can merely celebrate it, and in so doing the self as separate entity can happily disappear. But this can never be a resting-place. The next section of 'Song of Myself' brings Whitman firmly back into the flux of human life which is the only real ground for the poem. It is tempting to try to fit all American poetry somewhere within the movement enacted by this poem from the division of self and soul, through the ecstatic union, to the celebration of the details of the physical world, but more important is to remember the *interdependence* of the stages, in a process that is never ending.

One of the recurrent difficulties encountered by students when they come to read American poetry, especially when they are trained to read for symbol, depth and complexity, can be not the density of allusion or difficulty of language, but deciding the extent to which simple and self-evident details are being used to represent themselves or more than themselves. In deciding how to respond to a detail or event we search for clues to its significance, and traditionally we have been able to depend on certain literary and social conventions to 'place' an object, and guide us to appropriate responses. One of Whitman's most crucial actions, though, was to attack the hierarchies of taste and perception which decided what was poetic or spiritual and what was not. When the section quoted above ends with the mossy scabs and the pokeweed after the earlier biblical-sounding rhetoric, we are *not* intended to find anticlimax, since in the radiance which bathes the world in this passage there are no hierarchies or distinctions of value.

For Whitman this is not just a mystical moment, but a profoundly held political belief as well, in which the idea of democracy entails not only an equality of voice at the ballot, but a thoroughgoing cultural equality. This means too that the material of ordinary life, and of the contemporary city, is just as available and appropriate as material for poetry as the traditional images of Nature or history. Flux and change, crowds and cities are on the poetic agenda, and as a result the whole hierarchy of decorum and good taste is swept away ('I sound my barbaric yawp over the roofs of the world'). This also has implications for the sort of poetic self or persona presented, since he is no longer a focus of judgement, but a 'caresser of life', more a conduit of 'original energy without check' than a coherent or fixed self.

The celebratory and *inclusive* nature of Whitman's poetry contrasts interestingly with how English Victorian poets react to the world around them, and points to a significant difference between possible uses and adaptations of a fundamentally Romantic vision. Whereas the English poets saw the city as the antithesis of the spiritual wholeness to be found in and through Nature, Whitman made no distinctions, fusing his spiritual affirmations with an endorsement of America's progress and expansion. The danger with this is that the critical purchase available from being outside, and the potential political force of the utopian vision, can be lost, and it may look as if Whitman's affirmations become a sort of American triumphalism. Even if the English response did have the effect, as the nineteenth century went on, of steadily reducing poetry's ability to handle directly the new urban and industrial world, and making it an enclave of the refined and beautiful, it could also be said to have avoided a wholesale conformity with the values of the time. This is where, though, the idea of America as a prophecy is so important. For Whitman, it was the unique destiny of America to achieve that unity and harmony which his poetry both predicted and, he hoped, in the best traditions of prophecy, helped to bring about. America can be criticized in the name of what America is destined to be, a condition imaginatively already present in *Leaves of Grass*, so that Whitman's writing can be seen as simultaneously a celebration and a critique. These questions of the role of the poet in bearing political witness and the sources of his or her moral authority and responsibility will need to be returned to.

Whitman's inclusive and epic intentions were expressed in a form which seemed, in comparison with most other poetry of the time, to be formless and undisciplined, since it neither rhymed nor scanned, and was scattered with colloquialisms. In fact it was highly organized and rhythmic, but instead of the *end* of the line being tied, as in conventional verse (we know when the last syllable has to come, and what it has to sound like) the beginnings of the lines were what gave the effect of symmetry and rhythm, which gave a flexibility to the length of the line, and to its rhythm. In general, Whitman was aiming to produce a heightened rather than purely colloquial speech, a free and impassioned voice, and he refers to his work typically as songs, chants, or arias. Whitman's contemporaries, in England and America, who were at the time much more influential, also stressed sound, but for mellifluous and highly elaborate effects, which, combined with their restricted subject-matter made their work, in the eyes of the next important group of innovators, a genteel and bloodless affair.

MODERNISM

For Ezra Pound and T.S. Eliot, as young Americans in Europe before the First World War, Whitman represented a crude energy, but they saw it as provincial, not usable in the international scene in which they were establishing themselves in London. In Pound's poem 'A Pact' he makes a truce with Whitman:

> It was you that broke the new wood,
> Now it is a time for carving.[3]

The rejection of Whitman's and their own American dimension was not just part of a more general expatriate enthusiasm for Europe, as a reaction against the stuffiness and puritanism of America, but was a more fundamental stance towards what they saw as the crisis of Western cultural life in general.

In defining themselves in opposition to what they saw as the personal and subjective indulgences of Romanticism, these early Modernists stressed instead impersonality, technique and discipline. Going along with this is a conservative stress on the importance of authority and tradition, but we immediately encounter the paradox that these invokers of tradition effected no less than a revolution in Anglo-American poetry. Admittedly they did so by returning to older models of poetic excellence, but their very eclecticism, the way they chose and recreated the tradition which they were to follow, can in fact be seen as quite American. Invention, then, is always a renewal, a continuity as much as a rupture.

This anti-Romantic and impersonal stance expressed itself most programatically in the shortlived movement of Imagism, which stressed the virtues of the clear visual image, and the necessity of pruning out any subjective feelings, abstractions or literary ornaments which might obscure it. The influence of developments in the visual arts of the time, whether the impact of the Armory Show in America (see Chapter 13), or the first-hand involvement with European Cubism, Futurism and Vorticism of Pound cannot be underrated, any more than the constant involvement with American art by William Carlos Williams and, later, by a whole group of New York poets. Nevertheless, it is a dangerous mistake to think of the Image, as developed in Imagism, as exclusively visual; rather, the clarity and impersonality of a sharp-edged visual image should be seen as a model of what *could* be achieved in a language cleansed of nineteenth-century elaborations and musicality. It is crucial that the (capitalized) Image is not just a snapshot of surface reality, an impressionistic moment, but, in Pound's classic definition, 'that which presents an intellectual and emotional complex in an instant of time'.[4] Pound describes cutting down a thirty-line poem inspired by seeing faces in a crowd to a single 'haiku-like sentence', and the result has become the classic Imagist poem:

In A Station of the Metro

The apparition of these faces in the crowd
Petals on a wet black bough.   (p. 113)

In such a poem, he tells us, 'one is trying to record the precise instant when a thing outward and objective transforms itself, or darts into a thing inward and subjective' (p. 54). In this particular poem we can see quite clearly the way in which the juxtaposition of two visual elements creates the effect of recognition, of connectedness, which seems momentarily to unify both the poem and the world. It could be argued that in retrospect the most important and innovative thing in this poem is the gap between the two images, which allows or encourages an instantaneous grasp of the connection. The absence of 'like', or any explicit comparison or logical and sequential explanation, insists for a split second on the equal status and irreducibility of each image, so that one is not subordinated to the other. If the faces became just the incidental vehicle for the poet's emotions and associations we would have only the subjective and emotional world which Pound criticized in some of his predecessors. If just the faces, then we would have only impression and unrelated detail. What Pound is aiming at, and it is an important characteristic of early Modernism (as well as a more general impulse in American poetry to which we must return), is a way of including and unifying the disparate and threatening energies of the world in which he found himself. The poem fuses not only inner and outer, but urban and natural. Whether we finally want to read it as an indictment of the urban (these people are as lost and dislocated as fallen petals) or as a celebration of a fragile beauty found everywhere (the people are as beautiful and transient as the petals), the poem includes the city and the modern world as a subject for poetry.

WILLIAM CARLOS WILLIAMS AND OBJECTIVISM

Even so, it could be said that the ordinary and non-poetic is only allowed in here along with a more poetic image which can neutralize or normalize it within the poetic conventions of what is beautiful and appropriate. In this way, the use of metaphor itself, which is at the heart of Pound's unifying stratagem, can be seen as suspect, and was sometimes considered so by Pound's contemporary William Carlos Williams. In a metaphor, Williams argued, one thing was subordinated to another, was looked through, rather than at, in order to define the main object, and he saw this in democratic terms as unfair and unequal. In a poem such as 'Young Sycamore' he is at pains to present the object itself, without encouraging reverberations from higher cultural registers of language to interfere, since these would draw our attention to the larger context, and the specificity of the object itself would be obscured. Once again, though, we have to be careful not to see such poems as simply snapshots of reality, a realist prose scattered down the page; Williams is quite clear that he is creating a poem, 'a machine made of words'. There is an important distinction here between the use of words, as in realist prose, to recreate the object described, while the words efface themselves, so that we look *through* the medium of language, and don't notice it, and, on the other hand, 'lifting up a word and putting a space around it', as Harold Rosenberg describes it, which is a way of exploiting all the possibilities of language.[5] It is Williams's concern to use words not just as referential counters but as elements in a complex field of cross-relating semantic energies which makes his poetry different from realism, as we can see by looking at an early poem.

> By the road to the contagious hospital
> Under the surge of the blue
> mottled clouds driven from the
> northeast – a cold wind. Beyond, the
> waste of broad, muddy fields
> brown with dried weeds, standing and fallen
>
> patches of standing water

the scattering of tall trees

All along the road the reddish
purplish, forked, upstanding, twiggy
stuff of bushes and small trees
with dead, brown leaves under them
leafless vines —

Lifeless in appearance, sluggish
dazed spring approaches —

They enter the new world naked,
cold, uncertain of all
save that they enter. All about them
the cold familiar wind —

Now the grass, tomorrow
the stiff curl of wildcarrrot leaf
One by one objects are defined —
It quickens: clarity, outline of leaf

But now the stark dignity of
entrance — Still, the profound change
has come upon them: rooted, they
grip down and begin to awaken.[6]

In the first part of the poem we are confusingly situated in relation to the landscape, and the undistinguished and undifferentiated 'stuff' of winter. It is difficult for us to focus on it, or put it into an overall perspective, since there is no help from a controlling or centralizing eye (I) in the poem. Note the number of words which seem to offer a promise of location or direction which the overall syntax does not fulfill, either prepositions (by, under, beyond, along), or verb forms (surge, driven), so that the effect is confusing, like a finger pointing erratically. Then, with the first main verb, spring *approaches*, and the focus changes. Not that we have a single focus, in fact precisely the opposite, because now we have a huge multiplicity of foci, something which, if we try to situate ourselves or the poet in visual relation to the scene, is an impossibility. The observer can only focus on one thing at the expense of everything else, but spring is the bringing into definition of an almost infinite number of separate ('one by one') new foci. 'It quickens' implies not just the increasing pace of change and growth, but the point prior to that, at which the inanimate (it) becomes quick, in the sense of alive.

The use of the word 'naked' is bound to suggest that 'they' are human babies, but this association is dissipated as the poem goes on. This is typical of Williams, who does not avoid the inevitable associations which words carry, but neither does he let one set dominate so as to obliterate the literal meaning. The first line, for instance, which is often printed as the title, can be seen as the literal context for the witnessing of spring (Williams was a doctor), but contagion also inevitably links up with the germination of life in the poem. The result is that the idea of human efforts to limit it, as in the hospital, becomes absurd and contradictory, rather like the phrase 'contagious hospital' itself. Our relation to spring and to the creation of new life is thus decentred in the poem; in a more straightforwardly symbolic poem it could have been made central, and the natural world made to chime with the human (try substituting maternity for contagious).

Williams's concern for the specific, then, can be compared with Whitman's, even though he would not profess faith in any grand overarching scheme such as Whitman's Transcendentalism. Just as for Whitman the mossy scabs of the worm-fence are there both in their own right and as irradiated by his vision, so for Williams the role of the imagination is crucial. The poet must aim to 'perfect the ability to record at the moment when the consciousness is enlarged by the sympathies and the unity of understanding which the imagination gives, to practice skill in recording the force moving, then to know it, in the largeness of its proportions' (p.120).

The attempt to portray the true largeness of these proportions, whether metaphysical, historical or political, while avoiding subjugating the object itself to various sorts of symbolism, is perhaps the most distinctive theme in American poetry of the twentieth century, but it is also the most complex, because of the difficulty in sorting out the attitudes to language involved. Any faith in language's ability to represent the real world, with a corresponding faith that the world is knowable, runs into all sorts of (often productive) contradictions, as can be seen in the work of the Objectivists, a group often associated with Williams. Objectivism is mostly linked to the 1930s, though the finest work of its main figures, Louis Zukofsky, George Oppen and Charles Reznikoff, comes later. It can be seen as translating Whitman's democratic faith into modern urban America, so that the poetry has a concern for the ordinary and neglected which is political as well as aesthetic. Language *can* express the world which is objectively there, but to be able to work accurately language must be cleansed and rectified, as Oppen makes clear:

Possible
To use
Words provided one treat them
As enemies.
Not enemies – Ghosts
Which have run mad
In the subways
And of course the institutions
And the banks. If one captures them
One by one proceeding

Carefully they will restore
I hope to meaning
And to sense.[7]

Part of the sequence 'A Language of New York', this poem allows for an interesting comparison with a later New York poet, Frank O'Hara, who offers a more affirmative view both of New York and of the possibilities of the freeplay of language in his more surreal works like 'Second Avenue'. What is also revealing here, though, is the way Oppen's syntax allows 'I hope' to float free in the last section, rather than act only as a parenthesis, as it would be in 'will, I hope, restore'. The ability to hope, and hope itself, are restored as a dimension of meaning which had been destroyed by capitalism. For Oppen, to know anything in 'the true largeness of its proportions' was to see it in a historical and political context. To present something as an Objectivist, then, is to present both the thing itself and something yet to be brought into being, and this apparent paradox can be seen as a restatement of Whitman's prophetic vision, since the word vision also contains both of these dimensions.

For Whitman, buoyed up by his Transcendentalist faith, there was no real disparity between the ideal America and the developing nation of which he was a proud citizen. True, he could see the injustice and greed, and he was a personal witness to the horrors of the Civil War, but he was able to see these as temporary and necessary parts of a larger design. For him, history was a fulfillment of a prophesy. For later poets, without his faith and faced by world war and economic and political chaos, it was a nightmare, or at best a puzzle that desperately needed to be understood. Either way, it could not be escaped, and we have a whole succession of ambitious long poems – like the 800-page work Louis Zukofsky began in 1928, *A* (1978) – which represent in different ways attempts to come to terms with the contemporary world through an engagement with history.

THE LONG POEM: ELIOT AND POUND

In contrast to Whitman's organically unified world, in which humanist values were unchallenged, and which demanded correspondingly organic forms of art, the modernist experience was of fragmentation, discontinuity and the destruction of traditional humanist beliefs. Both Eliot and Pound tried to develop a form which was capable of facing this fragmentation head on, and even of utilizing it, by exploiting what actually happens when a reader is faced with a gap or discontinuity. In Pound's Metro poem, the conjunction of elements without authorial guidance makes the reader fill in gaps and make connections, so recognizing brokenness *and* responding constructively to it. Similarly, Eliot's *The Waste Land* (1922) uses descriptions of modern London intercut with scraps of quotations from many literatures and mythological traditions to create a densely textured collage in which we are able to trace recurrent patterns and connections.

Whether we take it as a statement about the modern world and its need for spiritual redemption, or an objectifying of Eliot's own psychological and spiritual despair, what we have is an act of salvage, in which permanent cultural and spiritual values to be found in the past are set up as a potential resource for the transient and confusing present. 'These fragments I have shored against my ruin'. If the political and cultural implications of this (pointing towards Eliot's later conservative use of the idea of tradition), were unpalatable to some of his contemporaries, as I shall show, the impact of the poem's thoroughgoing and brilliant use of effects of juxtaposition and discontinuity, not just locally but as a structural principle, was undeniable. Pound, whose ruthless editorial work on the poem no doubt increased its collage effects, himself went on to his lifelong enterprise of *The Cantos* (1925–60).

Like Eliot, Pound ransacks the past in order to discover patterns and recurrences, points of permanent value, but his commitment to what he calls the 'ideogrammic' method creates problems. He wants to build up complex meanings from concrete details, which are rooted in reality and therefore avoid the dangers of abstraction, but this depends on the reader actually *making* the connection, and the larger the conglomeration of these elements the more difficult it becomes to know which of the many possible cross-relations we are to follow. Pound's overall aim, following the general movement of Dante's *Divine Comedy*, was to lead the reader through the Inferno of modern life, through the Purgatorio of having to relearn and understand our past and its lasting values to, finally, the Paradiso of understanding and illumination. But as a modern man he did not have Dante's 'road-map', in the form of inherited and socially accepted beliefs, and instead he has to proceed like his other model, Odysseus, trying to navigate his way home 'as the winds veer'.

The poem becomes, therefore, a record of Pound's intellectual and political 'veerings', in which he explores, for instance, the founding of America, Chinese history, Italian banking systems and modern economic theory. As the poem goes on, though, his own life is giving increasing evidence that an overall pattern is *not* emerging. His confident support for Mussolini and Fascism in the name of the principles of Jefferson and the American Founding Fathers, his belief that he had an economic panacea for the problems of the Depression, was shattered by his postwar arrest and his lengthy committal to an American mental hospital. He continued to write, though, and in the most powerful of these later cantos he confronts the question of whether he is *finding* an underlying order and meaning – in which case his elliptical and discontinuous style would be a way of letting us see it too – or whether he is *making* his own local order, trying to create beauty and form in a chaotic world. The tensions between these two positions are never reconciled in *The Cantos*, and the last published pieces, which are not a closure or conclusion, contain both an assertion that 'it coheres all right/even if my notes do not cohere' and the recognition that the enterprise of trying to synthesize is doomed: 'I have brought the great ball of crystal;/who can lift it?'

Pound's career throws into clear relief the concerns of the long poem in general in this century. He claims to be discovering laws and patterns, in order to establish what is really a nineteenth-century model of cyclical history, and given where it leads him we may want to reject it out of hand. Where Pound diverges from Eliot is in the increasing tension between this closed model, in which all elements correspond in a predetermined poetic order, designed to reflect the cultural and spiritual order to be affirmed, and an open-ended engagement with new elements which arrive through sheer contingency. In both their writings and their lives Pound's and Eliot's careers divide along these lines. Eliot came to believe increasingly in the power of tradition and less in individual deviations from it, which corresponded to his Anglo-Catholic faith and social conservatism, while Pound remained eclectic to the end.

THE LONG POEM: CRANE AND WILLIAMS

Though Pound's open-endedness was taken up later, initially, for their contemporaries, Eliot was the figure to come to terms with. While his cultural pessimism and élitism profoundly influenced the Southern critics and poets who formulated the tenets of the New Criticism (see Chapters 5 and 16), some of his contemporaries reacted strongly against *The Waste Land*'s closing off of the possibilities of modernity. Hart Crane, for instance, used Brooklyn Bridge to represent the unifying and even transcendent possibilities of modern technology for America. He had explicitly designed an earlier poem as a rejoinder to Eliot's 'negations' and in *The Bridge* (1930) he draws heavily from Whitman's affirmations. He uses Brooklyn Bridge to represent the connection, the bridging, not only of parts of America with each other, but of the material America with the mythical lost world of spirit.

The problem was that Crane found it easier to assert the connection than to demonstrate it, in the charged and elliptical style which depended on connections being made in what he called the 'logic of metaphor'. If we compare his poem with Whitman's earlier 'Crossing Brooklyn Ferry' we can see that Whitman is a *part* of the crowd of people going back and forth, rather than standing back and aestheticizing it; he does not need to try to capture an inexpressible transcendence or eternity since the very movement is enough. Eliot complained that Whitman did not recognize the gap between the real and ideal, a charge which Whitman would no doubt happily accept, but in Crane we see an attempt at Whitmanesque affirmation in Eliot's rootless and hopeless modern world. In this way Crane connects up with a whole line of poets for whom such affirmation can never be assumed, but must be created anew in the poetry itself.

Crane was not alone in feeling that Eliot's example had to be resisted. Years later William Carlos Williams remembered the advent of *The Waste Land* as catastrophic. In suggesting that the generative sources which needed to be relocated were to be found in a cosmopolitan and heteroglot high culture, Eliot, as far as Williams was concerned, was 'turning his back on my world'. We have already seen how Williams concentrates on the objects of the ordinary world for their own sake, but he also wanted to build a larger structure. He faced the same problem as Pound in trying, as he put it, to 'interrelate on a new ground, difficultly' his materials, without imposing a narrative or discursive organization on them.[8] In his long poem *Paterson* (1946–58) he opted to use the New Jersey city of that name as his organizing principle, inventing also a man called Paterson, so that the identities of man and city are intertwined. Within this schema he can include documents, letters, historical chronicles, as well as characteristic accounts of ordinary contemporary life.

One of the recurrent concerns of the poem, which can be seen as Williams's equivalent to Eliot's search for a fixed point of value, is that of origin, but for Williams this is never imaged as a point outside or prior to physical and earthly existence. The river on which Paterson stands, the Passaic Falls, and its entrance to the sea are used for their symbolic possibilities, but these never cancel out their physical reality, and in fact Book Four ends with an eventual rejection of the mythological unity and closure which the sea as an image of death has traditionally represented. The appeal of the absolute is invoked through those inherited cultural reference points which have perpetuated this craving:

> You will come to it, the blood dark sea
> of praise, You must come to it. Seed
> of Venus, you will return . to
> a girl standing upon a tilted shell, rose

pink.

Thalassa!
immaculata: our home, our nostalgic
mother in whom the dead, enwombed again
cry out to us to return.

(p. 236)

But this temptation, which has a literary dimension too, in the appeal of
closed forms, 'this dream of/the whole poem', must be resisted, and
Williams offers instead a final, very specific, image of a man coming out of
the sea and heading inland. It would be wrong, though, to see Williams as
uninterested in questions of unity or recurrences and origins, since the
whole thrust of the long poem is to explore these questions, and its
organization depends on patterns and similarities rather than on the separate
objects and experiences of his more celebrated short poems. We do not
have pristine encounters with otherness or firstness, and when Williams
does try to image this he returns the mystery to the earth we can
experience:

Thought clambers up
snail like, upon the wet rocks

. . . .

Earth the chatterer, father of all
speech . . . .

(pp. 51–2)

At the source, then, is a diversity, and multiplicity, and Williams
elsewhere in the poem uses the figure of Marie Curie, and the properties of
'Uranium, the complex atom, breaking/down, a city in itself' to stress the
inextricability of destruction and invention:

A dissonance
in the valence of Uranium
led to the discovery
Dissonance
(if you are interested)
leads to discovery

(p. 207)

Williams is pointing to a relation between poetic and scientific creativity,
and he explicitly argues in his prose that Relativity should make us newly
aware of the purely relational nature not only of measurement but of
measure, by which he means the relative length and rhythm of lines in
poetry. Rather than being fixed, and the meaning poured into the form,
the new measure must be responsive to and inextricably part of the
content. As Robert Creeley later put it, 'Form is never more than an

extension of content.' This is *not* to say that form is less important. Williams insists that there is no such thing as 'free verse' since this implies that the only way that form and structure are operative is when they are limiting and pre-exist the material expressed in them. This is a crucial aspect of modern American poetry, and easily overlooked precisely because of the apparent simplicity and lack of recognizable 'form' of so much of it.

CHARLES OLSON

Perhaps the most important manifesto for these ideas, which in fact takes over the Creeley dictum above, is Charles Olson's 1950 essay 'Projective Verse'. Here he presents the poem as a field of force, in which the poet, during the compositional process, is led by the syllable, and its complex relations to the other sounds of the poem as it is being created, rather than by a preconceived goal. The poem *as* thought and action, rather than a *description* of it, is what he is proposing, and this has radical implications for the role of the poetic ego. As process rather than complete and preformed entity, this ego is clearly differentiated from that of the Romantic poet, whose sensibility was itself the subject of the poem. Olson proposes

> the getting rid of the lyrical interference of the individual as ego, of the 'subject' and his soul, that peculiar presumption by which western man has interposed himself between what he is as a creature of nature ... and those other creations of nature which we may, with no derogation, call objects.[9]

The poem involves a physical engagement, in breath and voice, as well as a mental or spiritual one, and this points forward to the increasing role of performance, in some strands of American poetry, and the printed poem as score for performance rather than finished or authoritative text.

The rejection of a lyric ego is, of course, very different from the impersonality adopted by Eliot, which encouraged detachment and irony. Olson's own poetry, and in particular his extended *Maximus* (1960, 1968) sequence, uses a personal voice, an 'I', extensively. It is in fact an important part of his rejection of universalizing and abstract modes of thought, and love of the concrete, that he embraces the specificity of viewpoint and personal experience:

> There are no hierarchies, no infinite, no such many as mass, / there are only eyes in all heads
> to be looked out of.[10]

Like Williams, who insisted that 'The local is the universal', Olson wants to prevent the specificity of his own and everyone else's experience from being subsumed under abstraction, symbol, or any overarching system of thought, and he grounds the poem in a locality, Gloucester, Massachusetts, equivalent to Williams's Paterson. But Olson is also much more concerned to insist on the universal as well as the local, and the poem includes within its 'field' mythology, cosmogony and a concept of politics. While he rejects hierarchies, repeating Whitman's democratic gesture, he does project an image of a 'polis', a community which does not violate or subdue the particular. In a multiple pun, he insists that 'polis is eyes'.

ROBERT DUNCAN

Olson's commitment to be both local and universal, and his insistence on process rather than unity or fixity presents problems in that it ultimately depends on a faith that we can and should dispense with oppressive systems because they obscure a more *fundamental* ordering. Robert Duncan, a friend and colleague at Black Mountain College (see Chapter 13) in the 1950s, insists that any order he can create is trivial in relation to the order he can find. We must resist the temptation, though, to see in such assertions a transcendental claim identical to earlier Romantic formulations. Olson and Duncan are as likely to invoke models from modern science as from religious systems, to express the idea of an order which can only be located in the act of finding rather than abstracted and fixed, and which cannot be totalized. Similarly the relation between local and universal is expressed without recourse to the conventional modes of symbolism, which would depend on an accepted scale of correspondences and gradations of significance.

Perhaps the most ambitious attempt to address this problem can be found in Duncan's 'Passages', a long poem which weaves its way through a number of his books, never quite separating itself out, or completing its themes, as the title's connotations of change, movement and fragmentariness suggest. He uses the characteristic form for the modern long poem of collage and fragmentation, and his description of his compositional practice applies also to how we are to read, in trying to be open to disruptions and discontinuities: 'The poem is not a stream of consciousness, but an area of composition in which I work with whatever comes into it.'[11] The collisions and disjunctures of meaning lead to a recognition of the larger order in which they coexist. 'Were all in harmony to our ears, we would dwell in the dreadful smugness in which our mere human rationality relegates what it cannot cope with to the "irrational", as if the totality of creation were without ratios' (p. ix). These ratios, like Williams's measures, are always relational and relative, making them different from the appeal to an absolute point of origin or centre expressed in earlier transcendental assertions.

THE VISION OF WAR

One theme in 'Passages' is America's involvement in Vietnam, and Duncan's way of handling it is worth pursuing. By intercutting material on President Johnson and America's actions with mythological and religious references as well as quotations from Whitman and Blake, he mounts a critique of America, as failing in terms of its own ideal. That is, Duncan's positing of a fundamental ordering, does not lead to quietism, or to an indiscriminate embrace of the universe, a leap above the level of politics and of individual responsibility. Rather, the vision of larger orders, 'the imagination of the Whole', is a critical resource, just as Utopian thinking as a whole can be seen, if sufficiently historicized, as political critique, rather than evasion. The Vietnam War, and the civil disorders that accompanied it, as well as the physical presence of large audiences at meetings and readings meant a new awareness of a public role on the part of many poets. Allen Ginsberg, for instance, who had since the 1950s written poems like 'A Supermarket in California' or 'America', which deliberately employed a Whitmanesque criticism of modern America, found the public role he had already assumed in his poetry. A poem like 'Wichita Vortex Sutra' exemplifies his belief in the need for both accurate language, along Imagist lines, and a moral vision which will not be swamped by the political and moral squalor he sees around him.

What happens, though, if, as in Denise Levertov's poem 'Advent', the concrete horror of events cannot be fitted into *any* vision of order, but instead seems to obliterate any faith in it?

> Because in Vietnam the vision of a Burning Babe
> is multiplied, multiplied, the flesh on fire
> not Christ's as Southwell saw it, prefiguring
> the Passion upon the Eve of Christmas,
>
> but wholly human and repeated, repeated,
> infant after infant, their names forgotten,
> their sex unknown in the ashes,
> set alight, flaming but not vanishing,
> not vanishing as his vision but lingering,

cinders upon the earth or living on
moaning and stinking in hospitals three abed;

because of this my strong sight,
my clear caressive sight, my poet's sight I was given
that it might stir me to song,
is blurred.

There is a cataract filming over
my inner eyes. Or else a monstrous insect
has entered my head, and looks out
from my sockets with multiple vision,
seeing not the unique Holy Infant

burning sublimely, an imagination of redemption,
furnace in which souls are wrought into new life,
but, as off a beltline, more, more senseless figures aflame.

And this insect (who is not there –
it is my own eyes do my seeing, the insect
is not there, what I see is there)
will not permit me to look elsewhere,

or if I look, to see except dulled and unfocussed
the delicate, firm, whole flesh of the still unburned.[12]

Levertov's poem is shocking, but not just because of the image of the burning babies. She invokes two different images of repetition: one is keyed to a redemptive larger order, in which destruction becomes renewal, the other mere reduplication, a circulation of images in a nightmare vision of the news media's capacity to transform by endless repetition rather than regeneration. The power of the imagination to transfigure reality, to see everything bathed in Whitman's radiance, has been destroyed by the horror of events. This is an everpresent threat, even acknowledged by Whitman, and is the staple diet of the Romantic crisis poem, in which the poet's vision has fled and needs to be re-awakened. What is alarming here is the problem of proportion. Put crudely, is Levertov complaining more about the dimming of her poet's vision than about what is happening to the babies? This would be a piece of monumental insensitivity and bad taste. One answer would be that she is taking on the role of visionary poet, who has the right to speak, who is empowered by her role and her vision, so that charges of personal egotism or narcissism miss the mark. Even so, the poem raises sharp questions about the role of the individual voice, and about subjectivity as moral touchstone. Such questions recur most strongly in the work of Robert Lowell, Sylvia Plath and others often called Confessional poets.

Levertov's poem examines the crucial interplay between outer and inner. At a literal level the poet must see what is there. At another level she must see beyond it ('the still unburned'). Yet the events of the world itself can corrupt that second sort of vision (the monstrous insect with multiple vision). As with Crane, the vision can be unsustainable. The endless interplay of the poetic imagination and the world 'out there', and the range of positions, from triumphant merger of outer and inner to desolate awareness of the poet's inability to be in touch with the fullness and vitality of the world, can best be seen in a poet whose whole career is a progressive reworking of these themes.

WALLACE STEVENS (AND OTHERS)

Wallace Stevens generally avoided both the political and the poetic affiliations of his contemporaries Pound and Williams, and his obliquity and apparently perverse and playful use of language seems to owe more to the French Symbolists than to Whitman. His approach to language, though, offers a useful reminder of the inadequacy of thinking of the world as a fixed thing out there, and language as a transparent medium for representing it. In Stevens poetic language itself becomes an exploratory epistemological tool, rather than just a medium of prior thoughts. He takes up the major Romantic theme of the imagination, but his language constantly thwarts any temptation we might have to settle into traditional assumptions, either of a fixed point of poetic presence, the 'I' of the poem, or of a reliable and recognizable natural world. Like Williams, his poetry rejects the consolations of Christianity, and of any fixed system:

> It was when I said
> 'There is no such thing as the truth'
> That the grapes seemed fatter.
> The fox ran out of his hole.[13]

But this does not mean he can accept Williams's faith in a cleansed language, since all language for Stevens is provisional within the terms of the poem itself. Even if we are urged to

> Throw away the lights, the definitions,
> And say of what you see in the dark
>
> That it is this or that it is that
> But do not use the rotted names

(p. 183)

we cannot assume that Stevens will offer a Williams-like concreteness.

Certainly his poems celebrate the senses and the concrete world, but it is part of his argument that though we must 'see the sun again with an ignorant eye' we must also 'see it clearly in the idea of it'; that is, we part-*constitute* it, through our perceptions and imagination (p. 380). There is a constant dialectical movement, for Stevens, which is reflected in our reading of his poetry, between the creation or discovery of order. We are separated from any original unity which might guarantee a harmony between our feelings or perceptions and any absolute state of affairs. This is a view of poetic imagination as creation, a lamp creating the world it illuminates, and Stevens accepts that 'to impose is not to discover' an order. And yet he insists,

> to find
> Not to impose, not to have reasoned at all,
> Out of nothing to have come on major weather,
>
> It is possible, possible, possible.
>
> (p. 404)

This endless movement between finding and creating is expressed within the poetry by an endless provisionality, in which statements have to be seen as temporary points in a larger landscape of ideas and feelings. We are like a figure in Stevens's major poem 'Notes Toward a Supreme Fiction', when 'normal things had yawned themselves away' and the old definitions had disappeared:

> The nothingness was a nakedness, a point
> Beyond which thought could not progress as thought.
> He had to choose. But it was not a choice
> Between excluding things. It was not a choice
> Between, but of.
>
> (p. 403)

Stevens is constantly trying to *enlarge* our sense of what the 'real' might be, and this is his final argument for poetry. His high reputation with post-structuralist and deconstructionist critics rests on their admiration for his endless provisionality, and the way in which he highlights and continues to work with Romantic concepts of presence and reference rather than refusing or abandoning them altogether as later poets have done, and it is interesting to note that one of the most celebrated poets of the last few years, John Ashbery, can be seen as offering the same experience. Originally connected with the so-called New York poets, particularly Frank O'Hara, and the Abstract Expressionist painters with whom they were closely associated (see Chapter 13), his poetry contains surreal conjunctions and a refusal of any extractable fixed meaning, but it also has a disturbing way of making sense in intense but unconnected clusters, so that we finish the poem with the feeling of having had profound thoughts but unable to put them together in any way which could have a critical purchase on our lives.

It is tempting to see Ashbery's popularity as connected to a sort of postmodern consumerism, in which we are allowed absolute freedom, because in fact it is completely irrelevant to anything we could do to understand or change the conditions of our life. In fact one way of theorizing postmodern society is to stress its ability to allow and encourage the local as the only area of meaning, thereby dismissing even the possibility of a total or unified view. A poetics which seems to offer all sorts of possibilities of meaning, but endlessly postpones or refuses to integrate them, could be said to fit very comfortably into this ideology, and certainly to have lost the visionary or utopian edge we have encountered earlier. Also lost, of course, is the anxiety and sense of loss which defined the Romantic crisis poem. Once we accept the impossibility of an overarching or transcendent meaning we can enjoy the present for itself:

> The luxury of now is that the cancelled gala has been
> Put back in. The orchestra is starting to tune up.

This orchestra, though, is an image of a multiplicity of elements, much more inclusive than most definitions of art:

> The conductor, a glass of water, permits all kinds
> Of wacky analogies to glance off him, and, circling outward
> To bring in the night. Nothing is too 'unimportant'
> Or too important, for that matter. The newspaper and the garbage
> Wrapped in it, the over, the under.[14]

By following through the ways in which the idea of poetic vision has interacted with a pervasive idea of America itself as an inclusive and utopian project this chapter has inevitably been partial. The most significant problem is that omissions and marginalizations could be seen as dictated by precisely those ideas of centrality and essence which many of the poets dealt with would want to reject, in the name of a larger vision of America. The project of finding a form which can allow for change and diversity without ultimately disintegrating, is both a political and a poetic one, and has come under severe pressure. Whether from postmodern scepticism about any totalizing or transcendent values, or from the self-identification and self-assertion of groups who have often been effaced rather than included in the whole which has been America, such as blacks and women, Whitman's vision has been tested. Perhaps politics as much as poetry will determine whether the vision can be inclusive enough, and whether Walt's promise in the name of his vision of democracy, that even now 'I stop somewhere waiting for you', can be fulfilled.

NOTES

1. Adrienne Rich, *On Lies, Secrets and Silence* (London, 1971), pp. 161–2.

2. Walt Whitman, *Leaves of Grass*, in Mark van Doren (ed.), *The Portable Whitman* (Harmondsworth, 1973), pp. 35–6.

3. Ezra Pound, *Selected Poems* (London, rev. edn, 1948), p. 91; subsequent reference in text.

4. J.P. Sullivan (ed.), *Ezra Pound: A Critical Anthology* (Harmondsworth, 1970), p. 41; subsequent reference in text.

5. Harold Rosenberg in Charles Tomlinson (ed.), *William Carlos Williams: A Critical Anthology* (Harmondsworth, 1972), p. 260.

6. William Carlos Williams, *Imaginations* (New York, 1970), p. 95; subsequent reference in text.

7. George Oppen, *This In Which* (New York, 1965), p. 39.

8. William Carlos Williams, *Autobiography* (New York, 1951), p. 120, and *Paterson* (New York, 1963), p. 30; subsequent references in text.

9. Charles Olson, *Selected Writings* (New York, 1966), p. 24.

10. Charles Olson, *The Maximus Poems* (New York, 1960), p. 29.

11. Robert Duncan, *Bending The Bow* (New York, 1968), p. vi; subsequent reference in text.

12. Denise Levertov, *Relearning the Alphabet* (London, 1970), p. 4.

13. Wallace Stevens, *Collected Poems* (London, 1955), p. 203; subsequent references in text.

14. John Ashbery, *Houseboat Days* (Harmondsworth, 1977), p. 14.

SUGGESTIONS FOR FURTHER READING

Useful general anthologies are Richard Ellman (ed.), *The New Oxford Book of American Verse* (Oxford, 1976), Geoffrey Moore (ed.), *The Penguin Book of American Verse* (Harmondsworth, rev. edn, 1983), and George Quasha's and Jerome Rothenberg's innovative and lively *America, A Prophecy* (New York, 1974). Broad critical agreement over the importance of both Whitman and Dickinson, soon breaks down with twentieth-century choices. Helen Vendler's edition of *The Harvard Book of Contemporary American Poetry* (Cambridge, MA, 1985) gives little space to poets in the Williams tradition like Olson or the Beats. By contrast Donald Allen's anthology *The New American Poetry 1945–1960* (New York, 1960), revised as *The Postmoderns*, ignores completely the Confessionals.

In criticism, Hyatt H. Waggoner's *American Poetry From Puritans to the Present* (Boston, MA, 1968) is a standard survey, but weak on post-1945 developments. Albert Gelpi's *The Tenth Muse: The Psyche of the American Poet* (Cambridge, MA, 1975) deals with nineteenth-century poets, as does A. Robert Lee (ed.), *Nineteenth Century American Poetry* (Totowa, NJ, 1985). Roy Harvey Pearce's *The Continuity of American Poetry* (Princeton, NJ, 1961) is an important book, which traces a distinctive American tradition, while Mutlu K. Blasing's *American Poetry: The Rhetoric of its Forms* (New Haven, 1987) comes further up to date in finding common linguistic strategies in very diverse poets.

The most useful general account of this century is Richard Gray's *American Poetry of the Twentieth Century* (London and New York, 1990), which is comprehensive, with bibliographies and brief biographies. Hugh Kenner's *The Pound Era* (London, 1971) make a strong case for a distinctive modernist tradition, as does Marjorie Perloff's *The Dance of the Intellect: Studies in the Poetry of the Pound Tradition* (Cambridge, 1985) and Albert Gelpi's *A Coherent Splendour: The American Poetic Renaissance 1910–50* (Cambridge, 1987). A wider range of poets is considered in Denis Donoghue's *Connoisseurs of Chaos: Ideas of Order in Modern American Poetry* (London, 1965), in Richard Howard's, *Alone With America: Studies in the Art of Poetry in The United States* (London, 1970), and in Helen Vendler's *Part of Nature, Part of Us: Modern American Poets* (Cambridge, MA, 1980).

Charles Altieri's *Enlarging the Temple: New Directions in American Poetry During the Sixties* (Lewisburg, PA, 1979) is one of the best of a large range of criticism covering the contemporary scene, including James E. Breslin's *From Modern to Contemporary: American Poetry 1945–1965* (Chicago, 1984) and Cary Nelson's *Our Last First Poets: Vision and History in Contemporary American Poetry* (Urbana, IL, 1981). Robert von Hallberg, *American Poetry and Culture, 1945–1980* (Cambridge, MA, 1985) and Walter Kalaidjian, *Languages of Liberation: The Social Text in Contemporary American Poetry* (New York, 1989) treat poetry in relation to society, in contrast to Helen Vendler's *The Music of What Happens: Poems, Poets and Critics* (Cambridge, MA, 1988), which insists on the importance of an aesthetic rather than an ideological approach. Such issues are to the fore in the renewed attention to specific groups indicated in Suzanne Juhasz, *Naked and Fiery Forms: Modern American Poetry by Women: A New Tradition* (New York, 1970); Harold Bloom (ed.), *American Women Poets* (New York, 1976); Eugene B. Redmond, *Drumvoices: The Mission of Afro-American Poetry* (New York, 1976); Donald B. Gibson (ed.), *Modern Black Poets: A Collection of Critical Essays* (Englewood Cliffs, NJ, 1973); Joseph Bruchac, *Survival This*

Way: Interviews With American Indian Poets (Tucson, AZ, 1987); and Cordelia Candelaria, *Chicano Poetry: A Critical Introduction* (Westport, CT, 1986).

CHAPTER SIXTEEN
American Cultural Criticism

Richard H. King

The centrality of cultural criticism in America can be explained by several historical factors. Founded, as Lincoln said, upon a proposition, the tension between promise and reality has generated a tradition of intense self-scrutiny which began in the 1660s, if not earlier, when the Puritan communities in New England confronted the difference between what their community had become and the 'errand' with which they originally arrived in North America. By the mid- to late nineteenth-century, it was becoming clear that the United States was not a people or nation (*Volk*) in the European sense of a collectivity possessing common linguistic, racial and cultural characteristics. Yet, except for the Civil War – admittedly a huge exception – the continued existence of the American 'experiment' has never been seriously threatened. This contrasts sharply with the debilitating civil wars and struggles against hostile powers that wracked France and the Soviet Union in the early years of their revolutions, the continuing threat of extinction that faces the state of Israel and the recent actual extinction of the Soviet Union as a state.

That 'objective' factors contributed to America's relatively stable heterogeneity is easy to forget. Geographical isolation played a significant part in ensuring the stability of the new republic. More importantly, perhaps, the explosive effect of the 'social question' was felt less in the United States than in nineteenth-century Europe. Just as there was no revolutionary 'Terror' in America, so there was no American 'counter-revolution' as had existed in France in the 1790s. To be sure, the first half of the nineteenth century saw the emergence of a (white) Southern cultural and political identity, that fed secessionist impulses and culminated in the Civil War and Reconstruction, the closest the United States came to a genuine social revolution (see also Chapter 3). Indeed many Southern patriots linked the War and Reconstruction quite explicitly with the depredations of the French Revolution. But though American cultural identity was implicitly, at times explicitly, 'white' (as opposed to 'black' or 'red'), that is, the United States was what George Fredrickson, in *The Inner Civil War* (1965), refers to as a '*Herrenvolk* (master race) democracy', the Southern option lacked the ideological or social appeal to deconvert the white population to a racial–feudal order that resembled nothing so much as the Old World that had been abandoned.

THE POSSIBILITY OF A DEMOCRATIC CULTURE

Beginning around the time of the War for Independence, the differences between America and Europe forced the question that French observer Hector St John de Crèvecoeur posed in an oft-quoted formulation in *Letters from an American Farmer* (1782): 'What is this new man, this American?' Cultural and political independence were to be inextricably linked in America. Over fifty years later, Ralph Waldo Emerson expressed the first full surge of cultural nationalism in his 'American Scholar' address of 1837 when he called for a distinctively *American* literary culture, while Walt Whitman, revoicing Emerson in *Leaves of Grass* (1855) and *Democratic Vistas* (1871), characterized American difference in terms of America's open, pluralistic and *democratic* character. Indeed, the incessant raising of the question of the nature of American culture was another way of wondering whether a democratic culture – a culture to which 'the people' had access and to which they could contribute; and one which reflected their concerns rather than the concerns of social and cultural élites – was possible or desirable.

Not surprisingly, the answers to the question about a democratic culture have ranged widely between two extremes. The tradition of cultural democracy proposed by Emerson and Whitman and echoed by such diverse twentieth-century figures as philosopher John Dewey, publicist Randolph Bourne and utopian social and cultural critic Paul Goodman, has answered in the affirmative. A democratic culture for these men was a matter of faith not proof. The radical implications of what was once at stake can be seen in Whitman's *Democratic Vistas*, where he asserts the revolutionary nature of the idea of a democratic culture: 'The great poems, Shakespeare included, are poisonous to the idea of pride and dignity of the common people, the life-blood of democracy . . . all smells of princes' failures.'[1] Divided between a vision of a democratic culture and the reality of cultural institutions run by the rich and well-born, champions of the

democratic cultural ideal have generally reacted to failures with disappointment rather than disillusionment.

Cultural conservatives, whether foreign or domestic, can of course
always respond with a 'we told you so' to democratic disappointment with
egalitarian culture. European observers have often expressed strong
reservations about actually existing democratic culture in America. Most
sweeping was the Comte de Buffon's peremptory (and premature)
contention, which Thomas Jefferson sought to refute in his *Notes on the
State of Virginia* (1785), that the natural environment of North America
itself generated inferior flora, fauna and aboriginal people. Clearly nothing
to match European achievement had appeared or could be expected to do
so in the future. Though the justly celebrated analyst of America, Alexis de
Tocqueville, was never the sceptic about political democracy his post-
Second World War celebrators presented him as, he did express strong
reservations, as we saw in Chapter 1, about the quality and depth of literary
and intellectual life of America in *Democracy in America* (1835; 1840). And
sociologist Max Weber's tremendously influential work, *The Protestant Ethic
and the Spirit of Capitalism* (1903) was only completed after Weber and his
wife had visited America. This suggests that the 'iron cage' of capitalist
culture occupied by the 'specialists without spirit and sensualists without
heart', evoked by Weber at the close of his book, was to be detected in the
heartland of capitalism, the United States.

Later, drawing as much from Weber as from Marx and Freud, left-wing
refugees from Nazism such as Max Horkheimer and Theodor Adorno
focused in their *The Dialectic of Enlightenment* (1944) on Hollywood as the
centre of a 'culture industry' driven by desire for power and profit. It was
all a far cry from the idea of a genuinely democratic culture shaped by the
informed tastes of autonomous citizens. Perhaps the only foreign observer
to maintain some modicum of faith in the democratic spirit of (white)
Americans was the Swedish social theorist, Gunnar Myrdal. And even his
An American Dilemma (1944) posited a split between an 'American Creed'
and the traditions of racism and history of discrimination that blocked the
realization of democracy in the United States.

But there were also distinguished home-grown conservatives, particularly in the first four decades of the twentieth century, whose opinions
deserve mention. They ranged from the old-line New Englander Henry
Adams and the cosmopolitan Harvard philosopher George Santayana to the
bumptious and irreverent Nietzschean H.L. Mencken, the expatriate-
turned-royalist T.S. Eliot, and Modernist-turned-Fascist Ezra Pound (see
Chapter 15). Such figures tended to see modern America as a vast historical
mistake, an object lesson in the cultural philistinism of the people
(particularly urban, proletariat or foreign-born), the hostility of democracy

to genuine distinction in thought and sensibility, and the false promises of capitalist materialism. By and large, such cultural conservatives were literary modernists at war with the modern world.

MODERN OR PRE-MODERN?

Attentive readers will have noticed a slippage of terms. Though I began by focusing on the theme of the possibility of 'democratic' culture, two other large concepts/phenomena have crept into the discussion – capitalism and modernity. This reflects the tendency for America to serve as a vast metaphor for and reservoir of the promises and perils of modern life, often taken as synonymous with capitalism and democracy. But despite – or perhaps because of – this identification of America with the 'modern', many American cultural critics have been drawn to two pre-modern traditions – the Puritan and the republican or civic humanist – to provide the resources for an internal critique of American culture.

Indeed, in dismissing American cultural life for being resolutely plebeian or *petit bourgeois*, many foreign critics have missed the critical role played by the Puritan and republican traditions in turning much American cultural criticism into a discourse of moral virtue and responsibility. Though America is often taken to be slavishly devoted to the ideal of modernity – historical progress mediated and enabled by reason as expressed in technology and science – American cultural criticism (and American life in general) has often been suffused by a sense of moral declension and historical nostalgia. The Puritan tradition had its roots in radical Protestantism of the Reformation era and the republican tradition its sources in pre-Christian classical culture. Yet the two traditions share a great deal: a belief in chosenness and an original unity of communal virtue in a 'city set upon a hill' or a 'virtuous republic' of yeomen farmers. But, so the shared narrative of declension goes, there has been a loss of virtue and unity, often attributed to the effects of modernity, particularly the corrosive effects of commerce and luxury, individualism and the pursuit of self-interest. The core message of such cultural criticism is the need to return to an earlier, pre-lapsarian state of communal virtue and unity.

Literary historian Sacvan Bercovitch, in his *The American Jeremiad* (1978), has identified the Puritan jeremiad, the sermon calling the community back to God's original purpose, as the generic form of self-justifying American cultural criticism. Just as important has been the secular, specifically political jeremiad deriving from the republican tradition. Examples in this genre include the popular rhetoric of the

'Fourth of July' oration in the nineteenth century particularly (and its anti-type Henry David Thoreau's 'On Civil Disobedience'), presidential inaugural addresses (John F. Kennedy's 'Ask not what your country can do for you – ask what you can do for your country' injunction in 1961 is exemplary here), and, from dissenting positions, Martin Luther King's 'Letter from Birmingham Jail' (1963) or Noam Chomsky's 'The Responsibility of Intellectuals' (1967), with its call for more vigilance in the face of American power, especially as exercised in the Vietnam War.

In the nineteenth century these two traditions had already become entwined in what sociologist Robert Bellah calls the American 'civil religion', which is composed of a political theology (the canonical texts being the Declaration of Independence and the Constitution), national holidays (Memorial Day, July 4 and Thanksgiving) and hero/martyrs such as Lincoln, Kennedy and Martin Luther King. Less oratorical and more complex examples of the jeremiadic tradition over the past few decades are C. Wright Mills's *The Power Elite* (1956) and, more recently, Christopher Lasch's *The Culture of Narcissism* (1978) and Bellah's *The Habits of the Heart* (1985). Most strikingly, such works often explicitly evoke religious or republican notions and display much ambivalence toward secular modernity. Indeed, the persistence of the jeremiad in American cultural criticism belies the conventional (European) wisdom that Americans lack a sense of the past or of tradition. Compared to the American obsession with decline from unity, the constant evocation of the virtues (and vices) of past leaders, the felt need to anneal past mistakes, and the continuity of the political culture, European national cultures look positively amnesic.

COMMUNITIES OF DISCOURSE/CULTURAL TRADITIONS

Just because individualism has played such a major part in American self-consciousness, it is tempting to claim that American cultural criticism emanates most typically from institutionally unattached individuals. In fact Emerson's 'Man thinking' does prefigure a certain type of American intellectual that philosopher Richard Rorty has characterized as the 'transcendentalist' intellectual, a figure who typically engages in a 'kind of name-dropping, rapid shifting of contexts, and unwillingness to stay for an answer'.[2] Lacking an academic discipline, in fact often contemptuous of academic life altogether, this sort of intellectual has typically written in the essay form rather than the academic monograph or systematic theory. He or she falls somewhere between the literary critic and the old-fashioned philosopher and publishes in 'little' magazines rather than mass circulation magazines or academic journals. But there is some evidence that this sort of 'public intellectual', to use Russell Jacoby's term, has in the last couple of decades become increasingly rare.

Yet to view American cultural critics as lone wolves and freelancers obscures the degree to which even intellectual 'isolates' work within a tradition of concerns and in reference to concrete institutions and groupings. There are in fact several ways to categorize types of American cultural criticism historically. One would be to see American intellectual life, at least in its (long) century of high achievement between 1830–1960 as a complex reprise of the sectional conflict between South and North. I have already alluded several times to Emerson and Whitman but there was a whole cluster of antebellum Northern writers and intellectuals, making up what F.O. Matthiessen later named (in his 1941 book of the same title) the 'American Renaissance', that established not so much a tradition of answers as a preoccupation with a set of questions – what was the relationship between self and nature, between self and society, between autonomy and democracy? What were the sources of spiritual sustenance in a world dominated by the business ethic and commercial considerations? How could the New World maintain its 'newness' in the best sense?

For these Northern intellectuals, largely identifiable with the Transcendentalist tradition (see Chapter 4), nature itself was the source of oppositional sustenance in a society where 'things were in the saddle'. There is a profoundly anti-institutional strain running throughout this Northern Emersonian tradition as reflected not only in its original hostility to slavery but also in its concern with keeping alive a democratic and self-renewing ethos against the large-scale institutional and organizational forces that emerged in post-Civil War America. Philosopher William James's life and thought illustrate some of the insistently individualizing tendency of the Transcendentalist tradition, though by the latter part of the century James himself had abandoned most of the substantive tenets of Transcendentalism and the political and social preoccupations characterizing it.

If James was concerned with *individual* renewal and spiritual vitality, young cultural radicals such as Van Wyck Brooks and Lewis Mumford spoke in the first two decades of the twentieth century – and later – of the need for general cultural renewal. Brooks's famous thesis, promulgated in such works as *America's Coming of Age* (1915), was that a deep split existed in American life between a 'highbrow' sensibility with its exalted ideals and a 'lowbrow' mentality informing a 'catchpenny reality'. Indeed, the two dominant figures of eighteenth-century (Northeastern) America – the brilliant minister-cum-theologian Jonathan Edwards and the ever resourceful and protean Benjamin Franklin – became standard representatives of these polarities in American culture. The rhetoric of Jamesian pragmatism itself divided along a cultural fault-line identified by Brooks and also by James's conservative colleague, Santayana, with his idea of the 'genteel tradition'. At times James could sound like the drum major of American philistinism when he spoke of the 'cash value' of ideas. Yet, in *Varieties of Religious Experience* (1903), he sought to salvage some cultural prestige and personal meaning for the individual soul in its search for transcendence. More generally, James embodied the beginning of a deep shift in American culture discourse from a moral and religious to a psychological, even therapeutic, orientation. Increasingly, the truth-value and the use-value of ideas became indistinguishable.

The cultural problem for Brooks, as for Mumford, was the lack of a literary and cultural middle ground where 'thought and action' could be brought into fruitful commerce. Mumford historicized this cultural self-division in his *The Golden Day* (1926) by nostalgically locating an original unity in what he identified as that 'unique moment in the American mind' between 1830 and 1860.[3] This originary highpoint was then followed by the post-Civil War Gilded Age in which the inheritors of the Emersonian tradition fell prey to what Mumford referred to as the 'pragmatic acquiescence', a mood in which Mumford felt that James had been all too complicit. Moreover this concern with the highbrow/lowbrow split in American consciousness, one which literary critic Philip Rahv, in his article 'Paleface and Redskin' (1939) collected in *Image and Idea* (1949), later identified in American literature as a conflict between 'palefaces' and 'redskins', reflected the historical distance of American intellectuals from the sources of political and economic power. This alienation of mind from power was registered with particularly strong regret by Henry Adams, one of the few American intellectuals whose inheritance included proximity to the world of political power.

Finally, it has been suggested that the countercultural impulses of the 1960s – the hostility to 'technocracy' and large institutions, the obsession with self-expression and self-discovery, the pursuit of new forms of spirituality, the attraction to pre-modern and rural modes of life and to traditional cultures; in political life, a commitment to participatory democracy and hostility to forms of racial oppression – were a recrudescence of the original Transcendentalist impulse, one that periodically manifests itself as cultural criticism and in political action.

Set over and against this New England tradition of cultural criticism has been a peculiarly Southern tradition. As it emerged by the 1840s, Southern cultural criticism was a distinctly conservative and 'unAmerican' matter. Often in contact only through periodical writings, antebellum Southern intellectuals scrutinized cultural matters through the lens of history not nature. Complexity rather than simplicity, hierarchy not democracy formed the baseline of cultural evaluation. The apogee of antebellum cultural and social thought below the Mason–Dixon line came in the work of Virginia's George Fitzhugh, such as *Sociology for the South, or the Failure of Free Society* (1854). He lashed out against the Northern culture of individualism and its emphasis upon individual rights, the contractual basis of society, and devotion to *laissez-faire* economics. Fitzhugh and other Southern organicist intellectuals offered a vision of political and social élites presiding over a hierarchical society, ordered as the family writ large. Their defence of slavery was only a particular example of the defence of inequality and hierarchy; their defence of religion a specific example of the defence of tradition against modernity.

Though there is little evidence of continuity of personnel or ideas with the antebellum Southern intellectuals, the best-known challenge to the American version of modernity in the twentieth century came from the Vanderbilt Agrarians, most notably in a collection of essays, *I'll Take My Stand* (1930). Though they generally choose academic careers, the Agrarians fancied themselves rebels against the academic, literary culture of their time. For the Agrarians, as we saw in Chapter 5, the South, past and present, represented the last line of defence against an urban, industrial way of life, an orientation toward the future, the hegemony of science and technology and a thoroughly secular culture. The best-known figures among them, such as John Crowe Ransom and Allen Tate, were above all else poets, novelists and literary critics. It was as such that after the 1930s the Agrarians had most of their direct influence, especially in academic literary criticism where the New Criticism, with its characteristic emphasis on the separation of formal literary and aesthetic judgements from political values or preferences, was the dominant force for more than thirty years.

More generally Southern cultural conservatives after the 1930s – Richard Weaver, author of *The Southern Tradition at Bay* (1963), being the most prominent – divided the world between those who reject modernity and those who embrace it. To the degree that the rest of the nation was committed to a secular society and culture, to domination of nature, to levelling democracy and to the 'Leviathan' state, the Southern ideal remained anti-modern. Though the 1960s represented the demise of Southern constitutional recalcitrance and dreams of political and racial separatism, the Southern cultivation of regional differences by no means disappeared. Southern conservatives from the 1960s onwards remained a fascinating conglomeration of organic conservatives, nostalgic less for republican origins than the ordered hierarchies of the Middle Ages, and libertarians scorning anything to do with political regulation or social engineering. Generally, Southern conservatives were cultural pluralists when facing outward, but cultural authoritarians in so far as they championed Christian values and anti-modern cultural positions at home. Indeed, the structure of the family remained the most widely shared image of the ideal social and cultural organization, even though most knew that it was fated to remain just that – an ideal form. After the 1960s, race was dropped as an explicit index to regional conservative reliability. Not surprisingly, Southern Afro-Americans generally found little in the white Southern tradition of cultural conservatism to entice them into its ranks.

But conservatives were not the only Southerners who raised questions about the nature of the national culture from a regional vantage point. In his *The Burden of Southern History* (1960), Southern historian C. Vann Woodward wondered if the rest of the nation might learn to temper its arrogance and innocence if it contemplated the South's historical experience of poverty, defeat, occupation and acquaintance with the tragic and ironic dimensions of history. Though embroilment in the Vietnam War and periodic surges of national chauvinism thereafter suggested Woodward's call for more realistic and tempered sense of national identity went largely unheeded, his suggestion that American exceptionalism was just that – exceptional – remained a powerful warning against the hubris embedded in the idea that because America was different, it was somehow better or more deserving of success than other nations.

The other coherent intellectual tradition from the 1930s through the 1960s was both the least American in origin and the most thoroughly committed to modern culture – the New York intellectuals. Emerging from predominantly Jewish, first and second generation working-class backgrounds in the 1930s, the New Yorkers were originally committed to modernism in culture and Marxism in political ideology. Later, as they moved away from their more radical origins, Freud and Weber as well as existentialists were major influences. As literary (not academic) intellectuals, the New Yorkers were committed to a Whitmanesque vision of the nation's literature as the privileged mode of access to the spirit of American culture. In his preface to his study of such twentieth-century writers as Theodore Dreiser and William Faulkner, *On Native Grounds* (1942), Alfred Kazin, perhaps the most 'American' of the New York intellectuals, wrote that his work was 'in part an effort at moral history, which is greater than literary history, and is needed to illuminate it'.[4] By 'moral' Kazin referred not to any specific ethical doctrine but to the cultural ethos, the world view, within which American imaginative and intellectual efforts were to be understood.

Beside their concern with the social, cultural and political resonances of American literature, New York intellectuals firmly encouraged modernist avant-garde experimentation and generally scorned mass culture. Figures such as Clement Greenberg in his 'Avant-Garde and Kitsch' (1939), and Dwight Macdonald in his work on 'mass-cult', 'mid-cult', and 'high cult' after the Second World War – in *Against the American Grain* (1962), for example – were distinctly uneasy with the direction American culture had taken, not because it was modern or democratic *per se* but because it had become synonymous with mass culture, devoted to the pursuit of profit, and a potential instrument of political authoritarianism. In this line of analysis they were close to Adorno and Horkheimer. Indeed, another refugee of the Frankfurt School, Herbert Marcuse, offered an analysis of American intellectual and cultural life in the early 1960s as 'one-dimensional', without resources for imagining alternative political, economic or cultural arrangements. Marcuse's analysis in *One-Dimensional Man* (1964) and *An Essay on Liberation* (1969) profoundly influenced the New Left and Counter-Culture of that decade. Yet for all their hostility to mass culture, New York critics pioneered American film criticism and championed Abstract Expressionist art (see Chapter 13) in the years following the Second World War.

If the New York intellectuals manifested little cultural nostalgia, at least in those early years, it was because they had no native ground, no nostalgia for some regional locus of past greatness, only a present and future to be imagined along modernist lines. But by the early 1960s, they, like the Southern Agrarian critics at the other end of the political spectrum, had lost much of their radical bite, having failed to develop any theoretical basis for their social and cultural radicalism. In their own work they exemplified what Daniel Bell, in his 1960 book of the same title, called 'the end of ideology'; and in assuming academic positions by the 1960s, they became – seen in retrospect – the last non-academic intellectual élite in American cultural life, one which combined exalted modernist standards with an accessible language of criticism.

No delineation of the traditions of American cultural criticism would be complete without mentioning the academic tradition of criticism, especially in the social and historical sciences. The late nineteenth century saw the rise of professionalization in American higher education. A generally though not exclusively 'progressive' tradition of social and cultural criticism flourished in these conditions up to the Second World War. No one was as responsible for undermining the scientific basis of white racial superiority as the anthropologist Franz Boas, who argued the case in a series of articles and books too numerous to list, while historian Charles Beard demystified the origins of American political culture and institutions in his *An Economic Interpretation of the Constitution* (1912) and made the study of politics and history in America the story, largely, of the pursuit of the main chance. In 1893, an historian from the Midwest, Frederick Jackson Turner, as we saw in earlier chapters, offered an explanation for what had made American culture and institutions uniquely 'American' and thereby trumped all efforts to identify foreign antecedents or ideas as explanations of the special nature of American experience. Turner's answer was the 'frontier', at once a place and a process, a dissolver and regenerator of culture that explained why America was different. The sources of American culture were precisely American; the future of American uniqueness, however, was dim, since Turner concluded his 'Significance of the Frontier in American History' by pronouncing a eulogy for its passing.

Still, academic critics of American culture could scarcely do without their European sources. But, for all the later influence of Marx and Freud on modernist intellectuals, probably the greatest single influence in the half century before the Depression was Charles Darwin. Yale sociologist William Graham Sumner used evolutionary theory in such books as *What Social Classes Owe to Each Other* (1883) to defend free-market capitalism and the cultural values needed to preserve it. Thus was initiated a tradition of American conservatism that re-emerged in the form of 'sociobiology' to dampen ardour for cultural and social liberation in the 1970s; the most articulate advocacy of the later manifestation, Edward O. Wilson's *Sociobiology* (1975), was subtitled 'a new synthesis' and likened human societies to those of insects. On the other hand, around the turn of the century, renegade academic, Thorstein Veblen, used evolutionary theory to suggest sardonically that the emerging industrial capitalist order, as described in Chapter 8, was a form of cultural regression not progress, while the way forward lay in the application of science and technology to the economy and the culture of consumption. And John Dewey's long and distinguished career as philosopher, educationalist and social theorist was built on the assumption that Darwin had undermined all philosophical notions of essential or eternal truths. With this in mind, Dewey saw philosophy's role as consisting in the discovery and shaping of those ideas that proved effective (or 'adaptive' in Darwinian terms) in the reconstruction of a democratic social, political and cultural order under modern urban conditions.

Finally, twentieth-century American cultural criticism would be unimaginable without the emigration to the New World of scores of Central European academics and intellectuals after Hitler's accession to power. Among the most prominent, at least in their later influence on cultural criticism, were psychoanalytic thinkers such as Erich Fromm, Wilhelm Reich and Erik Erikson whose contributions to the study of the psychological concomitants of modernity, particularly the connection between modernization and the rise of Fascism and Nazism, have been invaluable. Erikson in particular was fascinated with American national character and in research for studies like *Childhood and Society* (1950) joined American anthropologists concerned with the interaction of culture and personality in trying to identify the linkages among child-rearing practices, social and political institutions and culture generally.

As usual, while Americans liked to think of themselves as individualists, Europeans and post-Second World War analysts of national character such as David Riesman in *The Lonely Crowd* (1950) were struck more by their conformist character. Erikson's concern with the individual and cultural dimensions of identity formation revealed an American type who swung between excessive independence and a good-natured conformism, thus suggesting à la Tocqueville, that the extremities of autonomy and conformity were linked in subterranean fashion. Robert Coles, Robert Jay Lifton and Kenneth Kenniston, who were psychiatrically trained but academically based, followed Erikson's lead in the 1960s by investigating the preconditions and motives for political and cultural rebellion among the young. Indeed, Lifton speculated in his 'Protean Man' essay of 1967 that a global rupture in cultural continuity had occurred. As a result, young people in America, as well as in Japan and China, no longer found stable identities and life-long commitments to be functional in a world of cultural dislocation.

In the American and European context, sociologist of culture Philip Rieff pointed to the emergence of a new character type he named 'psychological' man, the product of a culture saturated with psychoanalytic notions and one who was highly self-conscious, ironic about everything but able to commit himself to nothing. Apparently a conformist, psychological man was in reality alienated from all binding faiths and forms of cultural authority. In *The Triumph of the Therapeutic* (1966) Rieff claimed to have detected another new type, the 'therapeutic', who sought to combine individual self-expression with cultural revolution. Rieff's work both reflected and most presciently foresaw the vast cultural upheaval that would mark America in the 1960s. On another level Rieff's analysis was yet another dissection of the individualist search for spiritual meaning that underlay Transcendentalism, Jamesian pragmatism and much of the more ominous examples of modernism's failure to offer a culture of belief to balance the critical spirit it so assiduously cultivated.

THE 1960s – AND AFTER

The cultural implications of the 1960s have yet to be unpacked and assessed. Still, it is safe to assume the following effects of the momentous changes of that decade upon American culture – and cultural criticism. First, since the 1960s it has been impossible to see American culture as a unitary or even dualistic entity. In fact is not clear that there is – or ever has been – an American culture or national character. Put positively, the plurality of American culture emerged with full force as an ideal after the 1960s. Cultural pluralism replaced the melting pot as the dominant conception of American nationality. More generally, as Rupert Wilkinson has noted, prior to the 1960s social and cultural conformity was seen as the American disease. Since then it has been the dangers of fragmentation, isolation, or Lasch's much discussed 'culture of narcissism', the final destination of the individualism Tocqueville identified in the 1830s, that has seemed most threatening.

The claims for cultural diversity have sounded from several directions in the last quarter century. The most powerful in many ways were the claims of black Americans whose Civil Rights movement in the 1960s gave way to a cultivation of black cultural consciousness and the rediscovery of a lost black culture by the early 1970s. W.E.B. DuBois in his *Souls of Black Folk* (1903) was the great precursor with his idea of the double consciousness or 'twoness' of Afro-Americans and his call for white American culture to recognize the immense cultural contributions of black Americans. The Harlem Renaissance of the 1920s and 1930s continued this work of cultural reappropriation and cultivation of racial pride, while more recent figures as diverse as Ralph Ellison, Albert Murray and Ishmael Reed continued this tradition of cultural pluralism in the 1960s, often in the face of harsh criticism from black cultural nationalists. In the eyes of the cultural pluralists, white Americans were not merely transplanted Europeans nor were black Americans displaced Africans. To be an American was to be a *mélange* of several cultures – European, African and Native American (for Reed, as we saw in Chapter 14, Asian too) – a claim that an Eliot or Adams or Henry James, but not a Whitman or Bourne or William James, would have found hard to accept.

Even more radically, the development of a black aesthetic and recrudescence of an Afro-centric perspective in the late 1960s – and then again in the 1990s – led some black cultural critics to reject the European tradition as an instrument of political and cultural oppression. Terms such as 'European', 'white', 'bourgeois', 'liberal', 'racist' and 'individualistic', became all but synonymous. Prior to the 1960s, the presiding binary opposition in American cultural criticism set America against Europe; by the end of the decade, America had been reconceived as the inheritor and perpetuator of cultural imperialism in the Third World, particularly Africa. All Euro-Americans looked, acted and thought alike. The American Adam differed hardly at all from his cynical European cousins.

These cultural polemics were augmented by scholarship in the post-1960s period which made it impossible to entertain the notion that Afro-American culture was only a derivative of Western values and institutions. Black literature, particularly fiction by Alice Walker and Toni Morrison and other figures featured in Chapter 6, demanded consideration as more than thinly-disguised racial self-justification or social protest. Finally, then, under this Afro-American pressure, all the vast generalizations about American culture and character had to be reassessed for their application to black Americans. So-called 'democratic' culture in America looked decidedly monochromatic, more like a *Herrenvolk* democracy than, in the famous expression used by black presidential candidate Jesse Jackson, a 'rainbow coalition'. From the new multicultural point of view, the point of cultural criticism in America was to reveal repressed cultural contradictions and the lost possibilities of what had once seemed a unified culture.

Yet, the most unexpected challenge to dominant cultural values in the post-1960s world came from the women's movement and theoretical feminism. On all fronts, women challenged the way men (and women) had previously thought of women and institutions such as marriage and the family, sexuality and violence. Betty Friedan's *The Feminine Mystique* (1963) offered a memorable title and cogent yet accessible analysis of the cultural complex that kept women in their place. Her analysis was later radicalized and generalized by Kate Millett in *Sexual Politics* (1970) into 'patriarchy', a transhistorical and cross-cultural formation which explained why, time out of mind, the second sex had always been second.

In some ways, the feminist challenge to male-dominated culture concentrated less on America *per se* than on the male hegemony which seemed so pervasive throughout human history. For American feminists, (male) American culture represented no important break in the skein of patriarchal domination, nor, echoing the charges of Afro-Americans, was it inclusively democratic. Democratic culture was now largely seen as a men's club. In intellectual, academic terms, the American feminists most clearly challenged the modern literary canon which, they claimed, had been largely constructed by male critics. Nina Baym noted that the obsession of many classic texts in American writing with autonomy and independence – those same ones that Kazin, without irony, had declared 'the American procession' – made them 'melodramas of beset manhood' rather than texts that spoke to all Americans of whatever gender.[5]

Again, as with Afro-Americans, women historians (and historians of women) rewrote American history to incorporate women into the national cultural narrative or, alternatively, developed a uniquely women's perspective on it. They questioned the radical nature of the Thirteenth,

Fourteenth and Fifteenth Amendments, since the male framers of these amendments refused to include women in their provisions for granting freedom from servitude and civil rights in the aftermath of the Civil War. Not only fiction writers such as Kate Chopin but the social and cultural thought of Charlotte Perkins Gilman in *Women and Economics* (1898) received new attention. Students of American and black literature rehabilitated the reputation of Zora Neale Hurston, the novelist and folklorist (see Chapter 6), while attacking black male writers for their celebration of dubious masculine values and the patriarchal family under the guise of black cultural liberation.

Since the 1960s the story of the New York intellectuals and Agrarian/ New Critics has been one of decline and fragmentation. Some former liberals, even radicals, such as Irving Kristol and Norman Podhoretz, took their cultural stand well to the right of centre and from editorial positions on such influential journals as *Encounter* (published in London) and *Commentary* (the leading Jewish magazine in the US) mounted a full-scale attack on what they saw as the cultural antinomianism, anti-capitalism and anti-Americanism of the New Left and Counter-Culture of the 1960s. With the exception of a few independent intellectuals such as Susan Sontag, avant-garde writing and criticism found an unexpected home in the universities after the 1960s. At the same time, the great achievements of modern painting and architecture began receiving a second, more sceptical look and commercial, 'vernacular' architecture a more positive one (see Chapters 9 and 13). More interestingly, the innovative and experimental techniques first propagated by the avant-garde reappeared in the mass media, advertising, popular music and film. Psychedelic and mind-expanding drugs, key elements in the counter-cultural ideal, were incorporated into and became central to whole sectors of the population. Finally, in the ensuing decades, the esoteric, eastern-orientated religiosity of the 1960s gave way to Jesus-freaks and a host of therapeutic cults, while on the cultural right the appeal of fundamentalist, charismatic and pentecostal messages grew apace (see Chapter 2).

What this all added – or adds – up to is far from clear. But Lasch's culture of narcissism did strike a responsive chord. According to Lasch, American culture, whether high or mass, encouraged immediate gratification, withdrawal from public concern and engagement, compulsive irony and jokiness, and an inability to imagine or maintain long-term goals or relationships. *The Culture of Narcissism* was an old-fashioned book in many ways. Despite Lasch's denials, it was nothing if not a jeremiad, a contribution to the 'literature of moral outrage'. Yet it also deployed a psychoanalytically-derived discourse in which narcissism strictly speaking refers to a border-line disturbance in individuals, not to a shared cultural character. Finally, Lasch's book revoiced the old Tocquevillean proble-matic of individualism *vs* conformity. As a tool of cultural criticism narcissism encompassed and helped explain both phenomena. Clinical – as well as cultural – narcissism was the state in which the individual vacillated between obsession with him- or herself (in quick quips, Quentin Anderson's 'imperial self' or Tom Wolfe's 'Me-Generation') and a sense of engulfment by others leading to abject dependency and loss of ego-boundaries.

Yet, while Lasch purported to describe a new cultural configuration, the characteristics he ascribed to the narcissistic type sounded for all the world like those identified by Lifton and Rieff in the late 1960s, those analysed by Riesman in the 1950s and even those pilloried by Puritan ministers in the late 1600s. From this cultural echoing, one inference would be that America had been and still was what Tocqueville had taken it to be – not some great exception to the vicissitudes of history but rather the wave of the future, the cultural entity that had already experienced the future other affluent societies were in the process of engaging.

Lasch's analysis was written from a position on the political Left. Yet he shared much of the cultural disquietude of conservatives such as Allan Bloom, whose *The Closing of the American Mind* (1985) identified the 1960s as the most proximate locus of cultural decline, and philosopher Alasdair MacIntyre, whose *After Virtue* (1981) was much more culturally and philosophically cogent than the analyses of either Lasch or Bloom. Closer to Lasch politically, Robert Bellah and those of his colleagues who produced *The Habits of the Heart* were disturbed by the evidence that individualism, whether 'utilitarian' or 'expressive', was the 'first language' of American self-understanding and expression. But they refused to dismiss the resources of two other more communally-orientated traditions – the republican one of civic involvement and the biblical one of religious commitment and community – as totally unavailable to counteract the privatising, self-absorbed tendencies of the culture. Thus for all the pessimism of the analysis offered in *Habits of the Heart*, its authors never quite succumbed to the shrillness of either Lasch or Bloom.

In the 1980s self-described 'liberal ironist' Richard Rorty found himself agreeing with much of the cultural analysis offered by conservatives and communitarians. Yet he refused to embrace the nostalgia for community and for metaphysical certainty that he referred to as 'terminal wistfulness'. If, Rorty reasoned, all metaphysical and religious foundations had been undermined, then the intellectual and cultural resources within the tradition of American thought, particularly the pragmatist tradition of James and Dewey, would have to suffice. Rorty refused the great lament for lost faith or absent community or the alternative of aestheticism.[6]

Finally, like Rorty in eschewing the jeremiadic mood, the work of Susan Sontag in the 1960s and academic Marxist Fredric Jameson in the 1980s set forth the lineaments of what had come to be called 'postmodernism' by the end of the 1980s. As early as her 'Notes on Camp' and other essays collected in *Against Interpretation* (1966) Sontag identified the emergence of a 'new sensibility' in which the defining tensions of high modernism between high and mass culture, art and technology, the ethical and the aesthetic had lost their compelling power. In such a situation, claimed Sontag, the point of art was to expand consciousness not provide edification or the materials for moral instruction. Thus the cultural dichotomies identified, and usually bemoaned, by everyone from Van Wyck Brooks to Dwight Macdonald were left behind as detritus of outmoded modernist worry.

Similarly, Jameson's ground-breaking analytic description of postmodernism called for a provisional suspension of moral judgement or historical condemnation. As a Marxist, Jameson identified postmodernism as the 'cultural dominant' at an advanced stage of multinational, consumer capitalism. Yet the characteristics he associated with postmodernism – the self as role and construct, the literature of self-reference or fabulation or dead-pan affectlessness, visual arts which live off a *mélange* of quotation and repetition, the past as pastiche and the future as unstructured by the goals offered by what French thinker Jean-François Lyotard called the 'master narratives' of general truths – seemed to rule out any ethical seriousness or grounds for political engagement and thus threatened his own political and moral commitment with irrelevance.

It was a major irony that the advent of the postmodernism was announced in the last days of the Marxist–Leninist bloc of nation-states, truly one of the great historical tragedies of modernity. Yet American cultural criticism seemed unable to offer a convincing idea of what a democratic culture might be under postmodern conditions. Intellectuals of a neo-conservative bent spoke of an 'end of history' marked by the triumph of democracy and free-market capitalism. But such pronouncements seemed to ignore the real inadequacies and failures of liberal regimes and cultures. If actually existing popular culture in postmodern America was democratic, it was also marked by the absence of any distinguished qualities of thought or feeling, the product of economic and media forces seemingly beyond the control of the 'people' at whom it was aimed.

By the early 1990s, it is not clear whether postmodernism is something or the loss of something, a form of belatedness and cultural byzantinism or the wave of the present and future. Though ostensibly more democratic and accessible than the allegedly élitist modernism that preceded it, postmodernism, if Jameson is right, is ethically tongue-tied and without political vision or commitment. Its deflecting self-consciousness suggests both the weightlessness of the traditional aesthetic sensibility and the impenetrability of esoteric theoretical discourse. Neither of these positions offers a convincing or appealing model for citizen or critic in a democratic culture. In focusing on difference, otherness and marginality, thinkers associated with marginal and oppressed groups have tried to turn the discourse of postmodernism to political ends. Yet in stressing marginality, difference and otherness, they have all but foreclosed the possibility of a broad-based democratic cultural discourse that implies more than a collection of marginalized groups (see also Chapter 7). Culturally, what Harold Rosenberg once called the 'tradition of the new' threatens to become what Rosalind Krauss has named 'the culture of the copy'; Walt Whitman's vision of democratic community is replaced by the idea of a society of 'others'.[7]

NOTES

1. Walt Whitman, *Democratic Vistas* in *Walt Whitman: Collected Poetry and Collected Prose* (Cambridge, 1982), p. 955.

2. Richard Rorty, 'Professionalized Philosophy and Transcendentalist Culture', *Consequences of Pragmatism* (Minneapolis, MN, 1982), p. 65.

3. Lewis Mumford, *The Golden Day* (New York, 1957), p. xv.

4. Alfred Kazin, *On Native Grounds* (New York, 1970), p. x.

5. Nina Baym, 'Melodramas of Beset Manhood: How Theories of American Fiction exclude Women Authors', in *The New Feminist Criticism*, ed. Elaine Showalter (New York, 1985), pp. 63–80; Alfred Kazin, *The American Procession* (New York, 1984).

6. Rorty, *Contingency, Irony, and Solidarity* (Cambridge, 1989).

7. Harold Rosenberg, *The Tradition of the New* (New York, 1959); Rosalind Krauss, *The Originality of the Avant-Garde and Other Modernist Myths* (Cambridge, MA, 1985), p. 170.

SUGGESTIONS FOR FURTHER READING

The topic of American cultural criticism could plausibly encompass just about everything written about America. Here I will confine myself for the most part to works not mentioned in the chapter and to more recent or accessible works that seem indispensable for the topic.

There has not been a synthesis of American intellectual history for quite a while, but Douglas Tallack's *Twentieth-Century America: The Intellectual and Cultural Context* (London, 1991) offers a stimulating, wide-ranging overview that focuses on the tension between modernism/postmodernism as well as surveying the major themes and movements of American intellectual history in this century. Giles Gunn's *The Culture of Criticism: The Criticism of Culture* (New York, 1987) and 'Beyond Transcendence or Beyond Ideology: The New Problematic of Cultural Criticism in America', *American Literary History*, **2**, 1 (Spring, 1990): 1–18 offer a stimulating set of probes into the role of cultural criticism in America and a position at odds with the recently emerging conventional wisdom. Russell Jacoby's *The Last Intellectuals: American Culture in the Age of Academe* (New York, 1987) suggests implicitly that one way to understand American cultural criticism is to understand the institutional settings – or lack of them – from which critics work.

Of studies of American national and cultural character there are no end. Robert Bellah and his associates' *The Habits of the Heart* (New York, 1985) exemplifies all the strengths and weaknesses of the genre; and the essays included in Charles Reynolds and Ralph Norman (eds), *Community in America* (Berkeley, CA, 1988) raise many important criticisms of the work of Bellah and his colleagues. Rupert Wilkinson's *The Pursuit of American Character* (New York, 1988) offers a valuable comparative analysis of national character studies since the Second World War, while Jean-Phillipe Malthy, 'Out of History: French Readings of Postmodern America', *American Literary History*, **2**, 2 (Summer, 1990): 267–98 ranges over far wider territory than the title of the essay indicates. One lesson of the article is that for foreign observers America tends to become a kind of Rohrschach image onto and from which they read their own preoccupations.

Important collections such as Henry Louis Gates (ed.), *Black Literature and Literary Theory* (New York, 1984) and Elaine Showalter (ed.), *The New Feminist Criticism* (New York, 1985) as well as Cornel West, *The American Evasion of Philosophy: A Genealogy of Pragmatism* (London, 1989) illustrate the theoretical sophistication of much recent cultural criticism emanating from Afro-Americans and women – but also its resolutely textual orientation. Indeed, works as different as Betty Friedan's *The Feminine Mystique* (New York, 1963) and Carol Gilligan's *In a Different Voice* (Cambridge, MA, 1982) have the merit of being based to a degree on talking to people rather than relying exclusively upon reading texts.

Finally, the issue of postmodernism which has come to dominate much recent cultural debate is an interesting way into the whole problematic area of the relationship between politics and culture, ethics and aesthetics, history and structure. Fredric Jameson's 'Periodizing the 60s', in Sonya Sayres (ed.), *The 1960s without Apology* (Minneapolis, 1984), pp. 178–209 and 'Postmodernism, or the Cultural Logic of Late Capitalism', *New Left Review*, **146** (July–August 1984): 53–92 are indispensable, even for those who are sceptical of Jameson's Marxist framework. Similarly, Alasdair MacIntyre's *After Virtue* (Notre Dame, IN, 1981) is always provocative, despite its author's Aristotelian and conservative orientation. Finally, Marshall Berman's *All That Is Solid Melts Into Air* (New York, 1982) and all of Susan Sontag's work are indispensable for understanding the efforts of younger members of the New York intellectual set to move beyond the moralizing modernism of their precursors.

Notes on Contributors

Glenn M. Andres is Professor of Art and Chair of the Humanities at Middlebury College, Vermont, where he concentrates on the history of architecture and urbanism. He has been a Fellow of the American Academy in Rome and Fulbright Professor in American visual culture at the University of Exeter. His publications, on Italian Renaissance and American topics, include *The Villa Medici in Rome*, *The Art of Florence* (co-author), *A Walking History of Middlebury*, and articles on American nineteenth-century building.

Christine Bold is Associate Professor of English at the University of Guelph, Ontario, Canada. She is author of *Selling the Wild West: Popular Western Fiction, 1860 to 1960* (1987) as well as essays on US cultural production in the 1930s and on various popular forms of the nineteenth and twentieth centuries. She is currently co-editor of the *Canadian Review of American Studies*.

Martin Crawford teaches American history at Keele University. He is the author of *The Anglo-American Crisis of the Mid-Nineteenth Century* (1987), editor of *William Howard Russell's Civil War* (1992), and has contributed articles to such journals as *Journal of Southern History* and *Civil War History*. He is the current editor of the British Association for American Studies (BAAS) Pamphlet Series and also engaged on a study of an Appalachian community in the Civil War era.

Stephen Fender has taught at Edinburgh, Williams, Dartmouth and University College, London, and is currently Professor of American Studies at the University of Sussex. His books include *Plotting the Golden West* and *American Literature in Context: 1620–1830*. Until the end of 1991 he was editor of the *Journal of American Studies*. *Sea Changes*, his recent study of the discourse of Anglophone emigration to the United States, *Sea Changes*, is published by Cambridge University Press.

Mick Gidley, Director of AmCAS at the University of Exeter, has written books, pamphlets and articles on Native Americans, literature, and photography. He has edited other essay collections, including *Representing Others* (1992), is UK editor of the *European Review of Native American Studies*, and chairs the Editorial Board for the BAAS/Longman American History series. He has been awarded fellowships by the American Council of Learned Societies and, in 1991–92, the Netherlands Institute for Advanced Study.

Cynthia Hamilton heads American Studies at Crewe and Alsager College of Higher Education. She is the author of *Western and Hard-boiled Detective Fiction in America: From High Noon to Midnight* (1987) and a forthcoming BAAS pamphlet on *Literary Responses to Slavery*.

David Horn is Director of the Institute of Popular Music at the University of Liverpool. He is the author of *The Literature of American Music* (1977) and co-author of *The First Supplement* (1988) to it. He is a coordinating editor for the journal *Popular Music* and managing editor for the international project to produce the *Encyclopedia of Popular Music of the World*.

Richard H. King is Reader in American Studies at the University of Nottingham. He is the author of *The Party of Eros* (1972), *A Southern Renaissance* (1980), and *Civil Rights and the Idea of Freedom* (1992), a study of the political thought and culture of the Civil Rights movement, as well as of essays on a variety of American historical and literary topics.

Robert Lawson-Peebles held posts at Oxford, Princeton and Aberdeen before moving to the University of Exeter to teach American and Commonwealth Arts. He has published widely on transatlantic relations and cultural history, including *Landscape and Written Expression in Revolutionary America* (1988) and *Views of American Landscapes* (co-editor, 1989). Among his current projects, he is editing a collection of essays on the American Musical.

George Lipsitz is Professor of Ethnic Studies at the University of California, San Diego. His publications include *A Life in the Struggle: Ivory Perry and the Culture of Opposition* (1988) and *Time Passages: Collective Memory and American Popular Culture* (1990). He is the book review editor of *American Quarterly*.

David Murray teaches American Studies and Critical Theory at the

University of Nottingham. His research interests are in American poetry and criticism, and in North American Indians. His publications include *Literary Theory and Poetry: Extending the Canon* (ed., 1989), *Forked Tongues: Speech, Writing and Representation in North American Indian Texts* (1991), and essays on various poets and Indian topics.

David E. Nye holds the chair in American Studies at Odense University, Denmark. He has been a visiting scholar at Harvard, Massachusetts Institute of Technology, and the Netherlands Institute for Advanced Study. Author of five books, most recently the award-winning *Electrifying America: Social Meanings of a New Technology* (1990), he is now preparing a history of the technological sublime.

Paul Oliver is a Fellow of the Royal Anthropological Institute and an Honorary Fellow of AmCAS at the University of Exeter. He is a former Head of Art and Design at Dartington College of Arts and Associate Head of the School of Architecture at Oxford Polytechnic. His many books on folk and popular arts include *Blues Fell This Morning* (1960; rev. 1990) and *Songsters and Saints* (1984). He broadcasts frequently, and is currently editing the *Encyclopedia of Vernacular Architecture of the World*.

Berndt Ostendorf holds a chair in American Cultural History at the Amerika Institut, University of Munich. His books include *Black Literature in White America* (1982), *Ghettoliterature* (1983), and *Die Vereinigten Staaten von Amerika* (2nd ed. 1992). He has also published articles on New Orleans, on American music, popular culture, photography and advertising, and is currently at work on problems of multiculturalism.

Stephan Palmié is Assistant Professor at the Amerika Institut, University of Munich, where he also received his PhD in 1989. He has published *Das Exil der Götter* (1991), a monograph based on fieldwork among practitioners of 'Santería' in South Florida, on the history and belief system of an Afro-Cuban religion, and a number of articles on aspects of African–American and Caribbean anthropology and ethnohistory.

Ferenc M. Szasz is Professor of History at the University of New Mexico, Albuquerque, and a former Fulbright Professor of American Arts at the University of Exeter. He is a specialist in American cultural history and has written essays on aspects of American photography, a book on the Manhattan Project, and *The Protestant Clergy in the Great Plains and Mountain West, 1865–1915* (1988).

Douglas Tallack is Senior Lecturer in American Studies at the University of Nottingham. His publications include *Twentieth-century America* (1991), *Literary Theory at Work* (ed., 1987) and *The Nineteenth-Century American Short Story: Language, Form and Ideology* (1993).

Ruth Vasey is a Lecturer in the Department of Theatre and Film Studies at the University of New South Wales, Sydney. She has an MA from the University of Hawaii and a PhD in American Studies from the University of Exeter, where she held a Commonwealth Fellowship. Her major research interest is Hollywood and its foreign market, and she is currently completing *Diplomatic Representations: The World According to Hollywood, 1919–1939* for the University of Wisconsin Press.

Map

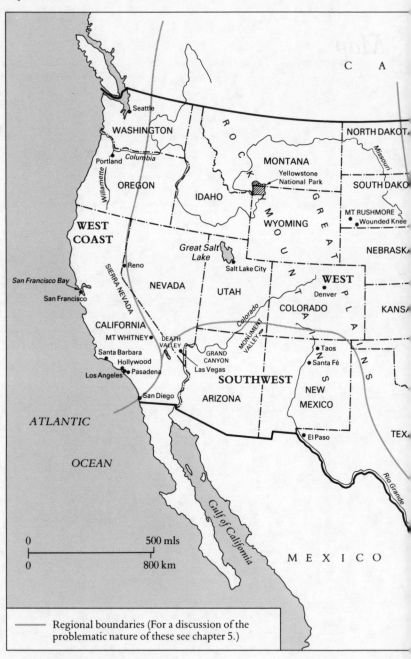

Map of the United States of America

Index

Index

Index

Hollywood *see under* films
Home Mission frontier, 30
Honduran refugees, 153, 160
Hood, Raymond, 199
Hoover, Herbert, 227
Hopi tribe, 113, 308
Hopper, Edward, 292
Horkheimer, Max, 363, 370
Hough, Emerson, 116
Houston, 113
Howard, Ebenezer, 200
Howe, George, 199
Howe, Irving, 33
Hubbard, William, 13–14
Huggins, Nathan Irvin, 130
Hughes, Langston, 122, 136
Humphreys, Don, 273
Hunt, Richard Morris, 194
Hurston, Zora Neale, 106, 136, 375
Hutchinson, Anne, 70
Hutterites, 33
Hutton, Betty, 276
Hyper-Realist painters, 303–4, 308
'hypo-descent', 122

I-Ching, 40, 256
Idealism, 72, 79, 80, 82, 83, 88
Imagism, 341–2, 353
immigrants; immigration
  artists, 289, 294
  Asians, 151–2
  Caribbeans, 152
  Central American, 153
  emigration to America, experience of, 7,
    10–12, 14–16, 21–2, 120
  and ethnicity, 142–65
  illegal, 152, 154, 155–6
  immigration bureaux, 145
  immigration policy (1965–), 128, 150
  intellectuals, 371–2
  Jewish, 31, 146, 147, 149
  Latin Americans, 152–3
  to Midwest, 109, 147
  new immigration (1880–1930), 63, 145–7,
    215
  to North West, 112
  numbers of, 142, 143, 146–7, 149–50, 152
  refugees from Fascism, 149, 294, 371
  restriction of, 147–8, 149
  return migration, 15–16, 146
  rival groups, 121, 148, 171
  Scandinavians, 109, 143, 144
  to SouthWest, 113
  and suffrage, 63
  and welfare capitalism, 173
  to West Coast, 114

  see also separate nationalities
Inclusivism, 207, 209–10, 211
Index of American Design, 293
Indian immigrants, 152
'Indian Territory', 51
Indians, American *see* Native Americans
Indochinese refugees, 157–8, 159
industrialization, 112, 144, 146–7, 166–88
'inferiority of environment' theory, 363
'installation' art, 301, 305
Institutional Church, 35
instrumentalism, 85–8
intellectuals, 46, 71, 87, 88, 146, 147, 365–6,
    367–8, 369–70
International Exhibition of Modern Art,
    1913 (Armory Show), 287–8, 290, 292,
    342
International Style, 197, 199, 201, 202, 203,
    205, 206, 207
Invisible Man (Ellison), 129, 137
Iowa, 145
Iranian refugees, 159
Irish immigrants, 143, 145, 146, 147, 243
Isaac, Rhys, 26
isolationism, 293–4
Israel, 39
Italian immigrants, 146, 147 and Hollywood,
    224
Ives, Charles, 244–5, 252

Jackson, Andrew, 57, 58, 62
Jackson, Jesse, 29, 105, 374
Jackson, William Henry, 111–12
Jacksonian Period
  'American Renaissance', 108, 366
  cultural criticism, 367–8
  democratic tradition, 45–6, 56–61, 67
  fiction, 317, 320, 325, 327, 329–30
  Gold Rush, 115
  immigrants, 143
  industrialization, 167
  Mumford on, 367
  Native Americans, 51
  the press, 214–15
  religion, 29–32
  temperance crusade, 329–30
Jacobs, Harriet, 136
Jacobs, Jane, 206
Jacoby, Russell, 366
Jahn, Helmut, 209
James, Henry, 373
James, Will, 113
James, William, 35, 68, 69, 75, 78, 80, 81–5,
    89–90, 93, 366, 367, 373, 376
Jameson, Fredric, 377, 378, 380
Jamestown, Virginia, 124

Index